KGALEMA MOTLANTHE

KGALEMA MOTLANTHE
A Political Biography

Ebrahim Harvey

First published by Jacana Media (Pty) Ltd in 2012
10 Orange Street
Sunnyside
Auckland Park 2092
South Africa
(+27 11) 628 3200
www.jacana.co.za

© Ebrahim Harvey, 2012

All rights reserved.

ISBN 978-1-4314-0438-4

Cover design by publicide
Set in Ehrhardt 12/16.5 pt
Job no. 001863
Printed by Ultra Litho (Pty) Ltd, Johannesburg

See a complete list of Jacana titles at www.jacana.co.za

This book is dedicated to my most wonderful mother Kulsom, who very sadly passed away during my research, to my dearest daughter Zina, who is my constant source of inspiration, and to all around the globe who fight for social justice.

Contents

Preface ix
An introductory reflection xxi

PART ONE: FORMATIVE YEARS
   1 Ancestral roots, youth and political baptism 3
   2 Life on Robben Island 33
   3 'Meeting the real world' 75

PART TWO: FROM ANC SECRETARY-GENERAL TO POLOKWANE AND PARLIAMENT, 1997–2007
   4 From Mafikeng to Stellenbosch, 1997–2002 123
   5 From Stellenbosch to Polokwane, 2002–2007 173
   6 The Polokwane 'revolution' and its aftermath 218

PART THREE: FROM POLOKWANE TO THE YEAR OF MANGAUNG, 2007–2012
   7 Kgalema, third ANC president of South Africa, 2008 257
   8 Kgalema, deputy president of South Africa, 2009 301
   9 A rough run-up to Mangaung, 2012 326

Endnotes 355
Bibliography 397
Index 407

Preface

> Political biography provides one set of tools by which to explore history and events from within the temporal and historical context of one life. It allows exploration of the events of history – from a micro perspective – looking at them through the eyes of someone who lived, breathed and was part of that history.
>
> Tracey Arklay, 'Political Biography'

The origins of this biography lie in a combination of circumstances, personal and political. I first interviewed Kgalema Motlanthe for the *Sowetan* newspaper back in 1999. From that first moment I found Kgalema to be refreshingly undogmatic, calm (too calm, some may argue), modest (too modest, still others may say), a very measured and dignified political leader.

Since then I have interviewed him more times than anyone else in this country, particularly for the *Mail & Guardian*.[1] I did a series of interviews for that paper when he became the third president (not 'acting president', as the media mistakenly repeated) of the Republic of South Africa on 25 September 2008, after the former president, Thabo Mbeki, was forced to resign after the controversial judgment by Judge Chris Nicholson.[2] As I got to know Kgalema better, the possibility of a political biography began to dawn upon me.

It was after the first national working committee meeting of the ruling ANC at Luthuli House in January 2009 that I asked him how he felt about my writing his political biography. It took him less than ten seconds to say, 'It's fine.' My interest in the idea had much to do with the fact that, though not uncritical of him, I respected him more than any other leader of the ANC since its unbanning. And though it is very easy to like Kgalema, as his biographer I had to distance myself enough to produce a text that was both critical and credible.

Since biographies are usually written about 'great men of history', some people have asked me whether Kgalema was a deserving choice. I believe he is. Many people tend to forget – partly because he has never really been an ambitious leader seeking attention, publicity or even power – that he has occupied strong leadership positions for many years. He was, significantly, the first chairperson of the ANC's most important and powerful Gauteng region in 1990, at a time when the ANC was re-establishing itself in the country. In 1992 he was elected acting general secretary of the National Union of Mineworkers (NUM), then the most powerful trade union not just in South Africa but on the African continent, and was formally elected its general secretary at NUM's 1994 conference.

In 1997 Kgalema succeeded Cyril Rampahosa at the ANC's conference in Mafikeng as its secretary-general, after its president, Nelson Mandela, Walter Sisulu and other senior party leaders persuaded him to accept that position and NUM to release him for the purpose. He was re-elected secretary-general at the 2002 Stellenbosch conference, a position he held until the ANC's Polokwane conference in 2007, when he became the ANC deputy president. In May 2008 he was elected

Preface

as an MP and in July became minister in the Presidency. Two months later, in September, he was elected president. His rise after Polokwane was meteoric and without precedent, though he was clearly a powerful leader as early as 1992, since when his stature has steadily risen in the ANC.

I would not have been prepared to write this biography if there was even the slightest chance of my soft-pedalling because I respect him so highly or because the ANC is such a powerful force in this country. The facts and analyses emerging from my research would not be diluted or modified to please Kgalema, the ANC and its allies. I intended to be fiercely honest, whatever my research uncovered. This steadfast approach would be crucial for an appraisal of Kgalema and the ANC, of which he is a major leader.

Unlike Mark Gevisser, prominent biographer of our former president in *Thabo Mbeki: The Dream Deferred*, I comprehensively unpack the dream itself, within which Kgalema's politics are situated. There has to be an intrinsic, causal relationship between the nature of a dream and its deferment, especially given our historical context, with which I deal in this book.[3] So we need to go back to the dream itself before we deal with its inevitable deferment. That dream has to confront the very nature of the decades-long struggle against political oppression (apartheid) and economic exploitation (capitalism) in South Africa and of the ANC's policies and strategies that developed in relation to those two inseparable historical realities.

Most fortunately, I had no need whatsoever to persuade Kgalema of the merits of such an approach. He certainly did not want a hagiography. As he put it to me later on: 'I did not think it would help me to let an ANC person do it, because I thought it was necessary that this be a really critical biography. That was very important for me.'

Kgalema Motlanthe

It was Gwede Mantashe who said to me that it was a measure of the man that Kgalema could allow a prominent and strong critic of the ANC to write his biography. How true. Kgalema often responded to me with the care and respect that most other ANC leaders would reserve for their own party's members – certainly not for prominent critics of the ANC. More than anything else, this raised his stature in my eyes and made me wonder deep down if his ready agreement to allow a critic of the ANC to write his biography was indicative of his own deep concerns about the party today, one that would hardly be recognisable to its erstwhile leaders such as Walter Sisulu, Albert Luthuli and Oliver Tambo.

My only surprise at Kgalema agreeing to this biography was retrospective: after interviewing some close comrades and friends, I discovered how intensely private he is.[4] Several of them could not credit that he had authorised anyone to write his biography, let alone a critic like me. Mantashe refused to believe me when I called him to request an interview and thought it was a hoax. Ahmed Kathrada and some others phoned Kgalema and those close to him to confirm that he had indeed approved the project. Indeed, it was a courageous decision for him. When I pointed out the need to produce an honest, critical biography, Kgalema's response was emphatic: 'That's fine, if it means dealing with substantive issues, but I certainly don't want to end up destroying individuals.'

He made another interesting comment: 'I think that because you are now able to talk to my family, friends and comrades about me, and what they think of me, including all the criticisms of me, it could enrich my life.' At another time he said that he found the series of interviews for the biography 'to be absolutely useful because it serves to remind one, refresh the past and rectify things'.

Preface

Perhaps more importantly, I hope this book will enable the public to get to know and understand Kgalema very much better than before, given his reticence to talk in public about his personal and family life. An authorised biography requires a degree of cooperation between subject and biographer – not only to conduct interviews but in my case to secure interviews with those close to Kgalema.[5] I often had no doubt that my political reputation had preceded me every step of the way, and that it was a factor in some of the delays and other difficulties I experienced. One thing is certain: political biographies are not for the faint-hearted. They are often rough territory for those who would traverse them, especially when dealing with an ANC leader at a time when there are so many conflicting and even brutal agendas at play in the organisation and its alliance with the Congress of South African Trade Unions (Cosatu) and the South African Communist Party (SACP).

However, where I had difficulty in securing interviews, Kgalema intervened on my behalf and in every case I got to speak to whomever I wanted to in the end. In such a situation a degree of closeness inevitably develops between the subject and the biographer, but never at any point did I feel that this personal closeness threatened to compromise the integrity of the project or influence in any way my assessment of Kgalema and the kind of conclusions I drew in this book about his personality, his leadership and his future in the ANC or government. Never did he even subtly indicate such an expectation. My clear goal was to get as close as I could to the subject in order to secure as much information, openness and cooperation as possible, without becoming too close. In this work I attempt to look squarely at all Kgalema's strengths and weaknesses in that complex interplay of personal, cultural, organisational, political and wider societal factors that frame any leader. My task has been to see and analyse the life in as detailed and balanced a way as possible.

Inevitably, a political biographer brings his own understanding and experience to bear on the representation of his subject and imparts his own views on matters that concern the subject's life. In my own case, I was a political and labour activist for many years, at the time when Kgalema joined NUM in June 1987.[6] As Cyril Ramaphosa's biographer Anthony Butler states: 'You cannot have Ramaphosa's life "as it has been", but only as it has been interpreted by the writer. However, interpretation is the prerogative not only of the author, but also of the informants, critics and readers themselves.'[7]

Mark Gevisser, Mbeki's biographer, on the other hand, is much more modest about the role of the biographer. Arguing against the traditional presumption of omniscience of biographers, he asserts: 'My starting point is that no biographer can be omniscient, and that the only person who can "know" Thabo Mbeki's story is Thabo Mbeki.'[8] Here, Gevisser seems to slide from one extreme to another. To see the subject as the only one who can 'know' is downright dangerous, especially if this is someone who may not be sufficiently open about his weaknesses or may have an exaggerated sense of his own importance. That is precisely where a critical biography comes in – to expose inadequacies the subject may not want to admit to. This critical approach has nothing to do with omniscience and in fact actively seeks to contradict it. With any political biography the author has to strike a fair balance between praising strengths and criticising failures.

I am acutely aware of the huge opportunity and responsibility entailed in writing this biography, especially in view of the current conflicting dynamics within the ANC, the ANC alliance with Cosatu and the SACP, and even in the government itself, most particularly around the 'succession battles' as the ANC

Preface

prepares itself for its elective and centenary conference at the end of 2012. It is not my intention here to use this biography, or let it be used, as a political intervention in these inner-party conflicts.

However, as a political biography is usually seen to be about politicians who 'are concerned with their image, ... with posterity and ... with public perceptions', how do we reconcile that understanding with the almost self-effacing, modest and apparently ambitionless reputation that Kgalema carries?[9] Does authorising this book indicate that Kgalema may want to modify his image and project himself more selfconsciously as a leader who has finally readied himself to assume and exercise power? This is an important and not necessarily ironical question that the biography must attempt to answer

The book draws on wide-ranging interviews with Kgalema and his family, with the comrades and friends he grew up and worked with in NUM, Cosatu, the SACP, the ANC and the government, as well as interviews with leading figures in other political organisations, civil society, academia and the media. I must mention that my interviews with Kgalema were all the more important for the biography because he has not written a great deal over the years; if he had, I could have derived much about his thinking from published sources. Kgalema, it must be said, like other leaders such as Walter Sisulu, has been embedded in an oral culture, which has a history of its own and which can have both strengths and weaknesses.

Kgalema's relations were very supportive of the biography of a man they had seen as their family and political leader ever since he was sentenced to imprisonment on Robben Island for ten years in 1977. Each interview with a family member contributed to the insights I gained. I warmly thank Kgalema's mother Sophia Masefako, his brothers Ernest and Sydney, his wife Mapula (whom he was divorcing at the time of writing), their children Kagiso and Kgomotso, and Ntabiseng, Mapula's daughter from a previous relationship; also his cousin Catherine and her husband Edwin, Teddy Matsitela, who tragically passed away months after I interviewed him, his cousins Michael Modipa, Raymond Madingoane and David Mahlamola Nkadimeng.

My particular appreciation goes to Kgalema's brother Ernest, who never tired of trying to help wherever he could. He arranged my interviews with members of the family, answered my endless questions about the family's history, and took me to meet their family from the maternal side in Ramantsho, near Marapyane, in Mpumalanga. A special thanks to Raymond, their cousin who lives in Loding, close to Marapyane, whose detailed knowledge of the family's history in that area was crucial for the biography.

I must warmly thank Professor Peter Delius, from the University of the Witwatersrand's history department, for agreeing to meet with Kgalema and me to share his knowledge about Polokwane and Mpumalanga, home respectively to Kgalema's maternal and paternal families. I found Vic Allen's *History of the Black Mineworkers in South Africa* an indispensable handbook for studying the South African mining industry and the history of NUM in particular,[10] while Anthony Butler's book, *Cyril Ramaphosa*, was also useful.[11] I relied considerably on the lengthy series of interviews that the researcher and author Padraig O'Malley conducted with Kgalema between 1992 and 2004. A series of interviews that Noor Nieftagodien of the University of the Witwatersrand's oral history project held with Kgalema in 2001 was also very helpful.

I most heartily thank my publishers Jacana Media for their patience and understanding when constant delays made it seem I would never get the book done. Bridget Impey, Maggie Davey,

Kerrie Barlow, Amy Flatau and other staff were wonderful, though at times I felt that they thought I was testing their patience too far!

I wish especially to acknowledge my editors Priscilla Hall and Russell Martin for their firm but sensitive and considerate handling of the manuscript. Professor Colin Bundy, who was its expert reader, also certainly made some very insightful contributions to its overall coherence, which I highly appreciate.

I wish to express my profound appreciation to those institutions and individuals who at various times provided funding to both kickstart and sustain the project over three years: the Oppenheimer Trust, Kuben Pillay, Manne Dipico, the Darene Foundation and African Rainbow Minerals, especially since many efforts to secure funding outside the private sector failed.

I particularly want to thank Pillay, the former NUM lawyer and currently CEO of Primedia, for his unwavering support through thick and thin. Nobody close to Kgalema supported his biography more than he did, in word and deed. During difficult and even depressing moments – of which I had many during my research – he was a constant source of encouragement. Another fervent supporter of this biography and a founding member of NUM, Director Matlala, assisted in various ways, giving me photos and arranging financial assistance when I most needed them.

I must thank Kgalema for the many hours he spent with me in interviews between May 2009 and July 2012. He generously allowed me over 180 hours of his time (probably a record), which gave me a valuable bank of information with certainly one of the best historians of the ANC I have ever met. Kgalema epitomises what Gramsci referred to as an 'organic intellectual'; he is a political activist who lacks tertiary qualifications but

Kgalema Motlanthe

learnt a vast amount through his involvement in the national liberation struggle and the ANC in particular; as a result he grew to understand the political situation and the dynamics of the broader society from his own experiences and from extensive reading over many years.

Kgalema's staff – Lerato Zimbili, Vincent Ngcobondwane and Malebo Sibiya – helped in arranging interviews with him and tolerated me when I placed them under pressure as a result of my own need to complete the research and the book. I also wish to thank Noor Nieftagodien for helping me to obtain books from the libraries at Wits University; the Mayibuye Centre at the University of the Western Cape for assistance with material from Robben Island; and the Historical Papers Department at the University of the Witwatersrand. Thanks, too, to Patrick Bond, Dale McKinley, Phiroshaw Camay, Director Matlala and many others, too numerous to mention, for the valuable insights they shared with me.

I wish to thank those who gave me time for interviews, many of whom did so generously: Vic Allen, Frans Baleni, Patrick Bond, Karima Brown, Anthony Butler, Phiroshaw Camay, Irene Charnley, Laloo Chiba, Neil Coleman, Saths Cooper, Jeremy Cronin, Manne Dipico, Jesse Duarte, Fiona Forde, Amina Frense, Steven Friedman, Howie Gabriels, Yusuf Gabru, Mark Gevisser, Daryl Glaser, Bobby Godsell, Gino Govender, William Gumede, Adam Habib, Ferial Haffajee, Anton Harber, Dirk Hartford, Ebrahim-Khalil Hassen, Barbara Hogan, Ahmed Kathrada, Paul Langa, Martin Legassick, Khetsi Lehoko, Seeng Letele, Phineas Mabetoa, Mondli Makhanya, Thabo Makunyane, Julius Malema, Jesse Maluleka, Xolela Mangcu, Mosibudi Mangena, Gwede Mantashe, Trevor Manuel, Thabo Masebe, George Mashamba, Daphne Mashile-Nkosi, Amos Masondo, Director Matlala, James Motlatsi, Don

Mattera, former President Thabo Mbeki, Dale McKinley, Moshoeshoe Monare, Thuli Mofutsanyane, Murphy Morobe, Mendi Msimang, Nathi Mthethwa, Gugu Mtshali, Derrick Naidoo, S'bu Ndebele, George Nene, Joel Netshitenzhe, Trevor Ngwane, Noor Nieftagodien, Siphiwe Nyanda, Blade Nzimande, Essop Pahad, Ebrahim Patel, Kate Philip, Mathews Phosa, Devan Pillay, Kuben Pillay, Cyril Ramaphosa, Ebrahim Rasool, Vishwas Satgar, Dinga Sikwebu, Elinor Sisulu, Bafana Sithole, Raymond Suttner, Ben Turok, Dominic Tweedie, Salim Vally, Zwelinzima Vavi, Eddie Webster, Mark Williams, Helen Zille, Lerato Zimbili and President Jacob Zuma. I regret that I was unable to interview Tokyo Sexwale and President Robert Mugabe, though this was not for want of trying.

Finally, I must mention Kgalema's closest friend and comrade, Stan Nkosi, who tragically passed away less than a year before I started this project. He would have been easily the most important person to interview and I am sure he would have made a huge contribution to this book.

An introductory reflection

Kgalema Motlanthe was born into a society with marked political, social and economic features, which influenced and helped shape him in myriad ways. We start with this wider context in order to understand the kind of child, son, brother, husband, comrade, friend and politician he became – allowing for the general fact that many different forces shape people as they grow up into adulthood and live out their lives.

From the time diamonds and gold were discovered in the nineteenth century, South Africa grew rapidly into a powerful capitalist country, by far the strongest on the African continent. The diamond and gold fields attracted jobseekers from across the globe. They also attracted capital in a rush for profits. As a result this country increasingly settled into the world capitalist economy, then still dominated by Britain and other European countries.

Alongside the burgeoning economy were the facts of race and racism. They had been defining features of South African history ever since the arrival of Jan van Riebeeck and other white colonists in 1652 at the Cape of Good Hope, but very seldom as purely independent factors shaping the society. Rather, race and racism have been largely used as instruments to achieve the rapid growth of local capitalism, which is why the most oppressed and exploited workers have always been black, whereas supervisors and managers under apartheid were almost exclusively white and white workers generally were much better off than their black compatriots.

But this did not change the fact that in the final analysis both black and white workers were – though far apart – still subjected to capitalist exploitation. That is why, from the very onset of colonialism and capitalism in South Africa, race and class were inseparably intertwined. The political (race) and economic (class) features have always been combined in our society. For almost the whole of the twentieth century the black working class led lives that were controlled by 'racial capitalism'.[1] This total system of oppression and exploitation dogged black workers and their families every minute of every day in some form or other. There were, and still are, hundreds of threads binding life in the factories and mines with life in the mine hostels, compounds and townships, whether urban or rural. Work, residence, housing, social amenities, welfare, education and so much more were all systemically linked to one another.

This experience has provided the content of the debates about the nature of South African society and about the kind of revolution needed to transform that society. The debates have preoccupied the national liberation movement over its entire history. Within the Communist Party they gave rise to a theory of 'internal colonialism', also called 'colonialism of a special type', which held that black people were oppressed as a race within the capitalist state. This in turn led to a 'two-stage theory' as a programme for action: first would come political liberation through the abolition of racist and undemocratic apartheid laws and practices (basically the national democratic revolution or NDR), followed by a struggle for true social justice and socialism.[2]

Starting in the 1950s, this theory began to gain increasing

An introductory reflection

ascendancy within the ANC and later became the orthodoxy of the liberation movement itself. But it is open to many criticisms and suffers from many contradictions, the most powerful of which is that it is impossible to compartmentalise people's real socioeconomic or material lives, especially those of working-class communities. According to the theory, the supposed 'leaders' of the working class were to divide the struggle into two stages. The first was to get rid of apartheid and introduce a nonracial democracy, but this nevertheless had to leave the capitalist system intact because the attack on it was to be held back for some unknown and indeterminate second stage in time: that would be the second stage of the revolution. The leaders, not the working class, would decide which of their demands and rights suited the first stage and could be won in it. The theory said nothing about when workers were to begin the struggle against capitalism, when they would be 'ready' to carry it out, and how they would do it.

Two-stage theory is the most ridiculous notion in the annals of revolutionary thinking. It is dangerously counterrevolutionary, as it directly harms people's living standards by holding back their demands just when families are ready to fight against the poverty, unemployment and hardship they have suffered for so long. After 1994, even the ANC's electoral slogan of 'building a better life' or its attempts in government to eradicate poverty would be subjected to the policy and budgetary constraints implied by the first stage of the national democratic revolution. The whole concept is unrealistic anyway. Nowhere in the world has poverty or unemployment been eradicated within a capitalist framework.

This is exactly why since 1994, in the revolution's first stage – the period of the unfolding of the national democratic revolution – conditions of unemployment, poverty and inequalities have in fact worsened in South Africa since the apartheid days.[3] The immediate question that arises is how a party supposedly representing the interests of working people can suspend a resolution of their daily problems to some vague period in the future. The best intentions of the ANC have been seriously constrained by fiscal rectitude, which has been pursued by the government in deference to capital. Moreover, in a highly developed capitalist society like South Africa, where as a result the black working class is the overwhelming majority of the population, the ANC resists nationalisation but supports the corporate sector, even extending it in the name of Black Economic Empowerment.

This occurs despite the ANC's claim to be 'multi-class', a description often used to justify its many neoliberal policies. The central problem about its 'multi-class' character is not that all classes are treated equally in terms of appropriate policies and budgets, but that it is the black working class – the historical support base of the ANC – that has borne the brunt of post-apartheid neoliberalism. This is why black unemployment and poverty actually increased after 1994 while big business was making more profits than under apartheid. The upshot is that the supposed 'leader' of the national democratic revolution – the black working class – has become worse off in material terms since 1994, while a tiny black elite has grown immensely rich in the same period, and a significant black middle class has arisen.

From the perspective of the present time, the strong and often violent public sector strikes since 1994 and the even more violent township protests from 2004 are the surest sign that the national democratic revolution is unravelling. We face a long period of mass struggles for the social justice, which the ANC has flagrantly failed to deliver.

These thoughts on the leading ideas of the liberation

An introductory reflection

movement are meant to provide some background to Kgalema's own thinking and political life, which have been inextricably linked to the ANC. What he has set out to do and what he has achieved need to be viewed in this larger context of ideas. Whether he has confronted the contradictions in the ANC's thinking and whether he has resolved or overcome them in his own thoughts and practice as a trade unionist, ANC leader and deputy president of South Africa, will become more evident in the course of this book.

In conclusion, it is important to point out Kgalema's attitude towards the independent left, who are vociferously critical of the ANC and its policies. Unlike most other ANC leaders, his attitude towards them is constructive. He respects all their leading figures, such as Ashwin Desai, Mazibuko Jara, Trevor Ngwane and Vishwas Satgar. He adds: 'There are no doubt some excellent people there. But I find that what makes the independent left go on short spells is that they tend to be issue-driven only instead of building permanent organisations, so that while they continue to take up important day-to-day issues they do so without a long-term political and organisational perspective.' With a warm-hearted laughter he recalls Desai saying to him, upon bumping into him at the entrance to the Anglo American head office in the 1990s, 'So I see you are now part of the bourgeoisie.'

PART ONE
FORMATIVE YEARS

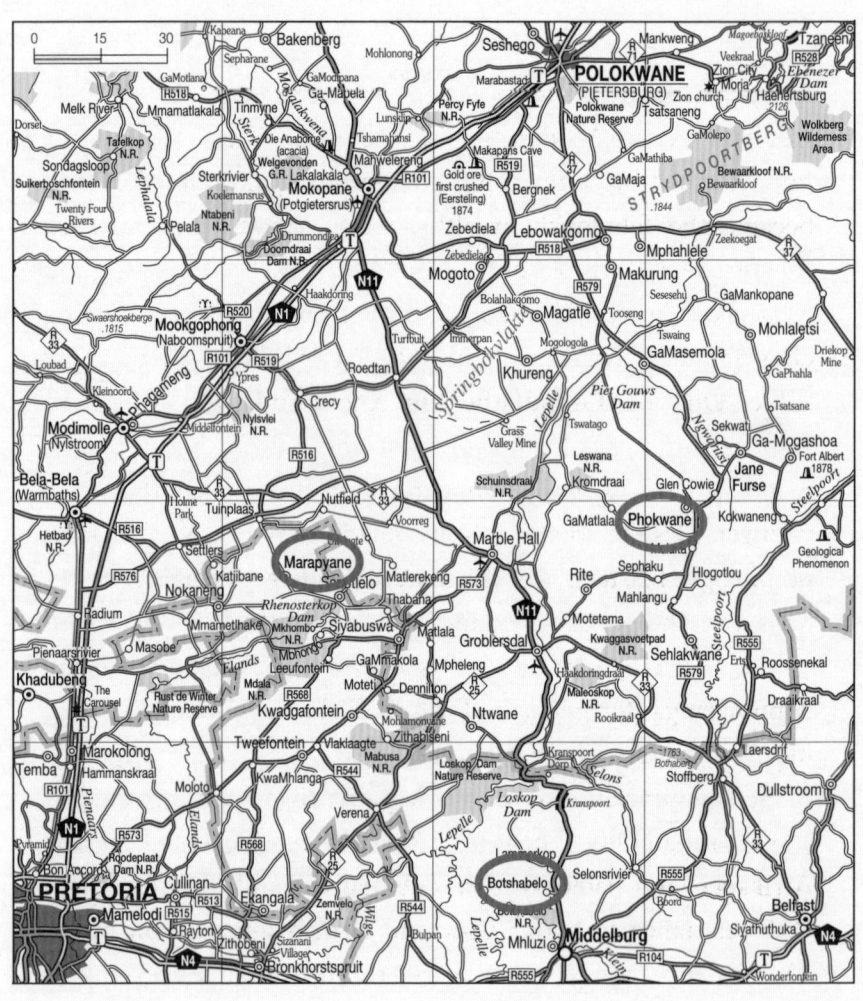

CHAPTER ONE
Ancestral roots, youth and political baptism

Ancestral family

Kgalema Petrus Motlanthe was born on 19 July 1949 in the impoverished black township of Alexandra, close to what later became the fabulously wealthy, white Sandton in northern Johannesburg. His parents, Louis Mathakoe Motlanthe and Masefako Sophia Madingoane, came from poor black working class families. Kgalema – also called 'Mkhuluwa', meaning 'Elder One' or 'Grandfather' in Xhosa and Zulu – has two younger brothers, Tlatlane Ernest and Lekota Sydney, with whom he has had close relationships, especially when they were younger. Despite what has been stated elsewhere, Kgalema has no biological sisters.[1] On the maternal side Kgalema's ancestry hails from the Sepedi-speaking Northern Sotho in the heartland of the Pedi kingdom or what is known as Sekhukhuneland in Mpumalanga (formerly the Eastern Transvaal), which in Sotho means 'the place where the sun rises'.

Sekhukhuneland, straddling Mpumalanga and Limpopo, has a fascinating political history, rich in the experiences of initially Afrikaner and later British colonialism and the legendary Pedi resistance to both.[2] Boer and British intervention in the Mpumalanga region, particularly the final brutal crushing of heroic Pedi resistance by the British in Sekhukhuneland in 1879, was among the worst manifestations of the ravages of colonialism in South Africa. The collaboration between British and Boer imperialism and racism against the BaPedi – when they were not at war with each other – was concerted and ruthless. Sekhukhuneland's historical significance is captured by the historian Peter Delius as 'the heartland of the once powerful Pedi Kingdom which under the leadership of Sekwati and Sekhukhune played a pivotal role in the nineteenth century history of the Transvaal. It held the Zulu, the Swazi, the Boers and the British at bay and had provided a haven in a dangerous and turbulent world. In historical maps of the Transvaal it was marked in bold letters, a place at the forefront of the hopes and fears of statesmen, missionaries and, ultimately, major-generals'.[3]

In more recent times, notes Delius, 'The ANC was no stranger to Transvaal rural politics nor to Sekhukhuneland, having a rich history of connection stretching back to the first decades of the century. Chiefs played a key role in the foundation and early years of the organisation.'[4] Some of the most senior royals of the BaPedi maintained close connection with the African National Congress (ANC) and provided financial support. ANC and Umkhonto we Sizwe (MK) veterans such as Flag Boshielo, John Kgoana Nkadimeng, Lawrence Phokanoka, Elias Motsoaledi, Godfrey Pitje and John Phala (who passed away in August 2009) were born and grew up in Sekhukhuneland.[5] BaPedi battles against the Boers were so heroic that King Sekhukhune II was invited to attend the founding conference of the ANC in 1912.[6]

It was also in Sekhukhuneland that Sabatakgomo was formed, an organisation forged in the interaction between workers in rural and urban areas. Migrant workers, moving constantly between the urban and rural areas, were the key players in its formation, in association with both the ANC and the South African Communist Party (SACP). They became the link between these organisations and struggles unfolding in both town and countryside.[7] But Sabatakgomo was more than just an organisation. It was also a community battle cry at the first sign of danger.[8] So closely tied is Sekhukhuneland to the history of the ANC in Mpumalanga that the formation of MK was inspired partly by the 1958 Sekhukhune Revolt.

Kgalema's maternal family moved from Phokwane in Sekhukhuneland to Botshabelo,[9] near Middelburg, when his great-grandfather, the Reverend Ramatoto Johannes Madingoane,[10] left to train as a priest. Upon completion of the training, he went to live and minister to a community in Marapyane, in Mpumalanga.[11] After falling out with this community in 1912, Madingoane bought a farm named Klipfontein. He met his wife, Sophia Mmateng Masefako Nkadimeng, in Jane Furse in Sekhukhuneland, where they were both attending the Lutheran church. She was the daughter of Kgosi Phaswane I and Mankwane Lekala of the Nkadimeng-BaPedi royal clan in Manganeng, also in Sekhukhuneland. At some point they married – it is unclear where and when – and finally settled on their land at Klipfontein.

The Madingoanes had five sons and one daughter. Their eldest son, Kgalema Marcus, was Kgalema Motlanthe's grandfather, after whom he was named. Kgalema married Louisa Mmope Sehole, a Mokgatla from Marapyane.[12] Their seventh child, a girl called Masefako Sophia, was Kgalema Motlanthe's mother. In 1939 Kgalema Madingoane moved with his wife to Apex, a squatter camp in Benoni Old Location, in search of work.[13] As such, he was a typical migrant worker. Trapped in cycles of poverty, unemployment and associated dependency, labour migration tends to cross from one generation to the next. Thus most of Madingoane's grandchildren ended up, like so many others before and after them, going to seek jobs and a living in Johannesburg. Kgalema soon got involved in community matters and eventually became a well-known community leader and later councillor in Apex. He was instrumental in establishing the township of Daveyton in 1955 and also moved into business, running a funeral parlour and general dealership there. After he died in 1956 two schools and a street were named after him.[14]

On the paternal side, Kgalema's grandfather Petrus Motlanthe was born in Sewaneng, a squatter settlement on the edge of a farm in Ga-Mothiba, some 75 kilometres from Polokwane (formerly Pietersburg).[15] Petrus and his family lived there with many other families until, with squatter removals, they had to leave in about 1940. They were moved to another farm, Melkboomfontein, a few kilometres away.

Kgalema's father Louis Mathakoe, the eldest son of Petrus, was also born in Sewaneng. Petrus was a polygamist and a traditional healer. A kinsman, Teddy Matsitela, remarked that Louis had 'contended' with the fact that his father was a polygamist, suggesting that he had reservations about that cultural practice. With polygamy, there were 'lots and lots of people' and Louis loved them all, Matsitela says. The home was called a 'location' to show how big the family really was!

When Petrus and his family moved to Melkboomfontein Louis did not go with them. Instead he decided to look for work in Johannesburg. He went to live in Alexandra and got a job as a cleaner at St John's College in Houghton. Kgalema's mother Masefako was then working as a domestic worker in Observatory and also living in Alexandra. It was there that they met. They dated for a while and married in 1946.

Kgalema's parents, like so many other black working-class people, had little formal education. Their circumstances – a product of apartheid education and urban control policies

– compelled them to take any job they could get rather than remain trapped in the poor black ghettoes of the then Eastern and Northern Transvaal. Louis would probably have realised that he was going nowhere if he had moved with his parents to yet another squatter settlement, on Melkboomfontein. His choice to move to Alexandra around 1941 and seek work was at least a better prospect in those hard days of apartheid.

Kgalema has a deep sense of family and history. As the research disclosed new information he said, 'These things fascinate me more than anything else, believe me.'[16] Born a year after the National Party came to power in 1948, he lived most of his life in the 42-year period of white racist brutality, oppression and exploitation up to 1990. His family's story still looms large in his mind, a significant backdrop to all that he has experienced in his own time.

Kgalema's family

Masefako gave birth to Kgalema, her first-born son, on 19 July 1949. It was customary that when a young woman was about to give birth she would go to her parents or relatives for support. This is what Masefako did. She went to the home of her sister Mantimu, where she was looked after. She gave birth at the Boksburg-Benoni Hospital and then returned to Alexandra with Kgalema.

In Alexandra, one of the oldest black townships in Johannesburg, his parents' home was 'just one big room', one of the thousands of 'houses' built by owners in their yards and often rented out. Sometimes ten or more families lived in one yard. Many of the yards were quite big, but the rooms were about nine by twelve metres. At night the chairs would be placed on top of whatever tables there were, to create space for sleeping. The Motlanthes often had at least six people living there, but often a friend or two or some family members visited over the weekends. These memories are still vivid for Kgalema.

Kgalema's family lived in several houses in Alexandra at the time. His grandfather Joseph lived along the same street, 16th Avenue. His aunt Sodi lived in 12th Avenue and his uncle Godfrey was in 6th Avenue. As a result, Kgalema says, he lived 'at different times in different homes.' Although he was only eleven when his parents were forcibly removed from Alexandra to Meadowlands in 1956, he could feel that Alexandra was a close-knit community and he missed it, 'especially in the area of football, which I loved to play as a young boy.'

Several sources say that the first school Kgalema attended was in Alexandra. In fact his brother Ernest says it was in Ga-Mothiba, in Limpopo, where his father was born. Ernest and Kgalema were sent there to their grandmother, Grace, for a few months just when Kgalema was about to start school because their parents did not have their own home at the time and other circumstances made it difficult for them to take care of their children themselves.

Kgalema resumed schooling for Grade 1 in Alexandra at the Anglican missionary school, known as Pholosho Primary. Before Bantu education began, Church schooling was the norm in Alexandra. Anglican, Catholic, Dutch Reformed and Methodist schools existed there until under apartheid almost all closed down. As a result of the Catholic Church refusing to close their schools, they continued to function. The other Church-based schools took a principled stand not to implement apartheid education and instead of working with the government, as they were invited to do, chose to shut their doors, including Pholosho Primary's. The Sotho meaning of 'Pholosho' is 'saved' but taking a more principled stand led, ironically, to the school's demise in Alexandra.

Ancestral roots, youth and political baptism

Kgalema's time in the Anglican school until it was disbanded had a huge formative influence on him, shaping his values and outlook at a still tender age. The Anglican Church 'is quite distinctive in Christianity. It tends to be more worldly.'[17] In that more progressive spirit, the official colours of Pholosho Primary were those of the ANC: black, green and gold. This was a conscious reflection of the huge influence of the ANC in Alexandra and more generally in Johannesburg, especially when Kgalema resumed schooling there in 1956. That time and its symbolism must have left an impression on him. In 1955 the Freedom Charter was adopted and in 1957 there was the massive Alexandra bus boycott.[18] Kgalema can still remember that his father bought a bicycle during the boycott in order to get to work.

After Pholosho Primary and the other mission schools shut down, Pholosho continued to operate covertly, under very difficult conditions. Kgalema remembers that the school 'was spread in different parts of the township, one room in a backyard, another in a garage and others scattered in other places. We went from one place to another to do our schooling.' Though his early memory of Alexandra is a bit vague, two very different images stay vivid: the regular police raids on shebeens, and always having a tennis ball in his pocket for playing soccer with his friends, either at school or on their way home.

From Pholosho Primary in Alexandra, Kgalema went to Totomeng Lower Primary in Meadowlands, then to Masekhene Higher Primary, also in Meadowlands, and thereafter to Meadowlands Secondary School in Zone 2. Though he stayed in Zone 8 he walked several kilometres daily from there to school in Zone 2 and back. Kgalema's parents finally placed him in Orlando High School because Meadowlands did not have high schools. He remembers those long walks he had to take from Meadowlands to Orlando High School and back each day. The extensive walking during his school years could well have inculcated his love of walking long distances in mountainous surroundings.

When Kgalema and his brother Ernest returned to Alexandra, they went to stay with their aunt in 13th Street because their parents still did not have a home of their own. With the boys fairly close by, their parents could at least see them more often and be closer to them to monitor their progress and attend to their needs. But two years later, in 1958, the parents got a house at 71, 16th Street and moved in, reuniting with the boys. They stayed there for less than two years before they were forcibly removed to Meadowlands in 1959.

At the time of the mass removals Kgalema's mother was still working in Observatory as a domestic worker and his father Louis as a cleaner at St John's. They were loving parents who took care of their three sons as well as they possibly could, under often the difficult circumstances of their menial jobs, low wages and imposed bad working conditions, especially in those years when black trade unions were not recognised and they had to contend daily with what was common for all African people in the urban areas then: the pass laws, police harassment and white racism in every facet of life. Kgalema's own family experience showed him that these inseparable daily injustices, political and social, made nonsense of the two-stage theory of revolution predominant in the ANC and SACP, which effectively separated political freedom from economic and social justice.

Like most African families, the Motlanthes struggled to make ends meet. Kgalema's brother Sydney recalls that at one stage his father gave him a kind of 'bread consumed by miners those days, called *mbonyana*. I think it was an inferior bread compared to what you bought in the shops. It was cheap bread you chewed forever.'[19] Kgalema agrees that they knew tough times but that 'there was always bread at least at home.'

Despite some needy periods Kgalema has no doubt that 'we grew up in a very stable environment. There were never really serious quarrels between our parents and though they were not perfect, on the whole it was definitely a stable family home. They respected and loved each other and they always warmly received family members who visited.' Sydney recalls that when he once wanted Kgalema to buy him something, he was scolded for not realising the need to be careful with money when times are tough. 'He said I was talking like a youngster who did not understand how money works.'[20]

Kgalema's parents came from stable family backgrounds and were religious, his mother Masefako probably more so than Louis. 'My parents were practising Christians and as a result I grew up in churchly surroundings,' he says. Kgalema adds that Masefako was tomboyish, by her own admission, and could do most of the things that boys did back home in Ramantsho, including killing snakes with a stick! She also had a temper, as he remembers candidly: 'If she was busy washing dishes and you were up to mischief the dishcloth would be thrown at you before you knew it. She was the disciplinarian at home, giving us many spankings.' Masefako was clearly an assertive, strong woman, even in relation to her husband Louis. Though a bit frail and suffering from Alzheimer's, at the age of 84 at the time of writing she is still very much alive in Meadowlands, Zone 8.

The brothers Ernest and Sydney did not think that Louis had as great a fervour for politics as Kgalema would have, but 'like any black person who lived under apartheid he hated it and sometimes spoke about many bad things that the white government did to black people', Kgalema says. Louis was a 'soft-spoken, reserved man and gentlemanly, a man of few words and almost reticent', as Kgalema puts it. It was Ernest who felt strongly that Kgalema took a lot after his father: 'He has some of my father's traits. My father was a great listener and never shouted at people or raised his voice.'

Kgalema says proudly that Louis never once 'lifted a finger on any one of us'. He recalls Louis telling him: 'I don't want to touch you because if I do I would do so much harm.' Yet he may have raised his hand occasionally. Sydney remembers Kgalema intervening to prevent his father from hitting him after he went to play for another soccer club, at a time when all his sons played for the same soccer club, Meadowlands Spa. Kgalema told Louis that it was Sydney's right to choose to play for whichever team he wanted. It seems that already in those days, when most parents hit their children, Kgalema was opposed to parents using violence to punish their children for any wrongdoing.

Though Louis had little formal education he was very interested in educational matters. Kgalema traces this interest to Louis' time at St John's College. Louis passed away in 1988, in the year after Kgalema was released from Robben Island. He was then retired. Sadly, Kgalema told how his father fell into an uncovered hole in Meadowlands while council workers were digging trenches for storm drainage pipes. After the fall Louis' health declined. Short of breath and vomiting most of the time, he finally 'just gave up.' With Kgalema already prominent in politics, there were many leaders and other members of the ANC, SACP, National Union of Mineworkers (NUM) and the Congress of Trade Unions (Cosatu) who attended his funeral.

Kgalema had a good relationship with his father, who visited him a few times on Robben Island. When he was released in 1987 he intended to spend as much time with Louis as possible, making up for the eleven years he had spent in detention and prison. Two months after his release, though, he joined NUM and ever since then his life has been consumed by commitments outside the family. It was very painful for him when Louis died.

Kgalema, Ernest and Sydney all recall, with nostalgia, how every year their parents took them during school holidays to either Ramantsho or Ga-Mothiba, to visit their grandparents. Clearly the Motlanthes have a deep sense of the importance of family. Nowadays they are fairly regularly in touch with each other. Many years ago the family formed the Mmope-Kgalema Burial Society, named after their grandparents. Kgalema's cousin Catherine took this initiative 'because our families did not visit each other much before'.[21]

In fact it is more than a burial society. It assists family members struggling as a result of unemployment, for example, to pay for debts or daily living expenses, as an act of familial solidarity. The finance provided is not a loan but a gift. One of the society's aims is to promote 'mutual and healthy social relationships among members of the society.'[22] The solidarity with members experiencing hard times could indeed be seen as promoting 'healthy social relations'. In recognition of the Makena-Madingoane familial links membership is open to all interested Makena or Madingoane offspring and their families. The family also consciously uses the occasion of the society's quarterly meetings to nurture family bonds. There are in today's atomised and atrophied world not many such families, weighed down as most working-class households are by the crushing weight of the current social crisis.

Having no sisters, Kgalema and his two brothers had to take turns attending to domestic chores when their parents were at work. The boys would rush back late in the afternoon to clean and tidy up before their parents came home. Kgalema laughed, describing this to me. As the eldest he had to make sure that all chores were done in time. But when it came to cooking, the conventional job for a sister, it was mainly Ernest who had to do it. Ernest had no problem with such sexism: 'Actually, I will say that I was the sister because I would cook and clean and so on at home.'[23] For Ernest, Kgalema was never really 'much of a cook but he would clean his own room, which was always very tidy and he was always dressed neatly. You will not find him just putting his clothing anywhere. Everything has a place for him and he keeps it that way.' He was so particular about how his clothing was ironed that he preferred to do it himself, and would do it even after it was already ironed but not to his satisfaction.[24]

Kgalema was no different from other African children in working class townships. Most of the family emphasise that he was a well-behaved and respectful child who listened to his parents and other elders and was fairly polite. The fact that he was an altar boy played a big part in his overall demeanour as a youngster. He adds: 'The values of Christianity broadly and the teachings of the Anglican Church particularly had a very big influence on my outlook on life when I was still young.' However, soccer was a competing commitment, and later it was politics too. From about 1970, when he was 21, he spent less time in Church activities, more with soccer, and increasingly got into politics, specifically with the ANC.

Phineas Mabetoa, his best friend during his teenage years, recalls that Kgalema was gentle, kind, ready to help where he could. For him, Kgalema the teenager was a 'very jolly and nice person and always accommodating.' He had a sense of order and discipline that seemed to come easily, having been instilled early on with the values of respect, selfless service, modesty and discipline. No doubt this reflects how he was raised at home by his churchgoing mother and within the regimen of the Church itself.[25] Kgalema's dedication to a cause has been notable in his political life, as we will see. Meanwhile, as a child his growing social consciousness made him averse to elitism and other inequalities. Why should certain cutlery be reserved for visitors? he asked his mother.

Kgalema was a keen, talented soccer player who for a while also played professionally. He played for Spa Sporting from Atteridgeville and Rockville Hungry Lions in Soweto. The manager at Spa Sporting was Russa Bud-Mbelle, son of the second secretary-general of the ANC, Isaiah Budlwana Mbelle, whose sister was married to Sol Plaatje. Kgalema held 'Uncle Bud' in high regard as his mentor. I doubt if there is any politician today who has as much knowledge of both the history of soccer in this country and the game itself as Kgalema.

His father himself had been a good soccer player and was fervent about the game; he played soccer in Alexandra and was called 'Lulu Mountain'. Kgalema's cousin Catherine and her husband Edwin Linala are sure that Louis's passion for soccer and the fact he was so good at it induced the same love in his sons, especially Kgalema, for the 'beautiful game'. At one stage Kgalema and his two brothers played for the same soccer team, Meadowlands Spar.

Mabetoa tells how Kgalema left the Shamrocks soccer team because he could not tolerate the ill discipline. Players were drinking before training and playing matches and sometimes missed training and matches as a result. After his pleas fell on deaf ears Kgalema quit, without regret, and formed another team, Spa. Ernest says it was Kgalema's positive influence that 'showed me the way and as a result I stopped a lot of the silly things I did as a youngster.' Kgalema was a role model for both him and Sydney and always their leader.

It was mainly through Kgalema that Ernest and Sydney went to church in Meadowlands. After many years as an altar boy, Kgalema intended to become an Anglican priest. As he told Padraig O'Malley in 1992: 'I was an altar boy for many, many years and I think that is really what shaped one's life.'[26] Through him, Ernest and Sydney both ended up as altar boys too for many years. Sydney recalls that they took turns to ring the church bell in the morning. 'There used to be a mass at 6.30 a.m. on Wednesday and then again that evening, and on Saturdays and Sundays.' There is a sense that it was not just that Kgalema was the eldest of the brothers but that he had the qualities that nurtured a closeness between them, along with their love of soccer and jazz.

Kgalema was also very much at home with the priests of the Community of the Resurrection, an Anglican religious order of which Father Trevor Huddleston was a member. He was particularly close to Father Kingston Erson, who visited his family in Meadowlands when Kgalema was imprisoned on Robben Island. Ernest remembers: 'Father Erson would usually take Kgalema over weekends to Rosettenville, where the church was, on a Friday night, and bring him back on a Saturday or Sunday night. If he did not get involved in politics he would have become a priest.'

This is so because after Kgalema had completed his primary schooling in 1964 the Anglican Church gave him a bursary to go to St Christopher's in Swaziland to do his secondary education and then train for the priesthood. Everything was arranged but he had to apply for a travel document to the Bantu Affairs Department. They turned down his application and said that he must continue to study in South Africa. Prevented by the apartheid regime from going to St Christopher's, he went to Meadowlands Secondary. It was a sad moment for him. However, had he gone to Swaziland, his life would have followed a very different course. He may well not have taken to politics and ended up where he is today. Ironically, he did end up going to Swaziland, not to study and become a priest but for the ANC underground, which he had joined in 1974 and which permanently changed his goals. From then on, Kgalema's life became tied to the broader national liberation movement and the ANC in particular.

Anglican, atheist or agnostic?

Many people asked me if Kgalema abandoned the deeply religious beliefs of his youth and became an atheist, a fair question of one who was at one time a leading member of the SACP – communists are usually atheists, though some call themselves Christian Marxists.[27] Kgalema's politicisation and resultant growth in social consciousness certainly led him to embrace Marxism. However, it was a Stalinised version of Marxism that he embraced, with the largely uncritical allegiance of the CPSA (Communist Party of South Africa, which later became the SACP) to the Comintern that began in the 1920s and continued as a political line long after the Comintern dissolved in 1943.[28]

Today Kgalema has a more nuanced response: 'I have an understanding as to why people believe in religion and also strongly believe in a spirituality, which is more earthly and not necessarily connected to religion. I am in this sense a deeply spiritual person.'[29] Human-centred, he accepts that many people practise a range of religious beliefs for many personal and historical reasons, just as he knows that there are different class interests and therefore possibly different political tendencies among the ANC members. It is the Church's early influence on his life, he believes, that freed him from being judgemental about the convictions of others.

He argues that Marxism still needs to get to grips with the sway of religion over the masses, rather than invoking dicta like 'Religion is the opiate of the masses'. He thinks that at this stage of society religion plays a balancing role as the 'easiest explanation of reality for ordinary people to remain sane.' But religious zeal can also dull the consciousness and be an obstacle to social self-emancipation if it promotes blind faith in the hereafter at the expense of a struggle against oppression. 'I believe in the dictum that says that for you to deserve to go to heaven you have to be good to your neighbours here on earth and take care of them when they are in distress, whatever the form such distress might take. In other words I could say that we should fight for heaven on earth, if you see my point. But I also agree ... that religion can be a form of escapism.' He believes we must strive to understand this escapism for what it is: a way of responding to society's multifaceted hardships, contradictions and resultant struggles, especially for working class families.

It seems that the more political Kgalema became towards the end of the 1960s, the less time he had for the Anglican Church. This was not because he overtly rejected it, but new political interests and commitments increasingly took over. By 1977 his political consciousness would have overruled his religious beliefs. From then on, the decade he spent on Robben Island in the company of many SACP-type Marxists such as Harry Gwala and Govan Mbeki (both outright atheists) appears to have consolidated his earlier growing scepticism towards established religions. More than ever before, he became committed to a specifically ANC political future. Asked if he had any regrets about not becoming an Anglican priest, without the slightest hesitation he said no, because 'a political cause embraces the entire nation in a national and even international project, whereas the Church embraces mainly its followers in a more restricted sphere. This means that through politics we can entirely change a society but through the Church by its nature one's goals will be much more curtailed.'

Political baptism

Kgalema's political interest began after reading Trevor Huddleston's *Naught for Your Comfort* when he was in high school. He found the book in the library of St Peter's Theological College in Rosettenville when he was still an altar boy at St Peter's church.[30]

Two chapters impressed him highly. One titled Education for Servitude 'explained the introduction of Bantu education, which happened to coincide with the closure of my school Pholosho Primary in Alexandra.' The other, Till There Be No Place, 'explained the forced removals in very lucid terms.'

At that time, he says, 'members of this Mission, like Father Erson, often used to visit our home. These were white people but they always cooked for themselves, cleaned and so on, whereas what I knew was that all white people did not do these things for themselves. Their conduct contradicted the picture we had of white people, as our oppressors and exploiters.' What seems to have most impressed Kgalema about these white priests was that they insisted on and never wavered from doing these domestic chores themselves. That sowed the seeds of Kgalema's firm belief ever since that nonracialism must be a fundamental principle of the national liberation struggle, in theory and practice.

There were many other influences Kgalema was exposed to in the late 1960s and early 1970s. The Black Power Movement in the US (particularly the Black Panthers) and the Black Consciousness (BC) Movement at home were on the rise and certainly made an impression on him. Writers and activists associated with Black Power such as Huey Newton, Eldridge Cleaver and Stokely Carmichael guided his thinking and so too did Steve Biko, the BC leader in South Africa who was tortured to death in 1977. At that time the ANC and Pan Africanist

Congress (PAC) were banned.[31] Overall, though, Kgalema tended towards the ANC 'because even where I grew up in Alexandra the ANC had a strong influence among people.' His parents were also supporters of the ANC, although 'they did not know a great deal', he says.

Kgalema was reading widely even before the BC-aligned South African Students Organisation was formed in 1969 by Biko and others. By then he had already read books like *Go Tell It on the Mountain* (1953) by James Baldwin, *Black Like Me* (1961) by the journalist Howard Griffin, a pocket-sized book titled *The Role of the Individual in History* (1898) by the Russian Marxist theoretician George Plekhanov, *When the Word Is Given* (1963) by Louis Lomax, *The Role of the Missionaries in Conquest* (1952) by Nosipho Majeke (a pseudonym for Dora Taylor) of the Unity Movement, and Frantz Fanon's *The Wretched of the Earth* (1963). He was then going on twenty years old. His favourite bookstore in Johannesburg was the old Vanguard, which specialised in leftwing literature. There can be little doubt that such wide-ranging influences enabled him, even after he joined the ANC underground and became a fervent follower, to take a broader view of things, both on Robben Island and ever since his release in 1987.

Contrary to some reports, Kgalema did not pass his final exams at Orlando High School in 1968. His favourite subjects were history and English, but in his final year he struggled with maths, switched to biology and then could not catch up what he had already missed in the new (compulsory) subject in time for the exam. The situation in African schools was deplorable at the time: Bantu Education condemned black pupils to inferior black teacher training, teaching, facilities and curricula so that they could not excel. He completed matric much later, during the first few years of his ten-year sentence on Robben Island.

For a while at high school Kgalema worked part-time as an assistant on Saturdays at Tollman's bottle store in Hyde Park.[32] He also got Ernest a part-time job there after he left. Kgalema says that when he started, all the black employees warned him not to drink the liquor, but they all drank! Working there, he says, 'I always had supplies, which I brought home. Sydney Khumalo, that great artist, used to visit my father. I would then take out a drink for them. They would listen to jazz while drinking and then late at night I would take him to his home in Rockville.' Kgalema has never been a drinker. He may take a sip of champagne during the festive season rather than be the odd man out, but apart from that he is a teetotaller. His reasons are his health and sport.

In 1969 he got a job in the Johannesburg city council's commercial unit. He supervised the liquor outlets in Soweto. Only from 1962 were Africans allowed to buy liquor, when beer halls were opened in the townships. These beer halls were deliberately placed close to railways stations so that workers could have a drink on their way home. Stan Nkosi, who became Kgalema's closest friend and comrade, Siphiwe Nyanda, former minister of communications, and George Nene, deputy director-general of multilateral relations in the department of international relations and cooperation, also worked in this unit at various times during that period. Together they later joined the ANC underground, Umkhonto weSizwe.[33]

Unlike other areas of the then white-dominated Johannesburg city council, the commercial unit did not have white supervisors. The workers and supervisors were all black, several of them ANC sympathisers. The unit ran the beer halls in the townships, did the stock-taking, banking, balancing books and other tasks. It was precisely this 'space' that enabled Kgalema to engage in underground MK work during the seven years he worked for the council. He recalls filling up his car, a Volkswagen Beetle, for just seven rands and almost weekly going to Manzini in Swaziland to take ANC recruits out of the country for military training.

Kgalema's immediate family

Kgalema met his future wife Mapula Mokate on a train, travelling from Johannesburg's Park Station to Soweto on 3 July 1970. Almost immediately they began to date. Mapula was then in Grade 11 and Kgalema was employed in the Johannesburg city council. She recalls that he was with a friend when he boarded the train and very soon got talking to her. Kgalema, to judge from letters he wrote to Mapula from Robben Island, had undoubtedly fallen deeply in love with her. They had a fairly happy relationship from all accounts. Their elder son Kgomotso was born in September 1972, they married in 1975, the year before he was arrested, and lived with Kgalema's mother Masefako in Meadowlands, Zone 8.

Mapula, a Tswana-speaker, was born in Sophiatown. She worked at Baragwanath Hospital as a radiographer and later at Leratong Hospital, where she was when Kgalema was sentenced in 1977, and later at the Alexandra clinic. Without Kgalema's income when he was on Robben Island, things became harder than usual for both Mapula and Masefako. At one stage accommodation became such a serious problem that Kgalema asked his lawyers to help Mapula get a house. When she finally found a house elsewhere in Soweto, she sent their son Kgomotso to stay with Masefako, with whom he lived for his whole childhood.

Mabetoa and Ernest both say that Kgalema and Mapula's early relationship was 'quite fine' and Kgalema's love letters show a very clear commitment to their marriage. Mabetoa does however note that Mapula tended to be withdrawn, someone more comfortable sitting back and keeping quiet, definitely 'not a very communicative person'. Some of the problems that developed in their marriage after Kgalema was released in 1987 may have reinforced this trait. Yet Kgalema says, 'She was also fine towards other people. Things went wrong when I went to the Island. As I was getting into the underground I did explain to her the responsibilities and risks involved. She accepted the situation.' He adds that her reserve was never a problem for him because 'we are all different people with different personalities.'

If Mapula was withdrawn and anxious, it may have been related to Kgalema's dangerous political work in the ANC underground. Mapula was not herself a political activist, although Kgalema says she was once fired for taking part in a strike at Baragwanath and when she worked at the Alexandra clinic she was a member of the South African Municipal Workers Union.

Looking for the ANC

It was while working at the Johannesburg city council that the idea of joining the ANC underground first came to Kgalema. Legally, the ANC was a banned organisation, having been outlawed, along with the PAC, in April 1960, in the wake of the Sharpeville massacre. The prohibition sent members of the ANC underground or into exile, and for almost three decades the organisation was hard put to maintain its presence inside the country. The banning of the ANC coincided with, if it was not exactly the root cause of, a not uncontested decision by its leadership to turn to armed struggle by setting up its armed wing Umkhonto we Sizwe, which at first engaged in isolated acts of sabotage and then regrouped outside the country, retrained and eventually launched a guerrilla campaign when it could gain access to South Africa.

The wisdom of the decision to turn to armed struggle has

been the subject of much debate, both within and outside the movement. There are those like me who believe that armed struggle failed to pose any real military threat to the powerful white state and was in fact counterproductive, channelling energy and resources away from key forms of struggle, like the workers' movement, and also invited massive state repression which affected all forms of struggle. Kgalema agrees to some extent: 'There was never any doubt at any time that we would not defeat apartheid because there was the understanding that this was a political struggle and that the armed struggle was really armed propaganda. In fact it was all along that realisation that sustained us. When I look back now we could not have got through that terrible period without a sense of optimism, which was that on the political terrain we will triumph ultimately.'

Useful as this explanation is, it does not reckon with the major disadvantages the ANC's guerrilla struggle posed for the labour movement and the resultant setbacks and defeats it posed for the ANC itself and the wider national liberation struggle. This is not to discount the psychological value MK's attacks on major installations and institutions had even for activists in the trade unions, especially in the 1980s. But a psychological boost for the working class movement was far less urgent than greater organisation of its ranks. The trade union movement, particularly the growing strength of Cosatu, happened in spite of the strategic emphasis the ANC placed on the armed struggle.

But in the late 1960s, when Kgalema first became politically conscious, these developments and reflections were still in the future. By then he had been reading wide-ranging political literature for a few years. Wherever he travelled around the country playing soccer he would look out for books and when he played for Rockville Hungry Lions between 1967 and 1969 he was already politically conscious. He recalls that he and his friends[34] formed a support group. They tried to assist people placed by the West Rand Administration Board at a transit camp in Meadowlands Zone 5 from where they were deported to various bantustans because they did not have Section 10 rights permitting them to live in white urban South Africa.[35] Though the group did not have radical solutions to these problems, they tried to provide relief for those people.

In 1973 and 1974 Kgalema, Siphiwe Nyanda, Stan Nkosi and George Nene became closer personally and politically. They formed a cell and sought to establish contact with the ANC, join MK and recruit ANC sympathisers to it. Kgalema's initial reason for joining MK was a 'generalised opposition to apartheid racism and discrimination.' They used a room which they rented in a coal yard in White City, in Soweto, to hold their meetings and plan their activities. So open was the group to working with all progressive political forces that when they once went to Botswana they met not only ANC leaders but also those of the PAC and BC. In 1974 Nyanda, Nene and Nkosi attended the funeral of the slain BC leader Abram Onkgopotse Tiro in Gaborone. There they met not only BC people but some ANC leaders too. The PAC and BC people struck them as quite disorganised, unlike the ANC. Anyway, they were all ready to 'take up arms'[36] and the ANC, having formed MK already in 1961, was best placed to enable them to do so. Kgalema himself, along with other Soweto activists, was also hugely influenced by the ANC veteran Joe Gqabi (who was also imprisoned on Robben Island, and later assassinated in Zimbabwe).

Kgalema recalls how their group had to organise bail money for someone who had been arrested for criminal activity and who knew a lot about their underground activities. They were worried that he would disclose this information if the police found out that he was associated with them, assuming their movements were being monitored. They got him out on bail and immediately made plans to send him out of the country at that dangerous time. In fact it was not long thereafter that Kgalema and Nkosi were arrested.

Kgalema's friend Phineas Mabetoa recalls that around 1973 Kgalema used to say to him at night time, when they looked at the lit and sprawling houses covering Soweto: 'Soweto is asleep.' 'He would say that people have eaten, perhaps read the papers, like the *Sowetan* or the *Star* and then go to sleep, which worried him.' It was only later that Mabetoa realised that Kgalema meant they were politically asleep. Kgalema expected that, given the appalling conditions in Soweto and elsewhere, blacks should already have risen to the challenge and acted to change it.[37]

In 1974, at twenty-five years of age, Kgalema quietly went to Matola in Mozambique, stayed with a man who had been a priest in South Africa, and tried to make contact with the ANC. The cell he was in had begun exploring routes from Mozambique and Swaziland to Tanzania, where the ANC head office in exile was based. Kgalema and his friends were by then all tuning in regularly on a Wednesday evening between half past nine and ten to listen to the External Affairs programme of Radio Tanzania, later called Radio Freedom, a station run by the ANC from Tanzania. Kgalema also went to the then Rhodesia in search of contacts with the ANC and routes to Tanzania.

While this was going on he began taking people out of South Africa to Mozambique and especially Swaziland. He would drive them on a Monday evening to the Swazi border post at Oshoek and after spending the day with them in Swaziland he would hand the recruits over to contacts and head back to Johannesburg in the early evening, in time for work the next day. This was made possible by a flexible working arrangement the unit had among themselves. He would do all the takings and banking every Monday so that he could arrange to be off every Tuesday in order to use the day to ferry people out of the country, return at about ten o'clock in the evening, meet underground contacts and be back at work on Wednesday.

The recruits would go out of South Africa legally on the same documents that other recruits had used before. The passports thus had many exit stamps but no entries; luckily the border officials did not bother to notice if the passport photos matched the people in the car. After entering Swaziland, more commonly, Kgalema would return with all the passports, to be used again by the next people to leave the country for training. Some recruits were taken out without documents, lying on the floor of the car while going through the border post. The group were so adept, they were never once caught. From late 1974 Kgalema and Nkosi took ANC recruits out of the country regularly for about eighteen months before they were arrested on 13 April 1976.

Arrest, conviction and sentencing

Late in 1975 the cell Kgalema was part of was instructed to convert from a recruitment unit to sabotage.[38] This decision was taken at a meeting in Swaziland attended by Jacob Zuma, whose main task was running MK's Natal–Swaziland operations, and Joseph Nduli, leader of the ANC underground network in Natal. Nduli trained recruits in handling the explosive TNT and supplied TNT to the unit Kgalema was in. Stan Nkosi had inadvertently given his real name to Nduli. When Nduli was arrested on 18 March 1976 and severely tortured, he gave Nkosi's name to the police, who were keen to identify the group operating from Johannesburg. Nkosi, who had never been detained before, in turn disclosed Kgalema's name, which led to his arrest on the same day Nkosi was arrested, 13 April 1976.

This was just two months before the Soweto student uprisings exploded on the scene. Kgalema was arrested at his home in Meadowlands. Under duress Nkosi had divulged Kgalema's identity to the police, who took Nkosi to Kgalema's home and waited for him to arrive in the evening. As soon as he did they pounced on him. He was arrested under the Terrorism Act for MK activities and taken to John Vorster Square. He recalls the officer who interrogated him saying: 'We have not just arrested you but we got the whole bloody lot of you.'[39]

Nkosi had handled his interrogation well until the police asked him about the TNT. He admitted later to Kgalema that he became so nervous that he made the admission. Asked about this episode, Kgalema says there was 'absolutely not an iota of betrayal in any way whatsoever. I trusted Stan with my very life.' His response shows a deep comradely loyalty and understanding of human vulnerability when in the hands of the most brutal security police, who killed many detainees during the terrible 1960s and 1970s.

Kgalema recalls that on one of his underground trips to Swaziland he met Jacob Zuma, Joseph Nduli and Tim Maseko, a teacher who later became South African ambassador to Swaziland. Zuma talked about his time on Robben Island, the gruelling conditions there and what was needed to survive the experience. This was a wry moment for Kgalema to remember, since he had been imprisoned there himself not long afterwards.

It was in Swaziland that Zuma met Kgalema and Nkosi for the first time. Zuma recalls how he drove them to a secret ANC house in Manzini.[40] A few hundred metres away, he instructed them to take a sleeping bag they had and cover their faces so that they could not know its exact location. Siphiwe Nyanda (later head of the South African National Defence Force in post-apartheid South Africa), who was part of the group, left the country and went into exile in 1975. The decision that he should leave was precisely so as not to place Kgalema and Nkosi at risk of detection and arrest, following some risks incurred by Nyanda during the dismantling of the recruitment machinery. By then only Kgalema and Nkosi were left in the machinery. The plan was to close it down completely and start a new unit, and this was in process when Kgalema and Nkosi were arrested.

Nelson Mandela made a telling comment that year in an article he wrote on Robben Island:

> Acts of sabotage were snuffed out because, in our enthusiasm for violence as a weapon to strike at the enemy, we neglected the important work of strengthening the political organisation by recruiting new members, holding branch meetings, conducting political classes, and using legal platforms to reach the masses of people. In almost all cases the members of the new sabotage organisations were from the liberation movement, which in the process was drained of many of its most active and experienced functionaries. The net result was a weakened movement at a time when it should have been raised to its feet.[41]

Before going to Robben Island, Kgalema spent just over a year in jail, eleven months of the time awaiting trial. For the first three he was held in the dreaded John Vorster Square, then eight months at Pretoria Central Prison, another notorious place. There he and the others of the group were kept in solitary confinement, communicating with each other by wall tapping. Using any tool, individual letters were tapped to spell out words. 'Abscond', for example, would start with one tap for 'a', two for 'b', nineteen for 's', for their place in the alphabet. It is not an easy system, and obviously best used with short words having letters early in the alphabet. People needed a good grasp of the language, and of course it was a non-starter for illiterate prisoners.

Masefako and Mapula, Kgalema's mother and wife, visited him during this time. So did his cousin Catherine and his father Louis, who went once or twice. Catherine, Masefako and Mapula went to court together. Catherine recalls that he and Stan were very brave throughout the trial, which lasted a few months. It was hard for Louis, then working at the head office of Anglo American Corporation in Johannesburg, to get to court but he succeeded a few times.

Kgalema, Nkosi and Joseph Mosoeu stood trial in the Randburg Supreme Court, before Justice Human. They faced three separate charges under Section 6 of the Terrorism Act 83 of 1967 and the prosecutor, the former Transvaal attorney-general Klaus von Leires, called for the death penalty. The defending lawyers were Raymond Tucker and Shun Chetty, with Geoff Budlender as junior counsel. They argued that Kgalema and Nkosi were reasonable people concerned about the future of the country. They were ordinary and good citizens who joined MK and resorted to planning acts of violence because there were no other democratic and legal opportunities for political expression by oppressed and aggrieved black people.

Kgalema and Nkosi were found guilty of furthering the aims of a banned organisation, the possession of explosives, and having undergone training for sabotage. They were sentenced to five years on each charge, in a fifteen-year concurrent sentence that was effective for ten years. Though the police found the explosives on Mosoeu, he was acquitted.

They were then held at Leeukop Prison. It was here that they were given a taste of what to expect on Robben Island: for the duration of their stay they crushed stones in a quarry. At the end of their time at Leeukop they were badly beaten up by the white Afrikaner warders. A copy of the *Rand Daily Mail* had reached one of them for secret circulation. Newspapers were prohibited and very valuable; unless one had access to a radio, they were the only source of information about what was happening in the country.

It later transpired that this was a set-up by the warders in order to compromise Kgalema, Stan and other prisoners. Suddenly these men found an unusually large number of warders waiting for them, who demanded that they strip naked for a body search. Kgalema and some others had already read the Prisons Act, which forbade officials to order prisoners to undress in public, and refused to do so. The warders did not know of the provision and believed that the resistance they encountered was illegal, so they went to lock all the sections in order to search the cells. Word flashed around that they would conduct a body search too. Kgalema and the others each grabbed a page of the *Rand Daily Mail* and ate it. In a few minutes there was nothing left!

When the warders returned they instructed all the prisoners to go to the communal cell. There they were told again to strip by warders armed with batons and rifles. Kgalema, spokesperson for the prisoners, was busy brushing his teeth at the time. Angrily the head of the prison shouted at him not to brush his teeth while he was talking. Kgalema responded by pointing out what they had said before: they would all strip, but in private. Immediately an order was given for extra warders to enter the cell and attack the prisoners. The warders far outnumbered them and 'they beat us up thoroughly', says Kgalema. Then they were all ordered out of the cell, the search for the newspaper resumed, and the prisoners were told again to strip by angry, baffled warders.

As a protest against this brutal and illegal treatment the prisoners the next day refused any meals and demanded to see the brigadier to lodge a complaint. This was on a Saturday, a day for prison visits. Kgalema asked Mapula to report the assault to their lawyer Raymond Tucker. Tucker applied to see Kgalema and the other prisoners about it. Immediately the prison authorities began to fast-track their transfer to Robben Island. Before Tucker could see them they were told to get ready to leave.

Early next morning, on 31 July 1977, Kgalema and Nkosi left Leeukop Prison together with Stan Nkosi, Sibusiso (S'bu) Ndebele, George Mashamba, Kehla Shubane, Ephraim Butshingi and Isaac Seko. While Kgalema and Nkosi were sentenced to ten years, Shubane and Butshingi were sentenced to 5 years each and Seko got over ten years. They were put in the back of an uncomfortable van to go to Cape Town, sleeping over at Kroonstad Prison. From there they drove to Beaufort West, stopping briefly to have tea and relieve themselves, then on to Victor Verster Prison in Paarl for their second night. Next morning they were taken to Cape Town harbour for the ferry to Robben Island. Throughout this long, tiring trip, they all wore leg irons to prevent them escaping.

Kgalema certainly had a full and eventful life before he was arrested, charged and sentenced to Robben Island. To say, as the *Financial Mail* stated after the 2007 Polokwane conference, that 'Motlanthe appears not to have existed until he was imprisoned on Robben Island'[42] simply displays a woeful lack of research. Here was a man who was an aspiring priest at one stage, a supervisor in his city council job, a professional soccer player for a while, who joined the ANC underground and took many MK recruits out of the country, and was setting up as a saboteur in the liberation struggle when the regime caught up with him.

CHAPTER TWO
Life on Robben Island

> Proletarian revolutions... criticise themselves constantly, interrupt themselves continually in their own course, come back to the apparently accomplished in order to begin it afresh, deride with unmerciful thoroughness the inadequacies, weaknesses, the paltriness of their first attempts, seem to throw down their adversary only in order that he may draw new strength from the earth, recoil ever and anon from the indefinite prodigiousness of their own aims, until a situation has been created which makes all turning back impossible, and the conditions themselves cry out: 'Here is the rose, here dance!'
>
> Karl Marx, *Eighteenth Brumaire of Louis Bonaparte*, 1852

Arrival and settling in

Kgalema, together with Stan Nkosi, S'bu Ndebele, George Mashamba, Kehla Shubane, Ephraim Butshingi and Isaac Seko, arrived at Robben Island on 2 August 1977. It was a cold, drizzly winter morning. Checking in at reception they were warned by a senior white prison official that they were no longer at Leeukop and that 'This was Robben Island.' Kgalema's response to the man was that he and the others were happy that the officials knew about Leeukop because they were going to challenge the brutal treatment they had been subjected to there, demand that those responsible be charged, and seek compensation.

Initially they were taken to E section, the orientation area which was separate from other sections. All new arrivals were sent there and were not allowed to mix with prisoners elsewhere. At the time the E section prisoners were mostly young activists from the June 1976 Soweto uprisings, arguably inspired mostly by the Black Consciousness movement at a time when the ANC was banned and as a result in lacklustre retreat on the home front. E section had its own facilities including a soccer field. F and G sections were the general ones, which E section prisoners eventually moved to. These general cells kept all the other prisoners except the Rivonia trialists, who were confined to the single-cell B section together with other non-ANC prisoners such as Neville Alexander, Dennis Brutus and Zeph Mothopeng. The quota of some 25 to 30 prisoners in B section shifted through the years and included Fikile Bam, Andrew Masondo, Joe Gqabi and Mac Maharaj. Namibian prisoners were kept in D section, and the single-cell C section was where offending prisoners were kept and punished.

It was in 1959 that Robben Island was designated a maximum security prison for 'non-white males.'[1] There is no doubt that Kgalema settled quickly into the harsh reality of maximum-security prison life. He had prepared himself mentally and spiritually for imprisonment throughout his detention, especially since it appeared that the state had sufficient evidence to convict even though he and the others were to plead not guilty. Among other factors the inner strength he derived from many years in the Anglican Church gave him a sturdy basis for meeting the often brutal conditions on the Island. He also drew strength from the fact he would be joining legendary ANC leaders such as Nelson Mandela, Walter Sisulu, Ahmed Kathrada and Govan

Mbeki, who had already endured over a decade of incarceration there.

Black political prisoners in the United States influenced Kgalema too, especially the heroic resistance of George Jackson, whose stirring book *Soledad Brother* inspired black political prisoners around the world.[2] But perhaps the biggest resource for Kgalema throughout the decade he was imprisoned was his powerful belief in the justice of the cause he had embraced. This conviction did not necessarily rest on theory and analysis about the nature of the South African revolution, as espoused by the ANC and the SACP, but on a fundamental belief in the nobility of the cause: the sheer unalterable necessity of fighting oppression, racism and exploitation. In the course of his years on the Island he was not only strong for himself. Fellow prisoners report that he succoured them and soon became a leader.

Kgalema recalled for me the layout of the prison so well that when shown an annotated photo of the Island in Charlene Smith's book *Robben Island*, he immediately pointed out a few errors. The tennis courts and the library were wrongly marked, for example, and he showed their true position.[3] Kgalema was moved from E to the general cells, first to F section and then G. Every year the prison board reviewed prisoners' conduct and performance to decide to what extent, if at all, they would enjoy privileges such as study, visits and letters, and what food they could buy. Today under our Constitution these would be considered human rights.

The general sections had some advantages over single cells. There was a greater sense of solidarity and companionship. People living together were more able to share ideas than those in the single-cell B section, where senior leaders like Mandela were kept. Of course the leaders devised ways to discuss and exchange information when, for example, they crushed stones in the quarry or went to the kitchen for meals. The divide and rule policy the Nationalist Party pursued among black people (Africans, coloureds and Indians) in apartheid society was purposely extended to the Island, even to the meals they ate. 'Yes, the darkies [Africans] got an F diet and coloureds and Indians a D diet, which were better quality meals, tastier and more nutritious,' Kgalema says.

In the general sections prisoners established a *kolkhoz*, the Russian term for a buying union, a kind of collective to help prisoners who did not have money or family and friends to rely on to buy things like sugar, tobacco and other basic provisions. One person was appointed to ration all the provisions received by the more fortunate prisoners. The system avoided creating any dependency complex among poorer prisoners, especially of a kind that would inhibit them from freely participating in discussions and collective decisions. For Kgalema the overriding merit was that the 'lack of money did not unfairly affect people and was a way of levelling the playing field. It was a politically inspired rule of sharing everything possible.'

Was Kgalema a leader in the making on the Island?

This question was put to several former prisoners who were together with him. Everyone answered in the affirmative, some eagerly. Murphy Morobe, who spent five years with Kgalema, said he made such a huge impression on him that he was sure he would be a major ANC leader one day. 'I can guarantee you that just about everyone who had the opportunity to engage with him not only learnt a lot but saw in him a future leader of the ANC. He is not easily given to rhetoric and not easily flustered, and having met ANC leaders of substance my sense was that Kgalema measures up excellently to what a typical ANC cadre should be. That is how I always thought of him. People like him are a special breed and, when I look at the kind of qualities a leader should have, I think of him.'[4] Kgalema, though, did not see himself as an ANC leader on the Island or even necessarily on release:

> We did not regard ourselves – certainly not I or the group I arrived with on the Island – as leaders of the ANC. No, the real leaders were those in B section who were the leaders of the ANC before being arrested, which we were not. I was very clear in my mind of such limitations, even when I was asked to go and strengthen the NUM. I went there to do just that and never at any point aspired myself to lead the union or later the ANC. I truly always saw myself as a servant of the organisations I have been a part of and think that it was an embedded notion I thankfully derived from the time that I served the Anglican Church. I have no regrets about what others may call my self-effacement.
>
> I still insist that it is not for members or followers of any organisation to want to be leaders. That is a decision which only the members of an organisation can make – if they so wish – but to want yourself to be regarded as a leader is too presumptuous and even arrogant, I think. That for me is what democracy in action is all about. To volunteer leadership is the antithesis of democracy, which is about collective decisions and not individual ambitions. If we don't make this distinction and instead entertain leadership aspirations we won't be able to build a powerful organisation and focus on the tasks at hand. Instead we will be consumed by feathering our own nests, which will spawn everything but organisation and the fundamental transformation of our society. That should be our focus.

So humble has Kgalema been all his political life that Paul Langa, a fellow prisoner, who shared a cell with him, said: 'Even when we once had a hunger strike we had to force him to represent us. He would argue with us and say that though he appreciates the trust we place in him he is not the right person and that there must be people stronger than him. But usually when we insisted he eventually relented and that is only when we told him that he has no choice in the matter and that the prisoners had spoken.'[5]

Langa went on to relate a useful experience they had with Kgalema in another strike: 'He stood up during the strike and said that there is no problem to go on strike but to do that may threaten the concessions we have already won, especially because it was not properly planned and we need to think of its effects on the elderly and sick. He is very open-minded when it comes to tactics and strategy – he can analyse a problem brilliantly and make you think about things that were furthest from your mind.'[6]

This account gives a foretaste of how later as a leader Kgalema could pinpoint what was important. In this case: a strike, especially about food, is a sensitive matter, so it needs to be properly planned; and planning for a strike must cater for the sick and elderly. We will see later that his response to the gigantic 1987 NUM strike also highlighted the necessity to weigh up the shifting balance of forces during a strike and let intelligent thinking guide tactical and strategic considerations, rather than being driven by anger and even the justice of the demands of the moment. This is the kind of pragmatism he seems to show now, in the ANC and government. His core approach is: take care that the action does not end by losing ground and compromising not only the demands on the table but the gains won in past struggles. Choose your battles wisely and, when you start them, be as prepared as you possibly can.

Kgalema could have been accused of conservatism by more

militant prisoners (and, later, workers) who reckoned that they had the strength to win their demands. We return to his attitude to this key question in the next chapter, when he joined NUM. Enough for now to say that apart from raising cautions he has never opposed mass action when it was the will of the majority, either in prison or in NUM. Discussing a particular case in prison, Kgalema says: 'A hunger strike is a double-edged sword, and therefore if you embark on a hunger strike your demands must really be achievable so that you can deal with [the authorities] almost immediately … so you can find a solution soon enough.'[7] He has confirmed that his experiences on the Island helped him a great deal in dealing with demands and conflict later on in both NUM and the ANC.

Kgalema seems to have made an impression quite soon after arriving on the Island. He was tasked from time to time to welcome, debrief, orientate and integrate new prisoners. His approach was to 'give people from other organisations the space to be themselves and not for the ANC to impose their integration into existing ANC structures.' Instead he provided them with whatever educational material they required that he was able to obtain, without any conditions. This was not a ploy either, towards recruiting to the ANC later on. Fran Lisa Buntman points out that Kgalema was sharply critical of younger and more educated prisoners who seemed sometimes disdainful of the views and experience of older but less educated people who could not absorb material as fast as them or participate as much in lessons.[8] Patience, understanding and respect are what he wanted them to show the older prisoners, often old enough to be their fathers. Kgalema's own sympathy and respect for older prisoners with little formal education but great practical experience in life and the struggle may have been reinforced by the fact that he too had been denied a university education.

He served on the political committee and through it had an influence on the content of political education. It was this experience that led him, after he was released, to place such great emphasis on the importance of political education wherever he worked. It is still a passion of his. In later years the media often reported him saying that instead of taking up any major positions in the ANC or even in government he wanted to go back to Luthuli House, the ANC head office, to focus on political education. Not that this was all he wanted to do; but he wanted to include political education among his tasks. In the run-up to the 2009 elections his detractors tried to spread the idea that he *only* wanted to work in political education – as a ploy to stop him being appointed deputy to President Zuma and hence being a possible candidate for the ANC presidency in 2012.

There is also no doubt that Govan Mbeki, as a teacher with huge interest in educational matters, had a big influence on Kgalema. Kgalema began to grow close to Mbeki on the Island. This was made possible because the ANC was organised to overcome the barriers to communication between the general sections and B section. The leadership in both sections would liaise through couriers to arrange for certain leading prisoners in the general sections to go to B section as part of the political organisation, under the pretext of maintenance work such as painting or carpentry. This often enabled them to interact with B-section prisoners. Upon Mbeki's release they became so close that every now and then Kgalema would go specially to visit him in the Eastern Cape. Bafana Sithole recalled that both Gwala and Mbeki held Kgalema in high regard on the Island and used to say he was going to be a leader in the country one day.[9]

From interviews with Kathrada and the group Kgalema was sentenced with, it appears that Mandela and others in B section were kept regularly informed of developments in the general sections, including about political education and those who were identified as potential leaders in the ANC. All documents authored in B section concerning the ANC and matters related to it on or off the Island were regularly sent to the general sections and responses sent back. They had a sophisticated communication structure which cut across all organisations: in every cell each organisation had a representative. All cells then formed a unit in their section and linked up with representatives from other sections in an overall commissar structure. Mandela makes the point: 'We regarded it as our duty to stay in touch with our men in F and G, which is where the general prisoners were kept. As politicians, we were just as intent on fortifying our organisation in prison as we had been outside.'[10]

Murphy Morobe, who attributes a great deal of his growth on the Island to Kgalema, said that on many Saturdays he and others would go to his cell and have 'special lessons' while others played sport. 'He had a way of making everyone feel warmly welcomed, someone you could confide in and with a deep sense of empathy for anyone distressed, even though he was in a similar situation to all of us. But he was able to elevate himself above his own personal situation, in which a kind of comradely ethos guided his relations with all the prisoners.'[11] Though not one to sing his own praises Kgalema does acknowledge that 'I always had good relations with all prisoners across the political spectrum. I can give you many names of PAC and BC people I got on very well with, to the extent where sometimes when they had personal problems they would come and share them with me. This also enabled us to sometimes switch to discussing political differences between us more constructively.'

Kgalema was on the disciplinary committee in the general cells, which communicated with representatives of other organisations on matters of common interest (Thabo Makunyane explains, 'That name [disciplinary committee] was just given to camouflage what it really did').[12] Kgalema and Stan Nkosi were leading members of the committee. The names of those who served on it were secret. Kgalema also chaired the inter-organisational structure that brought different organisations together. It dealt with issues all prisoners faced, such as grievances about poor food and warder brutality. No doubt he held this position precisely because he was seen not only as a leading figure on the Island but because he had a way of appealing to different organisations in the interests of all. He also for a long while coordinated political education within all the sections.

The works of Maurice Cornforth, the British Marxist philosopher, appear to have been widely read on the Island, especially the three volumes dealing with dialectical materialism, historical materialism and the theory of knowledge.[13] Kgalema still has most of his books. They influenced his thinking and guided him on general Marxist theory. At a more abstract level, Cornforth appears to have been useful for the prisoners with a philosophical interest in Marxism. Amos Masondo, former executive mayor of Johannesburg, who was also imprisoned on the Island with Kgalema, spoke at length about how passionately Kgalema loved engaging with new ideas and ways of looking at things, and how important reading was to him. With a distinct nostalgia Kgalema recalls how the late John Phala – whom he immensely respected – was 'our clock on the Island'.[14] Kgalema and others who wanted to read or conduct the early-morning political education class were woken up by Phala, who was unable to sleep much. He dutifully never forgot to wake them at exactly the scheduled time. Kgalema's closeness to and respect for Phala was partly because he was much older, with experience and wisdom to match.

George Mashamba recalls that Kgalema liked to tell jokes, whether in the cells or over meals or just lazing around, in order to keep the spirit of prisoners alive under harsh conditions.[15] Contrary to the public impression of Kgalema as a 'serious and staid character', as Mashamba put it, some of his closest comrades, like Paul Langa, remark how funny he could be at times, so that those listening would be drowning in laughter long after he had told the joke.[16] Says Langa: 'If anyone thought he is a very serious person they are terribly mistaken. He can be a great joker, I tell you. We saw this many times on the Island. He can defeat any situation in a very jolly way, especially when things are tough and people feel down. He likes to imitate.'[17]

Somewhere along the way, before he was sentenced, Kgalema had learnt the critical importance of how to survive under tough conditions. Since he and the others in his group received no formal training before they formed an ANC underground cell it seems that the background I have mentioned – the Anglican Church, the influence of his parents and his considerable reading – had helped. Telling jokes was a way of keeping himself and the others sane and resilient. But he prized other elements too. Buntman states: 'Kgalema Motlanthe commented that it would likely be [future] novels about Robben Island prison that would fully convey life as it was really lived in that prison. He emphasised that the "rich side of life at Robben Island" included the light moments, the social life, the discussion of family life, and how Islanders lived life beyond organisational infrastructure.'[18]

Langa says the prisoners called him 'Buddha' as a form of 'serious respect', as he puts it.[19] Kgalema and his closest comrade Stan Nkosi rewrote the constitution of the sports committee. Langa says: 'We had different sports bodies which they centralised under a unified constitutional dispensation for all sports. They drove that process.'[20] In fact Kgalema and Nkosi did not exactly rewrite the constitution but put it into a more coherent framework.

Langa says that Kgalema – obviously drawing on his Church background – had a tendency to quote from the Bible but could as easily switch in the next breath to the works of Karl Marx and Vladimir Lenin. This trend continues today and Kgalema explains why: 'I understand that most people in our society believe in Christianity and other religious faiths. To therefore be able to quote from the Bible to illustrate a point can be very useful and effective and I have seen this from my experience. A point made in that way tends to resonate more with many people.' Kgalema goes on to tell how the late Flag Boshielo, a former SACP leader, became a '*muti* man' because lots of workers went to traditional healers for help when they were in trouble. He did this to prevent workers being misled with bad advice by some of those healers, making him probably our first revolutionary *muti* man![21]

With the influx of new and younger people from the Soweto uprisings and the 1984 Vaal uprisings later on, Kgalema played a big part in trying to support those who were 'traumatised by the repressive violence and the torture they endured'. The political affiliation of such prisoners meant absolutely nothing to him. 'When I tried to help heavily traumatised prisoners, the last thing on my mind was political affiliation. No, it is our common humanity and compassion which then becomes of overriding importance.'

Since he had not completed matric earlier, he decided to do so on the Island in 1979 through correspondence study. After matric he completed a course in carpentry in 1984.[22] That same year he registered to do a BCom degree through the University of South Africa (Unisa) but for various reasons did not complete it. 'It was intermittent, some years I got permission to study and other years denied. I went as far as second year, doing economics, business economics, industrial psychology, banking, statistics and labour law. I finished six courses.' He completed these subjects in the first year of study but was not able to proceed further. His choice of subjects was inspired by clauses in the Freedom Charter that dealt with the economy: 'Clause three of the Freedom Charter made it important to understand how finance and the banking system worked and also to understand theoretically – as far as those books would permit – how capitalism works. I also had an interest in how savings are mobilised to work as capital and the vehicles that own them, through the banking system.'

An interesting assessment of Kgalema came from the prison authorities. There are several reports that describe him as 'very intelligent', 'well-behaved' and that he 'reads a lot'.[23] In July 1984, after seven years of imprisonment, the prison board report showed an unblemished disciplinary record for Kgalema.[24] He would not pick a fight with authorities for the sake of it, even when provoked. He was then, as he is today, cautious, thoughtful, measured and very patient in whatever he does. He combined those qualities with an incredible sense of self-control, never given to histrionics. One gets a sense that what was of utmost importance to him during those years was not just his survival but that he left there strong and resolved to 'continue the struggle'. He tended then, as now, to have a long-term perspective.

Talking to Kgalema and his fellow prisoners makes one thing clear: the extensive range of contacts he established in the decade he spent with senior figures of the ANC and SACP and the abiding respect everyone had for him played a big part in opening up doors for him after his release in 1987 and especially when the ANC was unbanned in 1990. That he became the first chairperson of the Gauteng ANC and later the ANC secretary-general for a decade was certainly a mark of the huge respect he gained.

Robben Island: ANC school of revolution?
After much debate on the Island, it was agreed that political education would be conducted under the aegis of the ANC. After the arrival of the Rivonia trialists, ANC prisoners from the mid-1960s onwards tried to win over supporters of rival organisations like the PAC and the BC movement, which in 1978 gave birth to the Azanian People's Organisation (Azapo). 'We worked systematically on the Black Consciousness group, which eventually led to people like Mosiuoa "Terror" Lekota and others joining the ANC,' Kgalema says.

How easy was this political education plan? His claim that the BC prisoners were 'heavily anti-Marxist' is hardly likely: at its founding conference in 1978 Azapo was emphatically socialist. In fact, along with the influx of ANC members from Eastern Europe, the influx of BC-oriented people – especially after the 1976 student uprisings – acted as a radicalising catalyst. As the former Island prisoner Saths Cooper notes: 'The post-1976 generation of prisoners were the ones who in a sense revitalised the Island by injecting a more critical consciousness which challenged the ANC hegemony and raised many uncomfortable questions.'[25] He adds: 'Not all BCM people were anti-Marxist. Most were anti-SACP on the basis of principle and its chequered historical record.'[26] Indeed, just like the ANC, the BC movement was never homogeneous. They also had members who eschewed socialism and tended towards a narrower African nationalism that stressed race and national liberation rather than linking the struggle against national oppression with the socialist class struggle against 'racial capitalism', its indisputable flipside.

Though Kgalema's zeal for political education began before he arrived on the Island, its most concentrated expression took place there, because in prison the one thing every inmate had a great deal of was time. Outside the work Kgalema had to perform, and playing soccer, he studiously imbibed every piece of political and other literature he could lay his hands on and was as keen on educating other prisoners. Of course the studying was seriously limited – understandably, with the constraints on debate on the Island – to the outlook of the ANC and SACP. It is for good reason that the ANC stalwart Ben Turok could say that the ANC is 'probably the most peculiar organisation in the world'[27] – his response to the ANC's often tortuous attempts to reconcile what is fundamentally irreconcilable, the interests of capitalism and the labouring masses, especially the black working class.[28]

Kgalema became a key figure on the Island in the important sphere of political education. For a long time he was responsible for the study material and had to 'ensure that when it was required it was either available or arrangements made for it to be received'. Though he and many others learnt a great deal, he adds, they also faced serious limitations on the kind and extent of material that was available, because of the official prison restrictions. 'There were always, given the nature of the Island, serious impediments to our development through reading and engagement.'

Though Kgalema was in complete agreement with ANC positions, his view is that the restrictive conditions on the Island and especially the absence of Marxist literature 'prevented a more intense, informed and all-rounded political and intellectual development of prisoners'. His fellow prisoners Makunyane, Sithole and Morobe agree that though they grew tremendously on the island, it would have been even better if they could have had access to more political literature. Fran Buntman makes the further point: 'Many of those who came onto Robben Island with little or no political understanding may have been persuaded less by the strength of the ANC's analysis of South Africa's political economy, and more by the fact that they had never been exposed to alternative explanations.'[29]

What is more, the ANC and especially the SACP were heavily influenced by orthodox Soviet thinking, which provided an intrinsic constraint on political education on the island. This was especially evident in the acceptance of the two-stage theory of revolution as the conventional wisdom within the movement. This theory, which was thought appropriate for the South African situation, held that 'colonialism of a special type' would be overthrown in two steps, first in a 'national democratic revolution' that would put an end to white supremacy and black oppression, and later through the victory of the working class over racial capitalism. Much of this thinking derived from SACP members of the Congress movement and reflected their captivity to Stalinist two-stage ideology.

Such adherence to the Soviet line also explains the lack of any acquaintance with the writings of Trotsky among Robben Island graduates like Kgalema or any familiarity, as part of their political education on the island, with robust critiques of the ANC and SACP, such as those propounded by the Marxist Workers' Tendency (MWT), a left-inclined group that was eventually expelled from the movement. After their expulsion, the ANC in exile spread word that the 'Trotskyists' of the Marxist Workers' Tendency must be condemned and isolated. This led in the 1980s to the younger activists of the UDF attacking them from public platforms in South Africa.[30]

Kgalema himself recalls: 'I remember Professor Ismail

Life on Robben Island

Mohamed always complained about MWT, I mean always. I don't know anyone who disliked them more than that man.[31] But I never once condemned them and neither did I have any serious problems with them. Vilifying and persecuting opponents of the ANC I have never done, no matter who they are. I can very strongly differ but that I will not do because I have never been a Stalinist and completely believe that everyone is entitled to differing views on any matter.' But one of the reasons why Kgalema can project such tolerance of opposition – as opposed to the exiled ANC leaders, who often witch-hunted, condemned and slandered opponents – was that he did not go into exile after being released from prison. He instead became part of the mass movement at home, which involved a wholly different experience of building mass organisations in a much more democratic, accountable, tolerant, comradely and enriching manner.

Kgalema makes a further point about the political education on offer on Robben Island: 'You see, you have a captive population and it is doing an analysis, which suffers from the obvious weakness of being a controlled community and there you could mistake someone who simply complies and conforms as a revolutionary because there is nothing else to do. Under the circumstances there was no opportunity within the ANC or SACP and in actual struggles to put into practice and test the ideas and differences that existed in what was a detached environment. But these debates were very instructive despite such serious limitations. That is where I learnt that nothing is cast in stone.'

Despite the limitations we have described, Kgalema valued these debates among prisoners on Robben Island to 'clarify the real nature of the revolution'. Robben Island was a key experience in his political life. Its strength lay in the fact that it had arguably – besides exile – the biggest concentration of ANC leadership at the time, representing the generation from the 1940s up to the banning in 1960, 'people who took a conscious decision to dedicate their lives to the struggle at whatever cost to themselves.'

But was he already a Marxist when he arrived on the Island? 'When I got there I had read Marxist literature to some extent but my understanding was still rudimentary and tentative. I had started reading Plekhanov but my most important development took place on the Island.' Kgalema recalls what Raymond Mhlaba once said, which may also explain his own role in the ANC: 'He used to say that the role of communists in mass organisations is to preserve their unity. He says that in your conduct and arguments you must be above factions and be able to be defended by the most backward in the organisation simply on the basis of how they perceive your loyalty to it. He also said that as long as you still just read Marxism you are students of Marxism but not Marxist. The only time you become a Marxist is when you apply the theory within the struggle to solve society's problems.'

'Man and His Country', an essay by Harry Gwala, played a big part in the overall political education of prisoners, including Kgalema. It is a basic introduction to the Marxist materialist view of history and the notion of class struggle. Gwala, in the same section as Kgalema, undoubtedly had a big influence on him, with his historical knowledge of the trade union movement – not to mention soccer, another favourite topic for both of them – though Kgalema by nature was so unlike him, not being very confrontational or adversarial.

It has been said that Kgalema was a protégé of Govan Mbeki on the Island.[32] The fact is that Kgalema was never a protégé of anyone in particular. For him, singling out anyone is unfair towards the other leaders who also influenced him. Walter Sisulu was one. On the Island they were in different sections, but they grew close after they were released. Kgalema says of Sisulu: 'He was overall the father figure for me and his wisdom was great beyond any doubt. I worked with him for a long while and though I cannot say he shaped my personality as such, what I can say is that the values he embraced and his conduct profoundly influenced me.' He also particularly mentions Johnson Mlambo of the PAC 'and many other well-meaning people in the Pan Africanist Congress, the Azanian People's Organisation and the African People's Democratic Union of South Africa, some really solid people.' So Kgalema, who was recruited into the SACP while he was on the Island, also learnt from people on and off the Island who were not ANC leaders or leaders at all. Some were ordinary members, for example, in NUM and later in the ANC after it was unbanned. These complex influences enriched him far more than a single mentor could have done.

But for Kgalema there was definitely something special about Sisulu. Several leading figures in the ANC spoke about this. Kgalema was clearly moved as he recalled: 'Even when he was quite sick he would come to Luthuli House and sit in his car and call me. He would tell me that he had come from Kliptown, Soweto or somewhere else and that he came to visit to draw some strength. He would give me a hug and say goodbye. The last time I saw him was at Milpark hospital. Though he was sedated, each time when he came around he would actually apologise for not being able to attend meetings because he was not well.'

'Inqindi and Marxism'

'Inqindi and Marxism' – codenamed Inq-M – was a discussion document that was circulated on Robben Island in 1978, a year after Kgalema arrived. *Inqindi* in Zulu and Xhosa means '(clenched) fist', the hand gesture symbolising the ANC or the Congress movement; 'Marxism' referred to the SACP.

The trajectory of the ANC, the SACP and Cosatu since 1990 and especially after 1994 makes reviewing this debate and Kgalema's place in it very important. It is arguable that casting the debate in these terms was false anyway, because the national (race) question was tied by countless threads to social and economic questions of the revolution – that is, to the capitalist economic framework within which it was located. This debate combined elements of theory, policy and programme, though not coherently. Basically it dwelt on the relationship between national oppression (racism) and capitalism, and in particular where the Freedom Charter stood in this debate and what type of society the Charter would usher in. Would it lead to a bourgeois democracy or a people's democracy? So acrimonious was this debate that it appeared less as 'Inqindi *and* Marxism' than 'Inqindi *versus* Marxism'. Mashamba says that the argument was so fierce that hardened factions were created as a result and old comradely relations were severely tested. 'It got so bad that many ANC prisoners were not talking to each other,' he commented.[33] Discussion got so intense, a fellow prisoner, Raks Seakhoa, recalls, 'that sometimes it could get very ugly.'[34]

Though regarded as by far the most important debate held on the Island, it has been neglected in the relevant literature. The initial document was written by Mandela (according to Kgalema, Mashamba and Ndebele) and sent to the other sections. But Mandela's authorised biographer, Anthony Sampson, says it came from 'the leaders in Mandela's section'.[35] It appears that after Madiba penned it, he passed it on to others in B section. Then it was sent to the general sections, where it sparked a massive and raging debate that produced several written responses. Kathrada was tasked with collating and summarising them in a document, which was sent back to the general sections with a covering letter written by Mandela.[36] Sampson cites from Mandela's note to confirm that the document was 'approved by the High Organ.'[37] According to Kgalema:

> The debate started off on the question of socialism because of an influx of young and militant MK people who had trained in the former Soviet Union and other East European countries. They had returned to the country, got arrested and sentenced to the Island. Their understanding was that we are fighting against apartheid and to establish socialism. They saw a direct link between fighting apartheid and socialism. It was very straightforward for them. These younger comrades were filled with Marxist language and when they arrived they were surprised that we were not talking Marxism. They had no doubts about the kind of society we wanted and also no need for a separation of the revolution into stages. But the older leaders of the ANC in the B section began to respond to this debate, which started in the general sections. Basically, they were saying that it's just Marxism in the main sections and that these younger people don't know the history and character of the ANC and therefore they needed to guide them. That is how the debate between national liberation and socialism arose which led to that discussion document, but they anchored a discussion of that relationship on the key question of the Freedom Charter, which led to differences about its interpretation.

As Kgalema understood it, 'Madiba's position was that the ANC has never decided to go the socialist route and therefore its policy document, the Freedom Charter, does not envisage socialism. What it does envisage is a bourgeois democracy. The other group, led by Oom Gov [Govan Mbeki], argued that the implementation of the Charter's vision and demands will not represent a capitalist or bourgeois democracy but a stage which will in fact lay the foundations for and lead to socialism.'

Kgalema adds there was another position on the Island, led by Walter Sisulu and Raymond Mhlaba, the two most senior SACP leaders while he was there. 'Their argument was that both Madiba and Mbeki were wrong because they argued that the outcome of a revolution does not simply follow an "either this or that" diagnosis but instead is a function of the mobilisation of social forces and clarity with regard to their political programme and strategy.' This view was apparently not documented or seriously advocated, probably partly because Sisulu was not given to writing. It also does not feature in Sampson's book and neither did Kathrada talk about it.[38]

The document 'Inqindi and Marxism', written and circulated by Kathrada, was significant for other reasons too. It conceded 'that some of the formulations in the original document were obscure, misleading or otherwise wrong. We also mistakenly assumed that our interpretations [in the leaders' B section] of the FC [Freedom Charter] was the same as that of comrades in other sections and that we all accepted the basic differences between the policies and ultimate objectives of the CM [Congress Movement] and CP [Communist Party].'[39] However, so intense was the impact on the top leadership in B section of the younger militant ANC members, who were advocating a socialist-oriented future for South Africa, that Kathrada found it necessary to point out: 'But the document warns that the growing interest in the study of Marxism ... should not be allowed to obscure the basic differences between the policies of the two organisations. ANC and the other Congresses are neither Marxist organisations nor communist fronts. They are national organisations which lead the struggle against racial oppression and not against capitalism. The FC, not Marxism, is the policy of CM.'[40]

This argument does not consider the fact that the Freedom Charter was then and still is today open to contending interpretations. Contrary to later positions that he took, Mandela himself, in 1956, asserted that the Charter was a 'revolutionary document precisely because the changes it envisages cannot be won without breaking up the economic and political set-up of present South Africa'.[41] In other words, the Freedom Charter can be interpreted positively from a Marxist perspective, rather than be seen necessarily in opposition to or at variance with it, as Kathrada suggested. The discussions have been far more nuanced and complex. Similarly, in the debates on the Island the 'national democratic revolution' was not envisaged to be open to more radical interpretations, but instead was seen as completely separate from socialism.[42] Kgalema put it like this: 'We had debates for years about whether the struggle then was for an NDR or a socialist revolution.' It was only after 1994 – when increasingly its nonsocialist, if not antisocialist, character became more problematically evident in relation to socioeconomic issues – that the national democratic revolution was injected with a bit more radicalism, but more as a belated catch-up than as part of a coherent revolutionary theory.

Among the leaders on the Island the strongest opposition to the views of Mandela and others in B section came from Govan Mbeki, whose response to the document can be found in his book published after his release, *Learning from Robben Island*. Mbeki argues that the emergence of a bourgeois democracy in South Africa was extremely unlikely, if not impossible, given the economic policy demands in the Freedom Charter; their fulfilment, on the other hand, would make possible the inauguration of a people's democracy instead. As Mbeki says: 'Nationalisation on a big scale is the only meaningful way in which the victorious liberation forces through their own people's government in a people's democracy could control the existing resources to the immediate benefit of the millions of the oppressed and exploited masses of our country.'[43] He adds: 'If a victorious people's revolution relaxes, instead of stepping up, nationalisation as envisaged in the nationalisation clause, it will have thrown away the main instrument in its hands to control the economy for the benefit of the erstwhile oppressed as provided for in another clause of the Freedom Charter. To relax this clause to provide individual ownership would be tantamount to sacrificing the interests of the overwhelming majority for an insignificant minority – bourgeois democracy – what a price!'[44]

There can be no doubt that Mbeki's arguments were powerful in terms of a theoretical analysis, but even his perspective depended ultimately on the situation at the moment of 'liberation' and on the balance of forces then obtaining. This is precisely why, although Kgalema was 'on the side of a people's democracy because the idea of a bourgeois democracy was totally unacceptable' (and in that regard he was in agreement with Mbeki), he 'always understood that the correct position was the one articulated by comrade Walter'. Kgalema puts it thus: 'Sisulu said that, though he was part of the team which drafted the Charter, he did not claim a monopoly of wisdom in interpreting and analysing it, because he said that what happened to it would mostly depend on the balances of forces at the time of victory over the Nationalist Party.'

In the event, the balance of forces in South Africa even after Mandela was released and negotiations began was not really in favour of the ANC and the Freedom Charter. On the contrary, the very release of Mandela and the beginning of negotiations were consequences of the initiative of the National Party. What is more, though the final constitution of 1996 enshrined huge gains for those previously oppressed, both political and social, the inclusion of a clause protecting private property was the strongest indication of the prevailing balance of forces in favour of capital in general.

While Kgalema was no doubt right in agreeing with Sisulu's position that everything depended on the power relations at the time of the transfer of power, Govan Mbeki and others like him could obviously not foresee what would happen later: the release of Mandela and all political prisoners, the negotiations and the constitution of 1996. The debate has not ended. In ideological, programmatic and policy terms it has never been resolved and still continues today: witness the storm that erupted in 2009 when the ANC Youth League raised the question of nationalisation.

So unclear is the ANC's current thinking on the relation between national oppression and capitalism that Kathrada could conclude: 'Unlike Marxism, which guides a CP [Communist Party] before and after the taking of power, the role of African nationalism is limited to the pre-liberation phase of the struggle. It cannot be used to reshape society after liberation, nor for the purpose of developing a new mode of production different from capitalism or socialism, as some political organisations claim.'[45] If so, one may ask: what has the ANC been doing since 1994, what was the RDP all about, and what is its commitment to eradicating poverty?

Marxist or African nationalist or both?
Arising from the 'Inqindi-M' debate, which raged on the Island for years, is the question whether Kgalema is more of an African nationalist or a Marxist – or is he both, as several leaders of the ANC and SACP had been much earlier, such as Moses Kotane?

Indeed, nationalism can live cheek by jowl with Marxism and has done so for very long, though it is the overall perspective and where the programmatic and strategic emphasis is placed between nationalism and socialism that is most important.

Through the years up to 1977, Kgalema came under the sway of both nationalists and Marxists (of the SACP type). On the Island Harry Gwala, Govan Mbeki and Lawrence Phokanoka had the most influence on him. It appears that because of their proximity in the general cells, Gwala had the greatest impact on Kgalema in terms of political education. 'We worked very closely under the guidance of Comrade Harry Gwala.' Kgalema had an even closer relationship with Phokanoka, with whom he was often in contact, an arrangement made possible by the networks of the ANC. These were major leaders of the ANC, but to a greater or lesser extent they were all in agreement with the politics, ideology and programme of the SACP. Mbeki tended to be the most independent of them all, especially in his views on the Freedom Charter in the 'Inq-M' debate.

Kgalema insists that 'in the South African context the most revolutionary native will be a nationalist because of the historical problem of white racism. It is inevitable. That is why on the economic front in our post-apartheid situation race is still so dominant.' But to recognise the validity and necessity of African nationalism in dealing with the legacy and continuation of race and racism does not in itself resolve either the problem of racism or the underlying socioeconomic problems of chronic poverty, unemployment and inequalities that bedevil the lives of the African majority. That is the nub of the matter when there is a disproportionate emphasis on nationalism, at the expense of the simultaneous transformation of the material conditions of the poor.

African nationalism, like all other nationalisms, can be and is a powerful social force for liberation from political oppression, but it does little to answer the social needs of those who have been both oppressed and exploited. This glaring weakness is one of the main reasons why nationalism can be easily captured by elitist interests, who use it to achieve other economic-class ends for themselves and even turn whole political movements, including those whose major support lies in the working class, in that direction. This is indeed what has happened in the ANC.

It is my view that Kgalema has not, either in the ANC or in government, come to grips with the fundamental contradictions between the African nationalism of the ANC and the material interests, needs and aspirations of the African working class. Nowhere has he written or spoken about this matter in a way that confronts the serious limitations of the ANC's conception of the national democratic revolution, as Karima Brown, Patrick Bond, Trevor Ngwane and others have pointed out in interviews. Interestingly, almost all of them are from the independent and critical left outside the ANC alliance. (Despite their criticism, they respect Kgalema probably more than any other ANC leader.)

True, some of his comments show that he is not of the mainstream, narrow and orthodox African nationalist school of thought. He recognises the real links between nationalism and socialism. But he has not faced fully the biggest limitation of African nationalism: that, beyond its unifying political usefulness, it obscures social and class divisions within the oppressed and between the leadership and their followers, which today run ever deeper. And because it does this, it neglects to prioritise the interests and needs of the African working-class majority. The much-proclaimed 'pro-poor bias' of the ANC is highly questionable. Besides other manifestations, the chronic township protests from 2004 onwards and what the protesters themselves have had to say about their plight in the media appear to contradict such claims strongly.

Kgalema combines, sometimes uncomfortably, African nationalism and socialism. Organisationally, the ANC has certainly been of paramount importance for him. When it came to the crunch in disputes between the ANC and the SACP or Cosatu, he defended the ANC vigorously when he was its secretary-general. He concedes that in the public domain his former leading role in the SACP – and thus as a socialist or communist – is little known. Kgalema's public image ever since he was elected ANC secretary-general is strongly ANC. One gets a deep sense that he wants it that way, that his loyalty to the ANC should not be confused with simultaneous membership of or leadership in any other organisation, including the SACP.

That is perhaps why, when he was secretary-general, his primary role was not properly or fully understood by leaders of the SACP and Cosatu. No matter what he thought of issues in the recurring conflict between the ANC and Cosatu, for example, he had consistently to try to preserve the unity of the ANC itself, first and foremost, and then its alliance with Cosatu and the SACP. So much did the ANC matter to him that he was not willing to be in leading roles simultaneously in the ANC and the SACP, and so withdrew from the central committee of the SACP soon after being elected secretary-general of the ANC in 1997.

Though Kgalema does appear at times to illustrate Eric Hobsbawm's warning of the dangers of Marxism losing itself in nationalism,[46] this has not always been the case. He has said, for example, that his role in NUM 'was to make the connections between national liberation and capitalism'. In his position at the helm of NUM, Kgalema did seem to be more forthrightly socialist than nationalist. This continued to some extent even when he became ANC secretary-general, as his attack on capitalism in the 2000 Cosatu May Day rally reveals, when he called on union members to 'intensely hate capitalism and engage in a struggle against it'.[47] And just over a week later he told Jaspreet Kindra: 'The ANC is itself not a bourgeois organisation. The country's leading socialist minds are in the ANC. Anyone who argues for socialism will find allies in the ANC.'[48] The truth of his claim is questionable, as many of the country's leading socialists who are outside the ANC will argue. But his answer has implications for the neoliberal policies the ANC has adopted since 1994 and the great difficulty of reconciling these policies with any socialist sympathies in the ANC. Why were such policies adopted – including the commercialisation of even basic services, like water, sanitation and electricity – if the struggle for socialism really finds allies in the ANC?

Another problem is that despite the ANC's commitment to nonracialism in practice, its African nationalism has not always been genuinely nonracial and broad-based but rather based on the 'African' majority. This is why Neville Alexander argues that often the ANC's nationalism was not all-encompassing and genuine but a 'pseudo' nationalism.[49] It was only in 1969 in Morogoro that membership of the NEC was opened to all and only in 1985 that ordinary membership was extended to all – incredibly, a mere five years before Mandela was released and the ANC unbanned. Kgalema's attempt to explain this is not convincing. He claims that this was unavoidable because other bodies were also organised on racial-colour lines, like the Indian Congresses, the Coloured People's Congress and the white Congress of Democrats. 'That is why it is important to understand that rationale. When they were legal here in the country, they organised themselves in that fashion. They did not open membership to all.'

But just as the Communist Party organised on a completely nonracial basis, so too could the ANC have done. The problem is that these race-based forms of organisation not only served to reinforce apartheid's racial distinctions along similar lines but continued to obscure socio-class issues that affected the black majority. The stubbornness with which race and nationalism persist in our society today is derived in no small measure from this past. All the same, Kgalema is not oblivious to the problem of a narrow African nationalism: 'Yes, there have been some crude Africanist currents at certain times in the ANC.'

The other problematic side of the coin of acceding too readily to nationalism is that 'socialists have been far too ready to concede the subsumption of the struggle for socialism'.[50] This has been seen as well in relations between the ANC and their allies, Cosatu and the SACP, over the years: the latter have all along played second fiddle in the alliance,[51] and the ANC has never really treated its partners as equals. Kgalema seems to have followed the trend of previous ANC leaders who were also leaders of the SACP: they all eventually subordinated the active, unequivocal and consistent fight for socialism to a diffusive multi-class African nationalism. Even Moses Kotane, when he was general secretary of the SACP and hence its most senior leader, deferred to the ANC's African nationalism. Indeed, Kotane's approach reinforces for Kgalema the centrality of the ANC within the alliance: 'Moses Kotane identified the ANC as the theatre in which the party can do its work because of its nature. The point is that you can become class conscious, be leftist, socialist and be on your own, whereas the ANC provides the theatre and space to grow your politics and reach out to all the strata and classes.'

It is tragic to see that even today, in the midst of the biggest social crisis we have ever faced, the SACP still defers to the

ANC, in respect of policy, programme and strategy, thereby contradicting the whole notion of its 'vanguard' role in the struggle. In the meantime – which could be for ever – the African masses must wait. For what and for how long nobody knows, neither the ANC nor SACP nor Kgalema himself. What the ANC, including Kgalema, has failed to realise is that it has for long needed a serious, systematic and rigorous review of its many political, ideological and programmatic weaknesses, especially in regard to its persistent claim that it represents the best interests of the working class and the poorest of the poor.

How can the ANC, including Kgalema, sustain such a myth in the face of overwhelming empirical evidence to the contrary? The constant but feeble attempt by the ANC to attribute post-apartheid social ills solely to the apartheid era, without itself taking partial responsibility, has long been exhausted.

Prison letters and a painful episode

We now turn to a personal side of Kgalema's life that was very painful but in the interests of the facts and transparency we have to deal with it. From the outset in August 1977 Kgalema had written regularly to his wife Mapula and in almost every letter expressed his deep and abiding love for her. A month after arriving on the Island he wrote: 'I doubt I can love anybody as much as I love you. You are an inspiration and ventilation for my vexed soul.' About his ten-year sentence he was brave and principled: 'It has not been easy but it had to be done, even at the price of not seeing him [his son Kgomotso] for ten years. However, I am on the right side.' In May 1978, after Mapula visited him, he wrote: 'You looked so good and fresh that you reminded me of a beautiful girl I met on a train on the 3rd July 1970. Her name is Mapula. Darling, if you run into her please tell her I love her.' In July 1978 he added: 'Thoughts of you inspire me to great heights. When two persons discover each other the way we have done, nothing can keep them asunder. Without your love I sincerely doubt whether the courage to strive for better things in life could have gained strength in me.' In August 1978, after a year on the Island he said they were 'two independent, complementary individuals who form a whole one in love. It is with great pleasure that I serve my sentence with you in mind.'

However, it was soon evident that they were not as complementary as he had thought. In March 1978 he wrote: 'There is only one weakness glaring in your make-up and that is detrimental to your whole outlook. Indifference to knowledge is a serious shortcoming. Combat it. Read the recommended books, more especially the last one.' The 'last one' was Maxim Gorky's *The Mother*,[52] which Mapula never got to read; by her own admission she was never a serious political activist.

The constant pressure to read could have been counterproductive. In 1980 he came to realise that he could have been wrong: 'I wrongly arraigned you for being indifferent to knowledge. I withdraw that. But we are on the threshold of a new epoch and it is the duty of people like you to keep abreast with the ever-changing present in order to prepare for tomorrow.'

From 1982, for over a year, Mapula stopped visiting and corresponding. Kgalema had no idea why. He and his family tried in vain to find out. It eventually transpired that Mapula was having an affair with another man. Kgalema wrote in April 1983: 'Try to imagine how I feel when all my letters to you seem to be swallowed by a big black hole which mockingly challenges me to fill it up.' Understandably, letters were very highly valued on the Island. And though visiting time was just for thirty minutes and 'no contact', Kgalema missed Mapula's visits terribly.

Then came the anguishing news: Mapula was pregnant by another man. His family had known months before and in a spirit of protection had not told him. A girl was born, Ntabiseng, and without rancour Kgalema wrote: 'How is Ntabiseng? Tell her I wish her good health and that I love her no end. My mind is spinning because it is so full of you.' He ended the letter: 'You, my love, represent my shining hour, the triumph of light over darkness. You are a fathomless fountain of inspiration without which my life would be a long night of dreary existence.'

A month later he sent this message: 'If you run into Mapula please tell her that I love her and give her a kiss for me. Tell her that one day I'll carry her across the threshold into a new life of ecstasy and fulfilment in so many ways. Remind her that tomorrow belongs to us and that she must brace herself for a hectic period of affection. It will be like old times, except that this time it will all be on a higher plane.'

Saths Cooper, a co-prisoner and a clinical psychologist, comments: 'There can be no doubt the news of Mapula's pregnancy would have hit him very hard, especially when the environment he was in was itself very tough. He would have had to draw on his innermost resources to deal with what was certainly a tragedy for him.'[53] He adds that this is all the more reason why Kgalema's decision to continue the marriage after his release was remarkable. 'That is probably why he is such a strong person and leader today. To come through both Robben Island and something like that takes a very special person, I tell you.'[54]

Kgalema's thoughts were running on dialectical materialism at the time, and the view that 'contradiction is the source of motion and motion is development – life itself.' Despite that, he wrote: 'Dear Mapula, love is not love that changes when it meets changes.' But indeed later, when he sought to divorce

Mapula, it was as a result of the fact that his feelings for her had eventually changed.

What helped him survive the crushing news was a circle of close comrades, people such as Stan Nkosi, Harry Gwala, Bafana Sithole, Paul Langa and others whom he confided in. They provided him with constant support throughout those dark days. One gets a sense that, after surviving that ordeal, little or nothing would faze him later in his life. Kgalema recalls too that some of the older ANC prisoners argued that when men suffer such a fate at the hands of their wives they need to try imagining what they would have done if their wives were imprisoned for ten or more years and they were at home alone and lonely. This understanding also enabled Kgalema to deal with the reality and stay sane with his equilibrium and integrity intact. Perhaps he also saw that the apartheid system jailing him for ten years would have been a big factor in the marriage breaking down, and may have been the main reason.

From 1984 Mapula began visiting again and once took Ntabiseng so that Kgalema could meet her. From the outset he saw Ntabiseng as his own daughter, so much so that it was only when Ntabiseng turned twenty-one that Mapula told her Kgalema was not her biological father. Mapula also took Kgomotso a few times, their son with whom Kgalema has a very close relationship. On his release, Kgalema spent as much time as he could with him.

Kgalema's reflections on family life appear to have deepened on the Island along with his growing socialist beliefs, as in this touchingly expressed letter to Mapula: 'A sage once averred that the chief guide that must direct us in the choice of profession is the welfare of mankind, and if we can choose work which can most of all benefit mankind, no burdens can bow us down because they are sacrificed for the benefit of all. Then we shall experience no petty, limited and selfish joy but our happiness will belong to millions.' Of his son he wrote: 'Kgomotso and all other children of the property-less class can never hope to rise above certain forms of labour for as long as the means to support life are primarily owned by a tiny section of our society.' Yet Kgalema himself says that nothing stays the same. At the time of writing, Kgomotso is a growing player in the diamond cutting and polishing business, thanks to black economic empowerment (BEE). Kgalema's links to his family remain personal, and he scrupulously avoids playing any role in businesses related to them, his friends or partners.

Meeting Mandela, soccer and other memories

Kgalema met Mandela in the reception area on the Island in 1980. Mandela was on his way to the Woodstock Hospital for treatment and Kgalema was too, for an operation on his knee after a soccer injury. Later on, when Kgalema was serving on the leadership structures of the ANC, Mandela spoke to him about ANC matters. Kathrada and others confirm that the leaders in section B were regularly informed about prisoners and developments in the general sections. Kgalema notes: 'You must remember that we were an organisation. We had certain responsibilities and from time to time we had to report to the senior leadership in B section and deal with problems.' Contact with Mandela was a valued part of the process for Kgalema.

From 1983 he learnt to play the flute on the Island. He bought a side flute and the *Encyclopaedia of Modern Improvisation*. With the help of a manual he could eventually read and write music to some extent, Bafana Sithole told me. Kgalema gave a modest smile on hearing that: 'No, he is exaggerating a bit about what I was capable of.' But Thabo Makunyane insists: 'Kgalema was very good with the flute and he often played by himself but with lots of passion and could talk for hours of music.'[55]

He was also a regular soccer player on the Island and loved the game there. Oddly, the authors of *More Than Just a Game*,[56] on the history of soccer on the Island, did not interview him or even mention his name,[57] although he was one of only two prisoners on the Island who had been a professional. He was also on the sports committee for years. Kgalema just says in response: 'Well, I was surprised, but that's okay. However, if you go and talk to any soccer player at that time they will tell you that I was very involved with the game on the Island.' As Korr and Close point out, 'Sport is a way of building character, of teaching proper values and of finding ways to persevere in the worst of conditions.'[58] Kgalema's love of sport definitely sustained him.

Much later on, during the late 1980s and early 1990s Kgalema sometimes wore a neck brace. Many people commented on this during our interviews and few knew the reason. When he was on the Island the prisoners used makeshift weights to do bodybuilding exercises, usually with galvanised steel as a bar and tins filled with concrete as weights. They used to do squatting exercises with these weights behind their necks. Kgalema ended up with a badly pinched nerve in his cervical vertebrae that continued to trouble him until Valli Moosa suggested he go for treatment to Linksfield clinic in Johannesburg. So skilled were the specialists there that after just three visits he had no more pain.

Kgalema speaks about the white Afrikaner warders with a tinge of sadness. 'Robben Island's white warders were poor and often orphaned, which is why they were found suitable for handling black political prisoners, but much as they tried to be hard on us and keep us in our places, so to say, there were moments when their own humanity came through and they were a bit considerate and even kind.'

Everyone from the Island remembers Kgalema as immaculately dressed always (even though it was the same uniform they wore daily) and that he always stood and walked very erect. Sithole says he 'stood out from other prisoners by his constant exemplary conduct and being well-mannered, easily approachable and kind. There was always something about him which was very dignified and as a result when you spoke to him it was with a lot of respect.'[59] Makunyane laughs: 'He is a great listener and he had this effect on me: when I saw that he was listening carefully and seriously, it inspired me to talk more!'[60] So morally upright was Kgaelma that Director Matlala, who worked with him in NUM, saw him as 'a symbol of purity'.[61]

Kgalema could be confrontational when he saw repeated injustices done. In one case, S'bu Ndebele recalls, the perpetrator was a black prisoner who bullied other prisoners. When Kgalema could not bear it any longer, he challenged the man to a fight. The bully walked away! – but then changed somewhat and was less aggressive towards prisoners after his embarrassing public retreat.[62] It was Sithole who said that Kgalema often argued that 'a person dies when he or she does not stand up for what is right. If you remain quiet you become a part of the problem and that negative force grows, but if you stand up and fight there is a possibility that you can win the war eventually.'[63] Kgalema adds: 'The better part of my life was governed by that ... principle, which I would use in many political conversations in order consciously to expand the forces for social change and recruit people to that cause.'

On the score of standing against injustice: the assault on Kgalema and the other prisoners in Leeukop was settled by their Cape Town attorney Lee Bozalek, of Mallinick's, in consultation with Raymond Tucker after they were transferred to the Island. They each received a paltry R925 in final settlement, which in a simple act of solidarity they donated to the South African Council of Churches to aid the families of prisoners of conscience, as political prisoners were called.

Before being released in 1987 Kgalema was transferred for three months in 1985 to the Rooigrond prison near Caledon in the Boland. This was routine for prisoners scheduled for release. It appears that Kgalema was sent there long before his release date in order to prevent an imminent hunger strike of prisoners (which he was centrally involved in organising) from being carried out. From Rooigrond he was taken to Pollsmoor for a while and then back to the Island.

Having to negotiate the adversarial atmosphere and the harsh realities of the Island seems to have shaped his role in NUM, the ANC and government later. The diplomatic role in all of them had elements in common. On the Island he had to deal with the racist and oppressive establishment and with the factionalism and opposing organisations among the prisoners. After the Island he had to manage a different set of struggles and contradictions. In the spirit of the Island, his skills honed there are free of arrogance or manipulation for political power. He shows great tolerance and understanding towards opposing views and actors.[64]

Did Kgalema consciously play this role on the Island in preparation for a role he could be called upon to play later on? Being modest does not preclude deliberately developing leadership qualities, nor is there anything wrong in doing so. Buntman observes: 'Prisoners on Robben Island self-consciously developed and cultivated the belief that their prison was a "university", a training-ground for young leaders, a lecture podium for the most senior leaders of the antiapartheid struggle, a tolerant community in which pluralism respected all political movements, and a centre of such profound and essential correctness that even warders and criminals could be converted to the "cause.""[65]

The references to 'correctness' and a 'cause' are persuasive simply because that is more or less what has happened with those ANC members and leaders whose conduct and ideas were seen as deviations from its policies or rules after they took office in 1994. In fact a similar corrective approach applied to those who broke from the ANC to form other parties. One can immediately think of Mosiuoa Lekota and others who left the ANC and formed the Congress of the People (Cope) in 2008 and, earlier, Bantu Holomisa. In fact, Kgalema and other ANC leaders have often spoken in this vein of ANC leaders who have 'gone astray' after 1994: give them an opportunity to learn from their mistakes, indiscretions and excesses and train them in 'moral rectitude' or even the more questionable 'revolutionary morality', all this done in a manner very similar to a Church, which must not discard those who have sinned but do all that can be done to rehabilitate offenders among the flock.[66]

Release from Robben Island and back to Soweto

On 14 April 1987 Kgalema, Stan Nkosi and others were released from prison. After their train journey from Cape Town to Johannesburg was delayed for three days due to a strike by the South African Railway and Harbour Workers Union, they arrived at Johannesburg's Park Station a day later. Daphne Mashile-Nkosi, who worked for the Detainees' Parents Support Committee (affiliated to the United Democratic Front), went to fetch them from the station. She remembers being somewhat awestruck because there was a big aura then surrounding anyone imprisoned on Robben Island. Also there to welcome them was Kgalema's brother Ernest and Father Erson. Mashile-Nkosi recalls vividly: 'The following week they came to our offices for assistance in settling down. We had to prepare IDs and other necessary documentation for them, because they had to start from scratch.'[67]

Kgalema spent the first few days after release with his family and friends, trying to get back into the swing of things in Soweto after a decade away. For about a week they could not travel around because of the strike. He and Mapula then stayed at her parents' place in Meadowlands Zone 3. Kgomotso was fifteen years old and Ntabiseng four. 'When I came out we picked up the pieces. I understood that what happened can happen when a man is away for so long and on that basis we reconciled. I even told her that we will have to work together to bring closure to that matter. But because she was not politically conscious there was a sense that the essence of what I said was not quite well received. However, though she was never a political activist her heart was with the struggle.'

Mapula said that the first two months after his release were 'fine' and without problems, but after Kgalema was employed at NUM from 1 June things were never really right because he was so preoccupied with his union work that he was hardly at home, even at weekends. Kgalema concedes that he was extremely busy after he joined NUM as an education officer. While working full time in NUM, in an extremely tough industry, he was also involved in ANC and SACP underground work, together with Stan Nkosi. Having just returned three months before from ten years' imprisonment, being new to the union movement, still trying to find his feet and acclimatise after a long absence and facing all the other demands upon his time, it was inevitable that he would not be with the family much – and that at a time when they should have expected to have more time together after his long absence.[68]

Reuniting was not easy from the outset, given what had

happened in the meanwhile, no matter how deeply committed both were to reconciliation. About her pregnancy with Ntabiseng in 1982, Mapula said: 'I was young and so many things happened in my life.'[69]

Kgomotso does recall a few times when he and his father spent some time together, especially doing gardening on a Sunday, the only day when Kgalema was sometimes at home. That ended when the workload grew. Mabetoa says he tried countless times for years to arrange to see him, in vain. People at NUM said Kgalema was often the first one at work, especially when he became acting general secretary in 1992. From his youth in the Anglican Church, dedication and discipline have come easily to him.

The marriage weakened as lack of time together meant the couple could not deal with their marital issues. Kgalema was still busier after Mandela was released and when he became the first chairman of the ANC in the PWV Triangle (later, the province of Gauteng). Kgomotso, even at fifteen, could see that the marriage would probably not work because it 'seemed impossible for him to become a normal father and husband to his wife and children.'[70] He adds: 'Because my father was so dedicated to his work I knew it will be difficult for him to sustain the marriage. They tried to give it a go many times but it did not work out.' Looking back, Mapula says: 'When he came back we did not really connect. We were together but there was little or no connection.'[71] Kgalema has repeatedly said that he came back with a commitment to make the marriage work, and the fact that four years later they had another child, Kagiso, must have been in itself the biggest incentive. Yet it failed and in 2010 he filed for a divorce.

An extra complication was that Kgalema had met such good companionship in Stan Nkosi. Mapula said he often seemed married to Stan instead of her. So close was the bond that Daphne Mashile-Nkosi – who later married Nkosi – could say: 'When Stan and I started a relationship and even after we got married I found it irritating because even when we went out he would say, "I first need to touch base with Kgalema."'[72] She adds: 'They used to go and buy everything together, clothing, everything, and were truly inseparable.'[73]

CHAPTER THREE
'Meeting the real world'

Kgalema's ten years in the National Union of Mineworkers rapidly educated him about the harsh realities of the racist apartheid world outside the Island. Here the brute force of management and state against the 1987 miners' strike showed him what unionists had to contend with. As education officer in NUM, he believed that miners needed a broad political understanding and he equipped many of them to rise to senior leadership in the union. In the same vein he pushed general union backing for the ANC and the Freedom Charter.

The wide respect he had earned both on the Island and in NUM led to him becoming the first chairperson of the re-established ANC in the then PWV region (later Gauteng). Returning to NUM full-time, he soon replaced Ramaphosa as general secretary in 1992. The next five years until he left in 1997 honed him as a leader: he had close insights into Codesa (the Convention for a Democratic South Africa), negotiated with the Chamber of Mines, worked hard alongside Walter Sisulu to defuse violence in various parts of the country, notably KwaZulu-Natal, and was central to setting up the Mineworkers Investment Company. His decade with NUM thus shaped Kgalema as a unionist, ANC leader and politician-in-the-making.

Kgalema joins NUM

The year 1987 was highly significant for the National Union of Mineworkers. At its February congress it became the first affiliate of Cosatu to adopt the Freedom Charter. Then on 22 April the NUM offices, in Cosatu House on the corner of Jeppe and End Streets in lower Johannesburg, experienced 'the siege of Cosatu House' when, in a combined police and army operation, two hundred heavily armed policemen aggressively searched the head offices of Cosatu and its affiliates for several hours.[1] The state had declared its battleground.

Also in April, Kgalema and Stan Nkosi met the charismatic general secretary of NUM, Cyril Ramaphosa, in Johannesburg, just days after their release from the Island. They were interviewed for NUM posts by him, the president James Motlatsi, the vice-president Elijah Barayi, and Howie Gabriels, head of the education department. Kgalema recalls his impression of the three most senior leaders of NUM at the time:

> Barayi was a miner at Blyvooruitzicht Gold Mine in Carletonville and was strongly ANC for a long time but he was not much of a theoretician. He had a knack however of saying things as straightforwardly and often bluntly as you can imagine. Cyril, on the other hand, was educated, a lawyer and sophisticated, and then we had James Motlatsi, who was also a miner at Western Deep Level Gold Mine in Carletonville and who I think was mainly responsible for building the union. He had a wide network of contacts among the miners, partly because he was selling blankets to them.[2]

Two months later, in June, Kgalema was employed by NUM in education. Stan Nkosi was employed in July in the legal department.

Ramaphosa was undoubtedly the most powerful trade union leader in the country at the time, and NUM its strongest trade union. Kgalema brought a firmer political tone to the job as NUM grew, but in the early days nobody played a bigger role than Ramaphosa did. Kgalema was highly impressed by 'a young lawyer who could have chosen to open a practice and be successful but he instead chose to be involved with workers.' This is how Kgalema recalls that first meeting with Ramaphosa:

> Coming out, I met the real world after an absence of eleven years. On the Island we had the luxury of debating. But my only wish was to make a humble contribution to the struggle for the overthrow of the system of oppression and exploitation, nothing more. I had no ambitions whatsoever to be leader of NUM, the ANC or South Africa. Other than snippets of him here and there I did not know much about Cyril but we got on quite well. I could remember an article by Mono Badela on the Cosatu 1985 launch and the role Cyril played in the unity process leading up to it. I also tended to associate him with that banner at the 1987 NUM congress, 'Freedom means socialism'. The impact of seeing this slogan emblazoned at the congress had a powerful effect on us [on the Island]. Those who were pushing for socialism in the debates now jumped up and said, 'You see the workers are ready!' It served to reinforce a particular perspective. So there were several elements which enabled us to click right away.

For his part, Rampahosa had no doubts about Kgalema. 'The very first meeting we had, I was struck by his analytical capabilities and powers and by his disciplined approach to everything. Here was someone who had great dignity and humility and was very keen to serve the union when he first joined.'[3]

The two men have played an important part in each other's lives. Kgalema's appointment in NUM was not a personal decision by Ramaphosa but an expression of the growing relations between NUM and the ANC. That in itself sealed Ramaphosa's political fate with the ANC, as his new political home. There was no turning back to his roots in the Black Consciousness movement. Kgalema became Ramaphosa's main link to the ANC when he recommended to senior ANC leaders that Ramaphosa be included in the internal ANC leadership group. Thus began his close ties with key ANC leaders such as Sisulu, Mbeki, Gwala and Joe Slovo. Vic Allen, NUM's historian, says of this introduction: 'Kgalema played a vital role but his presence was never very visible.'[4]

Ramaphosa's respect for Kgalema's achievements and especially for the kind of person he is came through clearly in an interview, when he said twice, 'He is my leader.'[5] Irene Charnley, who worked in NUM for many years, says that Kgalema was so knowledgeable and committed that Ramaphosa often asked his advice on political matters and sometimes deferred to him on important political issues. It was therefore unsurprising that Ramaphosa supported Kgalema to take over as general secretary in 1992. Ramaphosa's backing definitely paved the way for Kgalema's rise in the union, which in turn helped his rise in the ANC, and paved the way for him to replace Mbeki as president of South Africa for a brief period and thereafter to be appointed as the deputy president of South Africa after the 2009 elections.

There has been speculation about whether the employment of Kgalema and Nkosi in NUM was arranged somehow between NUM and the ANC on the Island before they left there – a kind of deployment – or whether some other related agreement was reached before they were released. Kgalema remembers: 'The matter was discussed on the Island by the ANC and a decision taken for us to strengthen the labour movement, particularly NUM because of the strategic importance of the mining sector. But it is not like an instruction came directly to the NUM leadership to employ us. However, there was a conscious decision that Stan and I will try to enter NUM. We had to go and talk to Cyril and other NUM leaders and after doing that we reached agreement.' Vic Allen puts it more strongly, that Ramaphosa 'was pursuing a deliberate policy of providing employment in his union for prisoners, as they were released from Robben Island.'[6] Ramaphosa explains:

> People like Billy Nair after his release were in touch with NUM. He had worked with Kgalema on the Island. We got quite close to him. In the course of discussion it became clear that we needed people who could add a lot of value to our union. And clearly from the Island's side they had been watching the emergence and growth of NUM and realised that it was going to be a fairly important organisation of workers going forward. So when Kgalema was released it was generally agreed by comrades on the Island and our discussions with people like Nair that Stan and Kgalema should come to the union. They came a day or two after their arrival from the Island. It was their first port of call and when they got there the chemistry was just unbelievable and we immediately told them that we needed to bolster the capacity of the union in political education and organisational work. And without much ado we informed the NEC that we should employ them. James [Motlatsi] and I met them and it was agreed that Kgalema be brought into education because we needed to give political direction to our educational work. Education before focused on the more technical and organisational, which Howie [Gabriels] was doing, but we needed to give education more content.[7]

At that stage – in the wake of huge, militant mass struggles and brutal state repression since 1984 – political direction and leadership were becoming essential in the trade union movement. In hindsight, Ramaphosa says: 'Kgalema and Stan ... joined us at just the right time. We had already adopted the [Freedom] Charter and now needed to consolidate and solidify it. The union was then strongly established and had become a force in the mining industry.'[8]

Six weeks after Kgalema joined the union, the Cosatu congress was to be held from 14 to 18 July. NUM was going to present a proposal that Cosatu adopt the Freedom Charter. This was to be the union's first-ever resolution to congress, and in the ordinary way the presenter would be an office bearer who was himself a miner. Instead, NUM chose Kgalema, and Cosatu accepted the resolution. Matlala recalls that in the union caucus beforehand the delegates, of which he was one, were struck by Kgalema's 'input on the political way forward for both NUM and Cosatu. It was the first time we were exposed to such a deep political perspective within the union.'[9] Paul Nkuna says that Kgalema was chosen because 'when it came to political issues he was very articulate.'[10] In addition, Kgalema appears to have been pivotal behind NUM's drive to get Cosatu to adopt the Charter. From the time he joined NUM he was widely seen as a man with a mission: to build NUM and the broader labour movement and especially NUM and Cosatu's relations with the ANC. A major effect of Cosatu adopting the Charter was to raise the stature of the ANC and its leadership role in the liberation struggle.

The great 1987 miners' strike
On 9 August, NUM embarked on the biggest strike in the history of the mining industry, for three long, hard and brutal

weeks. This legal strike followed a breakdown in the annual wage negotiations.[11] For someone new to NUM and the tough mining industry, and just released from a decade on Robben Island, the strike was nothing less than a baptism of fire in a key strategic sector of the economy. It rapidly introduced Kgalema to the basics of trade unionism. He soon realised that his lofty ideas on the Island needed to adjust to the reality of what NUM was up against, and that without a solid foundation in basic facts the most powerful politics would fade. This tough in-your-face experience taught him probably more than anything else about the resolve of miners to win their demands and the determination of management to suppress them.

Kgalema must have made a strong impression because the union gave him the vital task of coordinating support throughout the strike, where his capacity became steadily evident. As Matlala puts it: 'You see then already Cyril could hit hard and Mantashe could be worse but Kgalema could achieve the same objective without any aggression or loudness.'[12] His approach demonstrated the abiding values he had learnt from youth in his family home and the Anglican Church, and later from the ANC.

He met a heavy-handed, retrogressive and racist industrial relations management who had not only refused to come to terms with black miners asserting their power but was determined to crush them with a mine security system bristling with white right-wing elements. This is how Kgalema captures the scene:

> Anglo dismissed 50,000 miners. The mines had private armies at that time. Their brutality during the strike was something else, I tell you. While the final settlement was far from what we wanted it to be, at that point the decision of the workers was to settle and to rebuild. It was the first strike on such a large scale. In fact management was hoping to destroy the union by

such harsh action by deliberately targeting the leading strikers. Peter Gush, who was then heading De Beers, was the worst on management's side. In that conservative world Bobby Godsell was the most progressive and enlightened. The others were very rough. The worst employer then was Gold Fields, led by people who did not even want to talk to union leaders.

Under difficult circumstances NUM tried to conduct the strike in the best possible manner, which is why there was such wide support for it. Kgalema organised a team of students from the South African Council of Higher Education (Sached) to guard union offices while they studied. He also arranged for some supportive white women to prepare meals. He remembers that Billy Nair 'brought a paper bag with a quarter million rands to support the strike', that the late Willy Kalk 'also collected funds and Faith McDonald cooked a meal every day for the strikers', and he recalls the constant support of members of the National Medical and Dental Association of South Africa (Namda) as they cared for the wounded. Every NUM informant I met said that Kgalema did an excellent job coordinating such support, especially as he was totally new to the union and had hardly had time to settle in.

With 95 per cent of the strike ballot in favour of striking, NUM clearly did not overestimate the support of its members and their preparedness to go up against the mining giants. But it seems NUM badly underestimated the brutality the mining companies were capable of in the face of a union determined to win its demands.[13] Hein Marais dismisses the strike as 'a classical case of overreach',[14] and argues that the 'mining corporations exploited it as a chance to restructure the labour force' and that 'a little more than a decade later, half the mining workforce had lost their jobs.' But the massive vote for the strike showed how convinced the miners were about their cause; and the avalanche of job losses had a great deal to do with the increased mechanisation that was already under way years before the strike began.[15]

NUM settled the strike after about 50 000 miners were fired. It was when these dismissals took place that the NUM leadership realised they were in big trouble. Nobody had foreseen such vicious retaliation by the employers. Howie Gabriels, who was in the NUM negotiations team, said they had sat throughout the Sunday before the strike was called off and 'into the early hours of Monday morning debating whether to end the strike or not and decided, at a meeting of 400 stewards across the country, to end it.'[16] By then the companies had already started hiring buses to take the dismissed strikers home. 'It was a hell of a strike, 15 dead, 400 injured and some miners killed by other miners. A very violent strike with mine security leading the attack. We had a network of doctors helping us with the injured.'[17] The violence was all of a piece with the punishing conditions created as South African capitalism developed in the later nineteenth and early twentieth century, pivoted as it was on diamonds and gold. From then on, black miners had been super-exploited and politically oppressed to supply an abundance of cheap labour.[18] Management was not going to change its aggressive and confrontational style.

If the union had not ended the strike it could well have been destroyed, especially since 1987 was a time when it was simultaneously growing rapidly and busy consolidating the membership gains made since its launch in 1982. But this whole experience – particularly the savage treatment meted out by mine management, the state and mine security – seems to have hastened NUM's political decision to throw its weight, though diminished after the strike, behind the ANC. For Kgalema, fresh from the Island, it was a rude awakening to the combined brute force of mining capital and the racist state. 'We learnt that there was nothing like a liberal employer. We were expecting harsh action less from Anglo than from Gencor and others. But it came the other way round.' Kgalema could then see why the ANC on the Island were keen to place Nkosi and himself in NUM, to help strengthen union organisation on the mines, which by all accounts were, with white-dominated agriculture, run by the worst employers in the country.

Jeremy Baskin notes that a serious handicap for the strike was the lack of concrete support from Cosatu, which ironically had been founded upon the slogan 'An injury to one is an injury to all'.[19] Many will argue that, had there been strong support from Cosatu, the striking miners would probably have won their demands. Baskin makes it equally clear that both NUM and Cosatu could be blamed for this situation. Jay Naidoo, former general secretary of Cosatu, conceded its lack of support: 'There was a real weakness on our side in mobilising support for the miners.'[20] NUM was also criticised for poor strike preparations, its failure to send out speakers to rally support in affiliates, and inadequate information given to Cosatu and its affiliates.[21]

The debate still continues about whether NUM's termination of the strike was a defeat or a temporary setback for the union. NUM rejected those who saw the strike as a defeat, calling their view a 'very simplistic assessment of a very complex process'.[22] Kgalema himself did not agree that it was an irrevocable defeat but rather that it was a 'major setback'.[23] Gabriels and others felt it was a defeat because the wage demands were not only not met before the strike was ended but the subsequent mass dismissals were the biggest and most telling indicators of being outgunned.[24] Though the reinstatement of most miners did help, many thousands never got their jobs back. Add to that the fact that at some mines the workers were shot at and physically forced to go underground, and the sense of defeat only grows. However one looks at it, what is beyond doubt is that if there ever was a strike which taught NUM about the vicious collusion between state and capital, it was the 1987 miners' strike, especially since it was a legal one.

The systematic repression NUM faced after the strike ended only served to reinforce for many the sense of defeat they felt. Baskin writes at length about the multiple vindictive measures that mine management resorted to. A NUM report revealed actions including 'a marked tightening of mine security, compound admission rules and room searches.'[25] The report also stated: 'In almost every arena, the abuses of supervisory power are again manifesting themselves. ... Every branch reported an increase in dismissals since the strike.'[26] These heavy blows were only one side of the story. The flipside was that 'according to the union, strike action on the mines declined significantly after the strike.'[27] Morale in NUM sank so low that Ramaphosa's report to the 1989 congress stated: 'participation by miners in the June 1988 3-day strike against amendments to the LRA [Labour Relations Act] was limited and very uneven, which was largely the result of membership and leadership losses experienced during 1987 and the intimidation by mine security forces, the army and the SAP [South African Police].'[28]

This strike and its consequences had a lasting effect on Kgalema's approach to strike action in NUM and certainly a similar effect at crucial moments later in his political career. Robben Island had already made him readier to ponder situations at length but now he became much more cautious. Though the mandate to strike was very high, he often said afterwards that since he was not a miner he would never encourage a strike by miners, but would rather loyally support whatever decision they themselves took; as miners they, and not the leaders, knew best what was in their interests one way or another.[29]

> I was always very protective of the interests of miners, most of whom were migrants who had to historically endure great exploitation and hardships. I followed a simple guide I had developed – we will work things through and make sure that we win the best improvements for them and at whatever point they had to go into action in a deliberate sense I would always bring James [Motlatsi] in. I used to say to him: 'You are leading these workers, this is where we are now and these are the possible consequences of the action workers might take. What do you think?' He was an excellent worker leader, I must say. I often agreed with his advice.

Kgalema as education officer

Though employed in education, it was a while after the strike ended before Kgalema could get down to familiarising himself with the education unit and start to conduct training for shaft stewards. Jesse Maluleka, who worked with Kgalema, says he was so deeply committed that he had no problem at all when he was required to do training in outlying areas that could keep him away from home for over a week. In a rare comment, Kgalema touched on the sacrifices he made in his job: 'I was sometimes away on education seminars for ten days and would stay in a shack or in the hostel.'

Nearly everyone from NUM who was interviewed said that it is probably in political education that Kgalema made his biggest mark. He transformed the coursework into an instrument that opened the eyes of miners to the realities around them. As Maluleka points out, he started to change the department by emphasising the importance of doing open political work because he realised that you cannot limit education to bread and butter issues, union recognition and wage agreements. For him those matters were linked to political economy, society and class. As a result there was a big shift in the education department when he took over. This tended to affect how the union operated on the whole, including its role in Cosatu and in relation to the broader liberation struggle.[30]

A campaign that bore fruit was Kgalema's constant effort to prioritise health and safety through education and annual negotiations across all regions, where there was 'a very uneven emphasis on health and safety issues throughout the union, with some regions ignoring them completely.'[31] Kgalema knew that ignoring health and safety matters posed a threat to the lives of miners, discredited the union and played into the hands of mine management, who failed to take the necessary safety measures.

The rapid growth of NUM from the start and its growing politicisation – best expressed in its adoption of the Freedom Charter in early 1987 – had created huge challenges in the unit, which required large resources and competent education officers. Invariably there were problems in both respects. Vic Allen points out that Kgalema had 'only had five instructors working for him in the 16 regions of the union'.[32] A major contribution Kgalema made, Manne Dipico says, was to find candidates for training as educators to serve the swelling membership. He found some of them among both the former Island prisoners and returning exiles.

Allen adds what appears a groundless point: 'The constraints caused by the shortage of qualified staff were so great that Motlanthe faced the rare problem of not being able to spend the funds allocated to his department.'[33] While the staff shortage was indeed a big problem, what is unclear is the claim that the funds were not spent. It turns out that Allen did not check this with Kgalema, Ramaphosa or Manne Dipico,[34] who later acted as head of education. In interviews, they and other NUM officials rejected the idea. Anthony Butler in his biography of Ramaphosa also states without any verifiable evidence that Kgalema failed to spend the money allocated for education and goes on to say: 'He accomplished little in this role, leaving posts unfilled and funds raised by Cyril for this purpose unspent.'[35]

Ramaphosa was quick to deny this: 'That is rubbish. The result of Kgalema's work speaks for itself, look at all the leaders we produced and which were deployed to various sectors of our society. He did extremely well. Those are the results which his work helped to bring about.'[36] Dipico, Frans Baleni, Howie Gabriels, Matlala and several others from NUM also dismissed the idea. Kgalema blandly comments: 'Butler has no idea what he is talking about. This is partly the problem with these types of books. He made groundless allegations and did not even check with me or others in education or even with Cyril. I know journalists do that type of thing often, but I did not expect that from a high-profile scholar.'

Dipico not only dismisses the criticisms but adds: 'He did very well under the circumstances, especially from the time he was chairperson of the PWV region. His biggest contribution was in political education and teaching miners the history of the ANC and the labour movement. I doubt there is anyone in NUM who will deny that. You will find many miners who credit Kgalema more than anyone else for their better understanding of both the ANC and the trade union movement.'[37]

The reference to the history of the ANC and the labour movement is important because many accounts of Kgalema's 'political education' legacy in NUM fail to specify the important historical context he provided. Kgalema has an impressive knowledge of ANC history and that of the broad liberation and trade union movement, as Allen acknowledges: 'So detailed is Kgalema's knowledge of African history that I often thought that he should have been the historian for the black mineworkers.'[38]

Inevitably Kgalema had weaknesses too. One was that, under him, the NUM education unit failed to identify and confront from a working class standpoint the half-measured and in fact self-defeating limitations of the national democratic revolution – he did not seek to deal with these limitations in classes. But he made it clear to me that not once did he consciously try to implement a two-stage strategy there and by the time he became acting general secretary of NUM he began to question that approach. However, the very process of negotiations explicitly excluded socialism as the main goal of the ANC.

When Kgalema became acting general secretary in January 1992 he increasingly placed education at the top of NUM's agenda, having experienced first-hand the problems and prospects in that area and what was required to strengthen the unit. As Allen puts the point: 'Education was made a union priority when it committed itself first to improve the literacy and numeracy of its members and then to raise the general level of education to the equivalence of the school standards seven to eight. This commitment was seen as a necessary stage in the democratisation process.'[39] Kgalema saw that with education, raising the miners' level of consciousness, the top leadership could increasingly be drawn from their ranks. NUM could not pose a challenge to the mine owners for control of the industry in the interests of miners, he said, if the miners themselves did not control the union in the first place. His faith in miners who lacked the most basic formal education becoming leaders of the union never faded throughout the ten years he spent at NUM.

Two interrelated aspects were vital for him: knowledge and experience. He had the greatest respect for leaders such as Elijah Barayi, James Motlatsi, Gwede Mantashe and Frans Baleni, who were once ordinary workers on the mines, unlike Ramaphosa and himself. Motlatsi, who rose to become NUM president, was for Kgalema his most reliable informant and adviser on contentious matters.[40] Mantashe in 1987 had already opposed the two-stage approach: 'We cannot divorce the struggle for national liberation from the struggle against capitalist exploitation. We cannot have our struggles demarcated into a workers' struggle and a community struggle.'[41] That Mantashe and the others rose through the ranks in the tough, racist and reactionary mining industry certainly distinguishes them in the wider trade union movement and is a credit to the incredible tenacity of its members and to a committed leadership.

While working in the education unit of NUM, Kgalema was also busy in the ANC underground, not in MK this time but as a committed trade unionist. At the same time too, he played a part in the SACP and in the ANC's interim leadership core along with Walter Sisulu and Raymond Mhlaba, and then also Mandela on his release. In addition, he was a member of the central committee of Cosatu. Later he became the convener of Gauteng's interim regional committee of the ANC. For a short while he also chaired the disciplinary committee of the Gauteng provincial executive committee until, according to Laloo Chiba, 'he was consumed by so much work in the ANC and NUM, he was forced to relinquish that post to Amos Masondo.'[42]

To be active on so many fronts was exhausting and took its toll on his family life, which was already strained, as we have seen. The situation became even more demanding after Mandela's release and the ANC's unbanning in 1990, when Kgalema was appointed ANC coordinator of the PWV region, which focused on legally re-establishing the ANC. In fact James Motlatsi says that many people expected Kgalema to become the first premier of Gauteng, probably because he was its first ANC chairperson, 'but he does not jump at positions because they are available and there is an opportunity to advance himself.'[43] Allen reinforces the point that Kgalema was more senior in the ANC then than many knew during those hidden years when the ANC was banned. NUM asked him to look after Govan Mbeki when he was released from the Island and it was Kgalema who 'passed on Ramaphosa's credentials to Mbeki' and 'recommended to Mbeki that Ramaphosa join the new ANC executive'.[44] Instead of using his position to his own advantage, Kgalema just made himself available where he was needed.

Clearly Kgalema never operated solely as a unionist. He was already wearing several hats: NUM, Cosatu, ANC and SACP. Thus, he could not possibly have given his job in education undivided attention. Allen states: 'The Education Department ... was suffering most from the transformation in the political situation. Its head, Kgalema Motlanthe, was described as being so "overloaded with ANC work" that he needed to be provided with an assistant.'[45] The reality was that educational work in NUM had to cohabit with ANC and SACP work, each of which was potentially a full-time job. All of this reflected the growing alliance between the ANC, SACP and Cosatu and the overlapping membership between them.

Kgalema was deeply concerned about the effects his absence would have on the NUM education unit when he was busy with the demanding work of re-establishing the ANC in Gauteng.[46] He therefore insisted that he had to return to NUM full-time. 'When Cyril [Ramaphosa] was elected secretary-general of the ANC in 1991 I decided to go back to the union because at that time I was chairman of the ANC's PWV region and I said to them that I cannot remain on the committee and that at the next conference I would not continue to be chair. They agreed and then I went back to the union.' Loyal as he was to the ANC, he knew that NUM was his mass base and that he could not focus for any length of time on the ANC in Gauteng, even though it was politically and strategically the most important region.

Dipico played a role at this point: 'With Cyril [Ramaphosa] tied up in negotiations and Kgalema in the ANC in Gauteng, he [Kgalema] was worried if the union had the skills to negotiate complex negotiations. I therefore concentrated a lot on doing shop steward's training to equip them with negotiation skills.'[47] During this period before his full-time return to NUM, Kgalema went once a week to the NUM offices to ensure that educational work was carried on effectively. Dipico constantly consulted Kgalema on educational matters and welcomed his inputs, 'which were very valuable and without which I think we would have been in big trouble, not just in education but in the union on the whole.'[48]

But once the revival of the ANC was well on its way, Kgalema felt confident that the process was irreversible and that his absence would not have any negative effects, especially given the calibre of the collective leadership by then. He also had no doubt that, with Maluleka and others in education and Motlatsi and other leaders at national level, NUM would continue to grow.

As NUM's education coordinator, Kgalema served on the national education committee (Nedcom), which brought together the education units of Cosatu's various affiliates. Cosatu's former education officer Khetsi Lehoko recalls a 'highly impressive, dignified and disciplined NUM representative', who was 'more reserved.'[49] He recalls how clearly Kgalema got political points across, as when he used the tomato to illustrate the Marxist distinction between form and content. A tomato changing from green to red, Kgalema said, was also changing its content as it grew organically. Society also evolves, he went on, but 'unlike the tomato it does not develop in a predetermined way'. It depends dialectically on the conscious participation of social actors towards stated goals.

It was during his tenure as education officer that Kgalema came more firmly to distinguish between trade union consciousness and political consciousness. Political consciousness, he would say, does not arise simply because you belong to a trade union affiliated to a political party. You will come at issues in a trade union way that reflects your particular concerns and if your demands are not met you declare a dispute and perhaps go on strike. Yet, though unions organise in the workplace, their members don't live there but in communities – and to develop a political consciousness you have to be active in these communities and the party the union is affiliated to, on other matters that involve civic, Church, political and other organisations.

In fact our reality is more complex than this binary distinction between trade union and political consciousness suggests. South African history has fused political and trade union consciousness with its systemic linking of racism, apartheid and capitalism. Kgalema holds that, in the interests of their class, workers must strive beyond political consciousness to the perspectives, policies and programmes of both the union and the political party it is allied to. But the problems afflicting the ANC alliance show how limiting an undefined political consciousness can be.

'Education for liberation' – a popular slogan of the 1970s and 1980s – expressed Kgalema's own thinking in NUM. For him, 'education for organisation' was as important too. He saw the key to stronger organisation as a growing and critical class, social and political consciousness. Gabriels notes:

> While Kgalema was great at the political level he was also good at teaching shop stewards how to represent members. One must therefore not underplay the work he did as a trade unionist because I think he realised that it is useless to know the politics well but not the basic trade union stuff and in fact he seemed to have realised that you stood a better chance to have a political impact if you worked through the union stuff. This he realised and made the necessary connections.[50]

Kgalema as general secretary of NUM

Not known to many people is the fact that there was already a strong feeling at NUM's 1989 congress that Kgalema should stand against Marcel Golding for the post of assistant general secretary, But it was never Kgalema's plan to do so even after Ramaphosa was elected secretary-general of the ANC in July 1991 – Irene Charnley says that his style of leadership is like a shepherd's, leading from behind. Instead he urged that his work in education was of prime importance and that Golding was the logical choice as Ramaphosa's deputy.

He said this again at the NUM central committee meeting in January 1992 and that 'we must build this union so that regardless of who leads it we will continue to be strong.' He even enlisted Mandela's help:

> I told Madiba, who came to address the meeting, that Cyril and Marcel worked well together. I said to him that education is very important because we are a very strategic union, bringing together workers from villages across South Africa and that if we do this work properly NUM will be the backbone of the

'Meeting the real world'

ANC. So Madiba and I understood each other very well. I told him to please explain to the delegates my view because I come from the ANC into the unions and that you appreciate that the work the ANC sent me to do is incomplete and that I must therefore continue to do that work. So Madiba put it rather bluntly, which upset the delegates because they thought the officials spoke to him and not me. But I later explained this to the delegates and they understood. However, I lost the argument, even though Mandela intervened on my behalf.

The election therefore went ahead for the post of acting general secretary. The results showed 185 votes for Kgalema against Marcel Golding's 106. Afterwards Kgalema told Snuki Zikalala: 'I did not expect to be elected as the acting general secretary of the union. I had been out of the office for almost two months and was not aware that people had an eye on me. I even came late for the meeting and was not officially dressed for the occasion.'[51]

Kgalema's strong connection to the ANC and firm ties with ANC leaders like Walter Sisulu and Govan Mbeki must have played a big part in the decision, particularly as Golding was known in NUM to be critical of the ANC, SACP and the Freedom Charter.[52] But it was his own merit that won the top job in NUM. Paul Nkuna, the former NUM treasurer, said he 'possessed the leadership qualities the union needed after the departure of Ramaphosa: his gift of persuading people without an ounce of arrogance, aggression or force. His capacity to lead by example and immensely respectful and comradely behaviour towards others in the union and more generally, and his very tolerant approach to people, in a manner that never ostracises anybody, including those he may strongly differ with.'[53]

Maluleka spoke of how time and again Kgalema urged NUM leadership and delegates to Cosatu congresses not to throw their numerical weight around and instead treat all other affiliates with respect as equals, including the smallest unions. Kgalema told me he took this stand because NUM did sometimes abuse the fact that it had by far the biggest delegation at Cosatu meetings and tended to bulldoze its way through at moments of difference with other affiliates. I witnessed this myself at a few meetings I attended in 1986 and 1987.

Thuli Mofutsanyane, who later became Kgalema's secretary, said that what impressed her most about him was his coolness, 'so much so that even when he is upset you either won't … notice it because even the tone of his voice remains the same'.[54] Everyone I met who knows him well spoke about an incredible ability to control his emotions. I deliberately provoked him at times to check this. He took whatever I told him in his stride.

Another major reason for his election, Matlala says, was that NUM members had come to learn that he had joined them straight from the Island as a leading ANC cadre sent to help build their union.[55] For Kgalema, these twin loyalties captured the new political realities in the country, where work for NUM and the ANC was complementary – the two-way effect motivating the alliance between Cosatu unions and the ANC. Ramaphosa himself declares that though Golding was an excellent deputy, he favoured Kgalema to succeed him.[56] His view reinforced the dominance of political identity in the electoral tussle between Kgalema and Golding. It also showed how much Ramaphosa himself had changed since his days as a supporter of the BC movement. Matlala weighs the political relationship between Kgalema and Ramaphosa thus: 'Without undermining the huge role Cyril played and what he achieved in NUM, Kgalema had the biggest political impact.'[57]

Did ethnicity (Golding was classified 'coloured' under apartheid) play any part in the decision to elect Kgalema?

Kgalema rejects this. 'No, you see Marcel came from a different political tradition, one that was very critical of the ANC and SACP, which became known to the union over time. I think that played a much bigger role when he lost to me.' Ramaphosa is emphatic here: 'Their choice was Kgalema because he had more substance and political grounding. NUM since its origins was oriented towards the ANC because no sooner had we begun to organise workers from rural areas than we realised that some of them were once members of the ANC, like Barayi, who was an old ANC supporter.'[58]

The ANC held sway for NUM members and in the broader scheme of things. It was more central than ever following Mandela's release and its unbanning. Even if Ramaphosa had left under different circumstances, the union would probably still have chosen Kgalema, because by then NUM was embedded in ANC politics, partly through the work Kgalema had done there ever since 1987. Probably no other Cosatu affiliate was as actively committed to campaigning for an ANC victory in the 1994 elections and in all subsequent ones.[59]

Kgalema began as acting general secretary of NUM in January 1992, just two months before the start of Codesa, the Convention for a Democratic South Africa. This was a difficult time for taking over the leadership, when the Codesa process was at its most critical. Cosatu requested independent participation in these talks to ensure that the interests of the working class would be upheld in a post-apartheid South Africa. Kgalema personally did not support this position: 'This was my view, not NUM's.' There were already too many parties at Codesa, he says. His second point: the other union federations would also have demanded representation. Thirdly, Cosatu leaders had accepted being there as part of the ANC or SACP delegation (Sam Shilowa, then general secretary of Cosatu, was part of the SACP delegation, for example). Fourthly, as part of civil society, Cosatu needed to be independent of Codesa, as itse main purpose during the negotiations was to put pressure on the negotiators 'when things go wrong there or when people get cosy,' as Kgalema puts it.

At this time Kgalema was also chairperson of the ANC's PWV region. No evidence exists that this influenced his approach to Cosatu's presence in Codesa, but many will argue that it inevitably would have. Kgalema himself denies this: 'No, my leading role in the ANC did not cause me to adopt that position towards Cosatu's representation in Codesa. It was a whole new experience and uncharted territory and it was clear you could not win at the table what you have not won on the ground. That is why, whenever they deadlocked, those massive marches were mobilised by us to bring pressure to bear.' He adds that since the 'key representatives were there I don't know if Cosatu's presence would have made a difference.'

The assumption was that Cosatu was represented by the presence of their delegates in the SACP or ANC. It is debatable how right Kgalema was in not supporting Cosatu's demand for independent representation. If Cosatu had had its way, its socialist demands would probably have been strongly presented in the negotiations and the constitution itself might have been shaped more firmly in those terms. It is arguable that Cosatu's representation in Codesa would not have contradicted its alliance with the ANC. But the fact that in the late 1980s Cosatu, following NUM, adopted the Freedom Charter and largely opposed the Numsa-inspired Workers' Charter, which was explicitly and immediately socialist, also militated against a more revolutionary politics that went way beyond the Charter.[60]

Six months after Kgalema took office, on 17 June, Boipatong township exploded when over forty people were killed by hostel residents, many of whom were members of the Inkatha Freedom Party (IFP). The ANC in response immediately withdrew from the Codesa negotiations. Shortly thereafter the massacre in Bisho took place, which claimed 29 lives. Few people knew how active Kgalema was in trying to stem the violence that ravaged parts of the country, especially in KwaZulu-Natal and Gauteng, often going on trips for this with Sisulu. Barbara Hogan, secretary of the PWV region, recalls that Kgalema dealt busily with the violence raging in Daveyton and other parts of Gauteng, always at work behind the scenes and already 'very statesmanlike'.[61] Part of the ANC's difficulty in responding to such terrible destabilising violence was that it was still re-establishing itself in the country after an absence of nearly thirty years. To make matters worse still, on 10 April 1993 Chris Hani was assassinated.

It appears that Sisulu, perhaps more than other leaders including Govan Mbeki, had seen attractive leadership qualities in Kgalema and spent as much time as he did with him in order to hone those qualities for top political leadership. In many ways, the two men were alike: somewhat self-effacing, unpretentious and unambitious but totally committed to liberation. Sisulu may have seen much of himself in Kgalema. Kgalema certainly acknowledges Sisulu as mentor: 'He was overall the father figure for me and his wisdom was great beyond doubt. I cannot say he shaped my personality but I can say that the values he embraced profoundly influenced me.'

The fact that Kgalema was an *inzile*[62] helped to anchor him more solidly in the mass movement and impress upon him the key importance of democratic accountability and a deep and abiding respect for these processes in NUM and later the ANC. 'Working with mass legal organisations teaches you about honouring mandates and being loyal to those decisions, and to do that you need as thorough discussion as possible before decisions are made, especially big ones.' It also enabled him to resist the encroachment of the conspiratorial and factionalist politics that appeared to be the inclination of many ANC exiles who returned in 1990.

During his time as NUM general secretary, Kgalema never indicated that he had been recruited to the SACP on the Island. In an interview, he merely told Ferial Haffajee that he was 'agonising' over whether to join the SACP.[63] The most he said to Snuki Zikalala in another interview was: 'I have no problem at all with the [SACP] organisation, nor the collapse of the Eastern bloc' and warned that NUM 'should see itself as an independent organisation. Not an appendage of this or that political organisation.'[64] The ANC believed that for leading members of the SACP – those who were also ANC members and especially those involved in the negotiations process – to publicly declare their membership could compromise both the ANC and the party during negotiations. But since it was the National Party that was fearful of the influence the SACP could have on the ANC during the negotiations, it is arguable that these denials actually pandered to such paranoia. At that time and in fact all along, many people who were SACP cadres denied their membership for security and tactical reasons. In Kgalema's case, from his time on the Island into the 1990s – both before and after the 1994 elections – he was hardly ever known or seen as an SACP leader or even as an ordinary member. Even now, little of his life and times in the SACP is publicly known.[65] He pulled out of the SACP central committee after he became secretary-general of the ANC in 1997 but continued his membership until 2001, when he let it lapse. Overall, then, Kgalema was already seen after 1990 as a unifying figure who worked against factions in politics. 'He has the ability to avoid conflict and think through issues', says Barbara Hogan, who worked closely with him in the ANC's then PWV region.[66]

After acting as general secretary for two years Kgalema was elected to the post formally at NUM's eighth congress in February 1994. There were no contending candidates. He faced the heightened expectations of NUM members who, having borne the brunt of draconian labour laws for decades, were more than ready for fundamental changes in the industry at all levels. Ramaphosa had led NUM from the start and during the early negotiations. Now Kgalema was at the helm for the transitional and transformational stage. He would face big challenges just when several key staff, like Golding, left for government after the 1994 elections.

From 1992 on, Kgalema had been centrally involved in annual wage negotiations with the Chamber of Mines and was the spokesperson for the NUM team. According to Director Matlala, the other key NUM representative, Kgalema argued the need for a 'surgical overhaul', as he put it, to transform the Chamber into a less adversarial employer body and one that recognised that it had to keep up with the progressive political changes in the country. Matlala adds that Kgalema encouraged the Chamber to 'think outside the box' and constructively meet the huge challenges the mining industry faced in the 1990s, otherwise workers and employers would all suffer the consequences.[67]

Matlala, who led the negotiations for the first time as an office bearer who was not the president, appreciated Kgalema's attitude towards him. 'Although it was the first time someone other than the president led the negotiations with the Chamber he did not once make me feel uncomfortable or that I did not belong there.'[68] This is not at all surprising because Kgalema has always promoted grassroots leadership of NUM. Yet he was particular about protocol. Matlala recalls Kgalema telling an NUM caucus meeting, during the annual wage negotiations with the Chamber of Mines, how he had to curb Gwede Mantashe, his assistant, from singing revolutionary songs in the Chamber corridors. I have seen myself his abiding respect for others, cutting across all political, religious and other affiliations, including his opponents. He can easily spend the entire day with a congregation of the most conservative white Afrikaner churchmen or the most radical black thinkers who think that the ANC has made too many compromises.

Gwede Mantashe, his assistant, was very different from Kgalema, completely opposite in some ways – 'like yin and yang,' as Kate Philip says from years of knowing them in NUM.[69] How did they manage to work together so closely, especially for the three years between 1994 and 1997? Thuli Mofutsanyane, secretary to them both, found the relationship revealing of both men, but especially of Kgalema as NUM's leader. She said that not once did Kgalema pull rank on Mantashe in a meeting or in front of anyone in NUM.[70] Neither did she herself ever feel disrespected or undermined by him. If ever there was a disagreement between Mantashe and Kgalema, it never expressed itself in anger. Instead, Mofutsanyane says, at such moments Kgalema would call Mantashe into his office, close the door and have a constructive and comradely meeting, and when they emerged from the meeting both would look satisfied and sometimes even happy.[71]

Mantashe says Kgalema never robbed him of his dignity, however much they differed. This was particularly important for Mantashe as a straight-talking, at times brutally confrontational, personality. It was his no-nonsense mother who mainly shaped his temperament, he declares, which he has no regrets about 'because, at least, I am honest and truthful about what I feel and think, when others are often not.'[72] Clearly he needed a Kgalema to contain the working relationship, and there is little doubt that Kgalema regards him so highly that he unreservedly supported him for the top job in NUM when he himself left in 1997.

For the entire period that he was general secretary, not one fellow unionist had any serious complaints about Kgalema. The worst comment I met was that he tended to be indecisive when disgruntled staff came to see him. His usual response was to say their distress was fair but many people had much bigger problems and were much worse off. Some said they gained in perspective; others, that he tended to overplay the moral of the lesson without resolving the problems they went to see him with in the first place.

Motlatsi notes that organisations have not needed Kgalema when things were going well. 'When he took over from Cyril things were not well in NUM. When he took over from Cyril in the ANC things were also not going well, meaning that he is seen as the alternative when things are not going well and he is also not offended at all if people don't need him. In fact it makes him happy because it means things are strong in the organisation. Kgalema tends to emerge in troubled times when strong leadership is required.'[73] Indeed, this happened again in September 2008, when the ANC needed him to take over from the former president, Thabo Mbeki, after his effective dismissal.

Why has this trend continued? Kgalema consistently tries to avoid polarising issues by overt partisanship or extremes, both politically and personally. Without this balance crises can arguably easily deepen and reach breaking point, especially in a country with such a deeply conflict-ridden and explosive history. Importantly, it is a leader with this evenness that both sides at a time of crisis are likely to prefer at the helm. The role is often conciliatory, holding together differences in the ANC, in the alliance, and in wider society following some fundamental compromises the ANC made during Codesa. The social contradictions are so great that other than calling for an outright socialist revolution, a leader would at times have no alternative but to appease and placate both business and workers.

There is a clear-cut pattern for the general secretary of NUM to move on to become the secretary-general of the ANC. This happened with Ramaphosa, Kgalema and Mantashe. Kgalema states that he rated his experience at NUM very highly: 'I suppose that because of the role the union played – which has been a very important one – you can be relied upon to manage complex organisations like the ANC. I also suppose that the ANC membership are always looking for a radical edge to take things forward, but we also need a balance depending on the strength and organisation of the ANC and the overall balance and relationship of social and class forces.' Here again we can clearly see Kgalema straining towards some middle ground, catering for the ANC's 'broad church' almost as a matter of course.

The Mineworkers Investment Company

From about 1993 NUM held discussions and explored models with a view to setting up a Mineworkers Investment Company (MIC). The initial impetus came from Golding, persuaded by Johnny Copelyn and the South African Clothing and Textile Workers Union (Sactwu).[74] From there, Kgalema and Motlatsi drove the project leading to the launch of MIC in 1995. Some former NUM officials said how difficult it was for the union to even contemplate forming such a company, especially given its overt socialist leanings. Bafana Sithole recalls Kgalema persuading reluctant members of NUM about the need to create it: 'He told them that the investment wing of the union

'Meeting the real world'

is exactly that, a wing and not the union itself. If you take the wing of a bird you cannot say the wing is the bird but if you take it as a whole it is a bird. And that is how Kgalema got reluctant members to agree to form MIC and later to buy their own building.'

MIC's rationale and its formation are – as Kgalema and NUM described them at the time – very revealing of the mid-1990s in South Africa and elsewhere, when the balance of social and class forces called for new ideas. After the 1994 elections donor financial support for NUM dwindled to worryingly low levels. NUM had to maintain itself without outside help. In addition, with the ANC in power but the policy of nationalisation highly improbable, the question that arose in NUM was, as Nkuna put it,

> How are we going to be dealing with the many difficulties black mineworkers face? We realised that the earning power of miners won't enable them to buy and do a whole range of things many other workers take for granted, like furthering their own education or paying for their children's education. They cannot, for example, pay for a university education. Other than farm workers, miners were the lowest paid workers. We asked ourselves if we can support miners to do all these things through their subscriptions and the answer was no. That is why the idea of an investment company looked attractive.[75]

In 1995 NUM established a Mineworkers Investment Trust (MIT) with a R3-million nonredeemable 'shareholder loan' to launch the company.[76] Kgalema was one of the first directors of the MIT, as general secretary of NUM. The MIT acts on behalf of and in the interests of NUM. MIC pays a dividend from the proceeds of its investments to the MIT, which in turn deals directly with NUM by funding designated projects. The ability of MIC to repatriate a dividend to the trust depends on how profitable its investments are, which is why it constantly strives to increase its asset base and returns. MIC has substantial investments in Primedia, Tracker, Peermont, BP and FirstRand, among others.

NUM remains the sole shareholder of MIC, through the trust. From the start, the union was not allowed to invest anywhere in the mining, construction and energy sectors where NUM has members, to avoid any conflict of interest.[77] All the trustees are elected office bearers of NUM. The MIC board may include former office bearers of NUM; but, no matter what problems NUM might have, it may not use any of MIC's funds to save the day. MIC's former CEO Paul Nkuna confirms that, in the interests of NUM's principle of 'worker control', MIC has the power to appoint unionists to the board – and also to remove them if they think it necessary.

Kgalema played a crucial role in forming MIC. He also had a large part in creating the Mineworkers Development Agency, designed to serve the developmental and social needs of retrenched miners, their dependants and communities. The agency focuses on various projects to create full-time and part-time jobs and thus give retrenched miners an income to tide them through their difficulties, especially in rural areas, where there are little or no prospects of finding decent jobs. He was centrally involved too in setting up the JB Marks Education Trust, which provides bursaries to miners and their dependants, and the Elijah Barayi Memorial Training Centre in Yeoville, Johannesburg. And at the international level he was for a while on the executive committee of the Miners' International Federation, which took him on many trips abroad, especially to Australia, where NUM shared in exchange programmes with the United Mineworkers of Australia, which hugely benefited NUM members during the years from 1994 to 1997.

By its very nature investment in the capitalist world can be both profitable and very risky, as when MIC lost over R1 billion in the market crash of 2009. But by then the union had already received close to R400 million in dividends, which were used largely for education and skills training – a good return from laying out R3 million to form MIT and MIC in 1995. Kuben Pillay, chairman of MIC, emphasises that after the initial funding NUM members 'did not pay a cent more because we always held the position that workers' money can never be put at risk in terms of investment ventures.'[78] At its peak in 2009 MIC's market value was R3.5 billion. The crash that year shaved off close to R2 billion in market value (not cash), but the remaining estimated asset base then of over R1.5 billion is a staggering advance on the initial seed capital of R3 million.

How has MIC benefited miners and what did it cost them? From the initial R3 million NUM paid to establish the MIT and MIC, they have received close to R400 million back in bursaries and scholarships, covering various fields of study, without one more cent of cost to them. The qualifications enabled many who were ordinary miners to become leaders in those areas, with some rising to be senior managers and even CEOs of companies.[79] MIC has also had a positive influence by encouraging companies it has invested in towards 'a more nuanced approach to change management, transformation and the way in which they conduct business'. These are great achievements, given the serious limits of a capitalist society.

Union investment companies have faced many challenges in South Africa. So far, MIC has performed the best, judged by the interests of union members in terms of the returns of investment allocated to education and training for themselves and their immediate families. In 1999 MIC delivered R70 million to the trust. By 2008 that figure had increased to R368 million. In 2008 its total assets were over R2.7 billion and in its 2008 review MIC reported that it had made the largest-ever single distribution of R245 million by an empowerment company to its shareholder.[80] MIC has over the years won several awards for its performance, including the Best Established Black Business in 2009. It was voted the Top Unlisted BEE Company of the Year in 2006, the Barlows/Wits Business School Top BEE Deal for 2008, and the leader of Corporate Social Responsibility by *Black Business Quarterly* in 2009.

When Kgalema left NUM, the union had an unencumbered reserve of R40 million. Today NUM is by far Cosatu's richest affiliate, thanks largely to the income MIC has generated through its investments, and a substantial property portfolio yielding a lucrative revenue stream, which has enabled the union to do many things that would not have been possible otherwise. A major move initially was that NUM bought a building for itself instead of paying a fortune in rent over the longer term. The idea came from Kgalema, who eventually convinced the union after much resistance. NUM now wholly owns NUM Properties, created by MIT 'to hold, own and manage properties that would be required ... for the union to function effectively.'[81] These properties include the head office, regional offices and the Elijah Barayi Memorial Training Centre.

MIC's great advantage over most other union investment or BEE companies is that it is debt-free. It still shares in the market risk, but what MIC wisely did just before the recession started to hit in 2008 was to commit a lump sum for one of the top insurance companies to protect the capital and so ensure that MIC could still finance the projects of the MIT despite the economic downturn that soon followed.

'Meeting the real world'

The R245 million cheque out of the dividends that MIC handed over to the trust in 2009 was to guarantee that projects would continue unhindered.[82] But these gains must also be weighed against the fact that NUM officials who joined MIT and MIC were paid much more than the wages of skilled NUM members and they also received benefits that ordinary members did not, which Kate Philip said was a source of much unhappiness in NUM when MIT and MIC were launched.

Did NUM buy into the capitalist system, the heart of which is investments for profit? Kate Philip is 'not a great fan of union investment companies' but adds that 'to seek to be self-sufficient is a key political principle.'[83] Her main concern is that unions were simply naïve about how much money was involved and how unionists involved in these companies could get rich very fast. 'Once people got their eyes on millions there was no turning back.'[84] By contrast, MIC officials did not go that route, which is why they do not own any shares in it except for the salary, perks and incentive bonuses they receive.[85] In Kgalema's words, 'We took a conscious decision that because we had R3 million of workers' money in the MIT we decided that MIC will be 100 per cent owned by the union through the MIT and that we will never change that position.' Paul Nkuna, CEO of MIC at the time of interview, adds, 'There is no shareholder in MIC, other than NUM, through the trust. ... This model was Kgalema's brainchild.'[86]

It is a fact, though, that the unionists who were employed in MIC ended up being much better off financially than those who stayed in NUM. MIC was thus a gateway to self-advancement. Philip comments: 'The complete disparity in conditions between those who went to MIC and those who did not and the patronage about who got to go and stay became itself a source of conflict in the union.'[87]

Kgalema is aware of such things but remains satisfied with what MIC has achieved.

> None of the other union investment companies provide detailed and regular reports to members about investment activities and results as MIC does. They now have over 600 graduates from the bursaries for the educational and training programmes they were on. ... These were ordinary mineworkers and through such exposure some of them today are CEOs of companies. We also took an ordinary worker who ended up being the principal officer of NUM's provident fund through training and so on. But one of the weaknesses and therefore a challenge is to get these types of people to remain on the boards, so that the original values are not lost or compromised.

Ebrahim Patel, the present minister of economic development, agrees that MIC benefited its members through education and training 'but the much more important and harder question is whether it has benefited them to the extent that it potentially could have. ... It is a story of workers and their kids, financing HIV education, shop stewards' training and education for workers and their children and much more. For that we needed a long-term capacity to build and acquire financial independence because under apartheid we were dependent on unions abroad.'[88]

He raises another point: 'Are union investment companies operating under the ethos of the private sector or do we begin to conceptualise a social economy, which is not for profit but that is efficient and that produces quality goods and services but whose open purpose is social goals? ... For example, do we invest in casinos or only in the productive sectors of the economy and how do we handle the question of individual remuneration?'[89] That question is particularly crucial, given the extensive

'Meeting the real world'

evidence of how destructive and self-destructive gambling at casinos has been for black working class families, many of whom are probably members of unions who have invested in casinos. Kgalema makes no bones about casinos: 'No, it is not a responsible investment outlet. They reinforce negatives – such as that it is possible to become instant millionaires – and they are indeed destructive. But we should be asking why they are there in the first place.'

Some questions about MIC's underlying operations are still unresolved. Should MIC incentivise staff who are full-time? If so, what portion of a deal could staff buy into, understanding this could be only with their own money, which they had to obtain by their own efforts? How could NUM convey such options to all members and how would they access such opportunities?

Initially there had been the offer of co-investment rights where union members could buy into deals. But ordinary miners, who were still among the lowest-paid workers in the country, were never in a position to do so. As a result the co-investment rights fell away. Kgalema sat on the board when he was general secretary of NUM but he too did not exercise his right to co-invest in deals.

I was concerned, though, when MIC's CEO at the time, Paul Nkuna, refused to tell me the terms and conditions of the incentive bonus system MIC has in place for its directors.[90] Kgalema makes it clear that he would not sanction such refusal, adding that transparency would be in MIC's interests rather than against it. Nkuna's reason was that MIC was a private company. This was a serious contradiction: for years NUM had urged the right to access information in our constitutional democracy – and long before, under apartheid, NUM demanded that the mining bosses 'open up' their books when companies pleaded that they were unable to meet wage demands. This lack of openness reveals one of the downsides of union investment companies: just like other private sector companies, when it suits them they play by the rules of the market and its hegemony.

Many leftists have provided scathing critiques of union investment companies. It certainly is not easy to regard these companies as part of a socialist strategy. For Dale McKinley it is inconceivable: 'There is a world of a difference in unions becoming "players" in the capitalist game of accumulation and surplus distribution and unions seeking to use capital (in a capitalist-dominated world) as a means to undermine and transcend the game itself. It is ultimately the difference (and choice) between having a socialist strategy and making excuses as to why you can't have one (regardless of the difficulties).'[91]

Yet by the end of the 1990s most unions had formed investment companies, something nobody in Cosatu could have foreseen at its founding congress in 1985. So much did they become a new reality that Roger Southall concluded: 'Whatever the case against union investment companies ... their establishment was a fact of life, however much their critics might dislike them. Almost inevitably, therefore, the debate became far more pragmatic than it was ideological.'[92]

We know that many contradictions are unavoidable. Every day workers perpetuate capitalism by being forced to sell their labour and then buy (or struggle to buy) the very products they produce for a profit. Wittingly or unwittingly, we perpetuate and reinforce this system daily as large swathes of everyday life are owned and controlled by capitalist markets. The unions and other bodies including the ANC are very far from having the power to change the situation. Until that day comes, we live with a host of weaknesses and contradictions, and must see MIC and other entire union investment companies in this context. Until clear alternatives are found, investment companies will continue. The best approach for now is to assess the gains and disadvantages, as Kgalema does.

General appraisal of Kgalema
Aside from what follows, nobody I interviewed from NUM had any major criticisms of Kgalema, even when they heard that speaking openly would not be a problem, because he wanted them to talk freely. Some people were so impressed with him all along that they had never noticed any serious shortcomings. Others were even surprised at the idea of his weaknesses, seeing him as an almost flawless leader.

One or two staff members felt that Kgalema lacked the administration skills he needed as an education officer and later as coordinator of the unit. Irene Charnley disagrees: the education unit had good administrators; and it was not Kgalema's job to be an administrator but to run education and training classes and courses.[93] Kgalema admits he was not very good at administration but says little was required because the unit was funded by donors and when funds were received they was disbursed to various education projects. An irony here is that if an education officer required substantial administration skills, why was Kgalema not trained accordingly, especially since he had just returned from a decade on the Island, which was hardly a place to learn such skills? Charnley adds an objective test for gauging a lack of skill: 'Since every person has both weaknesses and strengths we must ask, "How did the alleged administrative weaknesses of Kgalema affect the organisation itself?"'[94] As it turned out, any lack of skill evidently did not seriously affect the head office and later the office of the general secretary.

Another concern raised by several of the staff was Kgalema's indecisiveness in dealing with problems they brought to his attention. They often left his office with the issues unresolved.

They said he was too lenient about staff issues and failed to act against those responsible. Kgalema's response was that some cases involved a desire by complainants for swift action against others – who could be entirely innocent – before enough evidence was gained and before the accused had the opportunity to state their case. He thought that sometimes people wanted to deny other staff their basic rights. He was not going to endorse any action against them without fairness and due process. Kgalema's sense of fairness is strong here, both of the case and how it is handled. Ironically, it was partly NUM itself which taught him about fairness in its cases against mine management. The conflicts on Robben Island also taught him to be careful before either attacking or labelling people prematurely, including political opponents. This caution had earned him huge respect on the Island, Saths Cooper says, including from opponents of the ANC and SACP.[95]

Some interviewees also said Kgalema tended to 'over-consult' when urgent decisions did not allow for such a luxury. This is difficult to gauge because the amount of consultation depends on the nature and importance of the topic. He certainly does prefer to maximise discussion on important matters and ensure that everybody is on board and understands the issues as fully as possible so that they can take part in deliberations and own the final decisions made. Overall, he would say, over-consultation is better than under-consultation. This timeless style seems to typify the more intellectual leaders. Raymond Suttner says that that is exactly how he found Kgalema on one visit: 'I thought I was taking up too much of the time of the SG [secretary-general] of the ANC but he had all the time in the world to talk about ideas.'[96]

The quest for facts has helped people adjust their sights. Seeng Letele described her disappointment with Kgalema over a perceived case of favouritism involving a white female staff member, then changed her mind when she heard the full story and said she apparently had not had all the information before she complained.[97]

Motlatsi recalls that Kgalema 'was always available to help and will never in a moment of need hold earlier disagreements against you. He focuses on the tasks at hand and organisational matters, rather than on individuals. And even when he may give you good advice, he will never tell others and want to claim credit for it.'[98]

Ebrahim Patel valued the fact that Kgalema tried to replicate the culture of open debate he had been schooled in on the Island. The NUM that Kgalema joined worked like a machine that had to get things done. Now here was someone who loved ideas and tossing them around. Some of the shop stewards were quite amused by this theoretician, Patel says, but also appreciated him as someone who wanted to go way beyond the routines of grievances and disciplinary procedure. He wanted to reflect on the bigger issues, not only in current politics but history as well. He liked to tell workers stories of South Africa's past.[99]

Patel expresses a concern he had back then: 'Because industrial relations in the mining industry were very hard and often brutal, I wondered whether this calm, very careful, reflective and highly dignified person would survive in such a harsh environment. His pace then seemed different from what the union and the industry demanded.' Indeed, Kgalema does often look like someone moving to the rhythm of a distant drummer, with an enduring 'unhurried sense' about him, says Patel.[100]

What emerges for me here is that the conduct of leaders – how they carry and project themselves in their relations with people, their organisations and the public – may be as important as the views and policies they embrace. Society is steadily awakening to the problems presented by machismo, aggression, disrespect, annoying impatience, self-centred ambitions and other decidedly negative features of many leaders.

Gabriels in the NUM education unit felt that sometimes Kgalema 'was too philosophical and blunt for the level of consciousness and debate among miners but at the same time he was pivotal in raising their political consciousness. Otherwise he was very dependable, diligent, disciplined and committed to his work and the miners.'[101] True, when Kgalema was less experienced he did tend to use abstract terms, like many young activists. His letters to Mapula from the Island had smacked sometimes of intellectual abstraction even before he joined NUM. Govan Mbeki and other intellectuals on the Island may have had some scholarly influence on him. He had shown no such signs before going to the Island at the age of 28. The very isolation of the Island could also have predisposed prisoners to intellectualise, especially since, as Kgalema has said so often, one of the biggest drawbacks of life on the Island was that no matter how strong one's views they could not be tested in practice. This was one of the main reasons why prisoners tended to defer to those who continued to wage the struggle outside jail.

Ramaphosa made an incisive point about Kgalema at the helm of NUM: 'I thought he would be much more political, but what he did instead was to concentrate more on the organisational aspects and the conditions of mineworkers, which I found truly refreshing.'[102]

Baleni recalls how Kgalema shed tears at an education workshop when he told the delegates about a trainer, Vuyisile Jonas, who had monthly deductions from his salary for traffic fines he had incurred in the course of his union work. Kgalema believed that it was unjust, and that the deductions seriously

'Meeting the real world'

affected his income at a time when union pay was low. Kgalema's stand soon resulted in the end of such deductions. This comradely compassion has been a constant theme in interviews with people he worked with in both NUM and the ANC.

Most of the NUM people interviewed said how impressed they were from the start with how humble and totally free from pompousness or arrogance both Kgalema and Nkosi were, even though people released from the Island were being revered at the time as heroes. Even more impressive, by all accounts, is that their manner never changed in the years after they joined NUM.

Because he hardly ever brings ego into his work and relationships with others, according to Kate Philip – especially in an organisational and political context – he also had no qualms about working under Ramaphosa or Gabriels.[103] On the contrary, he talked about how much he learnt from the leadership, shaft stewards and ordinary miners too. The learning curve included even the simplest things. Maluleka still laughs as he recalls showing Kgalema how to use an ATM when he joined NUM – because ATMs had been introduced while he was on the Island![104]

People also said that Kgalema was never a womaniser. Many men in the unions – both in leadership and the rank and file – have been heavy womanisers, including those who were married. Baleni recalls that when NUM men got together over a drink at the end of the month, when they got paid, Kgalema would sit with them but not utter a word when the conversation turned to women, as it often did.[105] Predictably he turned down an offer by NUM members to 'organise' him a woman when he once conducted shaft steward training at the Cullinan diamond mine near Pretoria. He told the miners that he was not interested and they needed to realise that 'women are not objects for sexual pleasure'. Combine this stance with the fact that he is also a teetotaller, disciplined and health-conscious – including being careful about what he eats – and it could even seem as if he is something of an ascetic.

A natural adjunct here is self-control. This should not be confused with a lack of courage: this was a man who in 1988 beat off two hijackers even after he had been shot in the stomach. Kgalema can be a site of calm in a storm that terrifies everyone else. He attributes his style to the scenes of his youth: 'I think it was the black township environment I grew up in where ruffians and every type of person were among my friends and so I learnt from young to deal with very different people and circumstances.' Gino Govender, who worked with him in the NUM education unit, says Kgalema particularly liked the poem 'If' by Rudyard Kipling, which extols the virtues of self-control.[106] There is no doubt that the tough life on Robben Island strengthened his mastery over emotions. Many leaders lack this, becoming conceited or arrogant when they grow to have power over millions. Kgalema often invokes these words by Abraham Lincoln: 'Many men have faced adversity, but if you truly want to test the character of a man give him power.' Mantashe observes:

> He has this disempowering, unassuming thing about him. He fakes weakness, that is how I describe him. When you deal with him you could think he was weak and not assertive. He does not throw himself around and you will never discover his strengths and his incredible knowledge until you really sit down and engage him. But his unassuming character is both a strength and a weakness. It is a strength in a sense that he does not expose himself unnecessarily but it is a weakness in that many people take it as a weakness, even though it might not be.[107]

Kgalema can be deeply pained by what he perceives to be falsity or duplicity. He was upset by Mac Maharaj claiming in his biography by Padraig O'Malley that he, through Operation Vula, represented the only underground structure and leadership in South Africa.[108] This does sound like the presumptuous arrogance of many exiled ANC leaders at the time. Surely the ANC cadres inside the country, like Kgalema, especially given his MK background, would know whether the ANC had an underground presence in the country and if it was significant. Kgalema responds: 'He is basically saying that he was the linchpin of the underground. The problem is that Mac did not know the facts. The internal leadership group of Govan Mbeki, Sisulu, Raymond Mhlaba and I were indeed an underground ANC structure. In fact on the day Mandela was released, we were in an underground meeting in Port Elizabeth. We had to adjourn the meeting so that Sisulu could fly to Cape Town for Madiba's release. When Madiba came out he became part of that group.'

Kgalema also strongly disputes an allegation in the O'Malley book that, according to Maharaj, he told a meeting of senior ANC leaders in 1989 that Govan Mbeki had confirmed to him Mandela was selling out: '"Madiba is drinking wine, dressing up, asking people to come and visit him. No one must go," Kgalema allegedly told the meeting.'[109] Maharaj claims to have heard this from Mohammed Valli Moosa, but Moosa has told Kgalema this was untrue. Kgalema firmly believes that the target of Maharaj's false claim was Govan Mbeki, with whom he had serious differences on the Island, and that he was using Kgalema for this purpose.[110]

Kgalema has never raised the matter with Maharaj. It is not that he avoids being honest with people but he would rather choose a moment for a one-to-one conversation to spare a person any possible public embarrassment and hurt. Failing that, he might simply drop the subject. This restraint could be a weakness, especially in the brutal world of politics, because sidestepping confrontations can be costly to himself and the organisation involved. His partner Gugu Mtshali says: 'Even in the ANC, if anybody did anything to him, he will pretend he does not even see it and that is how he deals with a lot of hurt he experiences. He pretends it has not happened but he will know where he stands with you thereafter.'[111] But does that mean he is, as Mbeki said, 'too soft' to be able to confront people when necessary? Mtshali says that anyone who says that he is too soft does not really know him: 'No, he was in fact upset when Mbeki said that about him. But I don't think he is too soft at all. He is more shrewd than soft but I also think that Mbeki said that, not because he really believed it, but because he wanted to obtain a particular outcome. But Kgalema will never do something that he does not really want to do or be party to something he does not believe in and accept. Every decision is weighed up carefully.'[112]

Since taking over from Mbeki and after being appointed deputy to Zuma in 2009, Kgalema appears to have become a little less restrained and more forthright. Yet his characteristic restraint has never been for lack of courage. Time after time, as we will see in the rest of this book, he has been bold on matters where many in the ANC would fear to tread.

PART TWO

FROM ANC SECRETARY-GENERAL TO POLOKWANE AND PARLIAMENT, 1997–2007

CHAPTER FOUR
From Mafikeng to Stellenbosch, 1997–2002

> I have never, I mean never, operated like a Stalinist in the ANC, NUM, the SACP or in government. My approach is simple: in debates you try hard to convince opponents of your views but if they refuse to be persuaded, then you must respect their right to differ.
>
> Kgalema Motlanthe, 2009

As secretary-general (SG) of the ANC, Kgalema was responsible for ensuring that the party carried out its adopted policies and programme. In his first term, as he saw it, his task included helping to build and sustain greater unity within the ANC and the alliance and liaising with government on some major matters – notably on Gear, iGoli 2002, HIV/Aids and Zimbabwe. There was unease in many quarters about the degree to which the presidency seemed to sway policy in the ANC rather than the other way round. Kgalema drew on a decade of experience in NUM but did find that he had moved into a far more complex arena, on a vastly bigger scale. This chapter mainly examines his entry into the role of ANC secretary-general and his stances and changing responses through the five-year period from 1997 to 2002, and attempts to evaluate how far he was 'his own man' and what he achieved.

Election as ANC secretary-general

In the run-up to the party conference at Mafikeng in December 1997, the ANC gave a great deal of thought to the kind of leader they wanted. Almost everyone who had some measure of influence in ANC circles – certainly among the most senior leadership – believed that Kgalema would be the best choice.[1] They wanted a strong SG who could unify and build the ANC after the departure of Ramaphosa and deal with the serious problems the ANC faced after 1994. Cheryl Carolus, the deputy SG, had been filling the gap while Ramaphosa was involved in the negotiations at Codesa and thereafter the constitution making. For Jacob Zuma, the 'ANC needed the most reliable, trusted and committed comrade because we were in a crisis in the ANC.'[2] Sisulu – who coordinated the re-establishment of ANC structures in the country – had wanted Kgalema to be the ANC's first Gauteng chairman after its unbanning and then its secretary-general; this spoke volumes about the confidence he had in Kgalema's leadership capabilities, based on years of close ties.[3]

Mathews Phosa notes that 'more than a year before the conference the matter was decided and that explains why Kgalema was not opposed in Mafikeng.'[4] Towards the end of 1996 Mandela went to the NUM offices to speak to Kgalema and other NUM officials.[5] Kgalema confirms: 'Basically he asked them to please release me for the post of SG of the ANC.' Kgalema immediately turned to Sisulu to persuade Mandela and other leaders to reconsider because he believed that NUM needed him to continue with them, especially as many leading figures had already left the union. He was also uncomfortable about how the choice was being made: he felt he was being parachuted into the post by the top leadership and that this usurped the constitutional authority of the ordinary members and the branches to decide by themselves. (Jacob Zuma says: 'It was a decision and a process that emerged from the top leadership. Once we got the commitment of NUM and Kgalema himself, we referred it to our structures.')[6] In the end Sisulu prevailed on him to accept the post. 'I then knew that I had lost the argument and had to accept.'

The election itself was an exhilarating formality:

> It was the biggest celebration of an otherwise rather taut week. It was as if, at last, with all the tension of the behind-the-scenes angst about the shift to Gear and the more public display of collective anxiety over Winnie, Motlanthe's election could release the pent-up tension of a thousand people stuffed into a baking sports hall. When the result was announced, he was carried from the back by a group of supporters. It took another fifteen minutes for him to reach the stage, struggle songs filling the air. There could be no doubting the popularity of this election.[7]

The writer here, Richard Calland, adds this impression of the man himself: 'Motlanthe appears a little older than his years, partly because his hair is greying, but mainly because he has a soft voice and is a gentle man, possessing an almost old-school politeness, with an engaging smile. There is a paternal aspect to him that is endearing. Yet, he is also tough and at times remarkably candid.'[8]

Kgalema became SG of the ANC at a difficult moment for the party and the country. On coming to power, the ANC had launched the Reconstruction and Development Programme (RDP) to address needs such as housing, land, health, education and services. Then in 1995 the RDP, then headed by Jay Naidoo, office issued the draft Urban Development Strategy, which flagrantly subverted the social justice framework of the RDP and laid the basis for differential class-based services, determined strictly by affordability.[9] This approach meant that the vast majority of the black population, who were poor, would be saddled with low levels of service for years and even decades ahead. By December 1997 unemployment, poverty and inequalities were rising. There was a whole range of related social injustices, most notably the increasing commercialisation and commodification at local government level of basic services such as water, sanitation and electricity, which later triggered various social movements and township protests.[10] Meanwhile, serious problems began to appear and deepen in the ANC alliance when Gear (the Growth, Employment and Redistribution strategy) was adopted in June 1996.

The ANC also faced the fact that the protection of private property had been enshrined in the new Constitution. This was one of many compromises made in the Codesa negotiations, probably through pressure from national and international capital, and nothing contradicted the interests of mineworkers and the broader working class more explicitly.

As for the capacity of the ANC to rule the country, Kgalema made it clear that, despite the ANC's policy conference of 1992 having produced guidelines called 'Ready to Govern', even by 1994 the ANC was in fact far from ready, with a serious shortage of technical, managerial and political skills and experience in its own ranks. Kgalema frankly admits this: 'Most ANC members deployed to government were not really prepared for its complexities because we had not deliberately taken people for training as bureaucrats and that kind of detailed political, technical and administrative preparation. That was really a steep learning curve for all.' The ANC's 1994 conference had taken place just months after the elections, too soon for a realistic assessment. Mafikeng was thus the first conference where the ANC could assess its performance on coming to power.

Kgalema was under no illusion about the huge task that post-apartheid South Africa posed for ANC rule, especially in overcoming the widespread problems of unemployment, poverty, homelessness and related social injustices.[11] But he did start with some points in his favour. As a leading ANC cadre from Robben Island and after his top role in re-establishing the ANC in Gauteng in 1990 and 1991, he was well abreast of developments in both the ANC and the government. His dedicated service in the previous ten years in NUM had strengthened his ANC credentials. His many qualities – especially his respect for others, commitment to the ANC and sterling discipline – were also well known by then. People in the ANC tend to have a strong historical memory about what their leaders have contributed, and so his election did not occur in a vacuum. His last position as general secretary of NUM had also kept him in close touch with what was happening in the alliance and government. In turn, there was general consensus within the alliance that he should become the new SG. Cosatu, particularly, pushed for this because they believed that a fellow leftist unionist in such a powerful position would help their cause. His election was thus seen as a victory for the left in the ANC and the wider alliance, especially since he was then also a leading figure in the SACP as a member of its central committee.[12]

Kgalema and Mbeki

Key to many people's reading of how Kgalema performed as SG is their view of his relationship with Thabo Mbeki. The two men were elected together at Mafikeng, Kgalema as SG and Mbeki as president. By virtue of their respective leadership positions, they were required to work closely together, which they did.

There are significant differences in how senior ANC, Cosatu and SACP leaders saw Mbeki and Kgalema and their relationship. Several leading figures in the ANC and its allies Cosatu and the SACP are convinced that Kgalema and Luthuli House were dominated and marginalised by Mbeki and the presidency, especially from 1999 when Mbeki appointed Smuts Ngonyama as head of the ANC presidency, a post that had never existed before, based at Luthuli House.[13] The perception is so strong that NUM's Baleni could say in hindsight: 'When he was secretary-general of the ANC all the powers of his position were taken by the presidency. Basically, he was like a mere clerk. It is only now, after Polokwane, that these powers are being restored. This happened during both terms but became worse in the second term. That was a debilitating factor which negatively affected his work.'[14]

It is debatable how far Kgalema was marginalised. He certainly has a different view: 'It is putting it too bluntly to say that Luthuli House and I were marginalised. You can perhaps say that Comrade Thabo had a poor way of doing things at times and also factor in the poor capacity of Luthuli House. We did not even have a researcher. I had to rely on Michael Sachs and Melissa Levin, whereas the presidency had numerous researchers. It was a whole institution on its own. So in terms of research, keeping abreast of developments and generating ideas, there was little capacity at head office, which has to be factored into an analysis.'

There were signs of Kgalema being marginalised in his first term as SG, his critics say, which became more blatant in his second term between Stellenbosch and Polokwane. Kgalema does not exactly agree but concedes that his relationship with

Mbeki and the presidency was much better during the first term, from Mafikeng to Stellenbosch, than the second. In fact, for Kgalema the first term started off on a very positive note: he found the first meeting of the top six officials was held on the last day of the Mafikeng conference 'constructive, positive and inspiring'. Yet, at the end of that term, he told the Stellebosch conference: 'Since 1994 the ANC policy capacity at HQ has been drastically reduced and this impacted on the ability of the ANC to effectively monitor implementation and the impact of our policies on the motive forces and our mission.'[15]

Despite this, when Jimmy Seepe asked him about Mbeki's alleged domination of ANC policies, Kgalema denied it: 'It's a wrong perception that has been spread around and it is based on lies. ANC decisions are not taken by a single individual. Look at Madiba. He is a powerful individual but he would tell you that he himself has to go through the structures of the ANC to put a certain view across. Everything is thoroughly debated within the ANC. There is therefore no basis to suggest that Mbeki controls the organisation's policies.'[16]

He also denied claims that Mbeki ran roughshod over him but added: 'Problems arose from 2003 when he [Mbeki] started using the state to run and determine ANC matters and when parallel structures were being created after Smuts [Ngonyama] became the head of the presidency. By the time of Polokwane there were no doubt parallel structures.' Xolela Mangcu grasps what was happening: 'When Mbeki became president he created a completely new unit called the presidency with Smuts Ngonyama as its head. This created tension between the office of the presidency and the office of the secretary-general – a position traditionally seen as the engine of the ANC. Suddenly Ngonyama was more prominent than Motlanthe – at least in the public domain, which partly explains why Motlanthe is still a stranger to members of the public outside the ANC.'[17]

Mbeki completely rejects the idea that he dominated Kgalema and Luthuli House or that they had a troubled relationship:

> We had a good relationship. The ANC officials would meet every Monday and the NWC [national working committee] every fortnight. That meant that I met him at least once a week and almost invariably after the NWC meeting we would have another informal meeting between him, Smuts and me in his office, talking more generally about things in the organisation. You could in fact say that throughout the almost ten years I was president I would have about two meetings a week with him. I don't know about any serious tensions that developed between Luthuli House or him and the presidency. If there were tensions at Luthuli House that was not conveyed to the presidency. The allegation that I marginalised Luthuli House was a deliberate campaign of lies. If you ask anybody what exactly does the marginalisation of Luthuli House mean, they won't be able to tell you.[18]

But too many people have said too many serious things on this score for them to all be dismissed. Karima Brown, always an astute political observer, says: 'One of the big reasons Kgalema was unhappy during Mbeki's reign was the serious lack of accountability of cadres the ANC deployed to government.'[19] And indeed this was the message coming through from Kgalema himself in discussions I had with him in 2006 and 2007. His sense was that leading ANC figures were trying to control the ANC through their senior positions in government and that their chief conduit for doing so was through the NEC.

This group was located in government and had massive

resources at their disposal they could use as they wished and they continued to insult our intelligence by saying that the problem was that we did not understand. That was in fact their starting point on many issues. Increasingly they regarded structures of the ANC with contempt, up to the point where a basic point evaded them: they were elected to the NEC by the membership of the ANC, but now all of a sudden the branches cannot be trusted to know certain things and it's almost as if they are the ignorant masses. But from what I can see we are still sitting with that problem, it's just that the leaders and personalities have changed.

Another related problem for him was that sometimes people were appointed to cabinet who had no serious standing among the membership of the ANC and the people as a whole.

Kgalema believes the most important factor in the whole ANC–government equation is the state of affairs in the ANC itself and whether it is strong or not. The ANC is incomparably more important for him than the government is. He says we would have far fewer problems in government if the organisation on which its rule is based and from which it is derived is strong, active and involved among its rank and file, to the extent that it insists on the strict accountability of those it has placed there. On this score, speaking at the ANC's national general council (NGC) in Port Elizabeth in 2000, he criticised lack of consultation and discussions between the government and the ANC: 'There is little understanding of or involvement in activities by ANC members and branches. Members are not empowered to engage in economic debates nor to initiate, undertake or participate in programmes to support economic growth and development.'[20]

The media have made much of allegations that Mbeki dominated the ANC (and hence Kgalema as its SG) and government, particularly on the issues of Zimbabwe and HIV/ Aids. Mbeki comments:

> Well, I have heard that informally only, because nobody ever told me that in an ANC or government meeting. Part of the problem was that ministers always felt that they had to prepare themselves very thoroughly in terms of their own portfolios when they made presentations to cabinet, because from their experience when presentations were made and debate followed the president will intervene and say this and that. Then you feel embarrassed because often the president would know more than the minister. But today I hear some ministers saying that they miss the serious discussions and debates we had in cabinet in the past. But to say that I suppressed debate is devoid of any truth.

I believe Mbeki completely in the sense that he did not overtly suppress any debates. In fact, in many of his speeches he encouraged them. Why wasn't he challenged in meetings? It was not that he suppressed debates, it was in spite of him not doing so. Once more it appears that, while Mbeki had strong views on many issues and would not hesitate to express them, the other leaders in the ANC had retreated to the margins of whatever debates did occur and did not openly challenge him even when they may have differed. That they took the line of least resistance was a symptom less of Mbeki's domination and more of the fact that the ANC was in serious trouble because senior leaders were afraid to do anything but toe the line. They chose a form of self-inflicted censorship (yet not even that stopped some of them from later blaming Mbeki after Polokwane).[21]

But there is undoubtedly quite a widespread feeling among those I interviewed in all the tripartite formations, including people who have been close to Kgalema, that Mbeki seriously undermined him and Luthuli House for years. Almost all of them sympathised with what they said he had to endure. Why then does Kgalema deny it? My reading is that, though he is a loyal ANC cadre and leader, he could not accept that Mbeki's attitude and actions, whatever they were towards him and Luthuli House, occurred in a vacuum, unrelated to what was happening to the ANC itself after 1994.

Questions arise here. Where were the NWC, the NEC, the cabinet and many other party and government structures? Where were all the seasoned members and cadres of the Congress movement, many with experience going back decades? Most importantly, where was the ANC? – the very question Kgalema later asked delegates in his report to Polokwane. If Mbeki really was a powerful authoritarian who utterly dominated everyone around him, what were they all doing to stop him and save the ANC of old? Kgalema agrees that people censored themselves to keep things calm for government and says this was happening all along, whether about Aids, Zimbabwe, Gear or any other controversial matter on which Mbeki had strong views during the course of his presidency.

There is more to it, though. Kgalema cannot accept that Mbeki did this or that to Luthuli House and himself and that he just passively folded his arms. He has spoken already and will say much more in later chapters to explode the myth that he was 'Mbeki's man' and that he did little or nothing to 'stop Mbeki'.[22] The question remains: did he do enough to rescue the ANC from Mbeki's alleged onslaught? But how much is 'enough' and who determines the answer to this question? However 'enough' is measured, for many people interviewed he did not do enough. If this is true, I am convinced it was not through his being weak or indecisive but because the entire ANC had become divided and vulnerable. It was impossible for Kgalema on his own – no matter how resolved he was – to put a stop to whatever was wrong in the ANC leadership or government.

Kgalema adds that the idea that Mbeki had a monopoly on thought within the organisation is ridiculous. 'The ANC is a multi-class organisation which debates any matter. When we emerge with a dominant position, it is an approximation of what was expressed in the debate, a product of contestation. When it is said there is no debate, it is due to deep ignorance about the nature of the ANC.' So why did the ANC allow Mbeki to become allegedly so powerful and domineering and later blame him for it? This question must lie at the heart of any probe into that period, but it is one that those who can only talk about what Mbeki did to the ANC will not like to explore, because their one-sided approach will not be vindicated – which also implies that Mbeki deserves some degree of rehabilitation. Mbeki definitely became a convenient scapegoat, as the president of the ANC and the country, for many of the ANC's own weaknesses and failures from the moment of its unbanning, through the negotiations and compromises of Codesa and thereafter the policies adopted after 1994, notably Gear. The same verdict applies to Cosatu and the SACP. If these two organisations could only be half as self-critical as they were scathingly critical of Mbeki, Manuel and other ANC leaders, the entire left in this country would be much better off.

We can say much the same to explain why Kgalema did indeed tend to tone down on Gear after Mafikeng. An Mbeki-fixated approach like Zwelinzima Vavi's will say this was due mainly to the negative influence of Mbeki. But it was really the combined result of many factors. Mbeki may have been a major factor but he could only play that role because a whole range of other conditions were already in place, in which Mandela and other leaders played a very big part.²³ Here we should include the fact that after Kgalema left NUM in 1997 and became SG of the ANC, he tended to become strongly critical of the left of which he had been a leader in NUM and Cosatu.

Surprisingly, he also criticised the 'ultra-leftists' in Cosatu – often the most convenient way of failing to confront the real issues that critics of the ANC's neoliberal policies validly raise – on the back of similar criticisms of Mbeki.²⁴ Ironically, his criticism coincided roughly with the period when it was said that he and Luthuli House were beginning to be marginalised by Mbeki, from about the time of the ANC's national general council in 2000. In fact it was more specifically Cosatu's anti-privatisation strike of 2000 that led to Kgalema's criticisms and the wider heavy condemnation of the ANC government. It was so severe that Vavi could say: 'We are happy to be declared extreme leftists; if fighting for the defence of jobs, free basic water, or affordable electricity makes us extreme leftists, so be it.'²⁵

Mantashe has an interesting explanation for what happened – that Kgalema has a steadfast loyalty to organisational decisions that forces him to respect authority and hierarchy, though there is no necessary link between loyalty and that kind of respect. Loyalty to organisational decisions is one thing and respect for authority and hierarchy, especially where it is elitist and stifling, quite another. But Mantashe says: 'Even when Mbeki did things that were clearly wrong, he would not confront him.'²⁶ He thinks Kgalema's personality may have made people say he was not assertive enough in challenging Mbeki's domination of Luthuli House.²⁷ Kgalema objects and says that when necessary – whatever others may think – he questioned and challenged Mbeki, and recalls Mbeki several times telling the NEC: 'I was thinking of suggesting … but knew that our SG would not be happy with it.' There is a strong sense from many, though, that if Kgalema did so, they did not see much of it.

Yet Mantashe goes on to say that 'Kgalema destroys idols ... if you want to make him into an idol he makes it his business to destroy that idol because he appreciates the fact that once you create an idol out of him, you create barriers between him and the people. That man will not think more of you because you have a powerful position in society and less of ordinary, poor or unemployed people.'[28] As we see, Mantashe here makes two statements at odds with each other. His own description of Kgalema makes it very unlikely that he would allow himself and especially the organisation to be dominated by its president. If Kgalema weakly allowed Mbeki to dominate him and Luthuli House, is this the personality that wants to destroy idols? Hardly.

Kgalema disagrees that Mbeki dominated. 'I was not marginalised during Mbeki's first term. I repeat that during his first term the collective leadership of the ANC worked well.' But to say that he was not dominated during the first term implies that he was or might have been during the second, from Stellenbosch to Polokwane. Back in 2002, Kgalema was even more emphatic: 'It's a wrong perception that has been spread around and it is based on lies. ANC decisions are not taken by a single individual. There is therefore no basis to suggest that Mbeki controlled the organisation's policies.'[29] He puts his case thus:

> The chief political responsibility of the secretary-general – though not spelt out in the constitution – is to keep the ANC together. That is why when the president of the ANC may have done certain things which were wrong, it was the responsibility of the secretary-general to raise them directly with him, which is what I have done when necessary, but I don't go and tell

the media every time it happened. Can you imagine what will happen in the ANC if I had to go public every time I had a difference with Mbeki? I would destroy the ANC by doing that. What message would it send to our membership and supporters?

He goes on to say that one of the problems with Mbeki was that he tended to react too quickly when he heard negative rumours about himself or his office, which Kgalema thought was very unwise, especially when he was the president of the ANC and the country. 'Precisely because people say lots of things about those in power, a president must be very cautious about how he or she responds to rumours.'

Kgalema acknowledges that Mbeki did say a few times, including at a conference, that Kgalema was a bit 'too soft'. He strongly disagrees: 'No, often this "too soft" characterisation occurred because I refused to go after people on the basis of rumours and whispers.' There is no doubt that some senior ANC leaders were critical of Kgalema, claiming that had he been more decisive it would have helped the ANC. Essop Pahad and Jacob Zuma are among those who shared this view. So, if indeed Kgalema was 'too soft', did Mbeki himself not exploit this sometimes?

Zuma has this to say: 'Mbeki had a style which almost hypnotised people. I'm telling you, Mbeki used Kgalema's gentle ways, I think. He [Mbeki] could move quickly on things, knowing Kgalema won't come after him quickly and strongly, and Mbeki did a lot of damage in the meantime.'[30] Some people have even blamed the persistence of certain problems on Kgalema not acting firmly at an early stage. But, assuming there is truth here, the fact is that hardly anyone raised these concerns directly with him. Precisely because the SG post is the most important to keep the ANC running daily and ensure its overall health, if there were such serious concerns then surely they ought to have been raised in both the NEC and NWC and appropriate decisions taken. Not once did any member of the NEC or NWC formally complain or criticise him in this regard.

Kgalema goes further: 'I think it was sometimes said that I was too soft when they did not get their way with me, when, for example, I did not do what they wanted me to do, like go after somebody they disliked or for whatever reason targeted. It's patently untrue. I did all that the ANC's constitution required me to do.' Yet some may hold that it is easier for him to say so now that Mbeki is no longer the president, when he runs no risk of censure that could dislodge him from his position or have any other serious consequence. This is not to say that Mbeki would have been vindictive had Kgalema been more forthright, but power relations are a major reality to sway politicians, especially at that time when Mbeki was a hugely powerful leader in the country. Yet I am reminded of the words of Irene Charnley: 'Kgalema is a very courageous leader. He does not care what position or authority you might have. If he thinks what you are doing is wrong he will take a stand against you – even if he is alone – and he will do so fearlessly.'[31] I tend to agree.

A further point: we habitually attach far too much weight to individual leaders and pay far too little attention to the dynamics within the organisations and, more broadly, the society that produces them. Attempts to blame Kgalema or hold Mbeki personally responsible for things that have gone wrong in the ANC and government are not only misguided. They miss out on a broader analysis and rob us of appropriate solutions. The glib approach also signals the decline of the organisation, because its fate and future reside with individual leaders rather than the membership's conscious and collective control.

Kgalema has never sought to deny that Mbeki had an influence on him or that he still has a good relationship with him. When the long knives were out for Mbeki after Polokwane and especially after the Nicholson judgment, he did not let this affect his bond with Mbeki. 'After working closely together for many years, I can say that Thabo Mbeki did influence my thinking on some things' – a normal effect indeed. Whatever happened under Mbeki's leadership, Kgalema says, he will always respect the huge contribution Mbeki made in exile and since his return in 1990.

We now turn to four main areas of concern during Kgalema's first term as SG, particularly with his relationship with Mbeki in mind – Gear and the RDP, iGoli 2002 and the anti-privatisation strike, HIV/Aids, and Zimbabwe – to see the dynamics in some depth.

Gear and the RDP

The decline of the RDP in 1995 and the emergence of Gear in 1996 were seen by many as the extended logic of catering for the interests of capital. Cash constraints became the hallmark. The original RDP had acknowledged the fiscal difficulties ahead, a fact often not conceded by the left, but the revised version, the RDP White Paper, saw the virtual demise of the programme after the RDP office was closed in 1995.[32]

Whereas Mbeki and Manuel saw Gear as the necessary financial framework for the RDP, the left generally argued from 1996 onwards that Gear contradicted it.[33] Mbeki's biographer Mark Gevisser says bluntly: 'Mbeki would go on to insist, repeatedly, that Gear was nothing but an iteration of the RDP, but the more he said it, the less anyone believed it.'[34] It appears that after the 1994 elections the RDP was increasingly discarded, except for the rhetoric. Cosatu saw the White Paper as reducing the RDP to 'no more than a social net to cushion the impact of job losses and poverty.'[35] The last remaining RDP structure, the RDP parliamentary portfolio committee, was abolished in the late 1990s.

Against the background of the horrendous damage apartheid had inflicted over a long period, the increase in unemployment, poverty and inequalities that followed Gear was devastating – and it was the black working class bearing the pain, not the white bourgeoisie or the ANC leadership. The significant increase in social grants from about 2000 could hardly compensate for the huge social damage Gear inflicted on working class communities, in particular between 1996 and 2000.

Where did Kgalema stand in relation to the ANC-led government's backing of Gear in 1996? He was NUM's general secretary at the time Gear was launched. NUM itself and Cosatu were staunchly critical. It has emerged that Kgalema did not openly oppose their stance but was quietly won over to the need for Gear.[36] It was Thabo Mbeki, president at the time, who had a major influence in changing his mind. Kgalema was one of several leading trade unionists who went to see Mbeki in Pretoria in a series of meetings on economic matters. 'The strategy was to identify key Cosatu leaders unhappy with Gear and to bring them into personal and informal contact with Mbeki, where, away from their constituencies and the need to project militancy, they might be swayed by his sweet reason.'[37] Said Kgalema, referring to Mbeki, 'He did the sums for us, he used logic to convince us, and it worked. Once I listened to him, my position changed. And I was not the only one.'[38]

Kgalema argued at the time that the huge inherited debt from the apartheid era compelled a fiscal regime that prioritised paying it off. He recognised that the bulk of this debt was not external but internal – linked to public provident and pension funds – and hence could not be sidestepped without massive legal and ethical implications, as he recalls:

> Paying the debt placed a huge burden on the state. Gear was therefore adopted as a policy which will enable government not just to service the debt but to eliminate it and thereby be able to defend the independence of the country, because at that point many were saying what is so magical about South Africa, why not go and borrow from the IMF and World Bank? But such a course of action would have led to these institutions to believe that they can determine our policies. Instead of taking that approach we decided to tighten our belts but defend our independence and therefore free ourselves from the influence and in fact dictate of multilateral institutions. Hence today South Africa can speak with relative independence and that is why on the continent most of the countries look up to South Africa for leadership, precisely because they are dependent for their budgets on donors and all the strings attached.

Zwelinzima Vavi says Kgalema spoke out strongly against Gear while he was the leader of NUM and criticises him for having changed his stance and soft-pedalled a bit after he was elected in Mafikeng.

> He seemed to have changed his tune when he got to the ANC. He started sounding like Mandela: 'We know that this is not the space we should be in, but circumstances dictated Gear, the Rand was collapsing, we were about to go to the IMF and therefore urgent austerity measures were needed.' … There was a feeling that he is not doing enough to defend our positions and struggles and therefore a sense of disappointment was certainly strongly there. But it was not only in him that we felt

disappointed but with all the Cosatu people who went to work full-time in the ANC and government. When we were angry with government policies and went to him he would say, 'Wait, comrades, we cannot throw away the movement.' Kgalema, I feel, could have done more to stem the Mbeki juggernaut. Sometimes it was terrible to see how Mbeki dominated the entire movement. However, Kgalema was popular in the Cosatu CEC [central executive committee] meetings. When he spoke you would not hear a pin drop.[39]

Kgalema is very clear that the need for Gear should have been properly explained, and wasn't. Further, he says, 'There was no real debate at all. Where was it properly debated?' A meeting at Mandela's home with a few leaders hardly constituted a proper consultation. None of the ordinary membership of the alliance partners had a chance to even discuss it, let alone decide whether they would support it or not.[40]

Kgalema goes on to say that Gear was not discussed in plenary at Mafikeng either. True, Gear had already been a fait accompli for eighteen months, but what Kgalema does not address is that the conference still had the constitutional power to reject it, which could in turn have led to the ANC insisting that it be abolished. 'I agree but it was not discussed in plenary' was, disappointingly, Kgalema's only response here.

While Kgalema did not seek to impose his views on NUM or Cosatu in the years following Gear's introduction, he also criticised the policy's lack of success. In August 1997, just over a year after it was introduced, he told Padraig O'Malley: 'I think that the government's macroeconomic policy has been a dismal failure actually. Whether you measure it against the employment situation, the truth and the reality is that there haven't been new jobs created, it has not even succeeded in attracting a flurry into South Africa of an influx of long-term investors who are willing to go into green fields investments. The trickle that has come into the country has only been directed at the JSE [Johannesburg Stock Exchange], more speculative investment than anything else.'[41]

In the same interview Kgalema states: 'In my view Gear was really aimed primarily at sending the message to foreign investors that South Africa was an attractive investment outlet for them. That's why I said its development should have been preceded by very clear assessments and questioning of all the assumptions that lay behind the kind of state machinery that this government has inherited, and also the needs and the massive problems, whether you are looking at housing, education, transport, electrification, all those things that need to be addressed.'[42]

Three years later, though, in September 2000, he sounds somewhat on the defensive about Gear: 'Gear has not created the number of jobs that it was expected to create, but there are other reasons as to why there have been job losses. Job losses were not as a consequence of Gear. Among the SACP there is a fixation about that and a simplistic attribution of job losses to Gear and yet the truth of the matter is that, to the extent that Gear was a macroeconomic policy, it had to address, among other things, if not the key element, macro stability.'[43]

What is evident here is a former leader of NUM who in his new job as SG of the ruling party is grappling with complex and constantly fluctuating economic indicators and who has to confront many other national and global considerations that his union post did not require him to address. His new post and its scope, environment and responsibilities were fundamentally different from those of his NUM days, something that Vavi and other critics clearly did not seem to grasp. Kgalema's own response is to ask himself if shifting to the new post changed his own consciousness and values. 'That for me is of the utmost importance, because a different terrain – like being in the leadership of the ruling party or in government – will inevitably bring with it new difficulties and challenges. In NUM I had to primarily concern myself with the mining sector, but in the ANC I have to deal with the whole economy and society. The scale is just vastly different.'

There is a sense that Kgalema became more pragmatic from the time he was elected SG of the ANC in Mafikeng. Some will argue that the pragmatism was there long before, as when he played a leading role in forming NUM's investment company and when he was persuaded by Mbeki's take on Gear. Kgalema does not deny the massive constraints of global capital; he concedes this is the universal problem and the supreme contradiction that socialists who get into office always face. On the post-1994 period and especially the aim in adopting Gear, Kgalema makes it crisply clear that he succumbed under pressure, in this case catering for foreign investors:

> I would still say it would have been a good idea and in fact necessary to make sure that we have more money available for social expenditure, especially against the background of the devastating social legacy of apartheid, but in the end in order to be attractive for investors certain sacrifices were made and as the liberalisation process started and was part and parcel of globalisation, you had no choice but to toe the line and pursue policies that will enable you to be attractive to foreign investors. That's precisely what was done.

IGoli 2002 and the anti-privatisation strike
Why was Cosatu so disappointed with Kgalema? The iGoli 2002

From Mafikeng to Stellenbosch, 1997–2002

programme had a lot to do with it. The city of Johannesburg designed this neoliberal plan to wipe out their deficit by commercialising and corporatising basic services such as Metro Gas, the bus service and the fresh produce market from 2002. Opposition by Cosatu, the SACP and many social movements was huge but not consistent or coordinated. Arguing that the scheme would result in job losses and tariff increases, Cosatu ran an anti-privatisation strike and met with vicious reaction from the ANC and government. Cosatu had other serious problems with the government too: the union was deeply unhappy with its policy direction; and the arms deal – which the government also mistakenly and unilaterally embarked upon despite many warnings – soon began to show signs of corruption. It was in this context, when Cosatu felt under attack from all sides, that it looked to Kgalema for support.

Cosatu underestimated the conservative forces he was up against in the ANC, pockets of opinion that quietly and privately began to see Cosatu as more of a threat than an ally, and considered what it would take to dislodge them. The goodwill and solidarity Kgalema may have had towards Cosatu meant little or nothing when he was up against forces that were steadily gaining the upper hand between Mafikeng and Stellenbosch (the strength of those forces began to decline between Stellenbosch and Polokwane, especially after Zuma was dismissed by Mbeki in June 2005).

Were his many strongly critical and surprising statements against Cosatu avoidable or understandable? Though he may not have been able to do a great deal to support Cosatu because of the nature of his job as SG of the ANC and the ideological confusion within it, why did it sometimes seem – from what I could gather talking to Vavi and other unionists – that he had not necessarily betrayed Cosatu's struggle for socialism, to which he had dedicated a decade in NUM, but that he had disappointed them, especially his attacks against them during the anti-privatisation strike of 2000? Vavi said that Cosatu was concerned and in fact infuriated by these public attacks at the time.[44] This reflects negatively on Kgalema, but more seriously on what was happening in the ANC itself and the enormous pressures he must have been under as a result. The unequal power relations inside the ANC and between it and its allies, Cosatu and the SACP, must have built up pressures to toe the line.

The following statements issued by Kgalema tell us just how dominant the more conservative forces in the ANC and government had become, which he appears to have sometimes passively reflected rather than challenged at source. At the start of the 2000 anti-privatisation strike he was emphatic about where the ANC government stood: 'The government is proceeding, correctly, to implement policies of the ANC determined at policy conferences and congresses of our party. Because Cosatu knows it cannot strike against us [the ANC], it targets the government. ... They can go on strike again next month and the month after, but there is nothing at all they will achieve. A great deal of their demands are ill-informed.'[45] This points to the unshakeable paramountcy of the ANC in policy making, where Cosatu and the SACP were junior partners who just had to accept that reality whether they liked it or not.

During the strike Makhudu Sefara wrote this about the 'restructuring' (largely a euphemism for privatisation) of state assets and after Mbeki's attacks against the 'ultra-left': 'Motlanthe continued the onslaught, saying members of the tripartite alliance who propagate socialism relied on "ready-made analysis of other countries."'[46] Kgalema had attacked the ultra-left earlier, in 2001, closer to home, in the ANC branches itself. Jaspreet Kindra wrote in the *Mail & Guardian*:

'Motlanthe said the branches were aware of the ultra-leftist tendency undermining the government and promoting counter-revolution', adding Kgalema's comment on the 'ultra-left': 'The general membership knows them and experiences them all the time.'[47] From a leftist – not ultra-leftist – perspective there are certainly big concerns with some of these remarks in the early 2000s, especially for activists in the SACP and Cosatu who were also ANC members and who had supported him so heartily as the new SG. His words do indeed resemble the criticisms Mbeki made of Cosatu and the SACP.

There can be no doubt that Kgalema's views changed significantly after Mafikeng. In 1992, as acting general secretary of NUM, he had told O'Malley: 'We have always professed independent trade unionism, that the labour movement should always remain independent of any political party. We think that the labour movement is an organ of civil society that helps to exert pressure on any government, including a democratic government.'[48] Furthermore, he told Snuki Zikalala in January 1992, immediately after becoming acting general secretary of NUM: 'Whoever belongs to the ANC or the SACP should not transform NUM into either the party or the ANC, NUM is first and foremost a trade union. I think we should try our level best to inculcate a spirit of independence in the union. The union should see itself as an independent organisation. Not an appendage of this or that political organisation.'[49]

Clearly, there will be grounds for criticism of Kgalema when we compare this stance with what he said above about Cosatu. In 1992 he strongly supported unions remaining independent of political parties and their right to exert pressure on 'any government', but when Cosatu went on strike, asserting their independence, he slammed them. Not to excuse his change of stance, but it does show that when you are in government or you are the SG of the ANC, the sustained political pressure you are under is very different from the worst you may have had in a trade union. The exercise and responsibility of state power, held by the ANC as the ruling party, hugely increase the scale.

At the 2000 NGC Kgalema had said that the relationship between partners in the ANC alliance was 'dangerously undefined' and that 'while the alliance had succeeded in winning elections, it had either failed or been less effective in ensuring a better life for all.'[50] Kgalema, however, had an approach to an aspect of a 'better life' that many on the left would reject as piecemeal reformism. While many have strongly criticised the cheap and poorly constructed RDP houses, he has this to say:

> Those who live in bigger houses say, 'How can the government build these people such small houses?' But they, looking at it in comparison to where they live, do not actually understand this person never had a house of their own before and lived in a shack which could be broken down at any time and from where they would have to move, but now they have a solid structure which belongs to them and they can do with it what they want. The sense of ownership and pride which flows from that kind of ownership is important.

There is definitely a greater sense of realism and pragmatism emerging in Kgalema's views after he left the unions. This has nothing to do with the influence of Mbeki or anyone else. Kgalema's experience in NUM, not least in seeing the need for the MIC, confirmed his view that you must do the best you can with what you really have, with a sense that material conditions will gradually change and increasingly so for the better. For him, RDP houses are 'building a better life' from the shacks homeless people lived in before.

Kgalema mentions that when he came in as SG there was no common alliance programme of action at either provincial or local level, which is why in 2000 he called on the alliance partners to debate and clarify the role each needed to play to improve the lives of ordinary people.[51] Though he did not say so in his report to the NGC, there was a direct causal link between the absence of a coherent programme of action binding the alliance and the failure to 'build a better life for all' more effectively.

The rapidly declining fortunes of socialism worldwide after his release from Robben Island in 1987 were probably the biggest factor that shaped his thinking. But after 1990 it was the resultant compromises the ANC made in Codesa and his own experience of the very tough and rough mining industry that had a decisive influence on him. He felt he had to take the state of play into account, as his response shows when Bafana Sithole urged him to be more assertive against Mbeki. Kgalema replied that the range of views within the ANC was not such that he could wage an all-out battle and certainly not one by himself.[52]

HIV/Aids

Did Mbeki also shape Kgalema's thinking on HIV/Aids? Kgalema spoke of how the drug AZT was being pushed by the pharmaceutical industry in its own profiteering interests. Mbeki, Kgalema and the ANC knew this was a major agenda in the debates about treatment. Kgalema says that once it was established that HIV causes Aids, the ANC never doubted the fact, but did argue that treatment should also cater for other factors, such as malnutrition, that could contribute to the compromise and collapse of the immune system, which is what HIV/Aids does. Speaking about these extra factors he told O'Malley in September 2000: 'Any other question, you are a dissident, you are bad, you are malicious, you are dangerous to society, you will be responsible for the deaths of so many children and this and that and so on. It's all crap from the pharmaceuticals.'[53]

In this respect he, like Mbeki, was unhappy that the world of Eurocentric medical science on HIV/Aids should be beyond criticism. Instead of being open to new questions, many in the mainstream media just said that Kgalema was slavishly echoing Mbeki on the subject. The media thus missed the area of concern, exaggerated the power of Mbeki's views and showed the president striding the stage like a megalomaniac. Kgalema also pointed out to O'Malley how the pharmaceutical industry concertedly mobilised the media to create the public impression that the ANC, Mbeki and the government did not care about people infected with HIV/Aids. There is no doubt that this is exactly what happened in South Africa and abroad.

Kgalema does say that the then minister of health, Manto Tshabalala-Msimang, and her department overemphasised the bad side-effects of antiretrovirals (ARVs) with little or nothing said about their desperately needed benefits. Their public relations were so bad, he says, that many people thought Tshabalala-Msimang was advocating nutrition in such things as beetroot and garlic *in place of* ARVs, instead of calling for both. This and government's delay in rolling out ARVs must have caused unnecessary deaths.

Kgalema also feels that Mbeki and the presidency should have told Tshabalala-Msimang and her department what the government stance should be; instead, he says, they were to some extent misleading him. My strong impression from interviews is that Kgalema held her and her health advisers more responsible than Mbeki for the mistakes and confusion.[54]

Tshabalala-Msimang and Mbeki did say things the ANC disagreed with. Kgalema drew a distinction between the ANC and government on these matters at the time. The ANC, through Kgalema's office, expressed its concern on some of the questionable public statements Tshabalala-Msimang and Mbeki made – but did not do so publicly, and it seems this did not carry much weight in the corridors of power. In fact it appears that the adverse international publicity finally did far more than Luthuli House to change government policy.

Kgalema at the time recognised some mistakes by Mbeki:

> The problem is that he made a few statements which may have sealed his fate on questions of Aids, like when he said he knows of nobody who died of Aids. But later the cabinet instructed him not to talk on Aids any more. To be honest, that was not his line of knowledge and expertise. Madiba's approach was different. He said that people must have a choice: if there are people who think the side effects of ARVs are too serious, then they must not use it, but if there are others who find it helpful despite side-effects, then they too must be free to use it.

Wryly, he adds: 'Somebody said to me that the irony of the government's stance was that there were no other people who wore the Aids ribbon badge more than ANC leaders in government.'

Kgalema shifted his position on ARVs after the government decided on a mass roll-out. It is entirely consistent with new insight based on the research findings, experience and further reflection, plus the fact that the final authority for the governmental decision was the presidency and not the ANC as such. But it does seem that Kgalema's views on Aids were influenced to a large extent by Mbeki. His earlier comments about Tshabalala-Msimang overemphasising the drawbacks of ARVs, as against their benefits, also seem to have occurred after government's decision to roll out ARVs and not before.

In 2008 James Myburgh stated: 'For a while, at least, it seemed Motlanthe was bewitched by Mbeki's views on the aetiology of Aids and the toxicity and lack of efficacy of anti-retrovirals.'[55] He went on to say, however, that after government's decision to roll out ARVs Kgalema's position 'shifted completely.'[56] He also recalled that Kgalema told *City Press*: 'We don't regret the way we have dealt with the issues. We have approached this issue very comprehensively. We are in the same boat with the TAC [Treatment Action Campaign] now. The government has been very cautious to ensure that when it embarks on treatment, such treatment should be sustainable. The ANC knew it was going to reach a time when the roll-out was going to happen. It was a progression of events that needed to be undertaken.'[57]

But how could there not have been any regrets in the face of the tragic gravity of the HIV/Aids crisis – especially the preventable deaths of a staggering number of people – while the ANC government was dithering and procrastinating, and especially given Kgalema's own criticism of Tshabalala-Msimang's catastrophic handling of the situation? In the end it was the loss of lives and the adverse publicity created that played a decisive role in government's change of mind and heart.

Zimbabwe

Zimbabwe was a difficult test for Kgalema. From his many visits to Harare when he was SG, he got to know the situation quite well and the parties and leaders involved. He also grew to see that people in the media have their own views and often their own agendas on Zimbabwe: 'They go on as if we have the authority and right to tell Zimbabweans what we want them to do in their own country. After all is said and done, it is only the Zimbabweans themselves who can resolve the crisis there. All we can do at the best of times is to play a facilitative role and try to share our views with them about problems in their country.'

President Mugabe has arguably been the biggest obstacle to resolving the crisis, but, as Kgalema says, 'Gordon Brown and George Bush and many of our people here at home don't care to familiarise themselves with the facts and can only come at Zimbabwe on the basis that Mugabe is a rogue.' There has indeed been a very pervasive and seriously mistaken sense in the media that Mugabe is not part of the crisis (which he is – even a big part of it) but that he equals the crisis.

Kgalema has been criticised for abiding by Mbeki's approach to Zimbabwe, but he was in fact strongly critical of both Mugabe's ZANU-PF and the Movement for Democratic Change (MDC), certainly far more so than Mbeki ever was. Regarding Mugabe's tenacious hold on power, he has been unequivocal about the hazard it presents: 'ZANU-PF is unfortunately still not fully ready to deal with and confront Mugabe's succession and until they get to grips with that fact they will have continual problems. If you have an organisation that does not have established internal democratic processes and practices, you will continually have big problems.'

Mugabe tried to convince Kgalema that the MDC was not a 'truly home-grown opposition but instead an extension of Tony Blair.' Kgalema was not impressed. 'I told him that the MDC is a legitimate opposition because election results have shown it, they were registered, they are in parliament and so on.' Yet he also told O'Malley in 2004 that the MDC 'was not a political party, it was a protest vote.'[58]

These two different views of the MDC lead me to consider that the world of politics and power is fraught with shifting sands as events shape and change perceptions of leaders. Sometimes there is tension between what is said at one moment and what is said at another. This seems to have happened several times with Kgalema, as it does with all politicians. Outright contradictions are more worrying, though, and these I have not come across much with him. He was also very critical on learning that the MDC had to apply for permission to have its own meetings, which included the police reserving the right to attend them.

Kgalema is abundantly aware that many Western countries, particularly Britain and the US, and businesses in South Africa too, have been supporting the MDC in their quest to get rid of Mugabe in their own interests and not because they really care about the Zimbabwean people. He knows these forces have conveniently equated Mugabe with the crisis in Zimbabwe, ignoring other major factors, especially the roles of Britain and the US, and at the economic level the enormous damage the World Bank and IMF have inflicted on Zimbabwe. Kgalema and the ANC have also tended at times to turn a blind eye to or downplay Mugabe's ruthless abuse of power, the many times he has violently crushed legitimate opposition, and his determination to stay in office at all costs. As SG of the ANC Kgalema could have been more critical. However, given the diverse and challenging concerns of his office and the presidency and the general quietude of the rest of the ANC hierarchy, how much more he could have done is unclear.

There can be little doubt that the mutual support between Mugabe's party and the ANC over a long period during the dark days of Ian Smith and apartheid greatly contributed towards the ANC's tolerance of Mugabe's antics. Kgalema is more critical of the ruling party in Zimbabwe than most people realise: 'ZANU-PF has had absolutely no experience in working in a multiparty democracy. They have had a virtual one-party state, if truth be told. Their history tends them towards a militaristic mindset when they are confronted with serious challenges, like how they have dealt with the MDC through brutal repression. ZANU-PF is actually a militaristic organisation. The brutality of ZANU-PF has in fact always been there, even in the 1980 elections. They massacred 20 000 people in Matabeleland.'

He also blames Mugabe and ZANU-PF for long delays in dealing with the land issue until it exploded: 'Even by 1990 they still had not strongly raised the land issue until he ran into budget deficits, which forced him to borrow and then as a consequence the structural adjustments came in and the rest is history.' For someone accused of following in the footsteps of Mbeki, this is strong stuff. But it is unfortunate that Kgalema did not express these criticisms publicly at the time. However, it is far from easy for an ANC leader to publicly criticise the president of a neighbouring country when the president of the ANC and of the country had not done so.

On the other hand, Kgalema thinks that the MDC leaders lack experience in the intricacies of negotiations in a complex environment, which leads them mistakenly to a cycle of demands, conditionalities and ultimatums, which itself hampers the process of negotiations, especially when dealing with Mugabe. 'They are not strategic in how they have handled negotiations. I told them that you cannot throw out countless demands and conditions all the time when you negotiate. You have to identify, isolate and target the key issues to take the process forward.' The hand of a seasoned trade unionist is clear here.

Kgalema's performance as secretary-general, 1997–2002

An assessment of Kgalema's first term as SG is bound to differ from one person and issue to the next, depending on political and ideological stances within the ANC and between it and other organisations, and also because of the kind of person he is. Probably the diverse 'multi-class' nature of the ANC is the biggest factor behind opinions that would vary in how people saw the role he played and was expected to play during his first term as SG.

Zwelinzima Vavi, as we have seen on the subject of Gear, was disappointed with Kgalema:

> I took my frustrations out on Kgalema after he went to the ANC because we came from the same union and Cosatu wholeheartedly supported him for the post of secretary-general at Mafikeng, because when he went to the ANC his respect in both NUM and Cosatu was very high indeed. I was a militant and felt he could have done more. Sometimes we got frustrated because that was the time we needed friends and he was not coming forward enough to support us. There were some moments, even in Stellenbosch, when he accused us of adopting an attitude that indicates that we are treating the alliance as a negotiating forum. I did not like it and we responded immediately. We were worried that, because he was so highly respected in Cosatu and the ANC, if he said anything negative about us the right wing in the ANC would exploit it against us, and they did sometimes. But because Kgalema is very loyal, the times he criticised us publicly were few.[59]

Jaspreet Kindra reported in 2001 on the disenchantment with Kgalema: 'Lobbying for an SACP–Cosatu-friendly candidate ... who was pushed through by the trade unions as "our man" at the ANC's Mafikeng conference has not worked.'[60]

Kgalema explains that from the outset he had to do what he could about the serious challenges the ANC-led government faced after 1994, all the while with increasing problems and fractious divisions in both the ANC and its alliance, with Cosatu in particular:

From Mafikeng to Stellenbosch, 1997–2002

> As the SG of the ANC, my understanding was that when all is said and done my main responsibility was to maintain the unity of the organisation. Therefore, if there was a suggestion of conflict and division, my job was to think very hard and find the means to intervene and try and resolve differences and marshal arguments which would hold things together in the ANC. Now, to do that, you cannot act blindly or hastily or take sides in disputes, because if you don't think very carefully before making any suggestions you will be attacked tomorrow for this or that. That is why to be in that position can be extremely challenging ... because everyone wants you to listen to their side of the story and hopes you would agree with them, but I steered clear of doing that and instead emphasised the need for unity in the ANC, despite differences. It is precisely why some people felt that I pondered too long on issues at times and that it was therefore a weakness, but there is no advantage to be gained from acting out of ignorance or a lack of information, or hastily and impulsively, especially in a big and diverse organisation like the ANC.

Yes, Kgalema had to conciliate and manage the diverse interests of a multi-class organisation. But he also failed to address social justice issues strongly enough, perhaps because he still shared in the ANC's lingering loyalty to the mechanistic two-stage legacy from the SACP: first, the fight against apartheid and for a nonracial democracy and, thereafter (when and how nobody knows), the struggle for socialism and social justice. A myriad of more radical permutations of the NDR by leftists in the ANC alliance after 1994, and especially after Gear in 1996, reflected a belated realisation that the inherent delay in this approach in realising social justice was in the first place false and mistaken.

Many ANC people interviewed spoke about the forthright

and courageous SG reports Kgalema produced. Every report he presented, at any kind of meeting, tended to stress the ANC's biggest weaknesses and dangers. This earned him many enemies in the ANC, especially when many other leading figures in the party and particularly in government were staying biddable, not wanting to rock the boat or even be seen to be doing so.

His conference and council reports were the result of input from the NEC deliberations, but the final report to the Stellenbosch conference was his work. This report in 2002 was very important because it reflected the most serious problems besetting the ANC and government since Mafikeng. Careerism, self-enrichment and corruption had begun to surface in the three-year period before he took office, from 1994 to 1997. Then the five-year period from Mafikeng to Stellenbosch saw a much more concentrated and dangerous expression of these problems. Their scale, frequency and severity exploded on the scene, so much so that as SG Kgalema felt compelled to reflect them squarely in his reports. Virtually every day the ANC had to deal with allegations and often evidence of corruption in different government departments and at all levels of government, including parastatals. He told the Stellenbosch conference: 'The ANC since its inception was an instrument at the service of our people. And yet, in the new conditions, some within our ranks regard the movement as an instrument to serve narrow self-interest and self-enrichment.'[61]

Bafana Sithole says: 'He called a spade a spade by exposing the ANC's weaknesses and did not hide anything, including that he too had to take responsibility for the ANC's problems.'[62] It was not only his candid assessments of what was happening to the ANC in government which were impressive but his reminding delegates and the country that the ANC was historically an organisation that encouraged 'enquiring minds, wide-ranging internal debates on ideological questions on the critical issues facing the country and discouraged dogmatism'.[63]

This was not the stuff the more conservative section in the ANC wanted to hear. But many will argue that the politics practised in the ANC alliance lacked a unifying set of principles and a common programme of action. Here the University of the Witwatersrand's Noor Nieftagodien asks: 'How did Kgalema reconcile and manage the differences and contradictions between the old ANC of the 1950s and the new post-apartheid ANC?'[64] In fact he could not, and never attempted to reconcile glaring differences that were irreconcilable. Karima Brown in an interview spoke at length of how much Kgalema emphasised to her that we need to deal with what the ANC really is today and the forces that changed it and where it is going, rather than hark back to the good old days.[65]

In his all-embracing role Kgalema did try hard to manage these difficult and, many will say, intractable differences in the ANC from the time he became SG. Sithole is sure that Kgalema did not abstract himself from the problems he presented in any of his reports or absolve himself from responsibility for the state of the organisation, and that in fact he was indirectly criticising himself too in his reports, a point Kgalema openly accepts. In his report to the ANC's 2000 national general council in Port Elizabeth, he dealt in detail with serious problems including a significant drop in membership, a decline in paid membership, poor recruitment and disorganised branches. There were a few goals the Mafikeng conference set itself that were either not achieved at all or only partly so by the time of the next conference at Stellenbosch. In his report to the NGC he had already stated: 'Without a unifying and politicising programme of action, branches often become little more than battlegrounds in which individuals and groupings fight each other for influence and resources.⁶⁶ Significantly, the NGC report emphasised the need for 'encouraging wide-ranging internal debates on ideological questions, on the critical issues facing the country and for theoretical clarity and discouraging dogmatism and encouraging questioning minds.'⁶⁷

Another weak area that Kgalema could not improve was the relationship between public representatives in government and the ANC's constitutional structures. The aim was to deepen this key relationship, but over a decade later little progress has been made. Mafikeng raised this as a priority, but the ANC has signally failed to implement its own resolutions. Responsibility must be borne by the entire organisation, especially the NEC and NWC as its top leadership structures. The SG has an important role to play in ensuring that conference resolutions are carried out, but he remains part of a team. Kgalema could not be held singly responsible. In fact it is the NEC that must carry the biggest responsibility when things go seriously wrong in the ANC because the organisational report of the SG is in fact the report of the NEC.

Patrick Bond says that though Kgalema 'came from a great tradition in terms of his own experiences, suffering, resistance and the university on Robben Island, he also had a machine-like way of working and an extraordinary loyalty to the ANC that seems to have displaced a real commitment to workers and the poor.'⁶⁸

Trevor Manuel has a high regard for Kgalema but says his reports to ANC conferences were far too long for delegates: 'Kgalema could happily give three- or four-hour reports but I don't know if our membership quite has that patience. There was just too much copious detail.'⁶⁹ Kgalema disagrees: 'No, he is wrong. The SG's report must strive to comprehensively cover the entire life of the organisation over a five-year period, unlike the president's political report. If it was considered too long by some, that is perhaps the unfortunate reality of these reports, otherwise I could have been accused of having left out or not given enough attention to important aspects or considerations, which could create serious problems for the organisation.'

Essop Pahad says about Kgalema's performance as SG that he certainly could have been more assertive, especially in meetings of the NEC, particularly 'when we identified certain serious organisational problems in the structures of the ANC.'[70] He adds: 'The other side of the coin is that if he had to be more assertive, that may have gone against the grain of his personality and could also have earned him more enemies. Perhaps for him to be more assertive might mean trying to change the person he is; and on the other hand, even when you are more assertive, and even very assertive, it does not mean people will listen and do what you suggest or want.'[71] Zuma basically agrees: 'When he was SG one sometimes felt he should have acted sooner. His more cautious style is also rare with politicians. There were some who felt sometimes that if he had not been so cautious and pondering, he could have acted to stop some of the problems going too far.'[72]

Yet it was Mbeki, Pahad and that inner circle who were accused in the first place of creating many of the problems in the structures of the ANC that Kgalema had to contend with. Kgalema says frankly in interview that by the time of Polokwane there were parallel structures in the ANC. There was plenty of talk about these serious problems after a while by Cosatu, the SACP and later on even some ministers who had been close to Mbeki, such as Mosiuoa Lekota, but when these difficulties occurred under the leadership of Mbeki they were silent – and not just that, but they were clearly complicit in what was happening. They found their voices after Mbeki was removed and suddenly became champions of democracy in the ANC. That is why the very birth of the Congress of the People was both opportunistic and hypocritical.

From Mafikeng to Stellenbosch, Kgalema constantly reminded the ANC of the serious ways in which it had compromised its traditional principles and the need to rebuild the organisation. In that respect he did a sterling job. Some leading figures in the ANC say he was the ANC's conscience and moral anchor, and continued to be so after his first term as SG. Significantly, the social movement revolutionary Trevor Ngwane, who was expelled from the ANC, says that, despite his weaknesses, he has more respect for Kgalema than any other current ANC leader.[73]

Kgalema's criticisms earned himself countless detractors among the more conservative pro-capitalist section of the ANC. Interviews with leading figures in the tripartite alliance confirm this and say the role he played particularly irked those who mainly wanted to use the ANC as a springboard for business self-enrichment. In a few interviews, including with O'Malley in the late 1990s, Kgalema predicted that aspiring black capitalists who arrived late on the stage of capitalist development in South Africa were bound to be even more vicious towards black labour than their established white counterparts. Many budding black capitalists resented such statements by Kgalema, especially when he argued for BEE to be restricted to one deal and that what was needed was genuine economic transformation that benefited the black masses rather than creating an elite club of black millionaires.

On the eve of the Stellenbosch conference in 2002, Kgalema wrote in the *Sunday Times*: 'Democratic change enabled the people to progressively take control of their own lives, to begin to shape their own destiny.'[74] But the reality was that basic services in townships were a sorry mess then. Water cutoffs for nonpayment were rife, as were poor and often terrible sanitary conditions, serious structural problems and shoddy RDP houses. Thousands of public sector workers had lost their jobs as a result of the severe fiscal constraints Gear imposed and social injustices were widely rising.[75] Here Kgalema sounds like the sort of political leader who plays down glaring social injustices and does not concede evident failures. This is one of the criticisms of his first term given in this chapter. But it is also clear that he was often courageous in talking truth to power and being self-critical of the ANC.

Kgalema's weaknesses and failures cannot be abstracted from those of the ANC itself. He could not reverse them on his own but he has never tried to gloss over them; every one of his SG's reports has raised some serious problems the ANC needed to face. The organisation cannot forever duck and dive around its deep contradictions or it will finally implode as social inequities worsen. The ongoing township protests may be a dress rehearsal for what lies ahead. Unless the ANC comes to terms with this, I believe its future and Kgalema's (as bonded with the ANC) will not be pretty.

Kgalema in the SACP

Kgalema had decided to keep his membership of the SACP not exactly a secret but low profile, as we have seen. When he was elected SG of the ANC at Mafikeng he left the SACP's central committee but remained a member of the Dobsonville branch in Soweto even after he moved to Midrand round about 2001. Then, shortly before the Stellenbosch conference, he let his membership lapse.

He says it was Raymond Mhlaba who first raised his membership of the SACP as a concern after Mafikeng. Mhlaba spoke to Mandela about it, who until then did not know that Kgalema was a member. Kgalema spoke to the general secretary, Blade Nzimande, and told him he would withdraw from the central committee but that they needed to work out how he would continue to interact with the party.

In hindsight he feels strongly that the SACP did not deal properly with several challenges their unbanning posed, including the question of open membership and whether to become a mass-based party or not. His decision to first pull out of the central committee and later lapse his SACP membership was more of a safer strategic move than a political or organisational one, he says, though there were both political and ideological causes and consequences. The requirement that a member be based in a branch also contributed to his dropping his membership.

Kgalema's decision to reduce his role in the SACP and eventually terminate his membership had to do with the inevitable political and organisational confusion of holding leadership positions simultaneously in the ANC and SACP, commonly called the two-hats debate in the ANC alliance. His take is that two hats at ordinary membership level is fine but holding two leadership positions simultaneously is not: 'There must be no doubt at all that as a leader of the ANC you are focused on the ANC, rather than having one foot in the ANC and one in the party. It is also meant to avoid the inevitable confusion when you are at the top of both.' He points to the problems Mantashe has had to illustrate his point.[76] True, several leaders of the ANC were also SACP leaders in the decades before they were banned. But this changed when the ANC government began in 1994, as people then held positions in state power, which opened a whole range of new and challenging difficulties.[77]

That Kgalema's membership of the SACP lapsed did not

mean that he abandoned the goal of socialism and his own commitment to it. Every time the party invited him to speak at its events, he dutifully agreed. However, Nzimande and, to a lesser extent, Mantashe did convey a sense of disappointment that Kgalema effectively withdrew from the party after Mafikeng.

There have been moves by the senior leadership of the SACP and ANC to discuss the repeated concerns expressed by the ANC in particular about wearing two hats. It appeared that some agreement had been reached, which is why it was later not surprising that Mantashe did not stand for re-election at the SACP's congress in June 2012. Meanwhile, Mantashe says he himself remained SACP chairperson without any serious problems after he was elected SG at Polokwane and did not see insurmountable problems in wearing two hats even at leadership level. Kgalema says that Mantashe needs to understand the centrality of the ANC over the SACP and that experience will show him that trying to strike a balance between the two won't work.

> When Gwede speaks in public there must be no confusion among ANC members about which party he represents, no confusion. The only way this continuous confusion can be avoided is not to have simultaneously senior posts in both organisations. To try and manage joint leadership is a waste of time and can create more confusion. That is the lesson since 1994. If I did not pull out of the leadership of the SACP after Mafikeng, I can tell I would have had serious problems.

Some have said that Kgalema is a hundred per cent ANC and, as we have seen, several leading figures in the independent left see him as more of an African nationalist than a Marxist. In the two-hats debate, he does not oppose joint ordinary membership of the ANC and Cosatu and the SACP, in fact he encourages it: 'I think it is a positive development ... when they join the ANC, Cosatu members cease to be Cosatu members in the sense that they cannot send members with a Cosatu mandate to an ANC branch, but it is a symbiotic relationship, which is healthy.'

But it is the very stance Kgalema takes in the two-hats debate that may have made it hard for him to reconcile his radical past in NUM and its explicit commitment to socialism with the pragmatism which both the multi-class ANC and the compromises they made during the Codesa negotiations demanded of him after he became SG. This is a pragmatism that rests primarily on African multi-class nationalism, which has meant downplaying sharpening class contradictions in the interests of the country, the nation or other such collective generalities – ultimately, however, at the expense of the majority black working class and poor.

A big question for the SACP after its unbanning was whether to remain a small, tight, highly disciplined and professional vanguard party or become a mass-based party in the new conditions of legality. Kgalema joined in the debates but now thinks they were inadequate, and that the final decision – to leave it up to individual members to decide whether to publicly declare their membership or not – was problematic.[78] He adds:

> I am not into those rigid arguments about either vanguard or mass. ... As the situation unfolds the party ought to be ahead of all of society and to lead society. Yes, there is a need for the party to have a legal presence, above board and with structures and so on and communists must be known, but there are those strategic placements the party must also make, because if it does not, I think it will create a situation where there will be the need to choose and I think it just sets the party back. There are

certain requirements or bottom lines membership of the party must require and the party must have the capacity to take you through a full understanding of Marxism-Leninism.

'Marxism-Leninism' sounds quaint today but Kgalema has always stressed that the quality of cadre training is critical to both theoretical and practical understanding of the tasks facing the party and the strategy needed to achieve goals. 'So I was not opposed to massifying the party but how they went about it,' he says.[79] Kgalema's view is that deciding to become a mass-based party must lead to much greater emphasis on training and education, to avoid an amorphous mass where quality has been sacrificed for numbers.[80]

ANC: Most peculiar organisation in the world?

Ben Turok said twice during an interview that 'the ANC is probably the most peculiar political organisation in the world.'[81] A stalwart of the ANC over several decades, he should know, and any serious scholar of the ANC will probably agree with him. Nothing depicts this characterisation more than trying to describe what and who the ANC represents. Its theory and practice depend on how we define South African society and the South African revolution.

It was during Kgalema's first term as SG that this crucial question of the ANC's identity emerged. He of all people knows that the class struggle and socialism have been indefinitely subordinated to the struggle against racism and national oppression. He senses the tensions but, rather than acknowledge the central problem, he is acrobatic about what the ANC really is and its relationship with the struggle for socialism.

In 2000 he said: 'The ANC itself is not a bourgeois organisation. The country's leading socialist minds are in the

ANC. Anyone who argues for socialism will find allies in the ANC.'[82] But in a later interview his response to the inherent problem – of reconciling the interests of the poor black majority and the tiny black elite – was this: 'Any living organisation can at some point transform itself into a more explicit socialist organisation. In the realm of possibilities that can happen. The ANC saw and learnt that the SACP was fully prepared to be in the trenches with the ANC against apartheid and social injustice and today in the fight against poverty, unemployment and inequalities. That has taught us not to oppose the goal of socialism, but the ANC is not meant to and is not structured to lead the fight for socialism.' In politics, can you logically 'not oppose' socialism and yet not be consciously in favour of it? But this is precisely the ANC's peculiarity that Turok referred to.

The ANC describes itself as a revolutionary movement and belong to the Socialist International but does not regard itself as socialist and denies it is waging a struggle for socialism. No wonder Karima Brown says: 'The ANC has mastered the art of speaking through both sides of their mouths. Over the decades you will see a great deal of double-speak in ANC literature.'[83] In socialist vein the ANC often calls for a resolute struggle against unemployment, poverty and inequalities, yet it is very familiar with the realities of life under capitalism, which are especially unyielding in South Africa, where racism and capitalism have such strong mutual interests. Kgalema in 2000 said: 'Our struggle will be achieved when people are no longer homeless and security of tenure is extended to everyone. Ignorance and poverty undermine our people's dignity.'[84] But there is no way that the poor black majority can secure an end to homelessness, poverty and unemployment under the capitalist system. Nowhere did Kgalema and the ANC make these points, which in his case is all the more irresponsible because the task of leadership is to define what an organisation stands for and state its corresponding tasks clearly.

Kgalema himself echoed and reinforced the ambiguities when, despite the non-socialist character of the ANC, he found it appropriate to attack the capitalist system in a May Day speech in 2000.[85] He did so, he explains,

> against the backdrop of the xenophobic utterances some were making just before I spoke. There were also at the time the flood disasters in Mozambique. I thought therefore that this was a moment to stress the importance of international solidarity with workers from other countries and in order to do that we need to understand how the international capitalist system works, where the pressure points are and where to exert pressure. I was worried that we had workers claiming to be left and socialist but who have no grasp of how capital works and the solidarity which defines left politics.

That is understandable, but less acceptable is his response on the compromises the ANC made during negotiations: 'Yes, it was open to criticism, but the type of organisation the ANC is could not really have led to more radical policies. On the other hand it was reflective of the balance of forces and therefore the strengths and weaknesses of those forces.' Here he succumbs to stock-in-trade cliché; the ANC often resorts to phrases like 'balance of forces' or the party's 'multi-class' character in a glib response to contradictions that cannot otherwise be explained away.

The indeterminate identity of the ANC is all too clear. In 2000 Kgalema said that the socialist systems of Cuba and China were good models for this country.[86] A month later, expressing an insight that many in the ANC agreed with, John Saul wrote:

'Colin Bundy acknowledged some years ago that to continue to hold out the prospect of a socialist transformation in South Africa may require something of a "leap of faith."' He added: 'To imagine that a milder-mannered capitalist order can secure a decent future for the majority of South Africans – or that deracialising bourgeois rule will meet the aspirations of the exploited and oppressed people – or that South Africa can be absolved of its economic history and enter a future like that of Sweden or Taiwan: now that requires a leap of faith.'[87] This reality we live with daily, beyond doubt.

I have mentioned Kgalema's deep loyalty towards the ANC and his firm belief that it is a very democratic organisation which members control. In 2004 he said that 'people love the ANC because in the ANC they have a right and the space to debate, speak and talk in a language of their command and [where] nobody can lord it over anybody else.'[88] When it was suggested that for many the ANC no longer represented the poorest of the poor, he replied:

> No, it still is, otherwise it would not be in a position to take steps against those who think that the ANC exists in order to create conditions for their own enrichment. .... It is in a position to do so precisely because there are sufficient people and the membership, general membership, who do not take kindly to greedy opportunists. We have no other power except in general membership. If something is not right we are able to take steps against anybody and the only authority that we have is from membership, we go to the membership and say this is what this comrade is involved in and this is un-ANC and we are taking steps. They say that is how we must act. Otherwise we ourselves would be thrown out.[89]

From Mafikeng to Stellenbosch, 1997–2002

His faith in the ANC is evidently deep and sincere, but is the picture he sketches a true reflection of what happens there? Many leading figures were publicly exposed in a great deal of wrongdoing (to put it mildly) but are still very much alive in the ANC and government.[90] The picture Kgalema has painted of good democratic policy decision-making is not quite true. Instead, the picture since 1994 is of a weak, fragmented membership far from being in control of their organisation. This is true not only in policy issues but other arenas. These are the very problems Kgalema reported on for the decade he was SG: corruption, self-seeking careerism, cronyism and so much more that flouts the values the ANC has espoused over many years and, Kgalema says, that would have Sisulu, Tambo, Luthuli and other stalwarts turning in their graves at what the post-apartheid ANC has become.

So, who has really been in control of the ANC since 1994? Not only have the ordinary rank and file not been in charge but they have arguably suffered in many ways, most tellingly from the social consequences of the policies the ANC leadership chose. Kgalema himself says the ANC of today is very different from pre-1994: 'When I look at the ANC today, I find that from its past policies and its history it was very progressively left, but in terms of the current understanding, interpretation and practices it is caught between living up to these progressive policies and being dragged into something else.' This is a refreshing bit of critical self-reflection which the ANC needs much more of.

Kgalema reflects all the tensions, contradictions and idiosyncrasies of the ANC but can also be remarkably frank about many of its weaknesses, probably more than any other leader after 1994. Many leftists inside and especially outside the ANC alliance have said that he has not done enough to confront these serious problems. Even if he raised them strongly in his reports, they say, what happened then? What did he and the others who supported his criticisms do about them after conferences? The concern is all the more valid because the same criticisms keep being made from one conference to the next, showing they were never resolved.

This is the context for weighing problems associated with Kgalema, Mbeki or any other leader of the ANC. When Kgalema asked that key and critical question later, at Polokwane – Where was the ANC? – it meant, where was the power of the membership to intervene and rescue the ANC?[91] Emphasising the failures of leadership, including Kgalema's as SG, often begs a more important question in turn: So what did the members do about it, in their own interests and that of their organisation? After all, the ANC is meant to belong to its members and not its top leadership. What has happened to the ANC since its unbanning and especially since it took office? A total focus on leadership leaves a seemingly helpless membership to continue to defer to their all-powerful leaders, which is decidedly not the empowering stuff for building strong mass organisations.

For Kgalema a memorable event, less than a year after Mafikeng, was when he accompanied the former Cuban president, Fidel Castro, on a visit to Soweto. They visited Walter Sisulu at home, and it turned out that a woman in Castro's party had been with Sisulu at a World Youth Conference in Budapest in 1953. 'They both remembered that meeting of forty-five years ago and I tell you it was a very powerful feeling we all had at that very moment.' That earlier time of idealism and real hope contrasts vividly with the political and moral decay in the ANC that Kgalema has had to face.[92]

CHAPTER FIVE
From Stellenbosch to Polokwane, 2002–2007

> I believe we must create material justice before we can hope to eliminate the kind of violence that has become a tragic habit in South Africa
>
> Nadine Gordimer, 2000

The period 2002 to 2007 saw the gap widening further between rulers and the ruled, the haves and the have-nots, plus incapacity and growing corruption in many offices. The ANC continues to be hamstrung by its multi-class emphasis and preoccupation with BEE and the black middle class in the face of the devastating poverty of the black majority. Kgalema, outspoken on principle, had nevertheless to mediate hard to keep the party united. As SG he also still had to work closely with government, whatever he thought of some policies and practices. He continued to strive towards establishing a political school and policy institute to educate leaders and grow the skills for policy analysis; neither of these establishments has yet seen the light of day at national level. As if this weren't enough, major scandals developed about himself and also Zuma. This chapter examines these matters and analyses the role Kgalema played and the stances he adopted.

Kgalema Motlanthe

Political situation in the ANC alliance

The five years between the ANC's Mafikeng and Stellenbosch conferences must have been extremely tough for Kgalema. Compared with the position of the president – though it is the most senior – that of the secretary-general of the ANC is far more demanding because virtually all the major problems on all fronts end up on his desk. The SG also has to deal at all levels with the day-to-day administration of the organisation and its complex relations with government. The SG's formal functions and role are exacting enough, but are even more so in a context of deepening social crisis with massive unemployment, poverty and inequalities. Add to that the enormous challenges which a negatively changing ANC has posed since 1994 – all the problems of careerism, corruption and self-enrichment, and abuse of the ANC by many for those purposes – plus trying to strike a balance to hold disparate parts of the ANC together, and it is clear that Kgalema was in a highly stressful job.

Even if the ANC's economic and social policies were socialist and 'correct', the party would have had a difficult time in government. Most of the ANC's cadres were never equipped for government, which today demands a high level of skills and experience. There is a powerful argument to be made that it is precisely in this situation – where many political appointees in government lack the most basic skills – that corruption, nepotism and cronyism tend to thrive most. The shortage of skills and experience meant the ANC's learning curve was indeed steep and intimidating. Yet, except for the ANC's deputy SG, Thenjiwe Mtintso (ill at the time and later South African ambassador to Cuba),[1] the top six officials were returned to office uncontested in Stellenbosch.

At the ANC's 2005 national general council, its second mid-term meeting since Mafikeng, Kgalema in his organisational report painstakingly dealt with problems afflicting the branches, the most important of the ANC structures. The most pressing included how branch officials were disempowering ordinary members and using them as little more than voting fodder for decisions that served their own interests. Here again he was consistent in identifying the new scourge that afflicted the ANC since coming to power: how money, crass materialism and privileges have seriously compromised it.[2]

In the next breath, though, he acknowledged that the Constitution allows 'all citizens to engage in legitimate business activity. Indeed, the Freedom Charter itself demands that "All people shall have equal rights to trade where they choose, to manufacture and to enter all trades, crafts and professions."'[3] This clause, he said, reflected the ways in which apartheid and colonialism had 'systematically suppressed the entrepreneurial talent of our people. Any path to the accumulation of assets among our people in general was ruthlessly crushed. Therefore, in abstract, the accumulation of wealth by our people should not run counter to the progress of the revolution.'[4]

Here lies the inherent contradiction of the multi-class character the ANC professes. The fact is that the ANC has for years been troubled by trying to serve the interests of all classes and being everything to everybody, at the expense of the poor black majority who suffer the brunt of 'racial capitalism' and whose interests after 1994 should have been the utmost priority.[5] The ANC was well aware of these contradictions, which is why at its 2000 national general council it saw the need to 'discourage dogmatism and encourage questioning minds'.[6]

On the eve of the Stellenbosch conference, in a *Sunday Times* article, Kgalema had again asserted the ANC's all-embracing character: 'The ANC is the people's organisation. As delegates gather in Stellenbosch, it will, in effect, be a meeting of all South

Africans united in their commitment to a better nation and a better world – a fitting tribute to those visionaries who gathered in Mangaung nine decades ago.'[7] He later acknowledged: 'The ANC has had to deal with problems of division and factionalism in a number of structures over the past five years, many of which can be traced to a competition among ANC members and leaders for positions of influence and the resources that come with them.'[8] In fact, after Stellenbosch it was more difficult for him to play the uniting role as he had done so from Mafikeng to Stellenbosch. In the next period, tensions between the ANC and Cosatu and the SACP often veered close to crisis as unemployment, poverty and inequalities grew.

But his steadiness in his multi-faceted role remained firm for his second term: 'Look, when I was in NUM I could afford, because of the terrain, a sharp and pointed stance on many issues. But in the ANC it is very different because there you find an array of different views, and the scope and forces that you have to concern yourself with are also vastly different.' By the time of the 2002 conference, for example, he was well aware that the 'sins of incumbency' were seriously taking their toll on the ANC: 'In fact already at our 2000 NGC we realised how this was eroding the defining characteristics of the ANC.'[9]

Kgalema began his second term as SG against the background of the big Cosatu anti-privatisation strike of 2000 and worsening relations within the alliance, particularly between the ANC and Cosatu. Once again, policy differences lay at the heart of this growing conflict as the ANC's 'broad church' style, especially in a deepening social crisis, limited its policy options. As Brown says:

> The ANC's policy gymnastics which they love and which is seen as a strength because it is this big broad church is also a great

weakness because the chronic ambiguity allows it to morph the Freedom Charter into the RDP, GEAR, then ASGISA and now the New Growth Path. Kgalema is just symptomatic of the ANC's own inability to come to terms with the necessity to provide definitive ideological clarity for themselves, let alone society at large, and I am not sure if they will ever reach such a point.'[10]

But while the key issues afflicting the ANC and the government (and posing problems for Kgalema) prior to Stellenbosch continued, new problems arose that developed into an unprecedented crisis for the ANC and government, with cataclysmic effect. Some concerned developments in the ANC and government more broadly, such as the dismissal of then Deputy President Jacob Zuma by President Thabo Mbeki in June 2005. Others directly concerned or implicated Kgalema, such as the Oilgate scandal, the ANC email saga and controversy about the Land Bank loan to Pamodzi.[11]

Though he would not say so publicly, there is a strong sense that Kgalema found it difficult to deal with Mbeki's repeated attacks against the ANC's allies, Cosatu and the SACP. Ominously, his second term started on a similar note as Mbeki again railed against the left in his closing address in Stellenbosch, which led a senior alliance figure to say: 'The pity is that the president has great diplomatic skills which he chooses not to use.'[12] Since Kgalema was also a leftist with a background in the SACP and the unions, Mbeki's repeated attacks put him in a difficult situation. He knew that if he differed with Mbeki publicly it would lead to serious problems in the ANC. Nobody was more acutely aware of how imperative it was to maintain unity than Kgalema himself. But the public hostilities within the alliance were so evident that a commentator could write:

'It is one of the many ironies of SA politics that the bitterest battles of our age have been waged within the ranks of the anti-apartheid movement itself – not between the movement and its foes. It is within the ranks of the ANC and its allies that SA has seen the worst fighting over race, class, gender, sexual orientation and many other questions of our times.'[13]

Nevertheless, Kgalema's second term essentially continued the primary role he had fulfilled in the first term, which was to keep the ANC together, no matter what. Responding to Essop Pahad's view that he did not use all the authority he had to deal with problems,[14] he agreed: 'Yes, that may be true but I was told that the chief role of the secretary-general was to keep the ANC together. It is a pity Madiba's office has declined you an interview because of his frailty – he would have confirmed that brief.'

Despite that brief, his second term as SG was in many ways different from his first. A number of factors coalesced to make it a difficult, dramatic and even explosive period for Kgalema, the ANC and government. Kgalema, in these years, was probably the senior political leader most frequently targeted and implicated in several major media scandals; but each time he walked away with his dignity and integrity intact and his accusers instead often left floundering in his wake.

The arms deal

Kgalema had no involvement whatever in the government's hugely controversial arms deal except when the ANC decided that Andrew Feinstein's disciplining over his basic opposition to the deal and its handling would be dealt with by Luthuli House, which meant by Kgalema. In his book *After the Party*, Feinstein says the disciplinary process was referred to Kgalema's office at Luthuli House, which required them to meet.[15] But Kgalema says Feinstein's visit had nothing to do with discipline; instead, they had discussions about the arms deal and other matters. As Feinstein confirms, they agreed that it was best for him to resign in the wake of the problems between himself and the ANC government over the arms deal, and this would be 'before the start of the next parliamentary session.'[16] After listening carefully, Kgalema asked him to put his concerns in writing so that he could ensure that the ANC would discuss them seriously. To his surprise Feinstein said he would rather not do so, as things had reached a stage where it would probably be futile to try changing the thinking and conclusions of the ANC on these matters. But in Feinstein's book he stated that he did in fact put down in writing the key issues that concerned him. Kgalema was adamant that he did not do so.

Feinstein's account of what happened with the arms deal is well researched and quite convincing – which is why his position in the ANC and parliament became untenable. He took a salutary stand while others appeared later to have acquiesced in the blatant cover-up into which the arms deal degenerated.[17] So what did Kgalema himself think about the arms deal, especially since Feinstein explained to him why he took such a principled position? Kgalema says that it was precisely because of what Feinstein had to say to him that he asked him to put all his concerns in writing so that the party could discuss them.

'Oilgate' and the Donen Commission

Then came what the *M&G* dubbed 'Oilgate'. Nothing in Kgalema's first term had implicated him in any wrongdoing, but suddenly in 2005 the *M&G* raised serious questions about how in 2003 Sandile Majali had arranged for PetroSA to pay his company Imvume Management an irregular advance of some R15 million against a delivery of oil condensate.[18] This payment related to a contract Majali had with PetroSA that was in turn part of the United Nations 'Oil-for-Food programme' (OFFP); so, through the contract, Majali's company was a participant in this programme.

The *M&G* claimed that documents in their possession showed clearly that Imvume was 'effectively a front for the ruling party'.[19] Whether Imvume really was a front for the ANC is another matter, but that it had very close relations with the ANC is beyond doubt. When PetroSA gave Majali the R15 million, instead of paying his company's foreign suppliers, Majali diverted R11 million to the ANC in December 2003, which was reportedly crash-strapped in the run-up to the elections in 2004, in what was dubbed 'the biggest political funding scandal since 1994'.[20]

Contrary to media speculation, the R11 million was not to pay for the ANC's election campaign but to meet an acute financial problem, particularly an inability to pay salaries. Faced with this difficulty in October 2003, Kgalema went to see Mandela, who gave the ANC R6 million of his own money to pay staff salaries for both October and November. But for December, the ANC once again did not have funds for salaries. It was then that some senior ANC leaders – not Kgalema – desperately turned to Majali. Majali approached PetroSA and requested an advance payment for his supply contract with the company. It is still unclear whether PetroSA knew that the money was for the ANC and therefore not an advance payment for the condensate, or whether Majali had informed them of how he intended to use the money.

Kgalema was implicated by the *M&G* as 'Majali's ANC patron', suggesting that since he was SG he probably had knowledge of the R11 million payment and its source.[21] Kgalema insists he did not know, and Majali has since died.

Patrick Laurence, after Majali's death, stated: 'The question that remains unanswered even today is whether the ANC secretary-general and its treasurer-general at the time, Mendi Msimang, were aware that public money was being used to pay ANC officials. The suspicion remains that they wilfully shut their eyes to the fact that public money had been diverted to the ANC.'[22] Kgalema's response is that many people wrongly see the SG of the ANC as the CEO of a company: 'Mendi was the treasurer-general of the ANC, who operates independently of the secretary-general. The finance department could take decisions without consulting me. Please check with Mendi. He will confirm that I did not at all know that the money came from PetroSA.' Indeed, Msimang confirms that Kgalema did not know at the time.[23]

When Majali could not pay the overseas supplier for the condensate because he had given PetroSA's money to the ANC, PetroSA had to pay the same amount again because they needed the delivery. Majali had not been able to refund the supplier because those who asked him to organise funds to pay ANC staff salaries had promised to have the money returned to him over the next few weeks but failed to do so.[24]

Kgalema felt strongly that the board of PetroSA should have taken responsibility and explained why they took that decision and why the matter was handled in this way. 'People in parastatals must not again act inappropriately due to political influence, because those who say that public funds were used for the ANC are correct and that is wrong and should never happen again. That for me is the most important lesson from that experience. The other related point is that because the ANC is obviously political, the main story was about the ANC and not establishing the facts first by asking PetroSA the right questions and then drawing the political implications and lessons.' The

M&G correctly stated: 'The deal puts the spotlight on PetroSA's management, which approved the payment.'[25] Yet they did not pursue that angle much further themselves.

It seems that the *M&G* made several attempts to get a response from Kgalema before the Oilgate story broke, via his office and the office of Smuts Ngonyama (then head of the presidency), and that there was some stonewalling by the ANC.[26] It must be said here (and also of the Kalahari story below) that the ANC's dealings with the media, the *M&G* in particular, left much to be desired. My own sense is that the ANC would have fared much better and gained in its own interests had it dealt more openly with the press.

What turned out to be perhaps more serious for Kgalema were the reports of the UN's Independent Inquiry Committee (IIC)[27] and later the Donen Commission reports, alleging that he was involved with Majali in irregular business dealings in Iraq. The thrust of the IIC investigation was to check if any of the companies from various countries involved in the United Nations' OFFP had broken any of their country's laws by paying kickbacks (euphemistically called 'surcharges'). Its report came out in October 2005. In turn, it triggered Mbeki's decision to set up the Donen Commission in South Africa in February 2006 to investigate alleged illicit activities of certain South African companies or individuals relating to the UN programme. But Kgalema strongly denies that he ever promised to pay surcharges or that he ever even requested that surcharges not be paid.

Kgalema had indeed been linked with Majali on Iraqi interests but only in the course of promoting party-to-party relations between the ANC and the Iraqi Ba'ath Socialist Party. In the period before the US attacked Iraq, diplomatic visits by Kgalema, Mendi Msimang and Smuts Ngonyama had prompted return visits to South Africa by the Iraqi deputy prime minister Tariq Aziz and his delegation and then a Ba'ath party group of veterans led by the businessman Khalid Tabra and including Aziz.[28] Following this last visit the Iraqi–South African Friendship Association was formally established on 20 October 2001, comprising the ANC and the Arab Socialist Ba'ath Party. The ANC decided to appoint Majali as its chairperson of this new body, largely because he knew Iraq quite well and was already doing business there. This appointment Kgalema had to confirm in writing to the Iraqis. In part it stated 'the ANC's approval of Sandi Majali as a designated person to lead the implementation process arising out of our economic development programmes.'[29]

When the IIC report appeared four years later, however, it claimed that Kgalema was alleged not only to have actively helped Majali in his pursuit of oil contracts in Iraq but that Majali had written a letter to say that Kgalema and Aziz were both at a meeting with him in Iraq on 10 May 2002 at which illicit surcharges were discussed.[30] These surcharges were to be paid to Iraqi officials behind the UN's back. Majali's undated letter, received by the Iraqi ministry of oil on 19 June 2002, was addressed to the oil minister Amer Mohammad Rashid and stated that Kgalema attended the meeting and promised to pay the surcharges.[31]

Kgalema has consistently said he never attended such a meeting. Majali later denied it himself, saying that Kgalema was in Baghdad at the time. Kgalema also denies ever being party to an official meeting where he agreed that Majali would pay kickbacks in any form. He once again strenuously denied that he ever requested or agreed that Majali pay surcharges and neither did he urge Aziz not to impose them. He insists that any mention of this in either the IIC or Donen reports is false and cannot be supported by evidence.[32] There is no verifiable evidence that he proposed Majali pay surcharges in instalments, as the IIC report indicated, and the question has never been put to him by either the IIC or the Donen Commission.[33]

On Majali's incriminating letter, Kgalema says: 'He was known, with all due respect, to drop names for his own purposes. He took a chance, probably thinking it will help him not to pay the surcharges and to in other ways facilitate his business dealings with the Iraqi authorities, but when he realised that he could not support that claim with facts and the possible implications that could have, he changed his tune and denied I was at the meeting.' This was the man whom Kgalema had recommended to chair the Iraqi–South African Friendship Association. Clearly he and the ANC had had great faith in him then.

On the matter of oil contracts, Kgalema says that Majali and his business partner, the Iraqi-American businessman Shakir al-Khafaji, who had close relations with Aziz, had been trading in Iraq long before Kgalema made his first visit there to build party-to-party relations between the ANC and the Arab Socialist Ba'ath Party. The media seemed unaware of this, which no doubt reinforced their idea that he had played a big role in facilitating Majali's business ventures in Iraq. As it turned out, the Donen Commission never gave Kgalema an opportunity to respond to the allegation. Kgalema adds that in helping BEE objectives in the oil sector, there was nothing illegal about the ANC trying to assist Majali to secure oil contracts in Iraq.

During the IIC investigation in South Africa the commissioners spoke to Majali but not to Kgalema. If indeed there were grounds for believing any wrongdoing on his part during his visits to Iraq and complicity in wrongdoing with Majali, why did they not talk to him? This was all the more unexpected because the IIC report did implicate him on the basis of Majali's letter. When the IIC report appeared, it declared the IIC's belief that Majali's company Imvume had used its relationship with South African political leaders to obtain oil allocations under the OFFP. The most senior political leader Majali travelled thrice with to Iraq was Kgalema.

Did Kgalema perhaps get caught up in a web of powerful interests and was compelled to play the role some people suspect he did, even against his better judgement?[34] He says no and repeats that he did not make any trips to Iraq, with Majali or not, on behalf of Majali but solely for international solidarity conferences and other party-to-party relations. He denies any suggestion or conclusion that he expressed opposition to surcharges and that he requested the Iraqis not to impose it on Majali.

The Donen interim report of 16 May 2006, addressed to Thabo Mbeki as president, adds this about Kgalema:

> The Secretary-General who is referred to in a letter [in the IIC report] proposing the above-mentioned payment of surcharges in instalments need not testify orally at this stage. Oral information provided by the US Attorney for the Southern District of New York (under terms of strict confidentiality) suggests that [Rodney] Hemphill will say that the Secretary-General was shocked by the Iraqis' request for surcharges and that Hemphill then assisted him to send a letter via the Ambassador of Iraq in South Africa to Mr. Tariq Aziz (the deputy Prime Minister of Iraq). A waiver of surcharge payments was requested in the Secretary-General's letter.[35]

The report comments that 'Motlanthe ... appears to be privy to information which is material to the resolution of these issues.'[36] Kgalema's response is that he never made such a proposal.[37] He also denies that Hemphill, a South African businessman, ever helped him write any letter.[38] The letter in question, he says, had nothing to do with oil surcharges but with party-to-party relations. It is not clear what the Donen claim rests on, other than simply accepting what these sources had to say. The Donen commission did not interview him on this or any other matter. Here we should note that for both the IIC and the Donen Commission, Kgalema was never a subject of investigation but, starting with the IIC report, he was regarded as a material witness. 'My sense was that some people were trying to implicate me but they were not supported by the facts' was his take at the time the IIC report came out.

Although Mbeki received the Donen interim report in 2006, final publication was held up until December 2011. We return to the story in Chapter 9 to discuss the five-year delay, which is now speculatively linked to other developments, and to assess the final report's findings as regards Kgalema.

Kgalema, Mbeki and the email saga
The 'email saga' took place in 2005 in the context of two matters that generated much tension and intrigue. The first was a deterioration of relations between Luthuli House, the head office of the ANC, and Mbeki's state presidency. This was related to the centralisation of state power in the presidency. Kgalema characterised the situation that developed after 2003: 'Increasingly there was a shift to government as the axis of power in the relations between Luthuli House and the government, especially the presidency.'

The second matter was the relationship of Deputy President Jacob Zuma and the businessman Schabir Shaik (indicted in 2003 and found guilty in May 2005 on charges of fraud and corruption). This also involved increasing concern in the directorate of special operations, also known as the Scorpions, and the national director of public prosecutions (NDPP), then Bulelani Ngcuka, that Zuma might be implicated in the arms deal, primarily through his relationship with Shaik. Although Ngcuka stated that there was prima facie evidence of corruption against Zuma, the NPA's 'prospects of success are not strong enough'. This meant 'that we are not sure we have a winnable case.'[39]

The email saga was a bizarre instance of ANC infighting long before the run-up to Polokwane. It was also an event in which Kgalema was a key figure and which brought to a head simmering discontent in the relationship between Luthuli House and Mbeki's presidency. On 12 July 2005 Kgalema received emails in the post, in a brown envelope. In an affidavit he said: 'When I read the correspondence I was shocked and disturbed. Of concern to me was the alleged involvement of senior leaders of the ANC in the email correspondence. The scurrilous and defamatory allegations against senior leaders of the ANC were the most disturbing feature of the email correspondence.'[40] Kgalema also received a second batch of emails on 18 August.

The emails purported to reveal correspondence between members of a pro-Mbeki and anti-Zuma 'cabal' of politicians including Deputy President Phumzile Mlambo-Ngcuka and her husband Bulelani, Ronnie Kasrils, the businessman Saki Macozoma, some staff of the Scorpions and 'white media personalities and opposition figures', as the *M&G* put it.[41] The emails were never made public but were selectively leaked to certain journalists. The *M&G* noted that 'the alleged "cabal's" purported aim is the destruction of Zuma and any other powerful figure who stands in the way of its political objectives, most notably Motlanthe himself and National Intelligence Agency director-general Billy Masetlha.'[42] Kgalema was implicated, as there was a perception that he had betrayed Mbeki by siding with Zuma.

Kgalema took steps to have the emails investigated, including a meeting on 25 August 2005 with the commissioner of police Jackie Selebi, also attended by Billy Masetlha of the National Intelligence Agency. Both men undertook to investigate the emails and revert to Kgalema. Selebi reported that in the absence of electronic versions of the emails, his investigations had stalled. An 'aggressive search for the document in the internet cyberspace' had yielded nothing,' wrote Selebi in October 2005; and added that it was impossible to progress with the investigation.[43]

In addition to the Mbeki–Zuma rivalries aired in the emails, Kgalema expressed concern at allegations that 'some members of the Scorpions were sharing information with Tony Leon and some journalists at the *Mail & Guardian*.' This concerned him as the Scorpions were bound by oath 'that information gleaned from investigations cannot be made public in any way whatsoever.' His acute concern, Kgalema says, 'was the conduct of a state organ in very sensitive intelligence matters.' As neither the original emails nor the report of the ANC's own investigation into them was ever made public, there is no verifiable evidence that the Scorpions were indeed involved in illegal activities or for that matter whether any of the many allegations in the emails were true in any way.

The *M&G* asserted that 'Motlanthe's decision to put this document before the ruling party's highest decision making body was audacious.'[44] Be that as it may, it was certainly at odds with the public statement issued by Ronnie Kasrils on 23 October, warning against 'sinister emails' and 'hoax emails' doing the rounds, labelling them 'clearly fraudulent' and 'reminiscent of Stratcom operations during the apartheid era.'[45] But those in the NEC who supported Kgalema's call for an inquiry did so in the name of the ANC rather than of government. Kgalema himself sought a separate inquiry as he was sceptical that Selebi's investigations would yield much. He therefore pushed for the ANC to do its own investigations, especially after he received a second batch of emails through the post in August.

Kgalema was later criticised by Siphiwe Nyanda and others for taking the emails to Selebi, an Mbeki loyalist, in the first place. It may be that Kgalema was naïve and that the constitution-embracing and organisation man took precedence over thinking and consulting informally within the ANC much more carefully, before deciding what to do with the emails. An independent ANC investigation into the emails might have been expected to clarify the issue; but when the report was submitted, Kgalema recalls, the NEC 'went further to say that the report had no status and therefore there was no report and the matter was dropped.' Apparently the investigations by the ANC task team committed particular acts that so compromised its work that the report was simply jettisoned. The email saga ended on that note and the ANC never revisited it.

The NEC's decision to abandon the matter had an unfortunate denouement: no clear findings were arrived at, yet the ill-will behind the emails has continued to define and redefine South African politics, albeit in oblique ways. As far as Kgalema was concerned, none of the details or rumours circulating during the email saga caused any lasting damage to his reputation and integrity. His actions in taking the documentation to the NEC did have consequences, though. As he puts it,

> The Mbeki group mobilised against me as a result of the email saga. But based on the facts, they could not succeed because the provinces knew what had happened and they understood

it. Furthermore, the fact is that I never took those emails to anybody except Selebi until he told me that he cannot do anything about it, which is when I decided to take it to the NEC for their consideration. They therefore cannot say that on the basis of the emails I went out to discredit anyone in the ANC, I was only interested in investigating the emails.

Kgalema always strongly disagreed with anybody who suggested he was either Mbeki's lackey or that he betrayed him in the email saga or any other matter. 'No, my role, as I understood it, was that I had to work with him and others in such a way that we pull together to get the work done. When I felt he or any other leader was doing us a disservice I had to take a principled stance and that is exactly what many did not like.' He is convinced that there was at that time a campaign by certain leaders in government – in collusion with particular major weekend newspaper editors whose names I will not reveal – to run negative publicity on him and that they used the email saga to do that. So serious were these attempts that some of them questioned his judgement and alleged that his views on the emails had driven him into the Zuma camp, something he contemptuously dismisses as insulting to both his intelligence and integrity.

Mbeki still insists that Kgalema was wrong about the emails. 'I thought it was a lot of nonsense but he thought it had some substance but there was no substance at all. But once the task team that was established by the ANC to investigate reported that whatever is in the emails it did not originate in government, he accepted it.'[46] This, however, did not mean that Kgalema dismissed everything in the emails. On the contrary, for him there were and remain elements of truth in them, but because a comprehensive investigation did not occur and the report was jettisoned, the facts will never be known.

'Kgalema's Kalahari friends'

On 10 November 2006 the *M&G* ran a story by Vicki Robinson and Stefaans Brümmer on Russian mining interests in South Africa.[47] A subtitle 'Kgalema's Kalahari friends' contained this report:

> Among the more curious episodes in the contest for manganese rights in the Kalahari was an alleged intervention by Kgalema Motlanthe, the ANC secretary general, against Chancellor House, the ANC company.
>
> It is alleged that Motlanthe presided over a meeting during the second half of 2004 attempting to convince Russian investment company Renova to team up with a company named Kalahari Resources, and not with Chancellor House.
>
> If this is true, why would Motlanthe have argued against the interests of an ANC business vehicle answerable to his colleague, treasurer general Mendi Msimang? One explanation could be Kalahari's composition – it reveals proximity to both the ANC and Motlanthe personally.

Kalahari Resources was a BEE mining company that had applied for prospecting and mining rights to what is known as the 'Kalahari Manganese Field' in the Northern Cape. The late Stan Nkosi, Kgalema's best friend and comrade, and his wife Daphne Mashile-Nkosi were involved in the company, and she was its chair. Other than the friendship between Kgalema and this couple, the newspaper's only basis for its allegation was the rather flimsy fact that Kgalema was called into a meeting Mendi Msimang was having with the Russian investment group Renova and introduced to them. This was not the first time that Msimang had introduced him to companies he had dealings with in his capacity as treasurer-general, but because Nkosi was very close to Kgalema this brief introduction to Renova – who sought BEE partners for mining manganese in the Northern Cape and therefore had discussions with Kalahari – was interpreted as Kgalema using his influence to help Kalahari Resources obtain a licence. This assumption was at least implied in the wording 'Kgalema's Kalahari friends.'[48]

Mashile-Nkosi is adamant that Kgalema had nothing to do with the licensing of Kalahari Resources.

> Stan and I read the story when it appeared and decided that we will not be prepared to justify our friendship with Kgalema to anyone, especially Stan who was very close to him for many years, before and after the ten years they spent together on Robben Island. But what does the *Mail & Guardian* know about Kgalema? That man would never get involved in underhand licensing schemes, no matter how close he and Stan were. It is actually an insult to him. Stan was very upset and said let them write whatever they want to. I reject with utter contempt the insinuation that Kgalema's close relations with Stan and I paved the way for our licence.'[49]

She gave a detailed, convincing background about both the formation of Kalahari Resources and their successful application for a mining licence, which was in fact a long and bumpy ride.

Msimang rejects the story as strongly:

> I really don't know how Kgalema gets dragged into the Kalahari matter. That fell entirely into my area, as treasurer-general. The only time he had any contact with them was when I asked him to very briefly come into a meeting I was having with Renova at Luthuli House to introduce him to them. He was far removed from those processes. Besides, if you know him he would never

have involved himself in such matters, simply because he always respects and strictly abides by the constitution. It is not an area the SG gets involved in. I see the *Mail & Guardian* also said that he opposed Chancellor House getting the deal with the Russians. It is a complete lie, whoever told them that. Besides, why would he want to exclude Chancellor House, which is an ANC vehicle, from such a deal? It does not make sense at all.[50]

Kgalema also would have none of it:

> Carol Paton first ran the story and then the *Mail & Guardian*. I had nothing to do with it but the media linked me with Kalahari only because of my close relationship with Stan and Daphne Nkosi. The story claimed that I said that the Russian guys, Renova, should have nothing to do with Chancellor House but there was absolutely no basis to that allegation. The person who dealt with that matter was Msimang, not me. He actually established Chancellor House, but it was run by its own board and CEO. Any attempt to link me with the licensing of Kalahari by the DME is arrant nonsense.

He has consistently said that he never attended the meeting in a scheduled official capacity but that he was simply called into Msimang's office so that he could be introduced to Renova. 'When I walked in they [Renova] introduced themselves and gave us some brochures, a CD and so on. Shortly thereafter I had to leave.' Though finance was not Kgalema's domain, for Msimang to want to introduce him as the ANC's SG to Renova is certainly nothing unexpected. It would have been more unexpected if Msimang had not done so, especially because of the nature of the post Kgalema held and the fact that his office was very near by.

Stefaans Brümmer for *M&G* explains why putting questions to Kgalema was important: 'I think what gave added impetus to our questions about Kalahari manganese things was the central involvement there of people who were close to Kgalema in one way or another – the late Stan Nkosi (his close struggle comrade), Daphne Mashile-Nkosi (Stan's wife), another Mashile who may be connected and of course Majali. His alleged involvement would seem to conflate personal and political roles, but, as said, it is very difficult to judge in the absence of any version from Kgalema.'[51]

One of the reasons why the writers Vicki Robinson and Stefaans Brümmer may have wondered if Kgalema had been involved was the fact that they got no replies to questions they put to him through his assistant Steyn Speed. Evidence they sent me shows that they tried several times, to no avail.[52] Kgalema sounded really annoyed, remembering the *M&G*'s attempts to get him to answer their questions:

> What riles me most is when I hear about anonymous sources having made this and that allegation. In fact when I hear that, I don't like it and I am not encouraged to respond to any related questions. And though I cannot recall seeing the questions, it is quite possible that Steyn gave them to me and said the paper is alleging I chaired that meeting and I told him it is nonsense. In other words even if I saw it [the list of questions] I may not have answered because their starting point was false because I had never chaired any such meeting. And if they said please state what the facts are, our stance was often that newspapers publish false stories with the aim largely of getting you to correct it and as a result we often stonewalled them on a whole range of things.

Brümmer's response was this: 'I am sure that Speed did not come back and say if we provide this or that further information, Motlanthe would consider responding.'[53] Indeed it does seem that Speed and Kgalema may have mishandled this request.[54]

But the *M&G* were at fault too. Their date for the meeting Kgalema was said to have chaired was 'during the second half of 2004', which is ridiculously vague. For someone as senior as the SG of the ruling party, the paper needed to have been much more firmly grounded than to merely state that someone 'alleged' that he presided over this meeting. And on Kgalema's supposed intervention against Chancellor House the *M&G* asks: 'Why would Motlanthe have argued against the interests of an ANC business vehicle, answerable to his colleague, ... Msimang?'[55] Perhaps because Kalahari consisted of his friends, especially Stan Nkosi and his wife Daphne? This seems an extremely simplistic deduction. Lastly, to say that he 'presided' over such a meeting is much more serious than to say he attended it, which demands in turn that the whole story be more solidly anchored to be credible. Kgalema said he could not recall exactly, but these may well have been among his reasons for declining to comment.

Brümmer does make a fair point about Kgalema not answering the questions and then not saying why: 'This is unfortunately quite consistent with the way Motlanthe often interacts with the media – a style perhaps best put as a complete non-interaction in the face of personally damaging allegations. I don't think this serves him well.'[56] Kgalema agrees that there have been times when he should have been more forthcoming in his dealings with the media: 'Stefaans may be right about my unnecessary silence at times, when it would have been better to respond in some way. They did articles on Iraq and I never also commented. Sometimes I did this because I was a bit too cautious.' For me, his reply shows how open and mature he can be when faced with a sensible argument.

The newspaper, surprisingly, seemed to have been naïve to accept the word of their source on the story. Luthuli House is a place where much is said and done by various people and it has its own dynamics, which are far from straightforward. It is most unlikely that the SG of the ANC would argue that its own investment vehicle should not be included in a potentially very lucrative manganese market. It is also highly unbelievable that he would do so in favour of his friends at Kalahari. The bias would have been so obvious, the kind of move that would inevitably surface. And had he played such a flagrantly contradictory role the ANC would have confronted him on it.

The Pamodzi–Land Bank loan saga

In 2005 the Land Bank granted Pamodzi Investment Holdings a controversial R800 million loan. The bank's own auditors expressed concern at 'the bank having overexposed itself by lending such a large amount of money to a single entity.'[57] It was reported in the *Sunday Times* that at the time of the loan Kgalema and Manne Dipico had 'a stake in Pamodzi through the Pambi Trust, which owns an 8% stake in the company'.[58] The assumption was that Kgalema and Dipico had used their political influence to secure this loan for Pamodzi to enable the 'buyout of a food empire for a company in which ANC secretary-general Kgalema Motlanthe and presidential adviser Manne Dipico have a stake.'[59] In other words, they would personally benefit from the loan as a result of the shares they owned in Pamodzi.

The two men were jointly named because both had unit trust shares in Pambi Trust, which was linked to Pamodzi, and both were also leading figures in the ANC – hence the notion that somehow they had influenced the Land Bank to make the loan. The story set this loan against the background of 'a time when rural community projects were battling to get access to funds' and 'when hundreds of desperate farmers were battling to get funding for tractors, seeds, shovels and fertiliser.'[60]

And what is the Pambi Trust? Years back, Pamodzi formed the trust and invited some two hundred black people to invest in it. Only about fifty did so. They pooled their money and bought an 8 per cent stake in Pamodzi.[61] Kgalema was one of those investors. This is the only link he has with the company. 'I have put money into Pambi Trust, which has a stake in Pamodzi. But I am not a trustee and I don't do anything there. I treat this investment in the same way I treat unit trusts I have with Standard Bank, which I have also declared in parliament,' he says. 'Because of my position as SG of the ANC I did not want to be seriously involved in business, so I decided instead to invest some money in Pambi. Dipico, then Mbeki's parliamentary adviser, was also invited and invested.'

Kgalema had just returned with Dipico from a conference of the Botswana Democratic Party in Gaborone, when they saw the *Sunday Times* placard headline: 'ANC bigwigs in dodgy Land Bank loan deal.' Kgalema asked Pamodzi to give him all the relevant documents. Together with these documents he wrote a covering letter to the public protector, Lawrence Mushwana. Tony Leon, then leader of the Democratic Alliance (DA), had already asked Mushwana to investigate the matter. In March 2006 Mushwana cleared both Kgalema and Dipico of any wrongful involvement. He found not only that both men were not involved in any way in securing the loan but that there were sufficiently good grounds for the bank to have granted the loan; it accorded with the bank's mandate and so there was no maladministration.[62] The company had told the *Sunday Times* that Kgalema and Dipico were 'not actively involved in any Pamodzi business.'[63] They also said that 'neither Motlanthe nor Dipico knew of the transaction while it was taking place.'[64] Despite these assurances, the insinuation that Kgalema in particular probably influenced the loan to Pamodzi continued in the media, and with it the suspicions.

Kgalema thinks the media's stories about Pamodzi and himself were partly linked to the email saga because of what the media had to say about these matters. 'The *Sunday Times* story on my involvement in the Land Bank loan to Pamodzi is discussed in the emails in fact before it came out in the paper. This is only one reason why I would never totally dismiss the emails, as I insist many have wrongly done.' Some emails said that a number of businessmen were trying hard to convince Pamodzi's shareholders to buy Kgalema's shares so that he would not have resources to help him in any political ambitions.

Kgalema explains an interesting twist to the story. The Land Bank loan was given over a ten-year period but by the fourteenth month Pamodzi had already paid it back with R100 million in interest. This happened before the *Sunday Times* story broke – which is why, Kgalema says, the journalist covering the story said then there was actually no story. These facts never came to light through Kgalema, largely because 'when you are very busy with many things you tend to forget about important matters, like this.'[65]

Shortly after Kgalema took over from Mbeki in September 2008, the DA wanted him to answer questions about Pamodzi. They did not succeed.[66] Since the public protector had investigated the case in 2006 and cleared Kgalema and Dipico of any wrongdoing, what need of question or answer? If the DA felt there was more to know, it was up to them to motivate the public protector to reinvestigate the matter by providing new

Kgalema's great-grandparents, the Rev. Ramatoto Madingoane and his wife Sophia Mmateng Masefako

Kgalema's father Louis Motlanthe (back row, far right) and other family members

At home in Meadowlands, 1972

In central Johannesburg, 1972

Kgalema (second from right) with Phineas Mabetoa (second from left) and other friends

With Phineas Mabetoa and others, 1972

Outside the family home in Meadowlands, early 1970s

In Zimbabwe, 1974

Brother Ernest (centre back) with family in Marapyane

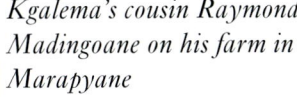

Kgalema's cousin Raymond Madingoane on his farm in Marapyane

Kgalema's mother Sophia Masefako in Meadowlands, 2010

With his close friend Kuben Pillay

Kgalema with his ex-wife Mapula Mokate

During happier family days

Kgalema's son Kagiso with his mother Mapula and her daughter Ntabiseng

Kgalema and Gugu Mtshali

With Nelson Mandela, 2001

At a NUM central committee meeting, 1992

With Director Matlala (centre) during NUM days

With ANC members

After an emergency plane landing in the DRC, 2009

With John Nkadimeng (left) and a Cuban delegate at a Cuban solidarity conference, 1995

On a visit to the Middle East, 2009

On a visit to the Middle East

At a reception in Palestine, 2009

On a visit to Palestine, 2009

At a Lead SA event at Liliesleaf, Johannesburg, August 2012

With Kuben Pillay at Liliesleaf, 2012

With young attendees at Liliesleaf, 2012

At his official residence, Mahlamba Ndlopfu, in Pretoria, 2009

evidence.

Kgalema's response at the time was appropriate: 'What is this suddenly all about? Upon the instigation of their former leader, Tony Leon, they requested an investigation by the public protector and I was cleared in a report they produced. What is the DA now up to, I ask, other than plain mischief?' Indeed, the DA's timing suggested a motive: Kgalema had just shortly before that become president after Mbeki's resignation. It could be that they wanted to discredit him. But even when smears are proved to be false, the dignity and integrity of the person targeted are often somewhat tarnished and sometimes never quite fully restored.

Oilgate and the sagas of the emails, 'Kalahari friends' and Pamodzi – they all appear to be attempts to use the media to discredit Kgalema during his second term. Nothing shows more strongly that they failed than his being elected deputy president of the ANC in 2007 in spite of it all. Evidently the delegates of the ANC did not give a damn what the media had to say about the ANC and their leaders. This might not be the healthiest attitude in a constitutional democracy, but when the facts contradict media stories that tarnish the reputation and credibility of a leader, then that attitude is probably appropriate. Even the 'political damage among Mbeki supporters' that Jeremy Gordin said Kgalema suffered as a result of his insistence that the ANC appoint its own team to investigate the emails saga had little or no effect at Polokwane.[67]

Mbeki fires Zuma

The year 2005 was probably the most momentous in the history of the ANC and certainly in post-apartheid ANC rule. Even if nothing else dramatic had happened, Zuma's dismissal, the circumstances under which it took place, and its effects on the

ANC, the government and the country would have made it a watershed year.

Pivotal to Zuma's dismissal was the conviction of Schabir Shaik shortly before. That these dramatic developments occurred just before the email saga may not be a coincidence, some people argue. Kgalema said that the dismissal of Zuma was mentioned in the second batch of emails he received on 18 August. The raids on Zuma's homes and offices also occurred in August. Some hard facts thus lay behind the smoke and mirrors.[68]

From the day Judge Hilary Squires convicted Shaik on 2 June 2005, a chain of events unfolded that had a huge impact on the ANC and the country. Squires found that Shaik and Zuma had a 'generally corrupt relationship'. If so, why was Zuma not charged alongside Shaik?[69] Gordin strongly suggests that the decision not to charge him was taken by the national director of public prosecutions, Bulelani Ngcuka, for political considerations, because in 2003 the powers that be were still protecting Zuma, as he was then the deputy president of the country and the ANC, and still 'their comrade'. All this changed when Zuma resisted Mbeki's request that he resign after the Squires judgment.[70]

Even before the judgment, Kgalema knew there were growing tensions between Zuma and Mbeki, partly because as the case against Shaik unfolded it seemed increasingly clear to Mbeki and his cabinet that Zuma was implicated, but there were also other conflictual dynamics between the two leaders. For example, Zuma informed Kgalema that when some provincial leaders in KZN told Mbeki negative things about Zuma he tended to believe them, which he said was increasing tensions between them. Kgalema went to Mbeki, told him of Zuma's concern and advised him to meet and discuss these matters before they got worse. Mbeki agreed, Kgalema says, but adds: 'that was the beginning of the problems which led to so much and finally the clash between them at and even after Polokwane.'

The growing conflict between Mbeki and Zuma was significant. There had been tense undercurrents for quite a long time. Kgalema, working with them and knowing this, was deeply concerned. He visited Mandela and told him that if these serious tensions at the top level of the party and the state were not immediately addressed, they would affect the ANC and the government. Kgalema explained that the trouble would not be readily seen in formal meetings 'but when the meetings are over they go in different directions.'[71] Mandela's response was that since the ANC was 'our movement we could not sit and fold our arms, do nothing about it and allow the ANC to implode and destroy itself.' Mandela offered to speak to them, which he did, seeing them separately. After that, Mbeki and Zuma had a meeting and produced a joint statement in which they denied there were any serious tensions between them.

Kgalema watched these developments with trepidation, especially the later cowboy-style raids by the Scorpions on Zuma's homes and offices. He knew deep down that the events were going to threaten the ANC seriously, which was already severely strained by many other problems and especially the presidency's worsening relations with Cosatu and the SACP. Kgalema condemned the raids and the Scorpions' cavalier style. 'I thought that just the practice of the NPA in the raids and how they conducted themselves and briefed the media about evidence they gleaned from their raids itself undermined the rule of law, which presumes you are innocent until proven guilty. What they were in fact trying to achieve was to discredit him politically more than anything else.'

After the Squires judgment (which did indeed seriously

implicate Zuma), Mbeki asked Kgalema and Msimang to go to him and ask him to resign.[72] Kgalema says he and Msimang had not agreed with Mbeki that Zuma should resign; that was a government and, finally, presidential matter and so it was not something Kgalema would express himself firmly on. Evidently then, the idea of resignation was Mbeki's.

He and Msimang dutifully delivered the message to Zuma but he would have none of it. His stance was both smart and tactful. He told them to tell Mbeki that he knew of nothing he had done that was wrong; and if Mbeki knew of anything serious enough he should fire him, failing which Zuma would refuse to resign. Kgalema is pointed on this: 'He said he won't make it easy for Mbeki by resigning and thereby playing into his hands. That's it, he said, and we left and went back to Mbeki.' As Mbeki recalls, 'They came back and said essentially that Zuma was saying that it would be wrong for him to resign because whatever language we use, the general public will come to believe that it was an admission of guilt.'[73]

Mbeki regretted that Zuma wanted him to dismiss him, 'which is exactly what I wanted to avoid because it then becomes a personal decision instead of an organisational one. We [the ANC] wanted to communicate a message that this was an organisational decision and not my decision alone, because this concerns the deputy president of the country.'[74]

Kgalema remembers that 'it was a Monday morning after the Squires judgment when Mbeki told me that he had no alternative but to relieve Zuma as his deputy. He said that he will have to brief Madiba about it and asked me to accompany him so that I am there when he tells him. So we went to see Madiba that night and Mbeki briefed him. Madiba asked Mbeki if he considered that Zuma was a man of the people and Mbeki said yes he did. Madiba was very concerned and raised his concerns

From Stellenbosch to Polokwane, 2002–2007

quite strongly.' The date was 14 June, just twelve days after the Shaik judgment.

Mbeki took the decision to dismiss Zuma before an extended NWC meeting in Cape Town. The idea of an extended NWC (including Cosatu and the SACP) to address this matter came from Kgalema, who felt it was serious, and Mbeki agreed. Kgalema also made it clear that the dismissal was finally Mbeki's decision. 'Mbeki needed as ANC and South African president to explain to the ANC and parliament his decision.' For Kgalema it was not only the ANC that Mbeki needed to explain to, but leading figures of Cosatu and the SACP – hence the extended NWC. He knew deep down that the dismissal was an earth-shattering political moment for the ANC, its alliance and the government.

Kgalema took notes but did not talk in this NWC meeting partly because Mbeki and Zuma would not be swayed from their stances: Mbeki decided that he had to dismiss Zuma if he did not resign and Zuma steadfastly refused to resign and instead wanted Mbeki to dismiss him if he no longer wanted him as his deputy. In any event, although Kgalema as SG had gone to Mandela on the burning issue. He explained:

> this was now a presidential decision and therefore a government matter. But we could deal later with his position as deputy president of the ANC differently, because he was dismissed as deputy president of the republic, not as deputy president of the ANC. Some people were truly stunned in the meeting, people like Fikile Mbalula and Zola Skweyiya. There was no real discussion and debate on the merits of Mbeki's decision – the way it was put was that this is a decision already taken by the president.

Usefully, Kgalema explains the nature of Mbeki's 'consultation' on this matter: 'When it is said a decision was taken "in consultation", this means that you are not dependent on that consultation before taking a decision, whereas taking a decision "after consultation" means you only arrive at a decision after you consult. Zuma's dismissal was a case of "in consultation" with cabinet and the extended NWC.'

A statement from Zuma after he was fired just does not make sense and flies in the face of the anger he felt at how Mbeki treated him, especially how he fired him and the flimsy grounds for doing so. He said: 'I accept and respect his pronouncement. I believe he has taken this decision not because I am guilty of any crime, but because of considerations relating to the constraints within which government operates.'[75] Why did he say this if he was strongly convinced that both the manner and reasons for dismissal were wrong? He expressed his deep unhappiness to Kgalema and Msimang and, later, Zuma's biographer Jeremy Gordin and myself in interviews. But so aggrieved were the delegates at the June 2005 NGC that they did not even consider this feeble attempt by Zuma to explain and even rationalise his expulsion, which Gordin referred to as 'mostly ANC-speak'.[76]

Was the decision correct? Mbeki is unrepentant:

> No, I have no regrets. All of us agreed that you could not get a determination like that [the Squires judgment] without it obviously meaning that JZ [Jacob Zuma] had been involved in some corrupt relationship. We spoke to some lawyers who said that Squires prepared his argument in a way that anticipated an appeal and he did not want to run foul of a superior court. It was impossible to ignore the judgment and the legal opinion on its merits. If we did that, it would have created lots of other

problems. There was no other way of handling it. We talked among the ANC officials about it and everyone agreed.[77]

But for Kgalema, the media's portrayal showed him that

> The law was more of an ass in Zuma's case because he was found guilty before he appeared in court. Laws are passed to protect citizens from the abuse of state power, but what you had in the case of Zuma was the state itself relentlessly pursuing him with charges. There is a question that has to be answered: if Mbeki and the others on that committee always assured everyone that the deal was clean, then how can Zuma, who was not on that cabinet committee and was Mbeki's deputy, be charged with corruption related to the deal? Zuma was in fact not involved in the arms deal. Mbeki chaired the cabinet committee on the arms deal. Other members of the committee were Joe Modise, Alec Erwin, Stella Sigcau and Trevor Manuel were on that committee. They should know far more about this deal than Zuma should.

For Kgalema, the biggest factor in Mbeki's downfall was probably his decision to fire Zuma and how he did it.[78]

Apparently Kgalema did not do much to try to persuade Mbeki that his decision to fire Zuma was wrong. For him, Mbeki was not only president of the ANC but of the country. This matter concerned his deputy in the state and the Constitution gave Mbeki the leeway to take such a decision, however cataclysmic. Kgalema's abiding and perhaps problematic respect for hierarchical authority had compelled him as SG of the ANC to tell Zuma that Mbeki wished him to resign, yet he did not feel justified to question the wisdom of Mbeki's decision, though he knew this was a grave step.

Kgalema adds that a deputy president is appointed by the president, who also has the prerogative to dismiss him for a variety of reasons. Once a president loses confidence in his deputy, even if the reasons are questionable, it is time for the deputy president to go because 'you serve in the cabinet at the pleasure of the president. If I get a sense that I am no longer welcome I would resign. When I put this to Zuma his response was "Well, if you know what I know you will not resign."' Kgalema says that if it was him he would have resigned rather than face an untenable situation after losing the confidence and trust of the president, and told Zuma so. As we have seen, Zuma refused, saying he would be 'playing into his [Mbeki's] hands'. Kgalema understood this stance.

Did Mbeki want to remove Zuma for reasons other than what he said?[79] Then Zuma had every right to refuse to resign and maintain that if Mbeki wanted him to go, then he must have the courage to fire him. The removal of a deputy president by a president must be taken on good grounds, otherwise the president's power here could become whimsical and arbitrary, which is not what a constitutional democracy needs.

Zuma made a shrewd move. He said he would resign all his positions in the ANC and as an MP after Mbeki dismissed him, knowing the ANC branches would want to know why and so the matter would be raised at the NGC. 'I took that decision because Mbeki was working things out in such a way that the NGC must not discuss my issue. Kgalema played a role in placing this issue on the agenda of the NGC when Mbeki did not want it to come up. But he badly miscalculated the NGC and everything.' But Kgalema did not exactly place this matter on the agenda of the NGC. It was contained instead in the Organisational Report of the NEC, which as SG he presented to the meeting.

The 2005 NGC meeting was a huge setback for Mbeki and

a resounding success for Zuma. Even though Mbeki had fired Zuma, and despite the dark cloud hovering over him after the Squires judgment, the delegates wanted him to stay on as deputy president of the ANC. Their immense vote of confidence in Zuma probably surprised Mbeki and his supporters. This was a crucial turning point in the ANC. Mbeki suddenly seemed to have his back to the wall.[80] As for Zuma, not only did he retain his post but this victory became the very platform from which he launched a dramatic comeback until he beat Mbeki at Polokwane and became the president of the ANC and, later, of South Africa.[81]

More than any other ANC leader, Kgalema stood by Zuma throughout. Until a court of law found Zuma guilty, he said, Zuma had full rights as an ANC member and a citizen. He made it clear that he would have felt the same if it had been Mbeki on the receiving end. Zuma appreciated his support: 'Kgalema played a role many people won't know about – because at that time Mbeki was ready to expel me from the organisation, especially in meetings I was not present at.'[82]

It was Kgalema who probably prevented Mbeki from expelling him from the ANC, Zuma declared. But it was in fact a decision of the ANC to support its deputy president. Kgalema put his modesty aside enough to agree: 'Let me tell you that if I did not take that stand – and he knows it – those targeting him would perhaps have finished him off politically.' Kgalema did not in fact do anything extraordinary but simply invoked the constitution of the ANC. Kgalema even went to court to support him during his trial, regardless of any adverse political cost to himself and much to the chagrin of Mbeki's cabinet.[83] His steady sense of principle may in turn be partly why Zuma chose him to be his deputy after the elections in 2009.

Would Kgalema also have fired Zuma if he were the president

under those circumstances? I doubt it. Kgalema said that if Zuma had been involved in corruption with Shaik, he should have been charged with Shaik and had the opportunity to defend himself. But further: his political style is very different from Mbeki's, as this comment shows:

> I think that if you are a president and you have a serious problem with your deputy or a minister, you should just sit them down and be straightforward about the matter and say that you think if is best for the person to resign because for whatever reasons the situation has become untenable. But to discuss the reasons face-to-face, even if briefly, in an open, comradely and sensitive manner, is very important. After all, Zuma was the deputy president of the ANC and South Africa.

Kgalema did once say, though, that 'good grounds may just be that you cannot get along with your deputy or even the realisation that you made a mistake to appoint such a person in the light of your experiences.' A complex matter indeed because we have seen that this approach can allow a whole range of negative subjectivities to influence a major decision.

Zuma was proving a very shrewd politician. If he had listened to Mbeki and tendered his resignation it is unlikely that he would have been the president of the ANC and the country today. It was his dismissal by Mbeki that ignited the indignation of the delegates and in turn fed a cascade of sympathy for him at the June 2005 NGC. From that point until the Polokwane conference, where Mbeki was unseated as ANC president, Mbeki's steady decline contrasted with Zuma's mesmerising rise. It seems that Kgalema's defence of Zuma at a crucial stage was key to that trajectory.

Nothing troubled Kgalema more than the fight between

these two leaders, which for him made even Oilgate and the email saga pale into significance. At the heart of his concern was the fate and future of the ANC. Yet even when the conflict was at its worst he strongly believed that it was 'not really ideological but for factionalist control and the power that comes with it.' There have indeed been no discernible ideological and policy differences between the two leaders all along. Kgalema's concern was premised on a thought he has repeatedly raised: once a leader is indebted to groupings and cliques, he or she will not be strong, unifying and inspiring enough to take the ANC forward.

From the NGC to Polokwane, 2005–2007

After the email saga and Zuma's dismissal, relations between Kgalema and Mbeki began to sour, politically speaking – politically, Kgalema insists, because remarkably, through every difficult moment he had with Mbeki before and especially after 2005, they still got on well personally. Until 2005 they had worked reasonably well together, largely because their positions as president and SG of the party demanded that they coordinate closely.

The email saga began the month after Zuma's dismissal, in July 2005, and as we have seen, according to Kgalema there was a reference in the emails to Zuma's dismissal and the raids on him. No final evidence has been presented that the mail messages were true or that there was any conscious connection between the emails and subsequent events – largely because neither the emails nor the ANC investigation into them was made public – but the sequence is certainly startling. There could hardly be a more deeply challenging situation for the ANC, the government and especially Kgalema in terms of what happened before and after the 2005 NGC. In the same month of July when the email saga began, the Oilgate story also broke in the *M&G*, and both involved him. They also came hot on the heels of Mbeki's dismissal of Zuma, which for Kgalema signalled the lowest moment in the ANC and government since the ANC came to power in 1994.

It is from about 2005 that Kgalema discovered that some people close to Mbeki were saying that he, Kgalema, defended Zuma when he should have been finished off and that without this support Zuma would not have survived after his dismissal. In the run-up to Polokwane he was reliably informed that Smuts Ngonyama and Essop Pahad went to the Free State province and told ANC members there that 'they could even compromise on Zuma as long as we get the SG out because they blamed me for not getting rid of Zuma. They were in fact campaigning on that basis.'

It was not only Kgalema who faced a tough time in 2005. Everything for Zuma seemed to go wrong too, except for the NGC, where he scored his victory over Mbeki. A suspicion arose that moves against Zuma were orchestrated because they happened in such rapid succession. From 2 June, when Judge Hilary Squires found Shaik guilty of corruption, the pattern was clear: six days later Vusi Pikoli announced that Zuma would be charged; twelve days later Mbeki fired Zuma; twenty-seven days later Zuma appeared in the Durban High Court on corruption charges; on 18 August the Scorpions raided Zuma's homes; on 6 December Zuma was charged with rape, for a trial to start on 13 February 2006.[84]

All these adversities that Zuma faced worried Kgalema greatly. He was convinced that to a large extent there were forces out to destroy Zuma's credibility. As he saw it, they meant to tarnish him to the point where he stood no chance of becoming the next president of the ANC and the country. Following widespread condemnation of the Scorpions and other attacks against Zuma, which many in the ANC alliance believed were instigated by Mbeki, Mbeki addressed a letter on 26 August to leaders of the ANC alliance requesting that a commission of inquiry be agreed upon to see if 'any member of the ANC and the broad democratic movement, including the president of the ANC, have been and are involved in a conspiracy targeted at marginalising or destroying the [ANC] deputy president.'[85]

Mbeki went further to project an image of deep concern with what was at stake: 'Specifically, our movement must act urgently and in unity to protect the ANC deputy president, and therefore our movement as a whole, from any hostile factional offensive, if it is established that such an offensive exists.'[86] And, to show that rumours that he was behind a political plot to block Zuma's path to the presidency were false, Mbeki added: 'I would like to assure you that I would be ready to appear before the commission.'[87] Mbeki gave the letter to Kgalema, who submitted it to an alliance meeting. The letter sounded sincere and convincing but his suggestion was not adopted, being opposed strongly by Cosatu and the SACP. After the raids on Zuma's homes, Cosatu and the SACP were positive that state agencies were being used to target Zuma. The fact that these events came soon after Zuma's dismissal and the NGC support for him left them so deeply convinced that they were unimpressed with Mbeki's offer and saw it as a face-saving gesture that was too late anyway. The battle lines were already boldly drawn.

Cosatu identified so strongly with Zuma, it was clear that they intended using the attacks against him as a rallying point to build an anti-Mbeki coalition in which Zuma would be the leader and alternative to Mbeki. At that point Cosatu and the SACP were so set on getting rid of Mbeki that a whole range of important considerations were not dealt with, the kind of agreements on principles, policy and strategy without which a strong coalition cannot be built.⁸⁸

The attacks against Zuma seemed strongly politically motivated, and elements in the state may even have been involved. Yet the way some people saw the case against Zuma was more opportunistic than the result of a sober appraisal. Cosatu also had a dangerously naïve view of Zuma as a kind of 'working class hero'. In a 2006 article in the *M&G* I wrote: 'The opportunism of Zuma's recent pronouncements, particularly at the recent Cosatu congress and in his speeches to Cosatu affiliates, is painfully obvious. But it seems most of Cosatu's leaders either fail to spot the contradiction of finding themselves as Zuma's most fervent supporters or are simply obsessed with the fact that their hero is not Thabo Mbeki.'⁸⁹

A huge and growing concern for Kgalema, especially after Stellenbosch, was the way in which increasingly the NEC and NWC were being deflected from fulfilling their constitutional tasks and becoming more the mouthpiece of the cabinet members present there. In his words: 'The central manifestation of the problem was that some ANC leaders were thinking mainly as government representatives, which opened up a divisive gap between the party and the government. In fact Mbeki was by far the best of the cabinet who realised that the ANC cannot be a lapdog of ANC leaders in government, but I don't know if he said different things to his colleagues in government.' Of course the ANC had not only the right but the responsibility to think independently of government, but when you have a ruling party as dominant as the ANC, the risk of blurring the lines between party and state is great.

Kgalema says this difficulty grew slowly but steadily over the years. 'It evolved over time as it became evident to ANC leaders in government that Luthuli House was becoming ... a thorn in their sides. This problem was linked to government salaries, perks and the power that goes with them. I have learnt that this is a compelling factor in what has happened. The real reason why this problem is serious and has to be dealt with is that, when the ANC wins elections, a cabinet is formed and MPs are chosen, people forget that all that takes place happens on the basis of the victory of the ANC at the polls ... but when you get to government you tend to forget where you come from and who put you there and instead you tend to become a power for yourself or a faction and even sometimes against the ANC.'[90]

The very fact that after 1994 many people rose from poverty into heady new posts in government or the private sector meant a sea change in their financial and social lives. Negative effects have included abuse of their power to use state resources, which can gain a momentum of its own, flouting their stated values and goals.[91] This pervasive ill prompts Kgalema to say frankly: 'All of us will state that we are committed to the ANC and its vision for social justice and equality and that we are not desirous of top, very well-paying and powerful positions in government, but watch what happens behind in the run-up to an ANC elective conference. And when the cabinet is being appointed you won't find anyone who says they would like to or are eager to be in the cabinet, but when some are not appointed they are unhappy. ... That is the sad reality.'

This is partly why he is not convinced that there was 'a real battle for the soul of the ANC' in the late 1990s and early 2000s on policy, ideological and programmatic grounds. 'Instead I think there was a battle for the influence that the ANC holds as a gateway to personal riches. ... People may couch their postures in ideological terms but essentially it was about who controls access to resources. The ANC, being the governing party, meant that once you take hold of the state you can determine what happens in a variety of ways, all of which in one way or another amounts to control over resources.'

In a limited way, though, there was a battle then for the soul of the ANC. In the wake of Gear and other neoliberal moves by the ANC-led government, Cosatu and the SACP really did struggle to take the ANC back to the more redistributionist policies of the Freedom Charter and the RDP.

We can only glimpse the footwork of the time in such things as records of ANC meetings, documents and media coverage. How does Kgalema rate his own performance in it? He recalls his effort to keep the government true to basic ANC commitments: 'Though there was a general tilt towards the government after Stellenbosch, I could still stop them in their tracks as far as the ANC constitution and policy is concerned and call them to order. The difficulty was that we had a presidency which was pulling in the other direction and even manifested itself in the ANC in a manner which created other networks, which became evident in the year of Polokwane. The cabinet was using the state to overrun the ANC and all kind of machineries were being established outside the ANC.'

A serious problem afflicted the ANC in the run-up to Polokwane:

> A big part of the ANC's problems in recent years has been the lists. The guideline issued by the ANC in fact debars lists ..., other than those coming from the branches. I raised this with both Mbeki and Zuma and in my organisational report to the Polokwane conference. The big problem for the ANC was that, though Mbeki and Zuma said to us they had no problems between them and even issued a joint statement saying that they ... pledge to work together, ... I pointed out

to an NEC [meeting] that this statement was untrue because as we approached Polokwane there was a list for Zuma which did not include Mbeki and one for Mbeki which did not include Zuma. There were now clear-cut factions in the ANC and once that happens neither of the leaders of the two factions can lead the ANC as it should be led: by one leader of one organisation. The ANC is not and has never been a faction [sic]. I urged all members of the ANC to belong only to the ANC and not to any factions because they are not the real ANC. These informal lists the papers talk of are lobby lists, which have nothing to do with constitutional processes and procedures for an election. That is why nobody would approach me about being on any list or to try and recruit me onto any list.

Kgalema was not all that opposed to Mbeki seeking a third term as ANC president, though he knew very well that it would lead to many problems if he retained his presidency of the ANC and Zuma was later elected president of South Africa. But what totally dismayed him was when he learnt that Mbeki was actually going out before Polokwane to canvass support for himself for a third term. 'If you have individual leaders who campaign and try to sway others onto their own lists, how are you going to prevent factionalism? Remember that those who do that know very well that the only legitimate lists are those nomination lists from properly constituted branches.' There can be no doubt that this is what alienated Kgalema more than anything else Mbeki may have done before.

In ANC tradition, leaders do not canvass for themselves. This does not make it wrong when it happens. Pushed on the matter, Kgalema said that while it might be Mbeki's right to canvass for himself, it was also the right of delegates to vote against him. For him that is democracy in action, but the process should be far more transparent. If people feel they can lead successfully, he says, they are free to announce their availability. Then it is up to branch members to decide about nominating them. The urgent need is for openness to stem the behind-the-scenes, often uncomradely and vitriolic canvassing for positions, which itself explodes the façade of a culture of selfless service.

What has happened to the ANC's goal of establishing a political school and policy institute, a commitment dating back to 1997? Breaking news at the time of writing is that the ANC in Gauteng launched its new political school on the Soweto campus of the University of Johannesburg on 12 August 2012, with Kgalema as main speaker. This is only a provincial start but a good stepping stone towards a school at national level. The policy institute is still nowhere in sight after fifteen years of waiting.[92] Kgalema was SG for ten of those years, dedicated to the idea.[93]

> I can tell you with absolute certainty that there are many in the ANC who will bear me out when I say that I put my head on the block for those two projects. I even spoke to the comrades with money to help start the projects. I am sure some people who could have supported it had selfish reasons not to have, but they all said it was a great idea but they failed to provide the money to start the projects. We even established the Stalwarts Trust, which was charged with the responsibility of launching these two projects. Eventually the documentation and people were in place but not the finance.

To me, his account suggests the delay is deliberate – all the more so because Gwede Mantashe told me that after he took over from Kgalema he was amazed to see that Kgalema had reached an advanced stage of preparation and that he himself just needed to take the process forward to completion.[94] We know that the ANC can find money for what they really want. The conference resolutions on these projects at Mafikeng came long before the 1999 arms deal, which cost the ANC government over R60 billion. So there were certainly other reasons behind the persistent lack of funding to start these two important projects. Surely the truth is that the political school and policy institute will put ANC policies under the spotlight and probably create more pressure for policy changes from some constituencies in the ANC and in its alliance. There may also be a fear of unintended consequences for the ANC, because wide unmet basic needs and the concomitant growing social unrest in the black townships will compel a critical analysis of the policies the ANC has pursued since 1994.

It certainly seems that deep down Kgalema knows the delay is not just for lack of funds, but the most he will say is: 'You may very well have a point but I can see no hard evidence of it being deliberately blocked.' Refreshingly he adds: 'If we have a resident political school and there is a coherent and confident political leadership who will not feel threatened by both the cadres which are produced there and by the lecturers and teachers we get, we could develop really powerful cadres in the ANC.'

CHAPTER SIX

The Polokwane 'revolution' and its aftermath

> Our concern is not about the flow of electrons between the turbine and the switch in somebody's house. Our concern is primarily about the framework of democratic and accountable resource allocations.
>
> Trevor Manuel, keynote address to ANC meeting on electrification, 1992

Against the background of hostile and debilitating factionalist relations within the ANC between the Zuma and Mbeki camps, which climaxed at the Polokwane elective conference, Kgalema became the presidential candidate of choice after Mbeki's resignation. First he helped to smooth the transition from Mbeki's presidency to that of Zuma and thereafter he became Zuma's deputy president. This chapter examines Kgalema's role in the Polokwane conference and its aftermath, including his deployment to parliament and the presidency.

Personalities *vs* policy at Polokwane
By the time of the ANC's 52nd national conference in Polokwane in December 2007, the socioeconomic side of the ANC's national democratic revolution left much to be desired. This mattered most to the poor black majority. They had secured a whole range of impressive political rights since 1994 but lacked

decent jobs, a living wage and adequate housing, among other things. Basic services such as water and electricity supply were so weak they had spawned radical social movements in protest, as we have seen.

Constitutional rights had not led to these material gains because of a budgetary constraint in the Constitution and the ANC's neoliberal policies after 1994.[1] Neoliberalism had begun just months after the 1994 elections, long before Gear in 1996, with the White Paper of November 1994 on water supply and sanitation requiring people to pay for these services even though racial capitalism had impoverished the black majority. The RDP White Paper, also of November 1994, stressed fiscal discipline and thereby eventually emasculated it, as earlier noted.[2] But clearly the seeds of Polokwane were sown when Gear was adopted in 1996: year in and year out since then, the centre of conflict within the tripartite alliance was the ANC government's economic policies. There was a clear and direct link between the fierce defence of these policies by the government and the simultaneous centralisation of power within the presidency, which wittingly or unwittingly tended to stultify criticisms by the left both outside and especially inside the ANC alliance.

The run-up to the Polokwane conference occurred alongside these devastating social inequalities, which silently defined how important the conference was. The build-up, in which Thabo Mbeki was pitted against Jacob Zuma for the post of ANC president and hence the country, was such a political drama that this context hardly featured in the campaigns. Matters of policy, far more of a priority, were eclipsed by the gigantic head-to-head battle. The sheer vitriol of the contest, which included pro-Zuma supporters burning T-shirts bearing pictures of Mbeki, made it likely that there would be problems at the conference and thereafter, and that they would not be about policy.[3]

Kgalema Motlanthe

Many people have said that Kgalema was included in both the Zuma and Mbeki lists, and the media have created the impression that everyone listed had given their blessing to being there. He says he was never asked to be on either list because everyone knew he was totally opposed to them, whatever opportunities they held for him. Here again, he recognised only the legitimate nomination lists coming from the branches. 'I have always been opposed to a divisive and factionalist politics and this is widely known in the ANC because my role as SG was to deal with such organisational divisions. ... Agreeing to be on any factional lists outside of that which issues from our constitutional structures, the branches, I will not do, because once you do that you get involved in and in fact promote factionalism.'

The unruly behaviour of many delegates at the start of the conference underlined the fact that voting was about personalities and factionalism. Mosiuoa Lekota, then chairperson of the ANC, was so heckled and booed that he could do nothing to restore calm. The protesters were boisterous Zuma supporters who identified Lekota as pro-Mbeki and thus in the enemy camp. At this fragile moment, when tempers threatened to derail proceedings, Kgalema took to the podium. Once he began to speak there was instant quiet.[4] For many observers he was the star of the show. Steven Friedman, for one, saw his authority over the four thousand delegates: 'Motlanthe did not really set the world alight before Polokwane, but after it he really emerged as a big leader. It's since then that I thought he could be quite an effective leader.'[5] Adam Habib says that his intervention was 'smart, mature and in fact very statesmanlike under the circumstances.'[6]

Kgalema comments mildly on how he reined in the meeting: 'All I did was to properly interpret the ANC's constitution, specifically the rules of conference, nothing more. It was based on my duties as secretary-general in terms of the constitution of the ANC.' He is far more forceful on the crowd's behaviour. 'In my report to the NEC I did say that members of the NEC went against their own guidelines and therefore the NEC itself was to blame for what went wrong both before and at the chaotic start of the conference. I appealed for a period of renewal at the conference after all the factionalist bloodletting in the run-up to the conference but what happened instead? We had a triumphalist faction, driven not by the ethos of renewal of the ANC but by labelling people they did not like as "Mbeki-ites", and that is the burden we still had long after Polokwane.'

Kgalema's report to conference

Kgalema delivered his last report as SG of the ANC with a profoundly deep sense of its history, which included its leading role in the struggle for national liberation but also its worrying organisational and political problems after 1994.[7] The tenor of his report was that unless these matters were confronted head on, the ANC's interests and future would be even more severely compromised. Predictably, since the ANC is multi-class, little or nothing was said about its chronic crisis being largely because of this very character.[8] Despite this limitation his report will probably go down in ANC and South African history as one of the most powerful ever. It was much more forthright than his previous ones about problems facing the ANC, covering the most serious issues the ANC had faced since coming to power, those between 2002 and 2007.

For a conference that had been so unruly at the start, Kgalema's first reflections were salutary, as Thebe Mabanga says: 'Motlanthe's opening struck a philosophical note, briefly elevating himself and taking everyone with him, above the bickering and politicking of the past few months. He reminded members of their commitment made at the last conference to be "living bearers of 90 years of struggle of the ANC" and implied with subtlety that anyone upon whom history confers such status does not conduct themselves with the mudslinging that has characterised the opposing camps in this campaign.'[9]

On the organisation, Kgalema did not spare the NEC, the NWC, the officials, the provinces and even the branches, and by implication Mbeki himself. Besides his usual targets such as careerism and self-enrichment he pinpointed the swathe of weaknesses behind the chief problems for the ANC and its alliance with the SACP and Cosatu since 2002. He also castigated the NEC for its lack of involvement in mass work and building the ANC and about ineffective deployments. His main focus was on the major problems between Stellenbosch and Polokwane: the dramatic events of 2005, especially Mbeki's dismissal of Zuma and its cataclysmic consequences for the ANC, the government and the country.[10]

Here he dwelt on what was probably the biggest problem then – factionalism – which arguably lay behind the email saga, the dismissal of Zuma and the many ugly anti-Mbeki scenes during campaigning before Polokwane. On the one hand he said, 'The ANC is not, has never been and will never be a faction', and on the other, 'When elected leaders at the highest level openly engage in factionalist activity, where is the movement that aims to unite the people of South Africa?' Going further: 'When the members of the NEC engage in factionalist activity, media leaks and rumour-mongering, how can we expect the membership of our movement to carry out their duties to observe discipline, behave honestly and carry out loyally the decision of the majority and the decision of higher bodies?'[11] Finally, 'When lists favoured by a chosen grouping are rammed down the throats of branches, without the benefit of political discussion, where is the ANC?'[12]

The Polokwane 'revolution' and its aftermath

'Where is the ANC?' That was the poignant question many remembered. It lay at the heart of his concern with what was happening in and to the party. For the first time, someone in the leadership squarely criticised those in the most powerful ANC structure, the NEC itself. When he declared that 'elected leaders at the highest level openly engage in factionalist activity' he was directly challenging the most senior leaders.

He contrasted their cruxes with the legacy of the old ANC greats: 'All of us have a duty to criticise ourselves and measure our conduct against the benchmarks set by our forebears, including JB Marks, Moses Kotane, Chief Luthuli, Dr Dadoo, Oliver Tambo, Walter Sisulu, Bram Fischer, Lilian Ngoyi, Ray Alexander, Govan Mbeki, Reg September and Nelson Mandela. All of us must reassess our contribution to building on the values and organisational practices that we have inherited from their sterling contribution. All of us have a duty to rectify our own behaviour and conduct, so that it meets the standards set by our forebears and the expectations of the generations that are yet to follow us.'[13]

Kgalema's report does not explain how the ANC's policy shifts between 1990 and 1996 perhaps influenced the deviating conduct he condemns. Very seldom will you find ANC leaders doing so. It means confronting what happened at a critical policy level. Two key documents, the Freedom Charter and the original RDP, suffice to show the divergences, somersaults and emasculation that occurred afterwards (but without addressing the structural and policy issues it is impossible to 'rectify our own behaviour and conduct, so that it meets the standards set by our forebears', as Kgalema put it).[14]

On the alliance and mass democratic movement structures,[15] he talked at length about the structural problems between the ANC and its allies and a serious lack of communication and coordination, but little on the huge policy differences, which lie at the root of the tensions and divisions in the alliance since 1994 and largely explain the chronic divisions that flare up so often.[16]

The report also does not explain – in fact the ANC has never explained – how it is possible that neither the policy institute nor the political school has yet got off the ground at national level.[17] In the words of the report:

> The ANC's 1997 and 2002 conferences passed resolutions calling for the establishment of an ANC Policy Institute. The role of the Policy Institute is to determine the extent to which ANC policies are implemented in the different spheres of the operations as well as to review the performance of the cadres deployed there. In addition it would act as a think-tank that could propose shifts in policy and evaluate the impact of government implementation. The physical infrastructure for the policy institute has been procured. However, to date the operationalization of the institute has been thwarted by resource constraints.'[18]

As we have noted, it is highly unlikely this is due to lack of funds.

Many years ago William Gumede stated: 'Motlanthe readily admits to limited ANC involvement in policy making, saying the party lacks capacity and resources to come up with policies or to effectively monitor them.'[19] Pressed hard, Kgalema finally gave me another response: 'Perhaps they don't want it, in the same way that the political school is perhaps not wanted, it seems. It does seem that every effort to establish these bodies has been thwarted. But most of our problems will be sorted out if they are established and work well.' He seems to hint here that the ANC may be concerned about possible consequences these institutions could have on the ANC and its allies, especially in combination. Whatever the ANC has said about a common programme cementing its alliance with the SACP and Cosatu is simply mistaken and misleading. The programme of a political party would be derived from its common principles and policies, but it is impossible to have a common programme between organisations with serious policy differences.

What did Polokwane really represent?

There have been many analyses of the significance of Polokwane, from overestimating to underestimating its radical political and policy potential. Karima Brown says that 'to a certain degree Polokwane was a leftist turn but that Steven Friedman sees nothing left in it when it certainly had more leftist content and potential than Mafikeng and Stellenbosch.'[20] Kgalema seems to agree with Friedman: 'Anybody who claims Polokwane was a revolution whose gains have to be defended against the "1996 class project" is both exaggerating and misrepresenting what happened there for their own agendas. It was an ordinary elective conference.'

Maybe he is right to minimise the significance in this way – and yet it *was* significant that the voice of ordinary members prevailed over factionalist attempts to manipulate them to vote for Mbeki or Zuma. Kgalema himself stressed that the majority of mandated delegates in their own interests removed a leader many said was very powerful, even unstoppable. Polokwane also showed that a national president with all the advantages of his position can be defeated by members of the ruling party. This was a victory for ordinary people, though their own class interests and needs did not feature much in the process. In this sense it looked to the development of a grassroots politics and even the resurgence of wider civil society.[21]

Did Polokwane really radicalise the ANC in some ways? Two months after the conference, Kgalema seemed to think so: 'The radicalisation in the ANC is a reflection of the reality of the country at the moment and should be welcomed.'[22] Here he was not referring to actual policy shifts but more to the mood in the ANC at and immediately after the conference. He felt that invaluable space for debate opened up after Polokwane, even if very unevenly. 'However, we still sit with similar problems as we did before. Power, for example, is still concentrated in cabinet.' The latter point is important; what has transpired after Polokwane, especially after the 2009 elections, does seem to bear this out. Cosatu's complaints alone indicate as much.[23]

For Mark Gevisser, 'Polokwane has come to stand, in the South African lexicon, as a turning point almost as significant as Nelson Mandela's 1994 victory and the transition to democracy.'[24] In hindsight we can confidently say that though it was significant in several ways, this and so much other euphoria elsewhere was seriously misplaced. Other than Mbeki's removal from ANC power – which in any case was largely expected following the ANC's provincial results a month before – Polokwane was not the political tectonic shift that many claimed at the time. That would have meant policy to change the lives of the poor black majority, not just a change of leadership and greater space for debates, important though these are.

About parliament itself Kgalema seemed encouraged: 'Self-confidence levels are a bit higher now. Before, MPs could not assert themselves because top leaders could easily pull rank. It will no longer be possible for a cabinet minister to simply wear an NEC cap and say we'll discuss this matter in the NEC and thereby control things.'[25] Not long before he took over from Mbeki he captured the character of the ANC after 1994: 'The ANC is both a national liberation movement and a ruling party:

it's about the management of that relationship. A liberation movement must always be with the people, take its cue from them and represent them. On the other hand governing parties tend to govern with a top-down approach, and in the ANC the challenge has always been to strike a correct balance between these two spheres.'[26] But the balance of control has certainly been in favour of a government whose economic and social policies have not really prioritised the black working class, for decades the majority constituency of the ANC.

Attempts by the SACP and Cosatu to make the policy resolutions at Polokwane look like a revolutionary breakthrough may have been strategic, to justify their past and continued alliance with the ANC in the teeth of criticism from the independent left and others, and also to signal to their conservative detractors in the ANC that they were gaining ground. But events since then have not measured up to idea, as Hein Marais concludes: 'In key respects, the succession battle was an undignified jostle for positions, leverage and influence. Individuals who had been slighted, wounded or marginalised during the Mbeki years now found common purpose with "comrades" nursing old grudges, those whose entrepreneurial or political ambitions had been thwarted, whose ineptitude or greed had upended their careers or those who had been shut out for politics or principles.'[27] Neither in the run-up to Polokwane nor at the conference itself were there any contentious policy debates.

The elections

Many have argued that Mbeki should not have stood for the presidency of the ANC in Polokwane. The *Financial Mail* said: 'His biggest mistake was to stand for election in the first place. Mbeki and his acolytes argue that no-one else from his camp is strong enough to defeat Zuma. The opposite is true. Countless

ANC leaders in parliament and the provinces say they will vote for Zuma because they want Mbeki removed.'[28] The *Financial Mail* went further to suggest that 'Mbeki's critics say his failure to see the outcome is due to personality flaws, including an arrogance which has blind-sided him time and again. Says one: "He never imagined ANC members could choose a peasant from Nkandla above him, with all his accomplishments and intellectual prowess."' The way I see Mbeki, the latter suggestion might very well be true, but this was his response: 'There were many ANC members who said to me that we may very well lose in Polokwane but the problem is that we are quite certain from what comrades could see that what we are going to have coming out of Polokwane is a bad leadership. And if you don't stand the world will say, "If only you stood we would not have had this outcome", so you must stand even if we lose, because we cannot just step aside.'[29]

Mbeki's supporters also alleged that fraud was committed in the nomination process and complained about it to the NEC before the conference. They said that Kgalema 'allowed regional officials who don't have voting rights at conference to vote in the provincial general council meetings.'[30] Kgalema contemptuously dismisses this allegation as probable bitterness in advance of the likely defeat of Mbeki through a proper process.

The electoral results of the provincial conferences over the weekend of 24–25 November 2007 already indicated that Zuma would probably defeat Mbeki: most provinces and branch delegates were opposed to a third term for him. But not even these results convinced the liberal media, who thought that Mbeki in particular was too smart to lose to the less cerebral Zuma. Marais says: 'Even as proceedings got under way in Polokwane, Mbeki's supporters clung to the belief that he would survive Zuma's challenge. Hardly any observers shared their optimism.'³¹ But some in the white-dominated liberal media also still thought Mbeki would win, or rather, wanted him to win. Not that they liked him – he focused too much for their liking on race and made them feel not only complicit with the apartheid past but that they continued to benefit after 1994 as a result of it. Myself, I believe they were scared of Zuma and his comrades in the SACP and Cosatu, seeing them as spectres of communism. In Moe Shaik's view, 'I think the media missed the depth of JZ's support, because they spent too much time analysing their own fears and prejudices. They were too busy with their own worries about "what will happen if JZ becomes president."'³² In the same article Shaik says, 'Journalists never understood the enormous fury that swept through ANC members when Mbeki fired Zuma. Journalists did not understand how difficult and painful that was for the ANC rank and file', a point Kgalema's report to Polokwane endorsed: 'The leaders, members and supporters of the ANC were, understandably, greatly pained by the events leading up to the NGC. It is a pain that each and every individual feels most acutely.'³³

There was another reason why the white-dominated liberal media hoped fervently that Mbeki would win, the same man they had castigated on race, HIV/Aids, Zimbabwe and much more: Zuma's closeness to the SACP and Cosatu threatened the country and their interests with radical economic policies. So for the media it was not just a backward, homophobic, singing and dancing peasant from Nkandla that worried them but his communist allies who imperilled capitalism and their class interests. That was the subtext.³⁴

Kgalema's election as deputy president was probably as certain as the election of Zuma as president was.³⁵ At Polokwane he beat Nkosazana-Dlamini Zuma, who stood on Mbeki's list. This was an indication that Zuma's supporters highly appreciated the fact that Kgalema had stood by Zuma in his darkest hour, when Mbeki fired him. After Zuma was fired and charged in June 2005 his supporters began to indicate that if he ran into legal difficulties from the court case they would vote for Kgalema to replace Mbeki at Polokwane.[36] No doubt his ten years as SG and his dependable work ethic counted too. He was also valued for not joining in the mudslinging that had become rife in the ANC. Mandela has said that 'Kgalema Motlanthe is one of the best men we have in this country. He never gets involved in conspiracies against his colleagues.'[37]

Kgalema firmly denies that he played the 'biggest role behind the scenes', as Karima Brown holds, in defeating Mbeki's attempt to win the presidency for the third time.[38] 'No, she is wrong. The only thing I did was to try to ensure that the members of the ANC exercised their right to choose their leaders. I did not care who they voted for in fact, just as long as all delegates understood their rights and that they were properly mandated by their branches, because once you have leaders who campaign that is the surest way of causing divisions in the organisation. It is only branch members who have the right to nominate leading candidates.'

Would Zuma have contested and won the presidency of the ANC and thereafter become the president of South Africa if he had not been fired by Mbeki in 2005? This is a mostly ignored but basic question. Just because Zuma was Mbeki's deputy this did not mean he would automatically succeed him in Polokwane, any more than that Kgalema will inevitably succeed Zuma in Mangaung. But it appears that Kgalema could have emerged as a major contender for the presidency in Polokwane if the trajectory after Zuma's dismissal had not occurred. The confluence of some important factors, some inspired less by support for Zuma than an intense desire to replace Mbeki, brought Zuma to power. Presidential interests of Tokyo Sexwale and even Cyril Ramaphosa – both of whom had for many years been immersed in the business world – might well have stood less of a chance if Kgalema had emerged as a contender. His decade as SG of the ANC would probably have been a major point in his favour, and his close relations with the branches, which hold the key to elections, could have tilted a closely fought contest his way. As I see it, the ANCYL and Cosatu as two major constituencies of the ANC alliance would have chosen him against Sexwale, Ramaphosa and even Zuma. But Zuma was fired and the rest is history.

Adam Habib believes that if Kgalema had stood in Polokwane he would have had a good chance of winning a sizeable percentage of votes, because many in the ANC alliance were looking for a third option. Many of Mbeki's supporters could have been swayed his way, Habib says – but only if they had a sense that Mbeki was bound to lose against Zuma. This could even have swung the vote in Kgalema's favour, though probably only by a whisker.[39] All this is borne out by the fact that Zuma received 2329 votes to Mbeki's 1505 – a comfortable victory but Zuma certainly did not demolish Mbeki. Kgalema, however, dismisses the idea entirely. He says it was virtually a Mbeki–Zuma two-horse race all through 2007, especially after Sexwale had withdrawn.

If Kgalema had stood for the presidency and Mbeki had withdrawn because he did not think he could beat Zuma and his supporters instead threw in their lot with Kgalema, then it was quite possible he would have defeated Zuma. But Kgalema is probably right in discounting the idea that he could have stood then, because Mbeki and Zuma were both so determined. Also, Mbeki and his supporters really believed they could defeat Zuma, though less so after hearing the provincial results in

231

November. Yet Gordin claims that two days before Polokwane Mbeki told a journalist that 'it would never happen' that ANC members would elect Zuma as president.[40] He does not give details but Mbeki's overly confident prediction is quite likely, since in my interview with him later he said that he and his supporters had underestimated what they were up against in Polokwane: 'We were not quite conscious of the serious and systematic work which had taken place until it was too late.'[41]

Post-Polokwane blues

Zuma's triumphant bliss lasted just a couple of days after Polokwane. Then charges against him were reinstated by the NPA. Within a few days of the conference, Mbeki provocatively went ahead to appoint a new SABC (South African Broadcasting Corporation) board that Cosatu and others strongly criticised. To crown it all, Mbeki failed to attend the ANC's annual January 8th statement,[42] a key annual event in its calendar. Kgalema did not mention Mbeki's actions to me, but they certainly must have contributed to the bad blood, as factions continued and in some ways intensified.

As for the Zuma faction, it soon became clear that they were acting on the same lines they had accused Mbeki and his cabinet of using before he was forced to resign. There was a pervasive sense that they had turned the tables on him and would stay in charge and that the axis of power had shifted decisively from the Mbeki presidency to Luthuli House.

Kgalema was deeply concerned with early signs that things were not going well after the conference and that the factionalist politics in the run-up to it would continue, he told me. This did not augur well for either the ANC or the government. He sensed that Mbeki and his supporters were still reeling from their defeat in Polokwane and some of them were probably bitter as a result, and that the victors were somewhat overconfident, too triumphalist and with not a small dose of arrogance and vindictiveness, even after Mbeki had lost. Moves within Luthuli House after Polokwane to unseat premiers said to be close to Mbeki worried him most because they were driven by the same factionalist manoeuvring and vices the Zuma-ites had accused Mbeki of not long before. If the period before Polokwane left him very worried about the state of affairs in the organisation he had dedicated his life to, then the period after Polokwane was not much better.

Increasingly, post-Polokwane soon stopped being what the victors over Mbeki had envisaged. Vavi soon began to express his dismay at some developments. Kgalema, who is close to and fond of Vavi, sees his growing disquiet thus: 'When Vavi said that unlike when we[43] were united at Polokwane we are now showing divisions, I said that was not real unity because we were united as a lobby group and not as a movement. After I had elaborated on this point, to his credit he thanked me for clarifying an important point which was a bit grey for him.'

Contrary to so much media assertion, Kgalema was never really in the Zuma camp before, at or after Polokwane. He knew the weaknesses of Mbeki and his cabinet and how undesirably they operated at times but he also had serious misgivings about several leading figures in the Zuma camp, having seen a lot of opportunism in their own interests. Contrary to some perceptions, he was never uncritically anywhere at any time. 'For me the conduct of ANC leaders after Polokwane was very important because we declared that renewal would be the key overriding theme going forward. But even after Polokwane many were still labelling some people as Mbeki-ites.' This told him that they did not understand what the main problems were in the run-up to Polokwane and seemed keen to blame problems on mere personalities and related skulduggery and brinkmanship without looking at both existing policy differences and why the former tended to overshadow the latter.

> Many in what was called the 'Zuma camp' did not clearly understand what really was wrong with the previous leadership, because if they really did understand, they would not in fact be repeating many of the problems committed by the previous leaders. With the earlier leadership, when they manoeuvred and were wrong in this or that, you could invoke the constitution, pull them into line and they would back off, but the leadership after Polokwane were extremely triumphalist and did not really listen when you invoked the constitution, instead they thought you don't understand power. For them the form and manifestation of the problem was simple: Zuma was victimised and we lined up behind him and removed Mbeki. But they failed to understand that other than and independent of this problem there were many other accompanying problems. It reminded me of what Mandela once said: a crisis or chaos can give rise to a leadership which is ill-suited to solve the problems and in fact can worsen them.

Kgalema knew well all the actors in this political standoff between Mbeki and Zuma and one way or another had worked with most of them. One of his biggest concerns was with the conduct of national office bearers, who constitutionally had far more responsibility than NEC members. It made him ask himself: what did Polokwane really produce? Media reports also suggested strongly that there was not a lot of trust among all the officials and the NEC members.

Despite all, Kgalema was confident that the ANC was big and durable enough not to fall apart:

This is because the greatest defenders and protectors of the ANC are its ordinary members. They are the eyes and ears of the ANC. Then you will have those in the various levels of the organisation who understand the cause and are committed to it. It is in tough times like these that they will serve to reinforce an understanding of our cause and commitment, which includes correcting those who go astray and clarifying matters to those who are stumbling along, because at the end of it all it is those same members who will have to elect a new leadership. The membership may seem passive at other times, but once conference convenes they become delegates with the power to both elect new leaders and to change what they don't like.

Is ANC deployment a myth?

At Mafikeng the SG's report stated that 'the ANC needs to urgently develop a deployment strategy for its cadres' and believed that 'a successful deployment strategy will greatly enhance the transformation process.'[44] It spoke of competition for positions and that 'election to an ANC leadership position is viewed as a stepping stone to positions of power and material reward within government.'[45] In the same conference Mandela himself, in his presidential report, warned: 'If we have learnt nothing else during these past three years, we have grown to appreciate the extent of the corrosion of the moral fibre of our society.'[46]

An NEC meeting in early 2008 eventually mandated Kgalema to both chair a new deployment committee (DC) and make proposals for its membership. Later that year, in the NWC meeting to discuss the new DC, he found the Polokwane spirit of renewal seriously violated. Some NWC members, such as Malema, rejected the names proposed for the committee and instead put their own names forward. I strongly objected and said that what they were doing was completely wrong and unacceptable. ... I thought it was very important to nip in the bud the practice of advancing certain people into positions on the DC. It was a very dangerous manifestation and I told them that I will never allow NWC members to nominate themselves onto the DC. They were taking out people like Trevor Manuel and Mohammed Valli Moosa and putting themselves there. I accused them of behaving in a factionalist manner.[47]

Kgalema set about putting the NWC discussion on constructive lines:

I insisted on a political discussion so that we can understand what we mean by deployment, the criteria for it and so on. 'Deployment' is in a sense a misnomer because we are in fact far from having properly and clearly defined the principles and objective criteria upon which such a committee must be based. What we have is a distortion and misrepresentation of deployment. It should not be called deployment. It should perhaps be called placement because 'deployment' has come to suggest a more serious, systematic and political approach to placing people in jobs. Such an important and strategic committee cannot afford to be influenced by lobbying and factionalist politics.

I told them that who gets deployed must not be based on who you know but on objectively determined criteria and procedure, which we have none of. In fact we should only deploy people who have the necessary skills and experience and are truly committed to the ANC and its work. We absolutely have to put an end to deploying members of the ANC who don't measure up to what is required but mainly happen to know senior cadres of the ANC or government officials.

We also therefore need to ask this key question every time we deploy someone, no matter who it is: 'Are those people truly skilled and equipped to carry out the tasks effectively and efficiently?' The strategic goal of a united, nonracial and nonsexist democracy has implications for deployment. It must inform our approach to the work of the DC in a more systematic and professional manner. In fact this is a shell of a committee we would be better off without. We have not even properly understood the capacity that would be required to have such a committee really working effectively.

Probably realising that his critical approach to these deployment issues was correct, the DC has tried repeatedly to get Kgalema more involved but his work pressures have not allowed him to. He has only been able to chair a few of the meetings, for lack of time.

He has clear views on what its role should be. They are probably a bit controversial for the ANC and certainly not what the media seem to think.[48] Deployment, he says, is not generally well understood. The ANC gets involved in deploying only the cadres for political heads, as for ministerial and director-general posts, he says. Even then, there is still a fairly rigorous process for candidates.[49] A big concern for him is that the DC's powers have been grossly exaggerated.[50] The committee itself has had so many problems that no serious, systematic cadre development seems to have occurred yet and it is hardly functioning today. Kgalema now thinks it should be either disbanded or fundamentally reviewed.

Understandably, the main focus in the media has been the widespread public complaints about poor performance of government departments, parastatals and much of the broad public sector as a result of a serious lack of skill and experience in those the ANC deployed to jobs at various levels. Many cases have been published linking these problems to charges of cronyism and corruption in the government and wider public sector.

Kgalema himself has long been worried about cadre employment.[51] Many under-equipped ANC members have been placed in senior jobs at fat salaries. Serious staffing problems exist in every government department. (Ahmed Kathrada has told me in exasperation: 'They are often a bunch of incompetents, I tell you.') In some cases all they had was membership of the ANC, some 'struggle' credentials and connections to the top decision makers on deployment. This is why for a few years Kgalema has emphasised in public speeches that we must use the best available talents, wherever they are. True, it is high time to move away from a narrow ANC-oriented cadre-deployment policy that has ignored skilled and even highly qualified people who were not 'African' or not ANC members, as he indicates here:

> It is important to get the country to understand that we need the best available talent to come to the fore because many people don't even apply because they are members of the DA or other parties and they say, 'Why even bother to apply because they won't even consider me.' But this is not only an ANC problem because the DA in the Western Cape is replacing people left, right and centre, precisely on the same basis.
>
> You must know that you have an equal chance for a post that requires skills and experience you possess and you must also commit to serve to the best of your ability regardless of who the political head is. The ANC needs to understand that the transformation of the apartheid state must reach a point soon where we target and reach out to the professionals regardless.

And no doubt this merit-driven approach (which also means being nonracial) should extend beyond professional classes to include all other skilled workers.

Kgalema under fire

Another serious matter after Polokwane concerned Kgalema directly. He has had a close but complex relationship with then embattled ANCYL leader Julius Malema and the league. After Kgalema's principled stand in the NWC meeting on the membership of the DC, some people in the ANCYL and the Young Communist League mobilised against him. Although the concerted public attacks on him by the ANCYL in particular in August 2008 purported to be only about his defence of the judiciary when they were challenging its institutions, targeting him also had much to do with what happened in the NWC meeting.

Media coverage included the *City Press* reporting that 'the ANCYL said Motlanthe behaved like a paragon of political correctness who is beyond reproach', appeared to have a 'hotline' to the media, unleashed 'unmandated attacks', had a political agenda and 'behaved as if he was already president of the ANC.'[52] The ANCYL did not substantiate these accusations. Their spokesperson, Floyd Shivambu, went further: 'Going around affirming the independence of the criminal justice system in the case of the ANC president is worrisome.'[53]

Shivambu also said that Kgalema 'would not say a word against Mbeki when he was president. He was not as assertive as he's becoming recently. It looks like there's a new-found energy to speak on issues. He had the space and time to articulate and re-assert his authority as secretary-general of the ANC, but he did not do that.'[54] To me this is just opportunistic sniping. The ANCYL never once criticised Kgalema in this way while he was SG. Malema made a very different response to me: 'No, no, Kgalema is a very assertive person when he needs to be, including in ANC meetings, and he is not afraid to stand alone on any issue or against the views of the majority. I have seen him do that many times.'[55] Harking back to the NWC discussion on membership of the DC, Malema added:

> When you push him to a point where he must respond to you he can be very firm and straight in what he wants to say and what he believes in but he will never be rude to you. He takes long to get upset, but when he does you will get scared when you see that side of him. There was a time that he took me on in an NWC meeting and everyone was shocked. It was about the names that should get into the deployment committee. I had problems with certain names he was proposing. He strongly objected and took me on in the meeting. Nobody could believe it. I could see the surprise on people's faces and when I wanted to respond the person next to me said, 'No, don't do that, don't.'[56]

Malema complains that things seemed to change after Kgalema was elected deputy president in Polokwane.

> We started to get very worried in 2008 when he started to say and do things which were very much out of character with the SG leader we knew. If we said something in the media he responded critically without even talking to us. We were seeing something we had never seen in him before, because in the past he would always try to understand why we said or did certain things. He was always this cool-headed leader who we could go to with anything and he always tried to understand where we were coming from before criticising us. After Polokwane

he was just lambasting us and not ready to listen and engage like before. But we did have a meeting about these matters and agreed comradely and amicably to engage with one another and not just accept as true what media reports say, whether it is us commenting about him or him responding to things we have said. As a result nobody can come to us and badmouth Kgalema or want to coerce us into a plot to undermine the deputy president of the ANC. That we will never do or allow.[57]

It does seem, however, that it was after the heated altercation in the NWC about the DC that the ANCYL suddenly found a lot wrong with Kgalema. Before then they had had a good and even warm relationship with him. No serious problems existed between the ANCYL and him until they launched their blistering attack in 2008.

Kgalema deployed to parliament

There had been media speculation soon after the Polokwane conference that the ANC wanted Kgalema to be deployed to parliament and the presidency to 'smooth the transition' to the Zuma administration. Luthuli House, fresh from the euphoric victory over Mbeki in Polokwane, was calling the shots in the months that followed and was certainly not shy to assert its new, if somewhat shaky, authority. There was clearly a sense that the triumphant Zuma faction did not quite trust they would get the wholehearted support of Mbeki's cabinet in facilitating the transition, especially since it was to stay in power for nearly another eighteen months until the 2009 elections. If a week is a long time in politics, then well over a year under those circumstances was far too long for Zuma and his supporters to wait for the elections and the power he would assume then. They had to create a political and institutional foothold to keep the Mbeki cabinet somehow in check and counterbalance the overwhelming support Mbeki still held in the executive.

Mantashe told the media after a national executive committee meeting: 'As part of managing the transition we agreed as the national executive committee that he [Motlanthe] should be deployed in government and in the executive.'[58] Naturally, the ANC could not speak publicly about any underlying fears it might have had and the deeper rationale for wanting to place Kgalema in government. But in his recently released book *Eight Days in September*, Chikane confirms that the underlying rationale was precisely that Luthuli House did not trust the Mbeki presidency and felt it could scupper things in the run-up to the 2009 elections.[59]

Certain developments – notably the NDPP laying charges against Zuma just three days after Polokwane, Mbeki's appointment of the controversial SABC board and his failure to attend the 2008 January 8th statement – clearly indicated that there was ongoing bad blood between the factions. There was definitely a sense of unease, unhappiness and even vindictiveness in the air after these acts, which may well have fuelled the antagonism that continued and probably worsened until Mbeki resigned in September 2008.

The ANC chose Kgalema not only because he was the ANC's deputy president but they needed somebody on the new NEC whom both factions trusted more than anyone else. The Mbeki cabinet did not have a hostile relationship with him even though there was a sense in Mbeki's camp that Kgalema had either disappointed or betrayed him by coming to the defence of Zuma and that, if he had not, Zuma would have been finished off after Mbeki fired him. All in all, he was widely considered the best person in the ANC to do the job at a very difficult, in fact fragile, moment in the ANC, government and the wider society, especially with his tenacious ability to mediate between the still-warring groups. The Zuma camp also knew very well that Mbeki and his followers had a lot of respect for Kgalema; if there was anybody they would cooperate with, it would be him.

Kgalema was deeply and for a while unswervingly opposed to moving to parliament.[60] He argued that if he was regularly briefed and interacted with the presidency and parliament to help smooth the transition, he did not actually need to be deployed to parliament or later the cabinet: 'If the sole purpose is to gain insight into the workings of government, could that not be gained simply by scheduled sessions with the director-general, with the president and others? Does it necessarily have to be gained by one going into cabinet?'[61] He went further to question the whole notion of Mbeki and Zuma camps: 'I don't know about "camps". The media has blown up this thing about camps. There are no homogeneous camps. Even within these camps there can be many differences about many things.'[62] If at the time his view was questionable, what happened between Polokwane and the 2009 elections has made it abundantly clear that he was right.

He had a further objection: 'I believed the ANC would be setting a wrong precedent, which says that once you have been elected at conference into a leadership position you have the right to be accommodated in the government, which is largely why I thought the whole politics of it is wrong – because down the line such precedents could be followed by the provinces and regions, and how then would the top leadership guide those people when among them a precedent has been set for that to happen?'

In the end the NEC's reasons prevailed. He became an MP on 20 May 2008. This was the result of a great deal of pressure the NEC placed on Mbeki to admit him as a minister into his cabinet. The expressed purpose for his becoming an MP was that it was the first necessary step to being appointed by Mbeki as a minister.[63] Some seven weeks later, on 12 July 2008, Kgalema was appointed minister and sworn in. He did discuss with Mbeki and the director-general, Frank Chikane, his reservations on going into government. Mbeki understood fully, he says, but they decided that it was 'best to just do it.'[64] He had no complaints about anything after he became an MP and, two months later, a minister. 'I was warmly received in parliament and in the cabinet, which, together with the fact that I knew everybody well there, helped orientate me a lot.'

Many in the media did not seem to realise that going to parliament and cabinet was not an intimidating experience for him at all. 'What people also don't know, perhaps, is that after an election, when Cabinet members are appointed, and the president speaks to them, one on one, I sit in on these meetings because it is the ANC that contests elections, it is the ANC that wins elections and it is the ANC that appoints ministers, otherwise I would not have authority over them.'[65] In the event, he only spent just over two months as a minister before he was elected president of South Africa on 25 September, following Mbeki's resignation.[66]

While an MP, Kgalema had a brush with Malema that the media made a great deal of. Malema had said at a June 16 commemoration rally, in Zuma's presence, that the ANCYL 'would kill for Zuma'.[67] Kgalema's response in a media interview was that this remark was 'intemperate and reckless'.[68] When the ANCYL rejected this and the fact that he had publicised his reaction, Kgalema emphasised that it was practically impossible and politically unnecessary for a leader to refuse to respond to media questions before consulting Malema or ANC officials. 'Why would I be in leadership if I have to each time first consult before I respond to the media?' Kgalema had taken the stand on principle, unimpressed by ANCYL fealty to the newly elected president of the ANC because it was uttered as a threat, and unconcerned about perhaps making himself unpopular.[69] Kgalema was to have many other encounters with Malema later on, as we shall see, responding in this same direct, measured way and not angling for political advantage.

A striking fact to end this section with is that Gwede Mantashe has had a more visible and firmer public profile since taking over from Kgalema as SG at Polokwane. It is quite likely that Mantashe was more in the media in 2008 alone than Kgalema had been over the entire five-year term from Stellenbosch to Polokwane, turbulent time though it was. Why? Kgalema is much more carefully considered than Mantashe tends to be. He will not think twice but five times before he makes statements or calls press conferences. Secondly, he has probably never once shot from the hip and been visibly upset at press conferences, being guided by protocol and his own judicious restraint, whereas Mantashe can readily tell a journalist where to get off. Personalities aside, the new political dynamics at and after Polokwane have put Mantashe far more into the public spotlight, as Kgalema says, adding that 'the media are much more into the ANC than before Polokwane.' In another context William Gumede remarked that the one thing he has noticed about Kgalema over the years is that he tends not to want to take risks and that it could be a problem – sometimes a leader needs to take calculated risks to get results.[70] But there is little doubt that Kgalema has become less overly cautious since taking over from Mbeki, probably because the different terrain of government demands it.

The Nicholson judgment and Mbeki's recall

On 12 September 2008 Judge Chris Nicholson delivered a judgment in the Pietermaritzburg High Court that was to shake post-apartheid South African politics like nothing before. His ruling had nothing to do with whether or not Zuma was guilty of the charges he faced, but rested on two other points. He found that the NPA had not 'given Zuma a chance to make representations before deciding to charge him, as is required by the constitution read in conjunction with the NPA Act.'[71] Nicholson also found that the Mbeki-led executive appeared to have interfered in the prosecutorial process and committed other acts that were 'indicative of political interference, pressure or influence'.[72] He therefore found the charges against Zuma illegal and invalid.

In the course of his finding, he held that the alleged moves by the Mbeki-led executive, particularly by Mbeki himself and the minister of justice, Penuell Maduna, were linked to the question of who the next president of the ANC would be. Here Nicholson concluded that Zuma had been unfairly treated and prejudiced in order to thwart any presidential aspirations he might have. Nicholson's judgment (later overturned) eventually led to the dropping of charges against Zuma a few months before the 2009 elections.

When we discussed this matter, Kgalema did not seek to assert that Zuma was innocent or guilty of the charges. He only focused on how unfairly Zuma was treated on the receiving end of the aggressive and prejudiced way the Scorpions (the investigative arm of the NPA) had acted against him, and condemned the incompetent and unprofessional way the NPA had gone about this matter. In law, procedure must obviously be fair and legal in itself for justice to be done.

Zuma's case has led to a lot of rethinking about legal process.

Billy Downer SC, the deputy director of public prosecutions in the Western Cape, speaking to an international jurist conference in 2010, addressed the decision by Mokotedi Mpshe, the then acting NDPP, to withdraw all charges against Zuma, which paved the way for him to become president of South Africa after the 2009 elections.[73] He deals with the serious limitations of relevant legislation about the authority and independence of the NPA and the NDPP. This arises because the NDPP is a presidential appointee and yet is expected to 'act independently and not take political considerations into account in making prosecutorial decisions.'[74] Downer says that 'a dichotomy arises from the fact that the NPA falls firmly within the executive arm of government and is thus subject to government policy and control, yet it exercises its functions in the judicial sphere, which requires such functions to be exercised independently of any such control.'[75]

The very fact that the ANC is the overwhelming majority party in parliament would make this dichotomy more dangerous, because the bigger the ruling party, the greater can and will be the political pressure for it to toe the line.[76] A crucial point here is that 'the central ambiguity regarding independence is contained in the provision in section 179 of the Constitution, that is, that the Minister of Justice – a political officer within the Cabinet – retains "final responsibility" over the NPA. How can the NPA possibly exercise its functions without "fear, favour, or prejudice" when this is the case?'[77]

Downer notes that a 'constitutional controversy has raged' ever since Bulelani Ngcuka, the former NDPP, decided not to prosecute Zuma in 2003, 'against the advice of two line prosecutors and indeed other members of the investigating team.'[78] The thrust of Downer's paper was to show that the decision by Ngcuka was completely wrong and that 'with hindsight Mr Ngcuka might wish that he had followed our advice.'[79]

Downer also points to other concerns that Wim Trengrove SC had raised in the Zuma case. Taped evidence was produced from people motivated by 'improper political purposes.'[80] The conversations had nothing to do with the merits and demerits of the case but only with the timing of the prosecution: 'The debate wasn't whether the NPA should prosecute or not prosecute.'[81] Mokotedi Mpshe as NDPP wrongly failed to proceed beyond the question of the possible abuse. He should have considered whether the abuse 'outweighs the competing public interest in ensuring that those who are charged with grave crimes should be tried.'[82] Finally, in a matter of such critical public importance it should have been left to the courts and not a prosecutor to decide what effect Leonard McCarthy's abuse of the process to manipulate the timing of the case had on the trial.[83] This last point is especially compelling in the light of the fact that the NDPP is appointed by the president.[84]

But it appears that if indeed there was a strong case against Zuma, it was compromised by the sheer mess the NPA made of it in a litany of errors, indiscretions, miscalculations and gung-ho arrogance. In fact this was so bad, it might even be argued that it compromised the case itself, which should thus have been abandoned. To have many serious allegations of fraud and corruption hanging over the head of the deputy president of the country and the ANC for many years without being brought to trial and resolved is itself an unacceptable persecution and intolerable burden to bear. And if the NPA could not act competently and instead allow itself to be manipulated by powerful politicians – which Nicholson alleged and for which there certainly does appear to be substantial evidence – then the institution itself is so severely compromised that a total review, reorganisation and renewal are required, from top to bottom, and from legislation to practice.[85]

The most dramatic consequence of Nicholson's judgment was Mbeki's forced resignation. A week after the judgment, on 20 September 2008, the ANC's NEC decided that Mbeki must be recalled from office immediately. The actual decision was reached in the very early hours of the next day. Trevor Manuel responded to this historic moment much as other ministers did:

> At 1.30 a.m. Derek Hanekom called to inform me that the NEC had just ended and they decided to recall Mbeki. I then decided that the right thing to do is to tender my resignation, which I sent to both Mbeki and Zuma. But I did not resign in solidarity with Mbeki. I was elected to the NEC and to parliament and had to sign nomination forms but I have no entitlement to the position of minister and have not been elected to it. You are appointed purely at the behest of the president. This is the principle I was trying to argue and, though I may have been naïve to deal with the issue as a matter of integrity, I have no regrets really.[86]

Early that day, a Saturday, Mantashe and Kgalema drove to Pretoria to break the news to Mbeki. It was not an easy thing for them to do. Mantashe, as SG, was an obvious choice as messenger. The fact that the NEC instructed Kgalema to accompany him indicated that they knew Kgalema not only had the organisational authority as deputy president but also the moral standing which the sensitivity of the crisis needed. They also knew that of all the officials it was probably Kgalema that Mbeki most respected. Mbeki received the news quite calmly and without any resistance, Kgalema says. On 21 September Mbeki tendered his resignation but by then he had already applied to the Constitutional Court to have Nicholson's judgment set aside and declared unconstitutional.[87]

Kgalema had problems with the decision to recall Mbeki: 'I felt that whatever the leadership thought about Mbeki at that point in time, it could not outweigh the need for a smooth transition from the old to the new leadership in both the party and state. In my view we could have kept him and brought the election closer, perhaps in April or even March. I think he would have agreed to that proposal and completed his term.' He felt it was a big risk. With Mbeki gone, much depended on how the ANC managed this difficult situation, including how they dealt with his profile and any further involvement he had in the ANC.

Unlike many other NEC members, Kgalema never sought to exclude Mbeki even after he decided to appeal the Nicholson judgment. In fact matters had been awry for months before the Nicholson judgment. When he was still in the cabinet and before Mbeki resigned, Kgalema told Zuma there was a serious problem because he was virtually the only one among the senior ANC leaders who spoke to Mbeki. 'I was also unhappy that after Mbeki resigned he was not kept in the loop and serviced as Mandela was when he retired. Right up to Polokwane I briefed Mandela on all important matters, but in the case of Thabo we were not treating him the same.' For Kgalema the point is that Mbeki 'was for long president of the ANC, remained in the ANC after his recall and accepted a very difficult and contentious decision and therefore cannot be made an object of permanent derision.'[88]

There were other problems Mbeki's recall created that concerned him:

> It was a huge moment and it created lots of doubt inside and outside the country about where we were going to as a country.

The Polokwane 'revolution' and its aftermath

I had to face many questions in Africa from leaders when I became president. Some African heads of state told me that the ANC is also their organisation, so how could we take such a serious decision without consulting them? I know there were those who criticised the role I played at times, but there is a big difference when you have a presidential responsibility in what was a crisis situation in South Africa. They could afford an oppositionist stance then, but in the light of the relatively stable and smooth transition we had after Mbeki's departure they wanted to claim a victory others fought for.

There was yet another point he considered about the recall, especially if it was seen as the result of accumulated failures and excesses: 'Mbeki's removal was in a sense tragic because an organisation and movement should protect you against your idiosyncratic weaknesses, especially if you are a longstanding member and a leader who has many strengths. An organisation is meant to draw out and encourage your strong points and undermine your weaknesses, because every leader has flaws.' Again we could ask in wider terms what was happening to the ANC itself that could allow Mbeki to be so domineering or to foster whatever other negative qualities were attributed to him.

Zuma did not want Mbeki to be recalled, Kgalema says, even after the Nicholson judgment alleged there was a conspiracy against him and that the minister of justice was involved. When the cabinet decided to appeal the judgment it could not do so because it was not party to the case. It could not appeal as if it were involved simply on the strength of a comment made against particular leaders by the judge, which had no legal effect anyway.[89] But, Kgalema says, the cabinet felt so strongly about the case that they still decided on the appeal and that it should be led by the head of the executive, Mbeki. 'It was then,

251

when Mbeki appealed, that Zuma felt the judgment had already concluded the matter and that therefore because he [Mbeki] was appealing he had to go.'

Kgalema describes what happened at the watershed moment when the NEC met after the cabinet decision to appeal: 'Every person spoke in the NEC of their experiences and what Mbeki subjected them to, but because you had to provide very powerful political reasons for recalling the president, none of them would be brave enough to say openly what the reasons they offered were for such a very drastic decision. But after everybody spoke it was like they did not want him to see one more day in office. The overwhelming majority decided he must go, but the officials did not speak.' Kgalema himself did not speak at the meeting that decided Mbeki's fate, but he has consistently said in our interviews that he did not think it was wise or really necessary.

What followed after Polokwane seemed to bear this out, though those who wanted Mbeki expelled would probably have no regrets. As Kgalema saw the aftermath of that conference: 'I am firmly of the view that Polokwane was no revolutionary breakthrough. There were no sharp ideological differences and debates really, but after the election results and the conference there was definitely a pervasive triumphant sense that "we are now in charge", which ironically partly led to some people being shut down for their differences with others. This behaviour no doubt contradicted the letter and spirit of renewal which the conference seemed intent on.'

Between Stellenbosch and Polokwane the debate about the 'two centres of power' became more strident, reflecting the growing conflict between Luthuli House and Mbeki's presidency. For Kgalema this was symptomatic of a larger problem afflicting the ANC and government:

The Polokwane 'revolution' and its aftermath

This notion of 'two centres of power' ... arises because of some who wanted to displace the leadership, who are ambitious for power and therefore who have an eye on going into government. The problem was also compounded by NEC members in the Mbeki government who often acted like they were much more accountable to cabinet than to the ANC and who continuously insulted our intelligence by saying that we did not understand what they were about. Increasingly they regarded structures of the ANC with contempt, up to a point where a basic truth evaded them: they were elected to the NEC by the members of the ANC, but now all of a sudden these members cannot be trusted and are instead treated like ignorant masses, who however put them in power. In fact, even after Polokwane that is still the unfortunate situation. It is just the personalities and leaders that have changed.

Personal matters

On 23 July 2008, the very day that Kgalema was to attend his first cabinet meeting as a newly appointed minister, his best friend and comrade Stan Nkosi tragically died in a clinic in Johannesburg after post-operative negligence. Kgalema rushed to the clinic at about 3 a.m. and then had to dash to the cabinet meeting in Cape Town. At the funeral he was the main speaker and in tears: 'Yes, I was very emotional and struggled to complete my speech.' Nkosi's widow Daphne says Kgalema took her husband's death very badly and what made it worse for him was that he did not have a chance to mourn because he was so busy in government.[90] Kgalema's wife Mapula chose to distance herself from the scene, which against a background of many years of unhappiness, finally ended their marriage. Media publicity and the pressures of his work had not helped the situation either.

Kgalema Motlanthe

From about 2002 Kgalema had been in a relationship with another woman, Gugu Mtshali. They had met when she worked in Cyril Ramaphosa's office when the latter was SG of the ANC and Kgalema was NUM's general secretary. Kgalema applied for a divorce from Mapula in 2010.[91] The divorce proceedings and the media stories about his relationship with Mtshali affected his relationship with his children, notably Kagiso, with whom he was very close while still at home.[92] The demands of holding the highest office in the land in 2008 and 2009 and then as deputy president meant he was unable to spend enough time with Kagiso just when he needed support most against the media stories on Kgalema's personal life. Mapula was not at his side at his inauguration as president. He was not going to pretend to himself, to her or the world that he had a marriage to speak of.

PART THREE

FROM POLOKWANE TO THE YEAR OF MANGAUNG, 2007–2012

CHAPTER SEVEN
Kgalema, third ANC president of South Africa, 2008

> In the struggle for liberation you do what you have to and can do. If you end up a leader it must be accidentally and not as a result of an ambitious goal that singularly drives you.
>
> Kgalema Motlanthe, 2009

After Zuma trumped Mbeki at Polokwane there was a power shift from the presidency to ANC headquarters at Luthuli House. Kgalema, coming in as interim state president, had to withstand what often amounted to domineering by other ANC leaders. His position was all the more difficult because he took office in the thick of the world economic crisis, for only eight months. He was also under strain from what appeared to be a campaign through smears in the media to scupper his chances of returning to government. He was definitely limited in what he would have liked to do, but he did help to stabilise a country in near-panic and made some firm decisions despite opposition, even from within the ANC.

Who really was the new leader?

When early in 2008 there was speculation that the ANC wanted Kgalema to join Mbeki's cabinet, this is how the *Financial Mail* described the situation and the man:

Amidst all the clamour from the ANC leadership for party deputy president that Kgalema Motlanthe to be promoted to a senior post in cabinet, one voice is missing: Motlanthe's. Why is he so keen to stay in the background? His politics are those of the old liberation movement where the organisation, rather than the government, is the primary force behind social transformation. Some in the ANC say Motlanthe 'still lives on the Island' – a reference to his ponderous political approach and fondness for quoting the words of ANC and communist stalwarts. Described by peers as a good historian, Motlanthe has a passion for books about the struggle that others have discarded, and he regularly reads and considers ANC history.[1]

A good description, except that it was not so much that he was 'keen to stay in the background' politically; he saw many careerists around him after 1994 who were keen to be in the foreground and had no wish to join them or be seen in that light. He was as committed as ever to the ANC, for him the heart of government and its irreplaceable foreground. He would not seek a position in government simply as his due and would only consider accepting one if ANC members nominated him. If he ended up in government, good and well.

What else? His reading, given his wider interests, extends far beyond 'books about the struggle'. Physically, as we have seen, he has always been a soccer fanatic. He is serious about fitness; he eats healthily and stays in good shape. He walks a lot, often ten to fifteen kilometres a day when he is holidaying. He is careful about everything he eats. No smoking, no alcoholic drinks, no fizzy drinks, no junk food and caffeine for him. Everything he wears expresses the man: simple and unpretentious, clean and neat, down to his Crocket & Jones shoes.

He would be comfortable discussing the history of jazz and

its cultural and social significance with the experts. He loves all kinds of jazz, especially Cuban music and the big jazz bands – Duke Ellington, Buena Vista Social Club, Ibrahim Ferrer, Ruben Gonzalez, Chris McGregor's Blue Notes, Mongezi Feza. He prefers Hugh Masekela's older music to his later, more commercial playing. There he finds Jonas Gwanga more innovative. He has visited Cuba about fifteen times on political and holiday trips and is fascinated by the people, culture, history and achievements. For a while now he has warmed to other music, especially the interpenetration of Khoisan and Batswana musical forms in the Northern Cape and North West regions.

Whether we call it charisma or not, Kgalema does command attention. Thabo Masebe, his spokesperson, mentions Kgalema addressing mass meetings in huge stadiums where his delivery and the response of the crowd were remarkably effective.[2] Ebrahim Patel says: 'If you asked me if Kgalema is able to inspire large numbers of people to passionately commit to some goal, I think he has that ability. The capacity for people to believe strongly in the ideal he is espousing I have no doubt is strong and well developed in him. I have seen him do that many times.'[3] According to Murphy Morobe, there are some who feel he is better suited to strategic interventions in smaller meetings, which he is 'very good at'.[4]

For Kate Philip, he has a 'quiet and dignified charm about him'. She recalls the first television interview he had after he became president: 'I was with my parents and they loved listening to him. He chatted about his youth, playing soccer, and he was very charismatic. He has a charisma of his own in interactive contexts. You warm to him easily.'[5] Dale McKinley warns that some political leaders use charisma to sidestep the burning issues, and refers to Zuma's penchant for singing and dancing at mass rallies,[6] when it is the ideas, policies and programme a leader advocates that people really need. Mbeki agrees: 'We had many real engagements in massive *imbizos* [community meetings] across the country around issues, which directly affected the lives of poor people. They were very fruitful and effective engagements with enthusiastic people, but we had no leaders dancing and singing there.'[7]

Most of those I spoke with said it is gravitas that strikes them most when they think of Kgalema as a leader. Kgalema has a dignified seriousness to him. In a mass meeting he would probably not be as spontaneous with the ululations as Zuma. In 2011 he told an NEC meeting: 'I can deputise Zuma for this and that but not for singing and dancing!'

Nelson Mandela, as a former president, wrote a letter to Kgalema that went to the media the day after he was inaugurated: 'We have known you for a long time and you are eminently deserving of this high honour. You are a quiet, firm and principled leader, one who puts reason above emotions and one who seeks to unite rather than divide. We know that our country is in good hands with you at the helm of government.'[8]

Taking over from Mbeki

Quite apart from the fact that he was the ANC's deputy president, Kgalema's intervention at the rowdy start of the Polokwane conference was so memorable that it was a major reason why the ANC decided to nominate him to replace Mbeki as president of South Africa. In Noor Nieftagodien's words: 'People were saying that he was so effective in restoring calm at a very fragile moment in the conference that it demonstrated the power he has. The impressive thing is that the conference was teetering at the moment when he made that intervention. That spoke volumes to me of the authority he had in the ANC.'[9] Pitso Tsibolane was as impressed: 'When the Mbeki people

Kgalema, third ANC president of South Africa, 2008

were booed off the stage, the chairman at the time, Mosiuoa Lekota, rose to chastise such behaviour, but he got an even bigger booing. It was only when Mkhuluwa (Kgalema) stood up and with a stern resolve and dignity called for order was there quietness. Only a giant of a leader could achieve that, and Motlanthe did it with calm and poise.'[10] He adds: 'When others chose which camp to join, he stood like a towering father above all circumstances, providing leadership, and supported Zuma through his ordeal when serving under Mbeki.'

He had made an exemplary stand when he supported Zuma by attending his trial in 2006. As we have noted, this was much to the chagrin of the Mbeki-led cabinet, who did not want the ANC to be associated in any way with the criminal charges Zuma faced. Though Mbeki was the head of the ANC and the state, Kgalema refused to defer to him in this. It took enormous courage, but my sense is that Kgalema felt anyway that his stance was in tune with the growing radicalisation within the ANC after the 2005 national general council. He could read the inevitable decline of Mbeki and the ministers close to him, which climaxed so dramatically at Polokwane. He had not been a publicity seeker or power-monger and was a relatively low-key ANC leader, but he had done enough to command the respect that would earn him a nomination to become president when the ruling party faced its biggest crisis ever.

His conference reports over the years, criticising much of what had gone wrong in the ANC, certainly weighed with his supporters. Even for the SACP leader Blade Nzimande, when Mbeki was recalled there was nobody else who had the stature and authority to take over: 'He was the most senior ANC leader at the time and had a very good understanding of the movement.'[11] For the ANC movement Gevisser suggests: 'A lot of the appeal of Motlanthe seems to be based on nostalgia, which is not a bad thing necessarily, of some glorious past in the ANC.'[12]

Indeed, given the terrible internecine strife among the ANC leaders at that time, there was a sense that people longed for someone who could try to heal the deep rift within the party. Many interviewees said Kgalema reminded them of the nobility of character of earlier great leaders like Tambo, Luthuli and Sisulu, being deeply humble and treating peasants and presidents alike and with equal respect.[13] The day after he became president, his mother Masefako described him growing up as a 'shy person'.[14] Today he comes across much less as shy, far more as deeply attentive to people, including those outside the ANC.

Mbeki resigned, with admirable grace, on 21 September 2008. The next day Zuma told the media at Luthuli House that Kgalema would take over. Gordin says that Zuma and his supporters did not want Mbeki's deputy, Phumzile Mlambo-Ngcuka, to continue and so they asked her 'to go quietly'.[15] On 25 September, following his nomination by the MP Ben Turok, Kgalema was elected by secret ballot, which was really a formality because the ANC then held 70 per cent of the seats in parliament.[16] He was installed as the third president of South Africa.[17]

The South African and world media, looking to Kgalema as a unifier, evidently felt he would be the most able to heal the deep wounds that the factionalist battle between Mbeki and Zuma had caused inside the ANC, use that effort to build bridges between supporters of both sides in preparation for the vitally important 2009 elections, and smooth the transition to the new Zuma administration later.

The week when Kgalema took over from Mbeki was a dire one for many in the country. The media reflected huge,

Kgalema, third ANC president of South Africa, 2008

crippling uncertainty and pessimism following Mbeki's recall. The sense of foreboding seemed contagious. *ABC News* described the outlook: 'Long seen as a possible compromise candidate, Motlanthe is praised as a unifier and conciliator, skills he will need as his party faces the worst crisis in its near century-old history.'[18] For the *Daily News*, 'Former trade unionist and freedom fighter Kgalema Motlanthe became South Africa's president yesterday in an atmosphere tense with fears of political and economic crisis precipitated by the ouster of his predecessor.'[19] Factionalism between Mbeki and Zuma supporters in the ANC and the state made matters worse, especially as the police, security and intelligences services also appeared to be involved.

The economy had begun to be battered by the financial storms surging through the world capitalist economy. Many did not envy Kgalema at all. It was one of the worst times in which to become president of the country. The situation led Kgalema to say four days after he was inaugurated: 'We have survived a week of uncertainty, hurt and anger.'[20] He was indeed thrown in the deep end and it did not get any better for him in the months that followed. The mainstream media, locally and internationally, were anxious that the recall of Mbeki might destabilise the ANC, the country and especially the markets, particularly after the downward jitters on the JSE immediately following the news that Trevor Manuel had resigned as finance minister.[21]

With the world on edge, bloodletting in the ANC hardly featured in the mainstream media. Most of their news, analysis and commentary on Mbeki's demise and the emergence of Kgalema focused on whatever would threaten to disrupt the economy. At a time when panic was dangerous, faith in Kgalema was important and appeared to be firm. The political analyst

Aubrey Matshiqi commented: 'When Motlanthe took over levels of uncertainty were very high. But he was the man for the moment, who reassured the world that South Africa would not go belly-up, at a time when we were generating headlines for the wrong reasons. And in that regard he did very well.'[22] Zuma's assurance that 'Kgalema has all the potential to govern and steer this country in a good direction' also helped to restore stability.[23]

'South Africa picks union stalwart as new president', read the headline of the *Guardian* the day after his inauguration, with this comment: 'Motlanthe is a left-leaning intellectual, widely respected by both radical leftists and business tycoons within the ANC. He is seen as a figure who could help heal the deepest divisions in the party's history.'[24] For *Time* magazine, 'Motlanthe is a cautious and low-key operator rather than a high-profile or empire builder, and is generally viewed as one of the intellectual anchors of the Zuma camp – which has challenged Mbeki's market-oriented economic policies from the left. Still, the widespread respect enjoyed by the former political prisoner and union organiser has positioned him as a bridge between rival factions, and the leader many see as the one best able to ensure a smooth transition to Zuma's presidency.'[25] The commentator Chris Landsberg said that Kgalema 'has played a very smart bridge-building role. He has been able to play a very detached role from the two camps. There were attempts to link him to one group or another ... [but] he was seen as neutral, and not balancing in favour of anybody.'[26]

The editor of the *Times*, Ray Hartley, wrote:

> Motlanthe is a very different prospect to the man he replaces: President Thabo Mbeki. He is a party man through and through. So much so that he had stood above the bitter fight

Kgalema, third ANC president of South Africa, 2008

between Mbeki and his rival, Jacob Zuma. Motlanthe has been willing to speak out against the rantings of the likes of Youth League motor-mouth Julius Malema when very few in the party had the guts to do so. That's all good and well, but what will happen when Motlanthe has to lead the country in the aftermath of its biggest post-apartheid political crisis?'[27]

This was the question many asked on Kgalema's inauguration day and there was nobody who could answer it. Meanwhile, observers like Hartley could at least see that he stood above the factions and at the same time spoke out on principle in any direction.

Mpumelelo Mkhabela warned that though 'South Africa's new president advocates collective leadership, he may well be covertly ambitious.'[28] But political leaders can at various times do both! In Kgalema's case, his stance is well known: 'I am not an ambitious person. I sometimes think that those who say I am ambitious for high office are being mischievous or they may be masking their own ambitions.'[29] And to Steven Friedman's remark that he could be using self-effacement as a tactic to mask ambition and get power he is emphatic: 'No, but that would be Machiavellian tactics. Make-believe and pretence cannot last very long. But politics need not be full of nefarious agendas. We can and must cleanse politics of all the filth we see today.'

Kgalema was not necessarily reluctant to become president of South Africa. His overriding concern was Mbeki being recalled in the first place. Months before he took office he had said: 'Well, that will be a daunting challenge, but as a loyal and disciplined member of the ANC I will rise to the occasion if and when the time comes.'[30] Yet he fought hard in debate about Mbeki's fate in the ANC: 'I took the view, after they made it very clear that they don't want him, that the best way to manage what was a huge problem was to let him finish his term but ask him to bring forward the 2009 elections, but I failed to convince them. Then when I was approached to replace Mbeki I just knew that it would be a lost cause to decline or resist.'[31]

How did Kgalema feel when the ANC decided he should replace Mbeki? 'When I was told about it I had to draw on my innermost resources to accept an immense challenge. But leadership also means achieving results from what others have made possible. I take my strength from the knowledge that this country has an abundance of talent: if we draw on that in a non-partisan manner we can make this country great.'[32] It was certainly the biggest political moment for the ruling party and the country since the 1994 elections. In his statement I see a maturity and sense of achievement and responsibility. Behind it, from interviews with him, I know he felt deep ambiguity and terrible pain at having to take Mbeki's job under such dreadful circumstances. This was the first time ever that a head of state anywhere in Africa had been recalled by their party in such a way.

His partner, Gugu Mtshali, says it was also the biggest moment in his own political and personal life and that never in his 'wildest dreams' did he think such a day would ever dawn for him, because he really never did aspire to be president of the ANC or the country.[33] For some, this could reflect a degree of subdued ambition that springs to life when the opportunity arises.[34] Even if this is true, he is probably the least ambitious politician in the top leadership of the ANC. I found him quite cool on the subject: 'Even being a member of the NEC I am not starry-eyed about it at all. You serve a term – no matter for what top position – and if you are not re-elected, for me there are no sleepless nights about it at all.' Mpumelelo Mkhabela said of Kgalema in 2009: 'He may well be the embodiment of an archaic ANC school of thought which holds that one need not overtly display an insatiable desire for a higher position to actually secure it.'[35]

Has he been too self-effacing? Ebrahim Patel has this to say: 'In a revolutionary movement, where loyalty and trust is fundamental, a degree of self-effacement is necessary because an overweening self-ambition could spell danger for the movement, in terms of internal battles over ego. There are few individuals who have absolutely no ambition, but Kgalema has an unusually high level of lack of personal glory-seeking, which is a mark of his exceptional strength. In fact his value is so much more enhanced by that rare quality.'[36] In this regard Kgalema was sincere when he insisted that he was never interested in government, even after Polokwane. 'I always felt that I could make a greater contribution in the ANC in the areas of political education, building the branches and, most importantly, building leadership. The ANC is far more important than the government is. Governments come and go. If the party is weak and flounders, the government drawn from it will be built on little more than dust. I have absolutely no doubt about or confusion about which of the two is the priority.'

Kgalema was not intimidated by the prospect of following Mbeki as president.

> Bear in mind that most of the people in both parliament and cabinet I had worked with over many years, both while with NUM and later the ANC. Besides, what helped me a lot was the fact that the transition did not disrupt or destabilise the state bureaucracy. It was largely intact throughout. I found a team of very efficient people there. Mbeki's advisers left with him but leading bureaucrats like Trevor Fowler, Frank Chikane, Joel Netshitenzhe and most, if not all, directors-general stayed

on. I also knew them well and had worked with them over many years. They were decent and professional people.

While he was SG he had also met leading party and government figures across the globe.

Kgalema did not have a sense that he had any inordinate powers. In the presidency, he says, 'you are always surrounded by advisers on every matter, although you naturally bring into the equation your own thoughts and experience. Together these determine decisions. For me the presidency or deputy presidency is just another platform from which you serve the party and the country as best you can. It is not permanent and I did not operate in the first instance on the basis of the power I wielded.' Though his powers were limited by various constitutional provisions (like the protection of private property and, with it, the capitalist system), he did have a great deal of leeway to be authoritarian if he so wanted to.

One of his staff, Dan Nkambule, who had also served under Mbeki, says how very impressed all the staff were when Kgalema became president. From the outset the man was so humble, they just could not believe it: 'I tell you, there were many times that he wanted to serve us with drinks and snacks! He often made us feel like each one of us here was the president or that he was just an employee, like us. We did not once [before] see that from a president.'[37]

The media made much of the fact that Mbeki did not attend the swearing-in ceremony, but Kgalema was not put out by it. 'No, I did not take his absence seriously. In fact he was one of the first people who called to congratulate me. There could have been a good reason why he did not attend but I did not read much into that. At that moment I had other very serious things to think about.' Among the congratulations he received from the ANC alliance, the one from the SACP says: '"Mkhuluwa" is well known within the ranks of the SACP. He is indeed a truly humble son of workers of our country, and truly understands the needs and aspirations of the ordinary people of our country.'[38] Though Nzimande and others in the party had not liked the fact that he pulled out of the central committee in 1997 and let his membership lapse too, they evidently still held him in high regard.[39]

In his inauguration speech he was sober and modest about the tasks ahead: 'Mine is not the desire to deviate from what is working. It is not for me to reinvent policy. Nor do I intend to reshape either cabinet or the public service. In a turbulent global economy, we will remain true to the policies that have kept South Africa steady, and that have ensured sustained growth.'[40] The rightness of the policies aside, his central theme was to assure all stakeholders that stability would be maintained after Mbeki's dismissal and assure investors that there would be no policy changes. Kgalema is too pragmatic to have said anything radical at such a vulnerable moment, especially since he would be in office for such a short time.

Mbeki's appeal against the Nicholson judgment

The decision by Mbeki and his cabinet to appeal against the Nicholson judgment must be seen against the subterranean conflict between Mbeki and Zuma supporters before and after Polokwane. Having been seriously implicated in Zuma's travails at the hands of the NPA, Mbeki and his cabinet believed it was absolutely necessary to defend themselves (even with virtually no prospect of success, as we have seen). As indicated earlier, this challenge was the last straw for Zuma. He now felt strongly that Mbeki had to go. According to Kgalema, Zuma felt Mbeki's prime motive was to get the NPA to charge and prosecute him

(Zuma); and speculation was that Mbeki wanted to use the case to prevent Zuma from becoming president of the ANC and then the country, which Mbeki strongly denies.[41]

Kgalema inherited this situation when he took over as president. He faced a lot of flak from Luthuli House, which wanted him to withdraw any financial state support for Mbeki's challenge. 'They [Luthuli House] asked me why should the state fund his appeal, but I said that if he is so aggrieved by the slur the judgment cast on him and his cabinet, he had the right to take such action.' Kgalema adds that those who insisted that he should not authorise such expense did not know how cabinet works.

> They wanted the cabinet minute to be changed, but I had to explain to them that since it was a cabinet decision we inherited, if it is to be changed we need a separate memo which rescinds that decision. Besides, their stance was crude because on the one hand they said that Zuma had a right to exhaust all his legal options to fight his case – which was funded by the state – but they wanted to deprive Mbeki and his cabinet of that same right. That is how I looked at this matter, though I did question the wisdom of Mbeki's challenge. But I proceeded from the premise of constitutional rights, meaning that since Mbeki was a sitting president when he was removed he had the right to challenge his dismissal.

For Kgalema, Mbeki's challenge did not necessarily mean that such matters damaged the image of the ANC. 'Rather, I think they are – though the manner in which some of these things have happened may be undesirable – a healthy sign at the political level of a growing, maturing, engaging and vigorous democracy.'[42] The *Sunday Times* then carried this lead story:

'Motlanthe's support for the NPA's appeal against the Nicholson judgment angered some in the ANC's NWC, who felt that he should not have lent credence to Mbeki's piggy-backing of the NPA. It was this move, according to ANC leaders, which led to tensions between Zuma and Motlanthe. In essence, by endorsing the appeal, Motlanthe was implying that Zuma was guilty.'[43] The conclusion was nonsensical. I did not even ask Kgalema to comment.

In the end, the challenge fell by the wayside. The appeal was thrown out in May 2009. Mbeki was going to take the matter to the Constitutional Court, but did not do so. The fact that Nicholson's judgment was overturned later on was indeed a degree of redemption for Mbeki and his cabinet. Politically it means that Mbeki was wrongly recalled. To this extent, history somewhat reinstates him but, unfortunately for him, it could not undo the event.

'Where was the First Lady?'
Extensive discussion in the media about Kgalema's marital status had its roots in the fact that at his inauguration he was not accompanied by his wife Mapula.[44] Fiona Forde made the point: 'What was conspicuous on the day Kgalema Motlanthe was inaugurated as president was the absence of a partner by his side. It sparked what I believe was natural interest in our newspaper group about the identity of the country's first lady.'[45] This was perhaps where all the media trouble for Kgalema began. It thrived further on scandal stories and public curiosity, piqued perhaps by the presidency's fumbling and Kgalema's own reticence.

For the *Financial Gazette*, 'The media's appetite was whetted by the fact that when the ANC issued a synopsis of Motlanthe's biography they were silent on his marital status.'[46] The media regularly asked who the first lady was but got no clarity from Kgalema or the presidency. The *Financial Gazette* complained: 'The ANC should by now have learnt that the best way to deal with media controversy involving the private lives of its leaders should be to make full disclosures rather than act as if there is something to hide, as seems to have been the case with Motlanthe.'

Kgalema did not make a public statement. This was not because he had anything to hide, but despite the fact that he had nothing to hide. There should have been some word at least from those around him who attended to the media and his public image. But the ANC's website was silent on his marital status and family in the week he was inaugurated.[47] Had a statement been issued by the presidency at the outset, it would have been much more difficult for smear stories later on to be carried with credibility. The lack of both a first lady and a statement clarifying the situation created a vacuum that Kgalema's detractors brutally exploited.

The presidency's mishandling was soon shown to be regrettable in the light of a story on 21 December, 'Blade plotting against Kgalema', when the *Sunday Independent* declared that 'a plot is being hatched to embarrass Motlanthe by claiming he is having an extra-marital affair, top ANC members claim. By dragging him into scandals, including one about an alleged love affair with a personal assistant who works at the ANC headquarters, Luthuli House, Motlanthe's enemies apparently want to make him less of a threat to the ambitions of Jacob Zuma, the ANC president. ... In the latest round of backstabbing, Motlanthe's love life is to be targeted.'[48] The main theme of the story was that Blade Nzimande was in a campaign to discredit Kgalema in the run-up to the 2009 elections because he and others believed Kgalema 'had ambitions to stay on if the ANC

Kgalema, third ANC president of South Africa, 2008

wins the 2009 elections.'[49]

Nzimande strongly denied the claim in a reply to Independent Newspapers (which their political editor Moshoeshoe Monare promised to publish but never did),[50] castigating the group for their cheap reporting: 'The ongoing treatment of the private life of the President of the Republic, Cde Kgalema Motlanthe, will perhaps go down in South African media history as the beginning of its "tabloidisation" and, much more seriously, the erosion of whatever credibility it still had. This dirty delving into the private life of the President, and the use of clearly discredited, if not emotionally unstable, sources constitutes reckless and highly irresponsible journalism.'[51]

The story should have forewarned the presidency that there was trouble brewing for Kgalema, but apparently it did not. Worse still, they declined to comment on a further piece (later proved false) about Kgalema having an affair with a 24-year-old woman.[52] If they had seen linkages between the two stories they would have been better prepared to support Kgalema. Various people I interviewed say the presidency failed him from the start. As Cyril Ramaphosa puts it: 'They messed up the first lady matter. They actually should have sat him down and said: "Chief, now that you are in this position your private life is going to be an open book because people will want to know all sorts of things, like 'Do you have a wife and children?'" And they should have said that if there are any skeletons in the cupboard, please tell us so that we know how to deal with it. In the presidency it is better that they are forearmed and told everything in advance.'[53]

Instead there was guesswork by Kgalema's spokesperson, Thabo Masebe: 'Remember Kgalema Motlanthe is the president, not his family. Any family can decide what profile they want to keep and we should respect that. She [the first lady] doesn't want to be known. Let's grant their wish to remain private.'[54]

The false impression of a family discussion when Kgalema and Mapula had been estranged for years just made their position worse.

The incompetent handling of the First Lady by the presidency severely compromised Kgalema, to the extent where a few people asked me if it was deliberate. That I certainly do not believe. But I note that Frank Chikane writes about 'the depth of emotion' one staff member felt when she watched him take Kgalema to what was Mbeki's office after the inauguration: 'It felt, said the staff member, like a coup d'etat.'[55] In that initial atmosphere, there may have been less sensitivity about how the media regarded Kgalema.

Given no other option but going public, Kgalema would far rather have spoken the truth than pretend he had a healthy marriage. As he says, though, 'Some matters are more personal' and 'There is no law governing a rupturing in marital relations. There were children, there is Kagiso. There were many things to work through.' In an earlier interview he said:

> The marital status and related matters of a president I believe is a very personal matter and it should not at all be a consideration in the performance of the president. There exist no constitutional or legal requirements for a president to present a first lady to the public. ... I often wonder why such a big thing has been made about this thing. This is not an ethical but a circumstantial issue which I should not have to feel obliged to explain in detail. But when you have tabloid media searching for sensational scandal they will come at it from that angle. You see, if they had been well-meaning and decent people they would have started by talking to me directly, which has not happened once. I am not saying that my personal life must be hidden and not be subjected to critical public scrutiny,

but it must not drag my children into it. The problems I have had in my family have been there for a long time, but why must I have to talk in public about it and thereby please the media just because I am the president of the country? That is where I have to draw the line.

Yet it is also true that the media's attempt to find out more about the new president was not easy because there was little about his personal life in the public domain. Years of keeping his personal life to himself meant that Kgalema was not very well known in society when he took over from Mbeki. Some friends and comrades said he tended to be too private. An exaggerated view of him when he became president was as a 'reclusive enigma thrust into the political limelight.'[56] Kgalema has this to say: 'It is true that I have found it very difficult to talk about myself or my family and that may lead some people to say that I am secretive, but that is not because I have anything I want to or need to hide from anyone. That is partly why I could authorise you to write my biography.' We could add that in an unhappy marriage he would be least likely to talk much about it.

But gone were the days when he could draw the line on family information to the media. When *Business Day* asked why there was not much information available about himself, he replied: 'I took a decision a long time ago that when I became actively involved in politics I would try to shield my family from the glare of public life.'[57] Obviously this was unrealistic from the moment he became state president, and arguably even before, as SG of the ruling party from 1997 and then deputy president of the ANC.

It was all very well for Pallo Jordan to say, 'Kgalema Motlanthe's private life is his own business and as long as it does not prejudice his performance of his official duties it should be of no concern to the public.'⁵⁸ Or Zuma to insist: We stand by our deputy president. His private life has nothing to do with the way he runs the country or how he executes his tasks as the ANC deputy president. That is his own business. We advised him to focus on his work in government and Luthuli House and ignore cheap attempts to discredit him.'⁵⁹ But actually there are valid grounds for probing into private life at times, including the need for a leader's conduct to be exemplary and the fact that a spousal office exists, funded by taxpayers. To say that public interest is not involved is simply untrue. The vital point for the media is to know their limits.

Jordan urges the media to think more carefully about the negative impact their stories can have on the lives of the people affected. This is not only to protect the dignity of people and, in this case, of the president but precisely because the scandal that was run about the 24-year-old, for example, *was* in the public interest and so the media staff should have taken far more care in their investigation.

The gullible and even complicit media certainly damaged Kgalema with that particular saga.⁶⁰ It must rank as one of the biggest lessons for the media to learn from, but all the apologies in the world cannot undo the pain and sorrow Kgalema and his family suffered. When Fiona Forde, who launched the story, finally confessed it was untrue,⁶¹ a tiny space was allocated for the apology at the bottom of the third page of the *Sunday Independent*.⁶² Not a word of regret was expressed for Kgalema's family and the enormous stress and embarrassment the stories created for them, especially for his youngest son Kagiso, who was still at school.⁶³

It also pained Kgalema that the peddling of lies by Independent Newspapers in particular later appeared in the international press, to his embarrassment when he travelled abroad. He feels these newspapers still need to answer the question – beyond an apology – of how the story was carried in the first place when their own guidelines required them to double-source and double-check the facts, 'but they did not bother to do any such thing.'[64]

After Independent Newspapers apologised, Carl Niehaus was reported saying: 'This is a clear demonstration of how glibly the media accepts information as facts if it goes to satisfy the agenda of some newspaper editors and owners. Not only is this practice unethical but it goes to show a lack of objectivity, bias and an intent to harm the good image of respected leaders of the calibre of Kgalema Motlanthe.'[65]

So damaging were these stories of Kgalema that some people thought they would destroy him. After the media flurry and simultaneous criticisms of Kgalema by Luthuli House, one observer, Pitso Tsibolane, concluded: 'The honeymoon is over. Just like the dramatic ending to the leadership of Dr Xuma, who was ousted for being too moderate by the radical elements within the ANC of the 1940's – namely the ANC Youth League and the SA Communist Party – Motlanthe's future seems to be written on the walls of history.'[66] Tsibolane was rather hasty in concluding that Kgalema was 'history'. But the attacks Kgalema faced were intense and vicious.

The smear stories have been seen as a concerted effort to discredit Kgalema in the run-up to the 2009 elections. Here is Forde's response to the suggestion that she was being used by Kgalema's detractors to destroy him: 'The reaction to the exposé this week is as much a reflection of the ANC's internal politics as it is of anything else.'[67] That was indeed what many people hinted at or concluded. From the interviews conducted it does strongly appear that this leak originated inside Luthuli House. In the same publication key questions about the story were asked: 'Where did this information come from? What is the motivation of the source? Who is trying to get back at whom?'[68] These were some of the questions raging at the time of the privacy debate in the media.[69]

Kgalema was strikingly noble about his appalling treatment by the media.[70] He met with the South African National Editors Forum (Sanef) soon afterwards in what Mondli Makhanya, Sanef chairperson, says was a very pleasant and constructive session. 'At the first meeting we had with him he calmly walked in with his leather jacket. ... It was a beautiful meeting, really cool. He set a very cordial and constructive tone from the outset.'[71] Another Sanef member, Amina Frense, recalls how highly impressed the editors were and that several of them felt quite embarrassed by the fact that after they had slaughtered him in their newspapers, he still hosted them warmly and was respectful, gracious and patient towards them: 'That was the time when some editors were attacking him and yet he was so polite and friendly, including with those editors who carried all that filth.'[72]

How well did Kgalema perform as president?

Probably no leader in South Africa's history rose as unexpectedly and rapidly as Kgalema did in the nine months from Polokwane, rocketing to dizzying heights in the last fortnight between the Nicholson judgment on 2 September 2008 and his inauguration at 2 p.m. on the 25th. This is how one publication saw it: 'It happened so fast. Motlanthe became a member of parliament only about eight weeks ago. By Thursday lawmakers elected this quiet and dependable favourite of the ruling ANC to South Africa's highest office. He, Zuma and Mbeki are forever joined in a political coming-of-age story for post-apartheid South Africa.'[73]

Kgalema, third ANC president of South Africa, 2008

It was all too sudden for Kgalema to be quite prepared. In what he called a 'unique combination of factors' he was shot up into the most powerful post in the country at a terrible moment for the Mbeki presidency and its staff, as Frank Chikane recalls: 'The mood in the presidency in Tuynhuys was sombre. Staff that had not been at the Union Buildings were still shocked by the unfolding events and the speed with which the changes were happening. They would have liked to have had a briefing to help them understand what was happening but there was no time for one.'[74]

Even if Kgalema had taken office at an easy time instead of going head on into a critical national and international situation, the time he spent there was much too short to be a gauge of his capacity and performance. Yet we can look at how he performed generally and note some important decisions he made.

His primary task at the outset was to address the general sense of decline and pessimism in the country following Mbeki's recall and the reasons why the ANC had decided he must leave. These developments had seriously disabled the renewal to which the ANC had committed itself in Polokwane and it was going to be hard to deal with the huge damage they inflicted on the ANC and the country.

Confidence in him was high when he took office, as Fiona Forde indicates about sentiments in the ANC: 'To them he is a silent but strong voice that exudes calm in a moment of panic – a man whose cool-headed outlook sees him through many a tough time. He is the voice of reason they regularly turn to in the sometimes disparate tripartite alliance. He is an intellectual of note, a comrade whose door is always open.'[75] At least Kgalema had the skills, style and temperament to prevent things from deteriorating further. 'Motlanthe's reassuring demeanour and the widespread respect in which he is held were partly responsible for the quick recovery', reported the *Financial Mail* on 3 October 2008, a week after he was inaugurated. At that most vulnerable moment there was nobody in the ANC with the respect in both business and labour that he had.

Kgalema's first three months in office were not bad, considering the wide-ranging adverse circumstances he faced and the ever-vigilant Luthuli House, which seemed set on stamping its authority on everything to do with parliament and the government. After the years when Mbeki was accused of centralising power in the presidency and marginalising ANC headquarters, it was not just understandable but healthy that, after Polokwane, Luthuli House resurrected the constitutional power vested in it.

But the ANC or particular leaders within it seemed anxious that Kgalema was receiving too much favourable media coverage – so much so that senior executives of the SABC were reportedly summoned to ANC headquarters in early December when it was felt that his popularity had reached proportions which got them worried that Zuma was being eclipsed. 'The SABC executives were read the riot act and instructed to cut down on Motlanthe and increase coverage of Zuma.'[76]

It is true that, though critical of his handling of several issues such as Vusi Pikoli, the arms deal and the Dalai Lama, most of the media seemed broadly to welcome Kgalema's presidency, with some even wondering if he should not continue after the 2009 elections. It was also noted with appreciation that, unlike Zuma, Kgalema swiftly rebuked those ANC supporters who disrupted the rival Cope meetings: 'I would really appeal to all those concerned to calm down and act in a responsible manner.'[77]

The year 2009 started off on a horrendous note for Kgalema. The *Sunday Independent* ran the lead smear story of the '24-year-old lover'. And just weeks later the *Sunday Times* ran a lengthy front-page article that focused negatively on some aspects of Kgalema's performance and on alleged differences and tensions between him and Luthuli House. But the overall thrust was that he had changed since he took over from Mbeki: 'Standing accused of not seeking consensus about important decisions is a new experience for Kgalema Motlanthe, who, prior to being elected president of South Africa, was praised for his ability to listen to divergent opinions and his consultative manner.'[78] The story went on: 'These days, many knives are out for "Mr. Consultation". Before Polokwane he extolled the virtues of consultation, especially when important decisions were taken, but after he became president "accusation started flying about his failure to consult with the ruling party's leadership about important government decisions."'[79] Kgalema was unfazed by this story: 'No, I was not really worried by that story at all. The point is that we had an elective conference where a new leadership was elected upon a common commitment to the renewal of the ANC, but some people wanted me to act contrary to that commitment and to go after certain people, which I was not going to do. That led to various attempts by some to discredit me.'

Steven Friedman says that the eight months Kgalema spent as president must have been a 'really torrid time.'

> I argued throughout that it was a disaster to be appointed that way. A lot of people close to Zuma felt that he was trying to take his job and that from the moment he took office they created a situation in which he was forced to keep a low profile. I think this affected his performance. He found himself in a situation where if he really wanted to make a mark they would make life hell for him. Though he was the constitutional head of state, he was often referred to as the ANC's deputy president, instead of

the President of the Republic of South Africa. All this affected his performance, I believe, because he must have realised that if he took any bold initiatives or did something unusual or unexpected he would be in trouble.[80]

He was obviously acutely aware that he had become president by default in the sense that it was due to Mbeki's sudden resignation. Zuma supporters were set on Kgalema not doing anything to upstage Zuma. Some were waiting impatiently for Zuma's rise to power to realise their own political or financial ambitions. Many feared that if Kgalema did well enough in leading the country, people might want him to continue after the 2009 elections, especially as (unlike Zuma) he did not have charges of corruption and fraud hanging over his head. This made him careful not to appear too eagerly presidential, which could be interpreted as wanting to stay in the post when he was only supposed to 'keep the seat warm for Zuma' until after the 2009 elections, as most of the media speculated.

Given the powerful ascendancy of Luthuli House over the state presidency after Polokwane, this could be true. Indeed there were times when he did appear to be consciously restraining himself, as some of his decisions indicate, despite his constitutional powers as president. Kgalema was also curbed by serious limits on issues affecting the working class. This was widely evident long before he took over from Mbeki in September 2008. At heart, Kgalema had been consistently sensitive about and responsive to the interests of the trade union movement and Cosatu in particular, as this typical statement reflects: 'Our collective responsibility is to work together to withstand the [economic] crisis and ensure that the poor and the most vulnerable are protected as far as possible from its impact.'[81] As already noted, though, I did get a sense from

Kgalema, third ANC president of South Africa, 2008

talking to Vavi and a few of the independent left that Kgalema did become much more pragmatic about the politics of being in government than in his NUM days or even when he was SG of the ANC, and this was a matter of deep concern to the left.[82]

Limited as he was in what he could do, I am convinced Kgalema did his best and certainly was not the 'lame-duck Motlanthe' that Moshoeshoe Monare described, if by that he meant ineffectual.[83] In a brief period he took several decisions that were firm and bold. The way he dealt with the SABC Bill, the Film and Publications Bill,[84] and the legislation dealing with the disbandment of the Scorpions comes to mind. In fact these were among the main areas of reported conflict between Kgalema and the ANC (or, better, Luthuli House) along with the Telkom/Vodacom sale deal, his decision to fire Pikoli without first consulting the ANC leadership, and his delay in signing legislation disbanding the Scorpions, plus the view that he had been faint in his criticism of Cope.

What also made it a difficult time for him to take over from Mbeki was the fact that the ANC was by then even more divided than it had been at Polokwane. The Nicholson judgment and the recall of Mbeki worsened matters to breaking point in both the ANC and government. Add to that the serious tensions that developed between Kgalema and Luthuli House about some decisions he took. The provinces and branches of the ANC were deeply divided after the gigantic clash between Mbeki and Zuma before Polokwane. Clearly his position was unenviable.

There was a great deal of media focus on bad relations between Kgalema and Luthuli House, some of it true or probably true and the rest just uninformed speculation aided by anonymous sources and rumour peddlers. It extended to a negative guess about his awaited state-of-the-nation address in February 2009 in the *City Press*: 'The current tensions come as the ANC decided to downgrade next month's state-of-the-nation address to a mere "presidential address". This is seen as an attempt to show that Motlanthe is just a caretaker president.'[85] This was simply nonsense. There was no such decision by the ANC, though some leaders anxious that Kgalema was eclipsing Zuma may have wished for one. And you cannot 'downgrade' a state-of-the-nation address, an appraisal of the state of the country, to a mere personal statement subject to the whims of politicians within the ruling party.

The 2008 *Mail & Guardian* Report Card criticised him for not acting decisively on the Zimbabwean question but praised him for the cabinet he appointed, which they said was 'probably his finest moment.'[86] He appointed Barbara Hogan as minister of health, replacing Manto Tshabalala-Msimang, which the newspaper said was 'an unexpected and inspired move.'[87] He also removed the safety and security minister Charles Nqakula and justice minister Brigitte Mabandla, and so 'finally relieved a long-suffering nation of the collective curse' of these ministers.[88]

We turn now to some controversial decisions Kgalema took in the eight months he was in office: terminating the services of the former NDPP, Vusi Pikoli; refusing the Dalai Lama a visa to enter the country; refusing to accede to yet another request to appoint a judicial commission of inquiry into the arms deal; his alleged delay in signing legislation disbanding the Scorpions, the investigating arm of the NPA; delay in signing the SABC Bill; and the Telkom/Vodacom deal.

Axing Vusi Pikoli
Vusi Pikoli, head of the NPA from 2005, was suspended from office in September 2007 by Mbeki, who cited an 'irretrievable breakdown in the working relationship between the Minister of Justice and Constitutional Development and the NDPP'.[89] Just

three days earlier Pikoli had secured a warrant to arrest Jackie Selebi, head of the South African Police Service and Interpol.[90] *M&G* journalists later speculated that Mbeki had suspended Pikoli as part of a bid to shield Selebi, his close confidant.[91]

Inheriting this matter, Kgalema decided to recommend to parliament that Pikoli be fired. This was controversial, given that the Ginwala Commission of Inquiry into Pikoli's suspension did not think he should be, though it was critical of Pikoli in certain respects. The DA severely criticised Kgalema: 'Motlanthe has failed the first real test of his presidency, which was to put South Africa's interests before the narrow interests of the Zuma faction of the ANC.'[92] They said he had focused on the 'peripheral aspect' of national security, which was the 'fig leaf of politicians with something to hide.'[93] The leader of the United Democratic Movement, Bantu Holomisa, was also scathing: 'It must be remembered that Mr Pikoli was the one who reinstituted charges against Mr Zuma; clearly he is being punished for not delivering a verdict that suits the palace.'[94] Many interviewed thought Kgalema should have exercised his mind more independently, since he was addressing the matter not as deputy president of the ANC but as president of the country.

It was well known that the new ANC leadership elected in Polokwane wanted Pikoli fired because many believed he had been gunning for Zuma ever since charging him in 2005. With the presidency of the ANC secured for Zuma after Polokwane, the anti-Pikoli voices were much stronger and they were calling the shots from Luthuli House. Even if Kgalema had agreed with the Ginwala Commission that Pikoli not be fired, he had little or no room to resist the wishes of Luthuli House, which seemed to be the new axis of power.

Everyone in the media certainly believed that Luthuli House

drove the decision on Pikoli. In an interview Kgalema took offence at the idea that he had no alternative but to do their bidding: 'It's an affront to conclude that my decision was politically inspired. Why don't they say the same thing when the president appoints ministers or judges: that it was influenced by Luthuli House? Furthermore, they do not advance legal arguments as to why my decision is wrong. Instead they conveniently politicised my decision.'[95]

He did have the constitutional power, as president, to recommend that Pikoli not be fired. But the fact is he would have faced serious problems had he recommended reinstatement, especially as the new NEC leadership had put their faith in him when they wanted him to replace Mbeki. It would have put his presidency under unbearable strain. Since the ANC suspected that if Pikoli were reinstated he would go after Zuma again, it would never want him back in the job. Too much was at stake for Zuma and his supporters. In this sense it could be argued that his dismissal was a fait accompli even before Kgalema recommended that his services be terminated. If Kgalema had differed, he probably would not have been able to do much about it. Some people did argue, though, that he could and should have taken a stand on Pikoli, not so much for the sake of the ANC as for that of the country.

The Congress of the People was very unhappy with Kgalema's handling of the Ginwala report: 'Motlanthe said he took the decision because the inquiry into Pikoli's suspension found him insensitive to national security matters. He did not explain why this alleged weakness – it remains unclear what the security danger was and Selebi has been prosecuted anyway ... overrode Ginwala's other findings in Pikoli's favour.'[96] It is hard to deny that it does seem that Kgalema, and Mbeki before him, tended to blow out of proportion this alleged insensitivity to national security, and that Kgalema downplayed the reasons in the Ginwala report why Pikoli should not be dismissed.[97] But Kgalema had no regrets: 'I have taken this decision with a clear conscience.'[98]

Kgalema may have erred in emphasising Pikoli's insensitivity to national security when that was not why Mbeki suspended Pikoli originally, even though Ginwala refers to it in her report. This is why Pikoli argued that Kgalema used 'insensitivity to national security' as a 'side issue' to fire him: 'What is of concern to me is to be removed on charges that were not put forward as a case against me. The matter [insensitivity to national security] is a side issue that was not even canvassed at the [Ginwala] commission.'[99]

Why, if Pikoli was so wrong about refusing to delay Selebi's arrest, did the government offer him a R7.5 million out-of-court settlement package?[100] Kgalema says nobody discussed the idea with him, to his surprise, but he came to see there could have been a good reason for it. The ministry of justice was eager to replace Pikoli with Menzi Simelane, because a new director-general was urgently required. A court case to defend Pikoli's dismissal could have taken a long while, which would have seriously compromised the work of the ministry.

There was a report, which Kgalema denied, that he had offered Pikoli a 'large sum of money to resign.'[101] There is, however, a lingering sense that, delay aside, the out-of-court settlement was made to avoid the government having to reinstate Pikoli if he won the case. Many wanted to get rid of Pikoli as the man who had laid charges against Zuma.

Kgalema's grounds for dismissing Pikoli remain highly contentious. It does seem certain that the state settled with Pikoli because the reasons for dismissal were quite possibly inadequate. But Friedman points out that the Pikoli dismissal was not an initiative by Kgalema but about the Ginwala report which he had to respond to as the president.[102] Even so, it was an unfortunate decision.

Refusing the Dalai Lama's visa

In 2009 the South African World Cup committee asked three South African Nobel Peace Prize laureates – Archbishop Desmond Tutu, Nelson Mandela and FW de Klerk – to invite the Dalai Lama to South Africa as part of the soccer World Cup celebrations in 2010. The Dalai Lama accepted, applied for a visa to enter the country, and was refused by the international relations department. Kgalema backed the decision and, as president, was finally responsible for it.

There was intense debate in the media about why the ANC took such an unpopular decision. Steven Friedman believed it was not mainly trade but 'probably party funding because there are many other countries that heavily trade with China but don't take decisions like that. China has a very focused trade strategy and would not care a great deal to fashion their trade with us on such a visit.'[103] But the political relationship between the Chinese Communist Party and the ANC–SACP was definitely a big factor. Party funding and many visits to China for a range of purposes were also at stake, along with trade. Probably for the ANC and the government, each of these factors was powerful in its own right and, when combined, they were irresistibly compelling.

The three Nobel holders and all of civil society strongly criticised the decision, but to no avail. Kgalema's spokesperson Thabo Masebe took this line: 'It would not be in the interests of the country to invite the Dalai Lama to South Africa at this stage because the attention of the whole world is on us as the host of the 2010 World Cup. The presence of the Dalai Lama here will divert such attention from us to other issues. We do have excellent relations with China and these relations have produced increased trade and investment. But this did not influence our decision.'[104] The explanation was hardly convincing.

Kgalema did not talk in those terms. Instead he said that he and the government had no principled objection to the visit but that the timing of the visit coincided with the fiftieth anniversary of the Tibetan uprising, and that could create serious problems in relations between South Africa and China. The outcry was immediate. Kate Philip expressed the view of many: 'That is the whole thing about democracy – giving free rein to various viewpoints. So even if the Dalai Lama used the opportunity to raise the question of Tibetan independence, what about it? Why must that right have been suppressed? I think that was one of the worst-handled issues when he was president.'[105]

Barbara Hogan, then minister of health, sparked a raging controversy in the ANC with her stance: 'The very fact that this government had refused entry to the Dalai Lama is an example of a government that is dismissive of human rights.'[106] Kgalema met her on the matter but refused to take disciplinary action against her, which also led to criticism from some quarters in the ANC alliance.[107] Themba Maseko, government spokesperson, strongly criticised Hogan: 'This position on the Dalai Lama is an official position of the government. It's unfortunate that she went on a public platform to attack a decision of this government when she is part of that collective.'[108] She was unrepentant.

In fact Kgalema and the ANC did not appear to take into account many important matters, including civic rights in China itself, that were of great concern to civil society everywhere, aside from the Dalai Lama's democratic right to visit South Africa. For many in the country, these reasons only made the decision to please China – which is what it turned out to be – still more unacceptable.

Kgalema, looking back at the condemnation as it became worldwide, says: 'The USA and others want to pontificate about the Dalai Lama matter, but they imposed sanctions on Iran, though much of our oil, for example for Engen, comes from Iran, without any care about how it will affect us. Twenty-nine per cent of our liquid fuel comes from Iran. As a result of the sanctions we had to frantically find alternative sources, but nobody condemns them for such unilateral action and says we need to take a stand in that matter.' That is true, but the question remains: Doesn't the refusal of the visa contradict the principled behaviour many praise him for? At the same time, as I see it, so resolved were the international relations department and the ANC on the matter, even if he had held a different view on the matter there was no way it would have prevailed.

I end this section with a concern about what I see as Kgalema's longstanding infatuation with China. For years he has been one of the leading voices for strong relations with that country. In 2000 he told O'Malley: 'The biggest nation on earth, the Chinese, do care and they are modernising their economy and they are committed.'[109] He insists that the ANC does not romanticise China: 'They are very methodical and you have to admire the discipline with which they pursue set goals.'

Unfortunately, in emphasising the benefits he sees in a Chinese relationship,[110] some of his statements suggest he has thought very little about the problems and contradictions it gives rise to.[111] He acknowledges the semi-colonial nature of trade and economic relations China has with Africa, the absence of independent trade unions and the suppression of civil society organisations in China. But when he accepts that capitalism has been restored in China thanks to cheap labour, for example, he tells me: 'Yes, I agree that it is cheap Chinese labour which is the basis of the growing foreign investment in China and that is why the South African Breweries have fourteen plants there.' That response in itself raises a whole range of questions about China and our relations with the Chinese. Our relations with China are arguably our most disappointing foreign relations story, these issues being what they are.

Refusing an inquiry into the arms deal

In December 2008 Archbishop Desmond Tutu and FW de Klerk petitioned Kgalema to set up a commission of inquiry into the infamous arms deal. He did not do so and was criticised for it. Since he was only going to be in office for about eight months, said some of those I interviewed, it was perhaps unrealistic to expect him to take on such a hugely controversial and combustible task that could not possibly have been completed while he was in office.

I think Kgalema would also have taken into account the allegations over the years that the new president of the ANC, Jacob Zuma, was himself implicated in the arms deal. Had he agreed to a commission of inquiry at that stage, it would have created many more problems for Zuma than he was already faced with. With an election looming too, it was even less likely that he would have found the timing appropriate.

Many in the media believed that Kgalema had little or no alternative but to yield to the demands of Luthuli House and reject the idea. 'Decisions on the Dalai Lama, Pikoli and Scorpions all indicated the long shadows of Luthuli House,' said the analyst Prince Mashele. 'You could then see that he was no president of his own. He was an implementer of ANC headquarters.'[112]

The fact that in 2011 Zuma felt compelled to institute an inquiry (with a projected life span of two years) only after a legal challenge by the journalist Terry Crawford-Browne was indeed a vindication of all those who had made similar calls over the years and a refutation of the government stubbornly resisting them. Until the terms of reference are known, and depending on how transparent the process will be, we still do not know how far it will be effective in yielding the full truth.

Delay in scrapping the Scorpions

The directorate of special operations (the Scorpions) was a unit of the NPA launched in 2001 to investigate and prosecute organised crime and corruption. After the Scorpions clashed with Jackie Selebi, the head of the South African Police Service, they were officially disbanded in January 2009. Already by June 2008 the ANC had decided to merge the Scorpions with the police, reducing their power. Preparations were made for the remaining Scorpions members to start work in a new police unit for priority crime investigation (the Hawks).

Kgalema delayed in this matter, as a convinced constitutionalist. Even with decisions with a sound political objective, the disbanding had to be done properly and comply with the Constitution. In the legislature, there are procedural steps for any major change that can be time-consuming, as Kgalema often told me. In this case he was scathing about the Scorpions' cavalier conduct but still insisted on due process.

The ANC criticised Kgalema heavily for delaying the legislation that would terminate the Scorpions, but he did eventually sign it. Then, sadly, the Hawks soon seemed to be even more at the mercy of political power than the Scorpions had been. Notably, they shut down the probe the Scorpions had been conducting into bribery among Zuma's allies in the multibillion-rand arms deal.[113] The decision to scrap the Scorpions was controversial. There was a huge outcry across the country[114] and from interest groups ranging from opposition parties to organised business. The DA accused the ANC of merging the Scorpions with the police in order to subvert investigations into the police force and to protect corrupt ANC officials.

Kgalema had no regrets whatever about ending the Scorpions and replacing them with the Hawks. In any case Kgalema and Luthuli House felt much the same about the unit, except that Luthuli House wanted the Scorpions disbanded faster than parliamentary and legal processes would allow. He could not conceivably have supported keeping them when for years he had criticised their conduct, especially in their aggressive and high-handed raids on Zuma's properties. No serious efforts were put into rehabilitating them, if that was what this called for. Instead the ANC was in a great hurry to get rid of them.

Quite apart from Kgalema's view that the Scorpions had often behaved disgracefully, this development exposed the fact that the demise of the Scorpions was, as with the Pikoli matter, most probably effected for political reasons.

Delay on the SABC Bill

The South African Broadcasting Corporation Bill was passed in parliament in August 2008. It was designed to amend the way in which members of the SABC board were both appointed and fired. The DA and other opposition parties said that the grounds for removing board members were much too broad: it 'leaves the door wide open for abuse by a majority party in parliament. In effect the board will now be accountable to parliament and, if it fails to do what parliament wants, it can be fired.' This, they argued, 'could kill off the independence of the SABC board and thus of the public broadcaster because the board will be beholden to the National Assembly for their jobs.'[115]

Luthuli House was impatient to get the Bill, passed but

Kgalema delayed signing it because he was concerned that certain provisions could be unconstitutional. He had to be sure that board members would not be fired willy-nilly without a fair inquiry and that members of the board must be protected by fair principles and procedures, as in other laws protecting workers. Perhaps his union past played a role in how he felt. Finally, on 14 February 2009 the Bill was amended to bring it into line with the Constitution. The DA was still unhappy that it gave parliament too much power to remove the board if the ANC, as the majority party, did not like its performance.[116]

There was a technical reason for his delay too: 'What the general public doesn't know is that when a Bill is presented to a president it has to be translated into a second official language, which takes time. That is partly the reason for long delays in many Bills – in November 20 Bills were passed, but by December only five were translated.'[117] He reportedly also pointed out to ANC MPs who were pressurising him to sign the Bill that, though they were eager to dissolve the SABC board, they were the ones who had recommended the board to Mbeki.[118]

He was correct to make this point, which can be attributed to the victory of Zuma over Mbeki in Polokwane, which created its own factional dynamics. He refused to be swept along by the overwhelming triumphalism that emerged after Zuma's victory in Polokwane; such arrogance, he felt, was the antithesis of the key theme of renewal to which the ANC had committed itself at the conference.

For him the pitfalls in the SABC Bill were evident, but many in the leadership refused to see the points that needed amending, driven as they were by their euphoria. As he puts it: 'The revolution has a right to exist and to succeed, but once you get people who style themselves as defenders and guardians of the revolution against "counterrevolutionaries", who are those who have different views, then they tend to become the revolution itself, so that there is no longer a distinction between the leaders and the revolution. In fact they no longer lead the revolution but are themselves the revolution. That is the basis of Stalinism.' His view is that, whatever views your opponents hold, you must never prevent anybody from expressing them or seek to crush them by intimidation.

Vodacom/Telkom sale deal

In November 2008 Telkom announced the sale of 15 per cent of its stake in Vodacom, worth R22.5 billion. The sale would result in Vodafone's share in Vodacom increasing from 50 per cent to 65 per cent. The Communications Union opposed the deal on the grounds that they had not been properly consulted and they feared job losses in Telkom. Kgalema signed the deal only when there was a guarantee that there would be no retrenchments as a result.

This is how a senior government official captured Kgalema's role in the discussions and, finally, the signed deal: 'A few weeks after [Kgalema's] taking office, the Vodacom deal came up in cabinet, which was the longest meeting he chaired during his short stint. From the decision-making point of view within government it was a feat for Motlanthe. He brought his own personality to the presidency: calm and the ability to listen to different opinions. He does not have the illusion of grandeur Mbeki had.'[119] He added that Kgalema 'handled the cabinet differences so well that once the decision was taken, the entire government was united behind the deal.'[120]

This achievement very early in his presidency meant that 'as the controversy around the Telkom deal raged, Motlanthe was getting safely ensconced in his position, securing a respectable media posture, causing some ANC leaders to quietly debate whether he, instead of Zuma, was perhaps the kind of leader the republic wanted.'[121]

But for the ANC's leftist allies, Cosatu and the SACP, the biggest criticism they had of Kgalema was the Vodacom/Telkom sale deal he signed. Cosatu underestimated Kgalema's own commitment to the deal. As we have seen, he signed it only after there was assurance that it would not lead to the loss of jobs in either Vodacom or Telkom. After ten years of working in NUM he was certainly not going to sign away the jobs of workers.

Kgalema believes there was another point behind Cosatu's resistance to the deal: 'It seemed to have more to do with their hatred of Cope and the people in it. They hated the idea of the largesse going to those people and for me there is no principle involved other than that there is no honour among robbers. I think it is as crass as that, because they don't allow the facts to speak for themselves. For example, their insistence that there will be no job losses, when in fact a condition of the sale is that there will be no job losses at all. Furthermore, their opposition seems largely to have been based on rumours that the deal would help to fund Cope.' When Kgalema refers to the 'largesse going to those people' he is referring to Elephant Consortium, which was reportedly involved in the deal and was known to have people involved in Cope and close to Mbeki in its leading ranks, such as Smuts Ngonyama.

Still, the way this matter was handled showed that as the new president Kgalema was in a difficult situation when he first took office. After Mbeki had been defeated at Polokwane and then removed from the state presidency, Luthuli House and the left in the ANC alliance were riding the crest of an unprecedented confidence, which often seemed to veer towards blatant arrogance in their new-found power and, as in the case of the Vodacom/Telkom deal, 'not allowing the facts to speak for themselves,' as Kgalema said.

Kgalema had to contend with sheer falsehood too. Long after the deal, in September 2009, an editorial in the *Financial Mail* asserted that Kgalema had met with Zuma and Telkom's CEO Reuben September two days after Zuma's inauguration as president, and that September was told that Telkom's deal with Vodacom must be overturned and Telkom must not sell its shares to Vodacom. The account implied he was party to a meeting that sought to undo a cabinet decision. Kgalema had never been at such a meeting, knew nothing of it and was particularly upset because the paper had never contacted him on it. In November the paper published a retraction and apology, [122] but only after Kgalema had got a lawyer to demand it.

Kgalema in the run-up to the 2009 elections

In the last few months before the national elections on 22 May 2009, there was much media speculation that Kgalema was so deeply disheartened by his experience as president that he did not wish to return to government. The *City Press* ran a story in January claiming that 'Motlanthe has told a few friends that he was under sustained attack from a group of people who do not want to see him return to the Union Buildings after the polls.'[123] In early February he said again that he did not want to return, speaking to John Carlin of the *Sunday Independent* in the wake of all the sleaze about the '24-year-old woman' and its suggestion of a campaign against himself. The smear saga was for him the worst manifestation of political and moral decay. If such blatant lies could be spread about him, apparently from within the ANC,[124] in order to besmirch his character to the point of preventing his return to government, his gut feeling was that he did not want to serve again.

Kgalema Motlanthe

So distressed did Kgalema sound in the Carlin interview, the commentator Jabulani Sikhakhane mistakenly concluded that he could not withstand the pressures of his life as president. Sikhakhane cited an Isaiah Berlin analogy: 'Whoever has chosen to make an omelette cannot do so without breaking eggs. It is the breaking up eggs in that hot kitchen of the presidency to make the omelettes of national interest that may have frightened Motlanthe.'[125] But Kgalema's concerns had nothing to do with inability to deal with pressure; they were about the dirty tactics of that 'group of people who did not want him to return to the Union Buildings.'

Kgalema may have been unwise and made the job of his detractors easier when he told Carlin that he was unhappy with his position: 'Being president means you have no life of your own. I actually don't like it. I think you have to be insane or very, very special.' Sikhakhane writes exactly what Kgalema's detractors were probably saying behind the scenes: 'On that basis we should accept his statement at face value. And in addition, we should be grateful to Motlanthe for the reminder that chopping limbs to save lives, as the job of the president often demands of the incumbent, is a bloody affair that is not for the faint-hearted. There should be no shame in admitting that.'[126] Yet, what Kgalema told Carlin was said in a moment when he was unusually candid about his emotions, about how alienated he felt at the time – deeply pained by the smear campaign and wanting to get out.

Apart from anguish on that score, Kgalema did not concern himself with ponderings in the media and kept his eye on presidential tasks while the rumours flew. Would he return to government and, if not, what would he do or where else would the ANC deploy him? Jessie Duarte prompted a lot of talk when she declared that he would return to Luthuli House to focus on

Kgalema, third ANC president of South Africa, 2008

political education.[127] There were stories that Blade Nzimande was eyeing the post of deputy state president: 'Several ANC sources confirmed that Blade wanted to be Zuma's deputy and that these are people who don't like Kgalema, including on the NEC, and that they had clashed in the NWC about the dissolution of the SABC board and the SABC Bill.'[128] Baleka Mbete, Kgalema's deputy at the time, was said to be eager to continue under Zuma and 'expected that Motlanthe would decline the DP [deputy president] post.'[129]

What many, including his detractors, did not appear to grasp was that once Zuma was inaugurated and had to assemble the cabinet and appoint his deputy, he would have to sit down with Kgalema anyway and discuss the composition of the new cabinet and Kgalema's place in it. That talk would clarify how far Kgalema was interested in serving in his government. Kgalema would be a key candidate as deputy state president, as deputy president of the ANC and outgoing state president. For the same reasons, it would be very difficult for Zuma to explain to the ANC why he did not appoint Kgalema as his deputy in the new administration.

Zuma was aware that no matter what he might have felt about Kgalema – after all the stories that Kgalema was still close to Mbeki and that he supported his appeal against the Nicholson judgment – he had little alternative but to appoint him as deputy.

The ANCYL was insistent on the idea at the time.[130] Altogether, though it could not be proved, it seemed clear that if Zuma did not appoint Kgalema as deputy, he was destined to have a very troubled presidency, which would probably also have alienated so many in the ANC that he could lose the post to Kgalema in Mangaung in 2012, assuming Zuma wanted a second term and some regions nominated Kgalema.

How do decent politicians who hold progressive principles

and are genuinely committed to the solution of society's most pressing problems survive the rough and tumble of our politics and an environment where skulduggery, opportunism and such filth are rife? Kgalema is among the first to say that politics must be cleansed, and is confident that it can be.[131] From his youth, he has held to the values of the Anglican Church.[132] As we have seen, his entry into politics, even before he discovered Marxism, was steered by those values, which led to a deeper, wider political awakening and awareness.[133]

Daryl Glaser said of Kgalema after Polokwane: 'I used to think that he was one of the Machiavellian plotters in the Zuma camp but later I began to see a much more principled politician than I earlier thought.'[134] For Gevisser there is something ascetic about Kgalema, whose political involvement seems not so much a passion as a calling for someone with a 'responsibility to lead the people because you can see further than them and it is your responsibility to educate them.'[135] Indeed, the epigraph of this chapter seems to bear this out; when Kgalema says, 'In the struggle you do what you have to and can do', he expresses a call to dutiful service. But for him it has been a passionate calling, an expression of his dedication to his beliefs.

CHAPTER EIGHT
Kgalema, deputy president of South Africa, 2009

> Kgalema is anything but a rah-rah politician and is decidedly not a statement of fashion but he communicates a sense of substance consistently.
>
> Trevor Manuel, 2010

This chapter explores Kgalema's role as deputy president, his performance and the key issues that confronted him during what has been a hectic and in fact dramatic period in South African politics since the 2009 elections.

Appointment as deputy president
In the run-up to the 2009 elections Kgalema had no ambition to return to any government post, including that of deputy president. 'I was not then in the least interested in grandstanding and speculation about the composition of a new Zuma-led government and my own place in it. Instead my main aim was to ensure that the new president is properly inaugurated. Others were more interested in presenting themselves as kingmakers and some very ambitious about securing ministerial and other senior posts for themselves.'[1] For him, the ANC came first. If Zuma, as elected president of the ANC, wanted him for state

president or deputy president, he would accept the post as another job the ANC wanted him to do.

The fact that Zuma chose him although Kgalema had not wanted to enter the running spoke volumes about Zuma's high regard for him, especially after all the criticism Kgalema had received from Luthuli House on matters during his presidency, not to mention the scandal-mongering in the media.[2]

Kgalema's approach to the new Zuma-led administration was cautiously optimistic at the outset.[3] However, his concerns grew from 2009 in the light of many negative developments, some of which we have already met and others that follow in this chapter. But he also argued that, unlike the previous regime with its sense of monopolistic invincibility, its arrogant confidence of being able to act with impunity, Zuma had not 'used the state machinery to overwhelm the ANC.'[4] Yet, when he became Zuma's deputy, he was under no illusion that (as when he himself became president) the people under ANC rule did not really govern as the Freedom Charter had promised. 'We in the ANC know that the people themselves are not really governing. That goal is therefore still an aspiration.'

Kgalema could have declined Zuma's request that he act as deputy. Though he had served as president for only eight months he was guaranteed an annual salary for five years of R2.1 million and all related benefits, such as two personal assistants and researchers, VIP protection and full medical aid, and free transport for the rest of his life. Precisely because of the scandalously painful stories he had to endure during the first few months of 2009, most people would have understood had he declined. No wonder he was upset when Moshoeshoe Monare said that it was 'legal daylight robbery' for him to be eligible for these benefits after serving for such a short term as president:[5] 'He forgets that to have accepted the job for five years was a

Kgalema, deputy president of South Africa, 2009

huge sacrifice precisely because I could have received similar benefits without doing anything and in fact retiring.'[6]

How powerful is the position of deputy state president? When Zuma was Mbeki's deputy his role was largely ceremonial, apparently through a conscious decision to limit its scope when Mbeki took over from Mandela in 1997. Kgalema's role as deputy for Zuma has been more substantial. Every Monday evening he gets two briefcases of tasks to perform, including the documents for cabinet meetings he will chair between Tuesday and Thursday where recommendations of the cabinet committees are formally considered. He often gets home between seven and eight at night and works as often until one or two in the morning.

The media appeals tribunal: Where does Kgalema really stand?

The proposal to introduce a statutory media appeals tribunal (MAT) after a resolution the ANC adopted at Polokwane was widely seen as probably the most serious threat to media freedom since 1994. A huge public debate took place in the media after the 2009 elections, with the ANC and the SACP arguing for the tribunal.

In early 2008 Kgalema and Pallo Jordan had met with Sanef in Cape Town to discuss the ANC resolution. Kgalema had already realised that the media perhaps had not grasped that this was not an ANC decision taken to impose a tribunal, but for parliament to investigate if it was possible and desirable, in the light of the ANC's concerns. As he told me at the end of 2009:

> The media conflates the conference resolution with the tribunal, but if the investigation shows that it is not a good idea we will drop it. They are also not engaging in constructive

debates about the matter but are often hysterical about it. I think there are genuine media concerns but they have a serious misunderstanding of the resolution and its intention. Besides, there was no way that we would impose a MAT on the media and the country. It was really meant to seriously strengthen the regime of self-regulation in ways which satisfactorily address the huge concerns the ANC has with it.

Earlier, while he was still president, he had a much more modest idea of the goals: 'This is a conference resolution to investigate whether it will be a desirable thing or not. The way I see it is that perhaps it will remain self-regulation, but the turnaround time and where an apology is printed must be done much more prominently because what happens is that they publish false things today and publish an apology months later. There is also no sanction other than just an apology that can be imposed by either the press council or press ombudsman.' He also noted that the ANC was well aware when it adopted the resolution that the Constitution enshrines the right of access to information and freedom of expression and a free media, principles the resolution did not intend to violate or abandon.

Another of his concerns was that 'access to the ombudsman was conditional because you have to first assure him that you will not pursue this matter in a court of law.' This is indeed a serious and unnecessary handicap: any suggestion that people may finally want to sue would make their appeal to the ombudsman a non-starter. To be compelled to give up a constitutional right in advance is a ridiculous violation of it.[7]

One might have thought that Kgalema would be the most ardent supporter of a statutory tribunal after all the pain he suffered at the hands of the print media in particular, in their hatchet job on him in early 2009. In fact this is why many in the

ANC alliance dug in their heels on the need for one. He did not make a hobbyhorse of the experience but it did leave him asking where the self-regulatory rules were that the media profess to apply in this story they got so horribly wrong.[8]

Tensions within the ANC about Kgalema's comments were quite obvious to the media. After his meeting with Sanef in October 2010 one report said, 'The ANC is silent on the deputy president Motlanthe's statement that the media be given the space to fix itself, rather than be subject to harsh punishments under the proposed media appeals tribunal', going on to cite Kgalema's view: 'If the process of reviewing the self-regulatory mechanisms produces mechanisms that can address the concerns about its shortcomings, we see no difficulty in accepting that right product, whatever it is – so we are in a sense allowing the space for the media to attend to that challenge.'[9]

Though the media were relieved at this conciliatory line, 'some in the media noted that while he has promised a softer approach towards the media appeals tribunal by strengthening self-regulation it is not clear how much authority he has on the issues, as others in the ruling party have contradicted him.'[10] In fact there is no evidence that any other ANC leader clearly contradicted him, but there was tension on whether the ANC wanted to get the media to a point where they would seriously investigate how to improve self-regulation or would rather focus anyway on parliamentary and ANC investigation into the feasibility of a statutory tribunal. Kgalema has strongly tended towards getting the media to do all they can to strengthen self-regulation, as long as it was to the point of satisfying the concerns raised by the ANC and not a half-hearted tinkering with the current model.

In 2012 Sanef's resistance to the idea of a statutory tribunal bore a little fruit when the ANC began to talk of 'independent regulation unencumbered by commercial or political party interests' but with parliamentary oversight.[11] This shift to a regulatory system apparently unencumbered by party political interests did not mean much, though, because it would be under the authority of parliament, where the ANC's dominance is overwhelming. The ANC continued to criticise the ombudsman system, which it said was flawed because 'it's funded by the print media, so they have to protect the newspapers from the public', according to Jesse Duarte.[12] Media funding of the press ombudsman does indeed raise concern about a conflict of interest, however much Sanef or the ombudsman pledges neutrality.

In April 2012 the ANC, including Kgalema, greeted new proposals by the Press Freedom Commission with much delight. The report recommends that print media move from self-regulation to 'independent co-regulation, involving public and media representatives without state intervention.'[13] Mantashe for the ANC explains: 'What is important about this report is that it has taken everybody out of their comfort zone, from the extremes of the [proposed] statutory regulatory framework and the total self-regulatory framework, to the centre, which gives legitimacy to the body, and gives a fair balance to regulation.'[14]

Sanef must take credit for having taken the initiative to establish the Press Freedom Commission. Kgalema, from several meetings with Sanef, was also pleased to see that they welcomed the findings. Of the top six ANC officials, it was mostly Kgalema whom the print media questioned on the ANC's MAT resolution, I think because they saw him as the most level-headed. He alone in the ANC leadership repeatedly said that if Sanef's review of self-regulation effectively addressed the ANC's concerns, the party might accept it. In his words to me in late 2011: 'I told Sanef that given the fact that they had set a review process in motion, if the outcome satisfactorily addresses issues raised by the ANC we will look at it and perhaps reconsider the idea of the tribunal.'

Protection of State Information Bill

This Bill had still not been passed by August 2012 after some amendments in November 2011 and May 2012 and ongoing public displeasure with aspects of the Bill and the inadequacy of the amendments to it. Kgalema feels that the media and public approach to the Bill had blown its intent out of proportion:

> Bear in mind that some information is already being protected by being classified as top secret, with criteria and a clear definition of who does that, so this Bill seeks to expand on that and from the manner in which it is crafted it is clear that it is open-ended, which creates a problem. But parliament has the right to narrow down the definition because that is how Bills are treated. However, the president will not assent to it unless it complies with the constitution. So we need to remove the hysteria from this matter, because Bills are Bills: they pass, are modified or get defeated.

Yet, as deputy state president and being in cabinet, he seems to have not fully realised just how sensitive and serious this matter really is to civil society. The 'hysteria' he cautioned against is a sharp indicator of mounting public anger at the most serious threats to the right to information, which the 1996 Constitution and especially the Promotion of Access to Information Act of 2002 enshrine. It appears the ANC is hell-bent on reversing these rights by creating new obstacles to access to information.[15]

Kgalema did think the parliamentary committee should have spent more time dealing with what procedure to follow and how settlement would be reached when differences exist between the parties involved if people already possess classified material, and what they must do when they wish to apply for permission to publish it. For him, judges should decide on disputes. On resolving differences, he told the committee they should do 'as we used to do in the unions: we isolate all areas of difference and then focus systematically on finding ways and means of reaching agreement.' He adds: 'But people must have the will and determination to find agreement. Some people say "to hell with classification" but they are wrong. They perhaps won't understand what this really means until they themselves get into government. There can be no doubt that some information is far more vital, sensitive and strategic than other information and the ability to decipher and distinguish is equally important.'

A key question is this: In a constitutional democracy and given the secrecy-ridden past we inherited in 1994, should the ANC, simply by virtue of its majority in parliament, have the power to decide on such a hugely important question in our society, especially given the very serious limits of public participation in the parliament-driven 'consultation' process?

When the ANC rejected the inclusion of a public interest clause in the Bill that civil society had fought long and hard for, Kgalema argued that the clause does not exist anywhere in the world.[16] Yet he also regards the decision making process as very important. Differences of opinion now, he says, are not the end of the road, as the Bill must still go to the National Council of Provinces and perhaps back to parliament. Just as he urged Cosatu not to bulldoze matters through with its sheer size when he was in NUM, he now urges the ANC not to do the same to ram the Bill through parliament. He adds that even if the Bill is forced through parliament by the ANC, the 'president can still object to the Bill if it does not possess sufficient checks and balances' (though it is very unlikely that Zuma would object after the ANC majority in parliament assented).[17]

The judiciary, the ANC and Kgalema

The relationship between the judiciary and the ANC has been one of the most contentious issues in the past few years.[18] Kgalema has differed somewhat from the ANC[19] in his understanding of the judiciary and its role in post-apartheid South Africa. He holds that there must always be debate between the judiciary, the executive and the legislature on their functions and the balance of power. 'It is common cause that constitutional democracies across the globe are characterised by the inherent, necessary and in fact healthy tension between the three arms of government, which must however always co-operate, even as they discharge their mandates. None of the three arms of the state are superior to any other and judicial review is a fundamental principle because no major policy or law can pass without complying with the Constitution.'

Unlike some in the ANC alliance, he does not regard the judiciary as 'counterrevolutionary' and thinks the idea both wrong and dangerous. 'When Mantashe and others say that judges are counterrevolutionary and that the judiciary is oppositionist, it reflects a completely wrong understanding of their constitutional role and their relationship with the other two arms of the state. ... The judiciary is a very important leg of our constitutional democracy and there must be no cutting corners in this vital sphere of government.' He opposes the inflammatory term and the generalising of individual acts: 'When we say judges are counterrevolutionary the uttered word cannot be taken back, which is why we must be very careful as leaders what we say in public. Besides, we cannot generalise about judges and judgments, because we have different kinds of judges and judgments, conservative and progressive, among blacks and whites, which is therefore much more complex than a simple black–white picture.'

He does have some other concerns about the judiciary: 'The Constitutional Court (CC) sometimes makes judgments which essentially amend the Constitution by stealth, with the result that the CC has tended to infuse into the lower courts political considerations in their judgments in anticipation that a certain matter may end up in the CC, meaning they factor into their judgments political considerations. I think that is a serious problem because the courts are not meant to make political judgments but on the basis of the actual evidence and arguments presented in court.'[20]

Kgalema also feels strongly that the executive must not appoint judges its members have personal ties with, because it can 'quickly prove very problematic, counterproductive and in fact perilous.' Senior judges must be as far removed as possible from the executive and their circle, precisely because of the sensitive nature of their responsibilities.[21]

At the lighting of the Eternal Flame of Democracy at Constitution Hill in 2011, on the fifteenth anniversary of the South African Constitution, Kgalema had this to say: 'The heart of any notion of democracy lies in the relationship between the executive, the judiciary and the legislature. As a result, the challenge that faced us has been the need to transform these arms of the state to accord with the vision of a united, democratic, nonracial, nonsexist and just society. In particular, I wish to pay tribute to the sterling work by the judiciary and the legislature, who have over the years dedicated themselves to building democracy.'[22]

Not once has he lambasted the judiciary (as others have done) although he knows they inevitably have weaknesses. For him, the judiciary still needs a more thorough transformation. Primarily, he says, it is imperative that the requisite skills and experience be acquired as soon as possible because the judiciary is pivotal to a well-functioning constitutional democracy. Given the decades-long racist nature of the judiciary the ANC inherited in 1994, it will take a long while to rectify the imbalances.

ICT, Mtshali and Kgalema

In 2010 the media ran a range of stories that involved Kgalema's partner Gugu Mtshali and some other people known to him, who were directors of a company called Imperial Crown Trading (ICT). They had applied to the department of minerals and energy for right to a 21.4 per cent stake in an iron ore mine, Sishen Iron Ore Company, owned by Kumba Mining, an Anglo American subsidiary. ICT and Kumba applied for this right, which became available at the end of April 2009. They both applied on 4 May, each insisting they had done so before the other. ICT won the case but the decision was subsequently overturned. ICT then appealed and the case is still pending.

There was so much groundless linkage made by the media between ICT's application and Kgalema on the strength of his personal relationship with Mtshali that one headline read 'ANC link to Sishen right'.[23] Had he used his political influence to secure the licence for ICT? Kgalema was not involved at all and (as in the case of Kalahari Resources) not a shred of evidence has been produced to support the idea; he is far too highly principled and experienced a leader to get drawn into any such underhand manoeuvring. Needless to say, Kgalema was dismayed by the insinuation and rejected it.[24]

Kgalema, Mtshali and the Iranian helicopter deal

In March 2012 the *Sunday Times* published a lead story that involved Kgalema and his partner Gugu Mtshali. The paper said she was implicated in soliciting a R104 million bribe to obtain government support for Aviation 360, a South African company trying to clinch a R2 billion sanctions-busting deal to sell helicopters to Iran.'[25] Kgalema was reported to have denied any knowledge of her involvement with Aviation 360.[26] Thabo Masebe in the premier's office said Kgalema 'at no stage discussed such a matter with any person, including the Department of Trade and Industry. The Deputy President did not meet with 360 Aviation in the manner suggested at all.'[27] But the company director, Barry Oberholzer, confirmed he had met Motlanthe in June 2011, although they did not discuss the deal.[28] Kgalema says he never met with Oberholzer and does not know him at all.

Kgalema, unhappy about what he regarded as false allegations, took the matter to the public protector, Thuli Madonsela, to be investigated.[29] Media speculation was that this move had to do with Kgalema readying himself to contest the presidency of the ANC with Zuma at Mangaung in December 2012. Kgalema denies this and insists instead that he just wants to clear his name after the serious allegations made.[30] The *Star*'s editor Makhudu Sefara got it right when he said the story had 'potential to gnaw away at the deputy president's credibility'.[31] Kgalema was evidently motivated by the need to defend his integrity as deputy president of both the ANC and the country. But it was also to clear Mtshali's name. Overall, though, he is sure that the real aim of the smear was to harm him politically.

It was significant that after listening to the recording of the meeting where the alleged bribery took place and viewing the transcript (both of which were leaked to the *Sunday Times*) the South African Institute of Corporate Fraud Management (SAICFM) reported that 'the facts are clear and that is that the

Kgalema, deputy president of South Africa, 2009

CIA and FBI appear to be directly linked to a very transparent attempt to offer a bribe to the partner of the Deputy President of a Sovereign State in order to attempt to implicate the Deputy President and that state in violating international laws and treaties.'[32] So seriously did the SAICFM regard the matter, they felt it should not have been referred to the public protector at all but that it 'calls for an urgent investigation by the Department of Justice, the Department of Foreign Affairs and our own Hawks and Intelligence Agencies.'[33]

There have been many stories of this kind, from the time Kgalema was SG. A few years ago it was sanctions-busting oil deals he was allegedly involved with in Iraq, now it is sanctions-busting arms deals in Iran, and none of this has ever turned out to be true. It seems his detractors, inside or outside the ANC, are set on looking for dirt to smear him with, though so far in vain. At the end of August 2012 Kgalema received the preliminary report from the public protector. The final report was due in the second week of September, but Kgalema said that it did not implicate him or Gugu in any wrongdoing.

An independent mind

While compiling this book I encountered Kgalema's own take on a range of topics along the way. Here are some that I find particularly notable.

Asked if he approved of Zuma's many references to Christianity in his speeches, especially since South African citizens, including ANC members, belong to various religions, he replied:

> We are a secular state and it is therefore important for a leader not to stir religious bias in favour of one religion or another. Mbeki used to send us a draft of his speeches for us

> to comment on because the question we need to ask is this: is this or that view what we would want the president of the ANC and the country to say in public? While ordinary members can say whatever they want to, the most senior leaders would need to be much more careful, especially on very sensitive religious matters.

He was displeased when Julius Malema criticised the dominance of racial minorities in certain ministries of government.

> If we raise matters crudely then we ourselves will reinforce conservative and even racist views among people. If you say we cannot include in government coloured, white or other people who have the requisite skills and experience, then you are setting us back by many years. We need to be conscious of the divisive legacy of apartheid and the likely repercussions of what we say in public. Sometimes Malema just says things on the spur of the moment and is then not conscious of the possible repercussions of his words and in this case it was truly a disaster. He needs to use the important platform he has much more responsibly, especially since it is not a permanent platform.

When Cosatu, others in civil society, and the media condemned expensive ministerial cars, Kgalema was not impressed.

> In a recession the responsibility of government is to help steer a recovery in the shortest possible space of time and get commodities – in this case all kind of cars – to be purchased so that production, consumption and workers' jobs can be sustained. Besides the manufacturing side they are also making the assumption that car dealers don't employ people and

they are not likely to lose their jobs if there is a slump in the market of all makes of cars. To single out cars in that way is a moralistic and in fact rhetorical argument. Furthermore, if government has to cancel orders or return cars somehow, what message is that going to send to the manufacturers in South Africa and what impact will that have on both investments and jobs? Finally, have those who called for the cars to be returned realised that as soon as you drive a new car out from the dealer its value immediately drops substantially?

While some of his points are credible, there is the distinct danger that his view can be seen by civil society as convenient and self-serving.

When Vavi said a few years ago that he was available for a post in the ANC leadership, Kgalema thought it plainly wrong.

On the one hand, it is actually most unfortunate in relation to Cosatu members because you would want them to decide this matter and not him, because he was serving at their invitation. Besides, not all Cosatu members are ANC members, which he should have thought of. On the other hand, it is the ANC members who decide who they want as their leaders, not somebody, no matter how important they may be, who volunteers his leadership. I don't think he actually thinks that way but that at that moment he just got a bit excited.

In 2010 the then minister of co-operative governance and traditional affairs, Sicelo Shiceka, proposed banning municipal workers from holding positions in political parties. This was Kgalema's response:

The minister arrived at the conclusion that most of the

problems in communities controlled by the ANC come from the ANC itself, because branch and regional leaders interfere in municipal administration. The key question is, what does the ANC and the South African Constitution say about this matter? ... The president endorsed what he said. But we are not a one-party state. You cannot also introduce legislation which will affect the DA, ID and other parties and basically tell them what they can or cannot do with their members. It was certainly in my mind a major error of judgement, though the minister may have meant well. But as we know the best intentions can pave the way to hell.

Addressing an ANC mass rally in Durban as state president in the run-up to the 2009 elections, he talked truth to power: 'The ANC must never take you for granted that you will always vote for them. It must rather work genuinely for you.' He urged the residents to 'remain mobilised and never withdraw from struggle' and that 'the ANC is an organisation of struggle because it believes that change can happen only through struggle; even if you have to march against an ANC councillor we view that as support. Life is only given to those who win it back through struggle. Please go out and vote for the party you prefer. I am not going to ask you to vote for the ANC – the ANC must earn its stripes – and if you feel that it hasn't served you, don't vote for it.'[34] And a few years ago he told the community of Thembisa on the East Rand not to vote for an ANC councillor who was a drunk.

Asked about whether Zuma's polygamy was a problem for women's rights, equality of the sexes and more progressive politics, he said: 'The ANC does not adopt anyone's culture and make it its own. Some people in the ANC practise polygamy and circumcision and others don't. That is why the question of polygamy is not something the ANC will adopt a position on at all. Our members are so culturally and socially diverse that we could create serious problems to adopt a policy either for or against polygamy.'

When the uprisings took place in Tunisia in 2010 there was a debate in the media about whether South Africa could be affected by the 'Arab Spring'. This was his comment:

> No, it won't happen here because we have a country of activists and activism, both of which we see much of daily. We don't repress opposition. Therefore I think if there is an uprising here it might very well be a socialist revolution, if you look at the overall militant character of strikes and township protests for almost a decade. But on the other hand the ANC won't be in trouble here because there is no logical imperative to preserve the ANC for what it is. There is nothing in politics that says it must forever remain an omnibus. If the rot in society manifests itself in the ANC and it can serve to concentrate the challenge to a tipping point which gives rise to a more radical alternative, that for me would be something really, not riots but revolution. The point is that we need to fundamentally transform our society and thereby eradicate by its roots massive poverty, unemployment and inequalities. Whatever it takes to achieve that noble objective must be done. That is how serious and urgent the situation is.

In an interview on the radio station SAfm about the ANC's alleged involvement in wanting to place its cadres in senior parastatal posts, he stated: 'The ANC has no business in pronouncing outside of internal processes, that our preferred person is so and so. It does not work like that. It shouldn't work like that. In fact it won't work like that. Anybody who makes a public pronouncement about the selection of this or that person is out of order.'³⁵

A brush with death

Kgalema along with a planeload of others narrowly escaped death in an emergency crash landing in 2009. He was returning to South Africa from an African Union conference in Tripoli together with Steyn Speed, who worked in the presidency, Sue van der Merwe, then deputy minister of defence, Khulu Mbatha, an adviser, and others. As a later investigation found, the crew had not prepared for the chance of bad weather that would prevent them landing to refuel at Bangui in the Central African Republic on the way home.

Seeking to land instead at Gbadolite in the Democratic Republic of Congo (DRC) in the middle of the night, the pilot and his crew came to realise that the airport there was completely inadequate because it was in fact no longer in operation. With only thirty-six minutes of fuel left, they had no other option. Desperately but with great skill, the pilot approached the unlit airport, using the plane's lights to find a runway, and somehow got the plane safely down even though some large potholes burst one tyre. As Kgalema recalls: 'The pilot decided he was going to crash-land on a path he could only faintly see, which he did, but one of the tyres burst so badly that you could put your head through the hole in it.'

Once they were back home, the ministry of defence was going to charge the pilot for negligence for not having fully prepared for the type of problem they encountered. Kgalema objected strongly. He pointed out that the pilot, a white South African, had saved their lives. While the later investigation led to precautions ensuring that this kind of crisis never happened again, no action was taken against the captain and his crew.

Kgalema, deputy president of South Africa, 2009

There was a worrying state effort at first to play down the event in the media. This was a ludicrous bit of dishonesty, done simply because the Defence Force and the presidency were too embarrassed to admit the truth that preparations for the flight had been inadequate. To Kgalema it was just counterproductive 'because the DRC had surely made a public statement about what happened. Besides, the UN people were also there, so to say that nothing happened was silly and embarrassing because the story given by the presidency did not accord with what those people disclosed happened there.' Sure enough, statements made in the DRC and by the UN spread to news agencies around the world.

State denial even extended to the need for an inquiry. Vusi Mona in the presidency reportedly stated: 'We have not asked for an investigation into the matter',[36] to which the *Sunday Independent* made this fair riposte: 'The presidency appears to be indifferent to the fact that Deputy President Motlanthe's plane had to make an emergency landing on an unlit runway at a deserted airport in the Democratic Republic of Congo this week because it was low on fuel.'[37] An aviation expert said pointedly: 'If their planning was done properly this incident should not have happened. Surely, there should have been additional diligence in place. They were transporting the deputy president of the country.'[38]

Kgalema has been particularly unlucky with his official flights recently. In September 2011 it was reported that a jet flying him to the opening of the Rugby World Cup in New Zealand missed its first landing due to a faulty warning light.[39] This was reportedly the same plane that failed again just a month later, in October, to get him to Finland on a scheduled official trip, due to mechanical problems. And in December 2011 the South African National Defence Force was compelled to ask South

African Airways to provide alternative planes for him when necessary. Unsurprisingly, both the near-fatal crash landing and other mishaps have not ruffled his calm nature. He continues to fly without any sense of trepidation.

Going public with Gugu Mtshali

Kgalema's romantic relationship with Gugu Mtshali had begun in 2002, but it was only in early November 2011 that they finally decided to go public about themselves in South Africa. The occasion was a dinner in Pretoria when Kgalema hosted Britain's Prince Charles and his wife, the Duchess of Cornwall.[40] His spokesperson, Masebe, confirmed that Gugu was his 'official partner' and added that she had been at his side before: 'She was with him when he went on his recent trip to the Nordic countries.'[41] He also confirmed that the divorce with Mapula was being finalised. But it was Gugu's appearance at the 2012 State of the Nation address that really put the couple in the spotlight.[42] The *Star* conveyed the moment: 'But it was the lady in the elegant low-back purple gown walking two steps behind Deputy President, Kgalema Motlanthe, who had observers and guests gasping.'[43] Gugu did indeed look elegant and composed in her role.

The delay in going public had been because of the divorce proceedings and because Kgalema knew the pain it would cause Mapula and the children, especially his son Kagiso, who has been very close to both his parents. When they finally saw a photo of him with Gugu, there was no going back. Kgalema is still sensitive about the privacy of his personal life. Any journalist trying to probe it is not likely to get far.

Kgalema's role as deputy president

Here we look at Kgalema's workload in office and something

of what he has achieved. For the *M&G* Report Card, 'So quiet has Motlanthe been that speculation about his succeeding Zuma has evaporated.'[44] The reality is that Kgalema has been extremely busy as deputy president ever since May 2009, to the point where access to him has had to decline markedly.

He performs in government at two intersecting levels: as deputy president of the country and as a cabinet member.[45] Knowing the ropes so well could partly explain why Zuma's office has kept him so busy. His familiarity with the different ministries and how government works has grown from a mass of interaction with them when he was SG of the ANC, the few months he spent in parliament and as minister in the presidency in 2008, and his eight months as state president. 'I do a great deal of work. Zuma focuses on the bigger issues, as it were. A big part of my responsibilities is dealing with director-generals and ministers of all departments when there are any problems or concerns,' he says.

As head of government business in parliament he has to meet regularly with office bearers to ensure that the executive is available to answer questions in the National Assembly. This task became all the more important as many ANC ministers often failed or refused to do so. Kgalema has approached this task with all the seriousness it deserved, since replies are the inescapable duty of ministers. When the magnitude of the problem grew, he wrote to all the ministers concerned 'requesting an explanation for each question that had not been replied to and to ensure that in future all questions are answered and in good time.'[46] As *Business Day* put it: 'parliamentary questions are a vital oversight tool and it is the convention that they be answered promptly and truthfully.'[47]

Kgalema's meetings with parliamentary office bearers to ensure that ministers were available to answer questions in the

National Assembly did improve matters slightly, but the problem persists. He raised this in cabinet, insisting that it be a standing item at every meeting. In June 2010 he promised the National Assembly that he was keeping records and tabling them in cabinet. While noting an improvement he reminded parliament: 'As ministers they are accountable to parliament directly, and it is up to the House to discuss the measures it should take to ensure that questions are answered.'[48] He also warned that if ministers continue to evade their responsibility their contracts will be reviewed.[49] But as the *Star* points out: 'the performance contracts system has come in for criticism because it does not envisage punitive action against erring ministers.'[50] This is precisely why it was also said that 'as leader of government business in parliament, he has committed himself to getting ministers to respond to questions, but, in reality, he has made little impact in enforcing compliance.'[51]

On other fronts: Kgalema is responsible for human resources development, where he works closely with the minister of higher education, Blade Nzimande. He is an ex-officio member of the National Planning Commission to develop a long-term vision and strategy for South Africa.

He chairs the South African National Aids Council. Since he began, there has been a very significant increase in state provision of anti-retroviral treatment, in both its amount and quality. The *M&G* writes that after years of disunity in the sector, Kgalema 'took a leading role in getting national Aids treatment guidelines revised to widen access to antiretrovirals.'[52] The *Sunday Independent* notes that thanks to his efforts 'the SA National Aids Council has been restored to its full strategic importance after becoming moribund under the previous government.'[53] According to Kgalema's office, 'he remains the pivot for all major changes in HIV/Aids strategies.'[54]

Kgalema, deputy president of South Africa, 2009

He chaired the FIFA inter-ministerial committee, whose job was to coordinate the preparations for the 2010 World Cup in South Africa, ensuring that stadiums, transport and accommodation were well organised and ready. His coordination was by all accounts splendidly performed. For him the key lesson of this event is that it showed that 'the government is capable of providing bulk infrastructure in the townships and rural areas, all those basic infrastructural necessities, like water, sewerage and electricity. If we could do it for the World Cup, why not for our people? If that can be done then we will indeed be building a better life for all, which will be better than the palliatives which we are now dishing out. We cannot also always conveniently blame everything on apartheid, like continued bucket toilets or other poor sanitation.'

He oversaw the appointment of Gill Marcus as governor of the Reserve Bank. A great deal else has not been publicised, for example his many important meetings with MTN and Anglo American. All this is besides the great deal of ANC work he still has to do.

Kgalema also leads the government's anti-poverty programme, War on Poverty, which has kept him busy visiting poverty-stricken areas around the country. It is difficult to measure exactly what impact the programme has had in dealing with widespread poverty.[55] A big obstacle seems to be the lack of a clear, comprehensive and coordinated campaign with unions and other sectors of civil society. It is probably this realisation that has prompted him to urge civil society to join the government as 'equal partners' in a coordinated front to fight poverty. He has proposed the formation of a council for that purpose.[56]

An experience in Douglas in the Northern Cape touched him deeply. An engineering firm made a mess of installing a sewerage system in the impoverished township, so the municipality decided to shut down the operation until the problems could be fixed. Meanwhile they had to continue using bucket toilets – but night-soil workers sometimes could not collect the waste for two or three weeks, a hazardous situation for families. He describes an 'old woman with snow white hair, who was paralysed and in a wheelchair,' who 'literally had to propel herself on her elbows because her grandchildren were too small to help her'. The municipality knew of this but did nothing to help her. Kgalema promised her that he would attend to the situation, which he did, and he had the satisfaction of seeing the system in place when returned to Douglas later on.

How would he regard his own contribution to the war on poverty? 'I am patient and take a long-term view but many people don't. Many people believe, and they are led to believe, that fifteen years is a long time and that therefore there shouldn't be people without jobs and there shouldn't be any poverty. But the reality is that it takes a long period to address these fundamental issues.'[57]

Kgalema also serves in international affairs. He appoints ambassadors and attends to important state functions like receiving courtesy visits from such people as the US secretary of state Hillary Clinton in 2009 and Prince Charles in 2011. He has made many working visits to the US, Europe and especially other countries in Africa. He also co-chairs the South Africa–Germany Bi-national Commission dealing with trade, investment and such matters.

Unlike the United States, we have no vice-president. This means that when circumstances require it, as when Zuma travels abroad, Kgalema as the deputy president takes on all the duties and responsibilities of the president.[58] When the media frenzy about Mandela's health scare broke in December 2010, it fell to Kgalema to address the dramatic concerns everyone seemed to have, since Zuma was out of the country. All the media praised his astute, sensitive handling of what was certainly a crisis moment, Mandela being the iconic figure he is worldwide. There is no doubt that his steady personality was exactly what this required. 'Motlanthe had to calm nerves and assure everyone that the quality of Mandela's medical care is under control' was the *M&G*'s summary.[59]

What was also salutary was both his apology for the initial media blackout on Mandela's medical condition by the Nelson Mandela Foundation and that he apologised that 'the government and the Foundation could have handled things differently', promising that in future the presidency would keep the country regularly informed. This moved the commentator Jovial Rantao to say: 'We should take our hats off to Acting President Kgalema Motlanthe and his communication chief, Thabo Masebe, for their important intervention. ... Motlanthe took the nation and the world into his confidence and explained what our former president was going through. What he did was to show respect to this nation, something which those who control all information about Mandela failed to do.'[60]

CHAPTER NINE
A rough run-up to Mangaung, 2012

ANC stalwart and MP since 1994, Andrew Mlangeni, is my hero, simply because he has dutifully served for eighteen years, has hardly ever been absent from parliament and has never been ambitious to get into higher office.

                                  Kgalema Motlanthe, 2011

The gloating bane of avarice
  Now abides among the newly-freed
Why the once steel faces
Of heroic stalwarts
Glows with the fat of greed
Ask why

                    Don Mattera, 'Sometimes, I feel' (1998)

This final chapter critically explores Kgalema's attitude towards the Zuma administration and some major developments he, the ANC and the government have had to face since the 2009 elections. The nationalisation debate, Malema's expulsion from the ANC and the upcoming Mangaung conference and related succession issues are rigorously analysed.

The Zuma regime: Kgalema's hopes and concerns

Though Kgalema accepted Zuma's offer to serve as his deputy after the 2009 elections, as a loyal cadre of the ANC, he had many serious concerns with much that happened since the December 2007 conference, during the eight months he was president and after the Zuma administration came to office in 2009. He had grown politically and personally in his time as president, short though it was. Most of all, he says, it made him see the strategic goal of the ANC more clearly: the creation of a united, nonracial and nonsexist democracy. 'It compels you to take a much broader view of matters and from the vantage point of the presidency you can actually pursue that goal more effectively, like on national days you talk to the whole country and get to know and understand the general situation much better.'

Kgalema was acutely aware at the start of the Zuma administration in 2009 that government is so complex and multifaceted, new cruxes arise even for the most experienced. For him they are a constant feature of governance, especially in South Africa where, important as nonracial political democracy is, there is a yawning chasm between it and the true social justice still seriously lacking for millions of poor people. The shortfall is compounded by the lack of requisite skills, education and experience, as ANC rule since 1994 has made all too evident.

Kgalema's hopes for the new Zuma term were dashed in several major respects, but he does not try to distance himself from the problems. The situation for the poor majority, relations between the ANC and its allies (especially Cosatu) and the state of affairs within the ANC itself are all on the whole very much as they were under Mbeki. For the poor, in fact, it is arguable that conditions have worsened, mainly through the growing economic crisis starting in late 2008 and the results of some of our own economic and social policies.

Kgalema Motlanthe

While acknowledging the positive changes that Polokwane ushered in, Kgalema's biggest hope was that the new administration would once and for all settle several major problems afflicting the party and government. He certainly did not expect that the new leadership would end up doing some things they had accused Mbeki of: witch hunting and behaving with an overbearing triumphalist arrogance (from the power that Polokwane had given the victors) and even a sense of vengeance. He is convinced that the central theme of renewal to restore the ANC's decades-long stand on values and principles of unity, solidarity, comradeship and selflessness was not realised after Polokwane, and thinks this was because many of the victors there had not grasped what the main problems were in the Mbeki administration. If they had, he believes, many of the troubles in that regime would not have been repeated after the 2009 elections.

On how people behaved in top positions, he had hoped that his discussions with the rest of the ANC leadership while he was president would help to correct those who were abusing their powers in the party and especially in government.[1] Here he was disappointed. At a time when many ANC leaders can be particularly self-seeking and arrogant, his hope is still to cultivate a much more considerate, sensitive and respectful leadership to serve the ANC and the country. His wish is to see the emergence of leaders with the qualities of Walter Sisulu, who for him best embodied the values of the ANC.[2] He is totally unimpressed by egotistic and pompous leaders.

Kgalema has been seen as something of a role model too. It was with his integrity in mind that Lord Robin Renwick said of him: 'There is no South African leader since Nelson Mandela who is more highly respected overseas, as he is seen to embody the best virtues of the old guard of the ANC.'[3] Clearly Kgalema himself is not a seeker after power. When he does acquire it he exercises it with caution, sensitivity and respect for others, whether he is dealing with ordinary voters or workers, his staff, a minister or a visiting president. He will accord the same respect to members of the chief opposition, the DA, that he gives to ANC members, for example. He conducted himself like that when he took over from Mbeki and he still does so as deputy president. Unsurprisingly, Adriaan Groenewald of *Business Report* found him deeply respectful of 'all people.'[4]

The country is still grappling to settle the relationship between the three arms of the state (the executive, legislature and the judiciary) and their individual powers, especially the role of the judiciary. Here Kgalema calls for less heat and more light in discussions. As we have seen, he deplores labelling the judiciary – and anything else – as counterrevolutionary (an expression of siege mentality among many in the ruling party).

Other concerns for Kgalema are the continued abuse of state organs for political ends; a lack of unity and trust among top party officials; a destructive preoccupation with succession issues and less with services to people; a steady departure from the fraternal, unitary and renewal themes at Polokwane; a corrosive factionalism and careerism that has become rampant. His hope was that with time these things would improve. Instead they have got worse since Mbeki's time in office.[5]

He is truly committed to the need for the ANC to be the real centre of power and is disappointed that, despite his efforts to strengthen its position so that it would control the government it elected more effectively, cabinet still appears to have the upper hand over Luthuli House. In fact it seems that since 1994 the executive has been far more dominant and even domineering.

Kgalema is deeply unhappy to see leftists from Cosatu and the SACP go into government with the intention of transforming it into a more effective instrument for emancipation and then, all too often, from one administration to the next, being sucked into the corrosive vortex of incumbency.[6] He believes that precisely because of this trend it is the duty of the ANC to intervene and put an end to such domination by the executive.

He is of the view that corruption in government, which has certainly increased since 2009, has much to do with a serious problem in the ANC itself:

> If you are in a position of power in the ANC you are also in a position to influence major decisions regarding tenders and decisions on all kinds of things. The system as a whole, the capitalist system, operates on the basis of buying its way through. So there will be many people who bring this and that present to you. Sometimes they don't want anything in return and yet the point is that they are opening doors. Some day they may knock on your door and say 'You remember...' That is how the system works. It consumes you if you are not very careful.

A main point for him is that, since it is the ANC that wins elections and deploys people to various state institutions, it is the party's responsibility to ensure not only that policies adopted are implemented in government but that problems in government that pose a threat to its policies and interests are speedily and effectively dealt with.

It is not enough simply to blame Zuma, any more than it was to blame Mbeki in the past. Matters are much more complex, with so many factors involved. It is true, though, that the buck stops finally with the head of state.[7]

Three years into the Zuma administration and after many disappointments, Kgalema still cherishes the hope that things could change to move the country out of a pervasive sense of crisis and paralysis in government on many fronts. Cosatu's Vavi sums it up: 'We will not get out of this crisis, comrades, while there is paralysis at the top.'[8] A great deal of damage has been done since 2009 that cannot be fixed quickly. Debilitating factionalist campaigning is already evident in the run-up to Mangaung. It is thus very unlikely that much will change substantially for the better in the rest of this presidential term, either in the ANC or in government. It is this state of affairs that gives Kgalema sleepless nights rather than what happens at Mangaung.

Kgalema and the Donen Commission

Is it right to pursue someone who was implicitly accused of conniving with the deceased businessman Sandile Majali about kickbacks (in the sanctions-busting Oil for Food programme we dealt with earlier) even when the commission of inquiry found him innocent? This is exactly what the *Mail & Guardian* did to Kgalema after the Donen Commission report of September 2006 was finally released by President Zuma in December 2011. The report of the commission, with all the information at its disposal, found that he was not guilty of any wrongdoing, but the paper persisted in suggesting that he had a 'case to answer'.[9]

What makes this worse is that the continued query in the newspaper left many wondering just what the truth was, a painful situation that had already hung over Kgalema's head for three years after Donen declared that his commission found he was 'exculpated'.[10] The *M&G*'s approach was fatally flawed: it drew its conclusion from the fact that Kgalema did not appear before the commission through circumstances beyond his control. Along similar lines the *M&G* states: 'The allegations against both Motlanthe and Sexwale[11] were not fully investigated and remain unresolved.'[12] Yet it seems that Kgalema was dissatisfied at not being given an opportunity to do so: 'I waited for the commission to summon me and prepared all the relevant documents but nothing happened.'

The delay in releasing the report did raise questions. Why did Mbeki not make the report public when Donen gave it to him in 2006? Mbeki says there were good reasons not to. Its objectives were deficient and that, for example, without proper investigation Donen was 'making determinations out of prejudice, like the South African government's relationship with Saddam Hussein. We thought, why release a faulty report which had several gaps and inaccuracies in it?' He also feels strongly that Donen seemed to be uncritically echoing much of what the UN report had said.[13] Frank Chikane expresses similar concerns.[14]

Yet there does not appear to have been any good reason why Mbeki could not have issued a brief statement to say why the report would not be made public. But in law he was not compelled to release the report of a commission he had established, especially if its objectives were not achieved. In interview he was not sure if he could have issued a statement, but did not say what would have prevented him.[15]

A lead story in the *Sunday Times* in 2009 reproduced unsubstantiated allegations about Kgalema from either or both the UN report and the Donen Commission report.[16] Why had Kgalema not released the report between September 2008 and May 2009 while he was state president? The *Sunday Times* claimed they had asked him to do so when he took over from Mbeki but that 'he also resisted calls for the release of the report'.[17] Kgalema denies this: 'There was no such request at all that I am aware of. They did not say who made that request and when. If I had received the request I would certainly have considered releasing it. After all, there was nothing in the report that could substantially and evidentially implicate me. I was always confident of that. But even if there was evidence against me I would have considered releasing it, because there were also larger issues of national and public importance.'

The final release of the report in December 2011 came after the *Cape Argus* and Independent Newspapers challenged Zuma in court. The timing of the release after a delay of two months, and just a year before the ANC's next elective conference at Mangaung, had some people guessing that this was designed to foil any presidential aspirations that Kgalema might have. But the reason for the two-month delay was reported as being 'intended to give those implicated an opportunity to comment.'[18] My own sense also is that the timing probably had nothing to do with trying to discredit Kgalema but with the fact that the legal challenge to compel Zuma to release the report could have succeeded. To prevent that embarrassing defeat, Zuma may well have decided to release it.

An anonymous source in the *M&G* claimed that Kgalema was 'deeply unhappy' and 'felt betrayed' by Zuma's decision to release the report.[19] He had no reason to be unhappy, simply because there was nothing in the report that could seriously implicate him. Informed in advance that the report was about to be released and asked if he had any objections, he made it clear that he had no problem with it at all and in fact welcomed it, so that it would finally put an end to a matter that has unjustly cast aspersions on his integrity for years.

The great nationalisation debate
Probably no other debate has ever divided the ANC, its allies and the whole country than the one on nationalisation since the ANCYL began to reassert its importance in late 2008. It had long been a topic in the ANC and broader national liberation

movement, and was discussed on Robben Island when Mandela and Kgalema were there. At its heart lie the economic clauses of the Freedom Charter. Ben Turok, who played a leading role in formulating them, explains that they broke new policy ground for the ANC. In a distinct shift to the left, the Charter demanded a sharing of the country's wealth and resources through the transfer of ownership of the mineral wealth, the banks and monopoly industry to the people as a whole; for industry and trade to be controlled in the interests of the well-being of the people.[20]

Though the term 'nationalisation' is not used, the wording can only mean that the state would own and control the wealth and resources of the country on behalf of the people. Since South Africa was a developed capitalist economy by the time of the Charter in 1955, the social implication was clear: the black working class was already the majority of 'the people' and race and class were inseparably bonded. Any attempt to emasculate the Charter of its revolutionary meaning could only be to serve other interests. Mandela himself spelt out the revolutionary intent a year after the Charter was adopted. It was 'a revolutionary document precisely because the changes it envisages cannot be won without breaking up the economic and political set-up of present South Africa. The Charter strikes a fatal blow at the financial and gold-mining monopolies that have for centuries plundered the country and condemned its people to servitude.'[21]

Malema uses this clause to argue: 'Whether we like it or not, ideologically the ANC is a Marxist-oriented political organisation. They have always been like that. The ANC has never come to the defence of capitalism but how best to bring down the capitalist system. That is why we are firmly asserting some elements of where we want to go and nationalisation is a part of that.'[22] This is also why Malema says, referring to Zuma: 'if you say it [nationalisation] is not ANC policy ... you are denouncing the Freedom Charter. Discipline means you must respect policies of the ANC.'[23]

Whether circumstances after the unbanning of the ANC in 1990 or under today's circumstances permitted such radical policies is another question.[24] As an alternative, if nationalisation is impossible, Kgalema has long advocated forming a state-owned mining company to benefit miners, communities and the state.[25] 'This could, for example, enable free and compulsory education, which will make me the happiest person.' Many in NUM said he was the first person to moot the idea.

Kgalema asks what the practical implications of nationalisation are, in today's conditions. No matter how correct the policy might be for dealing with rampant poverty and unemployment, he says (for example) that if the managers and bureaucrats in government departments and parastatals do not actively support it, it won't work.

> In fact the history of nationalisation is that if this layer does not wholeheartedly support the policy, they do the opposite, they subtly sabotage it. Besides, the debate about nationalisation must not stagnate at the theoretical level but must address the practical details of what you do once you have nationalised. ... Even if there is agreement on the policy, to win people over we must also produce a practical programme with which to implement the policy. ... The theory and especially the practical side must reckon with the present balance of forces in our country and the world. Included in this calculation must be not only an ability to start a serious nationalisation programme but to most importantly sustain it into the future. The question is therefore this: do current circumstances not only allow us

to start nationalisation but to sustain it? Otherwise it is pie in the sky. But the debate on nationalisation must be vigorously promoted in order to appreciate the pros and cons properly.

His caution tells him that adverse conditions in the economy, the labour movement and the state of the labour market – with the already very high rate of unemployment – are not conducive to a call for outright nationalisation, even if it were restricted to the mining sector.

This sector has already gone through a formal change to being state-owned. This happened in 2004 with the Minerals and Petroleum Development Act, which gave effect to clause 3 of the Freedom Charter. But the change hardly empowered unions and communities linked to the mines.[26] Instead of benefiting them, as intended, it parcelled out the mineral deposits willy-nilly to connected groups that became the biggest beneficiaries – so it mainly boosted black business groups and investors. It is thus highly questionable whether the state's formal ownership of the 'minerals beneath the soil' means the genuine nationalisation and socialisation of these assets, which is what Kgalema claims: 'The mines at the moment don't need to be nationalised because the 2004 Act restored ownership to the state and therefore the mineral deposits belong to the people.'[27]

The most disturbing feature of the debate has been the hysterical reaction in the media since Malema and the ANCYL started pushing for nationalisation in 2009, especially from white businesses and the mining sector in particular. This was certainly not helpful; overreaction from 'white capital' simply made the ANCYL dig in its heels. Kgalema once said that sometimes we breathe more life into things we oppose by the way we react to them. For him, it is vital that the debate stays rigorous and clean. He has been dismayed at the mudslinging between Malema and the SACP deputy general secretary, Jeremy Cronin, which debases the debate and deflects attention from the important issues.[28]

He does appreciate that the ANCYL's call for nationalisation stemmed from a growing socioeconomic crisis as worldwide recession began to affect our economy from 2008 and great job losses, the rising cost of living, and poverty began to bite deep. It was not just a manoeuvre to secure a state bailout for ailing BEE mining companies, as the SACP thought.[29]

Jabulani Sikhakhane notes with insight that the ANCYL made a big tactical blunder when it linked its nationalisation campaign to changes in the leadership of the ANC, which he said could disadvantage Kgalema.[30] But it just so happened that the start of the ANCYL's nationalisation campaign coincided roughly with incipient tensions between Malema and Zuma, which gave rise to the ANCYL's interest in a change of leadership.

ANCYL–ANC conflict and the expulsion of Malema

The growing problems between the ANCYL and the ANC began after the 2009 election of President Jacob Zuma, but there were tensions long before, as when Malema viciously targeted Mbeki before Polokwane as causing the wrongs in the ANC and the country.

Because the ANCYL and Malema were perceived to have played a big role in the election of Zuma as president of the ANC in December 2007, this almost certainly conveyed a wildly exaggerated sense of their importance and power in relation to both the ANC and wider society. Already in early 2008 Kgalema was repeatedly telling the senior leadership of the ANC, especially Zuma, that the ANC had to rein in Malema and other ANCYL leaders when they behaved unacceptably. Kgalema himself had been on the receiving end of a whole string of stinging false accusations from the ANCYL in August 2008, just a month before he took over from Mbeki.

Few, if any, heeded these warnings. It was not thought appropriate to take Malema, especially, to task at the time. In hindsight this was the biggest mistake the ANC leadership made, especially Zuma, who as president was the top official to curb indiscipline.

In truth Malema, with all his warts and misdemeanours, is a child of the ANC. His arrogance, excesses and especially his penchant for money, business and the high life follow the lead of so many ANC leaders who went this way after 1994. Kgalema agrees here, which is why he could tell Carol Paton a few years ago that the rot had spread across the board. His view is that only the ordinary members and their branches have the power to change matters and take the ANC back to its roots: 'The ANC must go back to the masses, and restore its credibility among them and their faith in it. The people must feel the ANC is their instrument.'[31]

Tension mounted between the Zuma-led regime and the Malema-led ANCYL soon after the 2009 elections and became really hostile after the public sector strike of 2010. They seemed to be heading for a showdown.[32] At this volatile stage Kgalema thinks relations had already deteriorated so far that the lines between Zuma and Malema in particular were drawn in sand. His repeated attempts at meetings and behind the scenes to cool tempers and resolve the serious divisions in a comradely way were in vain. He is convinced that the ANC leadership's failure to act created precedents that were exploited by the ANCYL to go ahead with greater force and almost a sense of impunity, as when they allegedly stormed the stage at the September 2010 national general council.[33]

For Kgalema, the problem perhaps began when the ANC

decided to charge Malema and the newly elected executive in 2011 for bringing the party into disrepute after they criticised the Botswana government. He says the ANC's disciplinary committee laid the wrong charges against Malema and the ANCYL executive; could have charged the ANCYL instead with defiance because it had deliberately and publicly contradicted the ANC statement about its attack on the Botswana government; should never have taken up the Botswana issue because the ANCYL had apologised for it; should not have conducted their proceedings with lawyers, which simply made matters more adversarial;[34] should not have allowed NEC members to be involved in the hearings;[35] were conflicted among themselves about what they said about Malema and the ANCYL before;[36] did not allow those charged to plead in mitigation; meted out drastic sentences to Malema and others when some of them were first offenders; did not monitor Malema (who did not go for anger therapy in 2011) or make it clear that misbehaviour during the two years really could mean expulsion;[37] and more. But though these were his concerns he, as always, respected decisions taken by all ANC structures and did not seek to oppose them.

Kgalema certainly feels it was not necessary to expel Malema. Properly addressing the issues by settling them amicably in meetings between the ANC and its youth league could have prevented charges being laid against Malema and other youth leaders in the first place, but this process was not really given a chance.[38]

With the benefit of hindsight, Kgalema's approach to the entire matter of the charges against Malema and other ANCYL leaders is both simple and thoughtful. He says that after the ANCYL had its conference in 2011 and submitted its report and resolutions to the mother body, the ANC should have pointed out if there were any inconsistencies between that and the ANC's own constitution and resolutions on relevant matters.

> We in the top leadership of the ANC should have constructively engaged the ANCYL on any matters arising from their conference we were not happy with, but the fact is that we did not do that. Instead we rushed punitively into laying charges against our own youth league, whereas our actions should have been driven by the guiding, nurturing and corrective role we as the mother ought to play in relation to the ANCYL. The fact is that the ANC had a constitutional obligation to act in that manner, but because it did not do so it failed to discharge such a responsibility. That was not right. It was in fact fundamentally wrong of us.

It may even be with a degree of paternalism, but Kgalema has always believed that his first responsibility towards the ANCYL is to teach and take care of them, as in this example: Kgalema reprimanded Malema for turning up at schools during teaching time and said the authorities should not allow him to disrupt schooling. Malema defied him and said he had no reason to listen to Kgalema, and questioned his authority. Kgalema did not clamour for disciplinary action against Malema. Instead he spoke to him, after which Malema discontinued going to schools while classes were in progress. The rehabilitation was what mattered.

For the disciplinary committee to have inflicted the drastic sentence of expulsion on its own youth leader seems totally wrong and for Kgalema it goes against his own belief in rehabilitation.[39] Had Kgalema been approached to help settle the conflict between the ANC and its youth league there would have been a resolution without any expulsions or even probably suspensions. Having learnt so well in NUM about negotiating on the toughest terrain, he would have been up to the task, especially since this matter concerned the fate and future of the youth wing of the ANC. For him the youth are a priceless asset and indeed represent the future.

Malema makes this profoundly important point: 'Maybe our ideas serve as a threat to the current leadership. What is ill-disciplined about thinking? ... Your right to think must be protected.' Steven Friedman says that whereas there were grounds for disciplinary action against the ANCYL, 'instead they were punished for expressing opinions.'[40] The ANCYL must have the right to criticise whatever it thinks necessary, including the ANC leadership, which is why Kgalema has repeatedly said that the role of the youth league is to think radically and bring new and challenging ideas into the ANC.[41]

On the other hand Kgalema had this to say when he addressed the ANCYL at its centenary rally in Limpopo: 'The ANC has no use for a passive youth league. We need our youth to be militant, creative and determined. It is the ANC's duty to show and lead the ANCYL if it strays from the path. We must guide it all the time.'[42] He has been consistent about this approach to the ANCYL. In 2009, when he was asked about the controversial utterances of Malema, he said: 'When you have a youth that is energetic but erroneous at the same time, you cannot shirk your responsibility of correcting them and bringing them into line. The ANC never gives up on anyone.'[43]

Kgalema recognises that some of Malema's actions just deepened antagonisms instead of healing the rift. There is no doubt that Malema is sometimes his own worst enemy. Malema also has no sense of choosing his battles strategically, in Kgalema's view, but throws himself into everything and shoots from the hip far too often. In the rough, brutal world of

South African and specifically ANC politics, such an approach is terribly unwise.

Kgalema has been concerned about the seeming hatred that Malema and the ANCYL had for Zuma:

> They must not be driven by bitterness and hatred and a determination to hurt. That kind of politics I want to have nothing to do with. I do not support it because such anger and bitterness can destroy an organisation. But discipline must also not be used to vindictively get even and settle scores. Discipline must never be mixed with and motivated by anger. Besides, in the final analysis the struggle has always been about love. We fought hard for what we believed in out of love for human beings and hatred of oppression and exploitation, not for people as such, but the systems that ruled our lives and reduced us to poverty and misery.

After being expelled in November 2011 Malema tried many times to seek a 'political solution that does not involve disciplinary action.'[44] It was said that 'his supporters believe that party leaders, including Kgalema Motlanthe, Phosa and Sexwale, favoured this to resolve the political impasse between the mother body and its youth wing.'[45] Kgalema did indeed share this view.

There can be no doubt that this episode is going to have long-term consequences for the ANC itself and especially its relations with the ANCYL. For Kgalema, the most unfortunate thing was that whereas the ANCYL sought a political solution after Malema's expulsion, which the ANC did not appear to be interested in, it was precisely such a solution that the ANC should have pursued before laying charges. If this had happened, Kgalema is confident it would have obviated the charges and the use of lawyers on both sides, which tended to complicate matters much more.

Kgalema has refrained from public comment. As is clear, though, he never supported Malema's expulsion – and would never support that of any ANC member, especially not from the youth wing – but feels bound by the decisions of the structures of the ANC.

Electioneering before Mangaung

The topic of succession in the ANC presidency arose just a month after Zuma was inaugurated as state president in May 2009, when Vavi declared that Zuma would have a second term (this ignores the fact that he can return only as a result of the election in December 2012, even if he stands unopposed). Never before had comment about the next election surfaced so soon after a president had been chosen. Never before, either, had a Cosatu leader pronounced on a matter that concerned the leadership of the ANC. This reflected the pro-Zuma euphoria in Cosatu at the time, which distracted many from thinking about just what their unity in Polokwane as the 'coalition of the wounded' had been based on, aside from a common desire to remove Mbeki.

But once the first signs of tension arose between Zuma and the ANCYL in early 2010, it became increasingly clear that Malema wanted Zuma to be replaced by Kgalema. Malema later told me as much, and that this had been the ANCYL's plan when they voted for him to be deputy president of the ANC in 2007. Kgalema objected strongly when he heard this: 'You serve strictly only for one term. If I am nominated for the position of president and elected in Mangaung, that cannot happen because of any earlier position I held, even though the practice has been for the deputy president to become thereafter the president. It is a matter that is entirely in the hands of voting delegates. Each conference is a new conference for a new term.'

Being preferred by a constituency as large as the ANCYL did not sway Kgalema at all; instead it distressed him. He says ANC elections 'follow explicit guidelines and procedures which constitutionally must be adhered to and from which there can be no deviation. But the more serious problem is that such premature talk of succession was distracting us from carrying out the tasks and implementing the policies we agreed to in Polokwane and in fact from building the branches and a more united and stronger ANC.[46] Besides, it also feeds negatively into other things, like affecting the environment in which we work in the ANC, the alliance and especially in government.'

He says the ANCYL knew they were wrong when they said publicly that they wanted him to succeed Zuma. As we know, he disapproves of choosing leaders in that way. 'There is no problem in discussing leadership issues or even desirable qualities but they mention specific names, which becomes a very big problem because names should only come up in the nominations process. Nobody has approached me because they know what my response will be. Any member of the ANC who engages in any way with succession is violating the authority of the constitution because nomination can only arise organically from the branches.' When the ANCYL wore T-shirts bearing his face as the next president he rebuked them so hard that the *Times* remarked: 'This is the first time an ANC leader publicly chastised his own supporters for contravening party policy and internal campaign decorum.'[47]

Where provinces act factionally before elections Kgalema has told them that two opposing groups cannot either be right because neither of them are the ANC. Members should leave the group they belong to and 'properly belong to the ANC because [otherwise] new members are recruited into your faction and not into the ANC as such, which is wrong, divisive and unacceptable.' Over the years he has emphasised that ANC leadership is elected, never prearranged. In a North West ANC conference in Rustenburg in 2011 he said: 'Never allow anybody to own members of the ANC. Please, please, do not join the groupings in the ANC.'[48]

Kgalema was greatly saddened by the hostile divisions reported in NUM's elective conference in June 2012, some allegedly about the ANC election. They were so deep and ugly that NUM's president, Senzeni Zokwana, was furious that some members brought 'their own security guards into the conference hall.'[49] Never in its thirty-year history had one of the strongest and most united unions in the country experienced such vitriolic clashes at a conference. The report continues: 'NUM is suddenly finding itself drowning in the same sea of corruption and factionalist politics in which branches and provinces of the ANC are mired.'[50]

Campaigning has even gone underground. In May 2012 the ANC provincial secretary in Gauteng, David Makhuru, said that certain unidentified people in the NEC were inviting party members to secret meetings, a matter the ANC in the province was investigating.[51] It appears they were campaigning for Zuma to be re-elected and probably trying to make inroads in a province Kgalema hails from, which is rumoured to want him to replace Zuma.

Kgalema rejects attempts to link him to provincial bases or biases but has encountered some of the rivalries. In North West province in July 2012, he says, 'I found literally two parallel structures. The people who are supposed to be in the leadership are actually involved in the factionalism. In Potchefstroom, where there were two separate branch meetings, I insisted that one meeting be held, which they finally did.' Serious factionalist divisions within the ANC and much underhand manoeuvring are said to be afflicting Mafikeng and many other areas. This must be addressed speedily, otherwise it may affect the validity of the electoral auditing for Mangaung.

A sly trick emerged in March 2012. The *Sunday Times* reported that Zuma's supporters would support Kgalema as his deputy, but only if he did not challenge Zuma in Mangaung. The story cites a Zuma supporter saying that 'the general view is that Motlanthe should stay on as deputy president, with the view that he will then take over from JZ at the next conference in 2017.'[52] The tactic here is to try ensuring that Kgalema will not stand against Zuma, with the threat that he could lose out on any state office if he does; and the bribe is that if he stands down in 2012 he will have the votes for president in 2017. This just flouts the constitutional authority of the branches to decide on the next president, let alone the one elected five years down the line in 2017. Predictably, Kgalema through his spokesperson has replied that 'he will not be party to any arrangement with Zuma's supporters to not stand against him in return for being returned to the deputy presidency' and the branches 'should be allowed to nominate leaders and no one should engage in attempts to make leadership arrangements.'[53]

There has been much speculation in the media about Kgalema and Mangaung.[54] Among the deluge in 2011 the *M&G* reported, 'Despite the growing backing for Motlanthe as the next ANC president, the debate was sensitive, said ANC caucuses, because the party's deputy president "does not want to talk about it."'[55] Later the *Times* columnist S'Thembiso Msomi guessed, 'Although Motlanthe has not publicly stated that he wants the job – he is reportedly just as reticent on the subject in private – I don't see him declining if he is nominated by the majority of branches.'[56] The *Sunday Times* said that 'intense lobbying for deputy president, Kgalema Motlanthe, to succeed Zuma as head of the ANC has begun in earnest in South Africa's economic hub, with the party's Johannesburg region positioning itself as a springboard for his campaign.' Kgalema said he knew nothing about this and 'distanced himself from any campaign to become ANC president.'[57]

The *Sunday Independent* stated that 'Motlanthe, quite strategically, has said he would not avail himself if Zuma is still available for the top post.'[58] Kgalema's responds: 'No, it is not true at all, but nobody has approached me. My position is that nobody must try to canvass for themselves in the run-up to elections. It is up to the will of the branches. But if I am nominated for such a position when the electoral commission approaches me and says I have been nominated for such a position, I will then either accept or decline. However, I will not be party to any manoeuvring outside the prescribed constitutional structures and processes.'

Kgalema has never gone out to canvass for himself and says he will never do so.

> Never, I say, never, because once you do that you get ensnared into factionalist politics and it is tantamount to promoting yourself as the best in the party. You also become indebted to cliques and for me that is a weak and uninspiring leadership. No, I will never deviate from that fundamental principle, which is that decisions about leadership must rest solely with branch membership and voting delegates. We must never manipulate and manoeuvre because we are ambitious for power and in the process rob the membership of their inalienable right to choose their leaders. What I am much more interested in is a strong and united ANC rather than being preoccupied with becoming the president.

Whoever gets the top job, what difference would it make? Some, particularly on the left outside the ANC alliance, think policy will continue as before instead of changing fundamentally, especially for the macroeconomic framework. This observation relates to the ANC and the state, since it is the ANC and government that decide policy, not the president. A court ruling in 2012, that the case against Zuma on corruption charges may be revived, could complicate matters for a second-term presidency for him.[59] Thus far, Kgalema has resisted being tied to any faction and the kind of patronage networks that have plagued the ANC and the government.

Whither the ANC?

As we have seen, Kgalema is acutely aware of the ills in the ANC and that, unless they are dealt with sooner rather than later, the future for the ruling party will be bleak. Years of township protests over basic services and the many struggles waged by organised labour, especially by Cosatu, have raised the stakes sharply. Any complacency about the rapidly expanded social grants system to help highly impoverished, mostly black, households is seriously misplaced. Besides, the DA has made some significant inroads into former ANC strongholds.

The ANC's recent policy discussion documents are frankly not inspiring. The same old language and themes are churned out from one policy or national conference to another, shedding little true light. There is hardly any real clarity about the current situation and where the ANC wants to take the country. 'Social transformation', 'transformation project', 'ideological capacity', 'organisational renewal', 'developmental state', 'capable state', 'balance of forces' are among the vague terms used.[60] Meanwhile the black masses, who are supposed to be the beneficiaries of social transformation, grow poorer and more restless while the ruling elite who urge them to be patient live in luxury. The ANC is likely to come under so much pressure from the discontented masses that it could indeed lead to our own Prague Spring.

Kgalema thinks this will not happen because protests and strikes are not suppressed and they air democratic opinion enough to avoid revolutionary explosions. Only time and events will tell, but his approach sounds mechanistic. Vavi, for Cosatu, still warns the ruling party that a grassroots revolution may overthrow it if it fails to wake up to the dire situation the poor black majority still faces, eighteen years after the dubious 'miracle transition' occurred in 1994.

There is also a deep sense that grand themes and resolutions seem to dissipate soon after conferences. 'Organisational renewal' was noted as the key guiding theme the ANC emerged with from Polokwane in 2007 and was the key theme again for the ANC's policy conference in June 2012, with no explanation of what, if anything, had happened in between. Kgalema said at the Harold Wolpe memorial lecture in June 2012 that renewal 'must be preceded by rigorous analysis of the ANC as it exists today' and that the ANC should 'stand back, pull back and take a hard look at itself and free itself of sentimentalism. If we don't do that ... the reality is that there will be a realignment of forces.'[61]

The ANC will degenerate further if it fails to carry out a rigorous self-critical review of what eighteen years of its rule have really achieved. But because the party is weak on self-critical analysis this is unlikely to happen. In the words of Pallo Jordan: 'The movement's reluctance to undertake serious study of the outcomes of freedom has rendered it less capable to manage the contradictions produced by its own policies. The ANC's capacity to lead will depend on how it addresses the societal changes its own policies have generated.'[62]

The 'second transition' (ST)[63] is the latest ANC buzzword on social transformation and is probably meant to prevent a Prague Spring. It is a belated attempt to deal with the disastrous social results of the ongoing dominance of white capital, the elitist nature of BEE and the consequently moribund national democratic revolution. Whatever 'revolution' there was has left the poor majority materially with not much more than the vote.

Kgalema is familiar with the system from which these contradictions ultimately arise. Addressing a University of South Africa audience on the centenary of the ANC in 2012, he said: 'National oppression and its social consequences cannot be resolved by formal democracy underpinned by market forces. While formal democracy may present opportunities for some blacks and women to advance, without a systematic national effort, led by the democratic government, to unravel the skewed distribution of wealth and income, the social reality of apartheid will remain.'[64] This is Kgalema's abiding wish, which he fervently hopes he will live to see fulfilled in his lifetime. The fact still remains that the ANC has not seriously got to grips with how its own policies have contributed to the contradictions facing it in 2012.

In his Wolpe speech Kgalema also criticised the ST: 'Second Transition! Second Transition! Second Transition! From what, from where to where? What constitutes the first transition? What were the tasks of that phase, have all those tasks been accomplished or not?'[65] These are valid questions, but Kgalema could as well have posed similar ones about the fate and future of the national democratic revolution, because the second transition is a direct consequence of this 'revolution' failing in a supposed first stage to deliver social justice in countless respects to the poor black majority. Not even the false distinction between politics and economics in the ST document can obscure a

A rough run-up to Mangaung, 2012

related failure: the mechanistic 'first transition' and 'second transition', which are just as false as the two-stage theory. Both the NDR and the 'transitions' offered the black masses political freedom and the many liberties of 'bourgeois democracy' but they stop short of dealing with the systemic causes of growing unemployment, poverty and inequalities, which are inherent in capitalism.

In its fatally flawed analysis, the ANC pretends that the past eighteen years were all about politics and that the ANC is not to blame for the blistering poverty ravaging the country.[66] Yet, as we have seen, its many neoliberal economic and social policies since 1994 have worsened the poverty and inequalities that apartheid bequeathed. This is obvious in many areas but none more appallingly so than in the most crucial ones: the poor quality of RDP houses and water and sanitation services in black townships since 1994, which not even their huge spread to many more people can conceal. The commercialising and commodifying of the most basic services (beyond paltry free 'lifeline' supplies and inferior RDP houses) is the biggest problem facing poor communities.[67]

Why is there so much emphasis now on the stark, terrible poverty that for years has daily stared the ANC in the face? Wide speculation in the media is that Zuma is playing up these issues in the run-up to Mangaung in order to affect the electoral outcome there and secure a second term as president, especially by appearing to appease disgruntled grassroots ANC delegates and voters whose patience has run out with their deplorable lot. But the theme probably also has to do with the fact that this conference coincides with the ANC centenary, which in the midst of devastating poverty is indeed a time for strategic reflection and is therefore not necessarily opportunistic.

One thing is certain: the ANC's fallback of invoking its own (in many ways glorious) past has now been exhausted. Millions of people have had more than enough of formal democracy, historical memory and symbolism. Instead they want decent jobs, houses and sanitation, adequate food and water and the dignity that goes with it all, which is why Kgalema in his Wolpe speech warned: 'When you celebrate the past as the beginning and the end, then of course you are conservative, you are preserving the truths of yesterday.'[68] For the vast majority of its members, past glories cannot compensate for the inadequacies and failures of the ANC any more. The police massacre of 34 striking miners at the Lonmin mine in Marikana in August 2012 is just the latest desperate attempt to quell the growing impatience with poor wages and poverty. Kgalema was appalled and deeply pained: 'This must be the worst industrial relations disaster since 1994 in the mining industry, an avoidable tragedy of immense proportions. It is therefore also the biggest wake-up call in the industry and in fact a severe warning that the mines either address the underlying causes of the strike or face many more explosions in the future.'

Wherever the ANC is going, it will have the benefit of Kgalema's presence in the party. Here let me quote the tribute he paid to that sterling stalwart of the ANC, Walter Sisulu, on his death in 2003:

> Thousands of voices have concurred that he was a great freedom fighter, a trusted leader and a worthy friend. In the days that follow ... much more will be said to offend his modesty. He would remind us that the African National Congress always operated as a collective – that no one person can take credit for what was essentially the achievements of the masses. Yet there is nothing I have heard in the past few days that has been untrue, nothing exaggerated, no stories embellished. What

emerges from these stories is not the portrait of a saint, but a vivid and multilayered picture of a human being, who though not lacking in faults, was generously endowed with compassion, understanding, humility and reason.[69]

Without realising it, Kgalema could have been describing himself.

Endnotes

Preface
1. *Mail & Guardian*, 25 January 2008; 8 February 2008; 3 October 2008; 9 January 2009. These interviews were particularly important because, bolstered by the Polokwane conference, Kgalema spoke with greater confidence and certainty than in previous interviews.
2. According to the South African Constitution it is only when the president is absent from the Republic or otherwise unable to fulfil the duties of president that the deputy president or a minister designated by the president acts as the president and is therefore 'acting president' for that period. If a vacancy occurs for whatever reason, the person filling that vacancy for however long is the president, duly elected by the National Assembly. See Sections 86–90 of the Constitution.
3. Mark Gevisser (2007), *Thabo Mbeki: The Dream Deferred*, Johannesburg: Jonathan Ball.
4. It is my considered view that by the time uncomfortable questions were raised about the absence of his wife Mapula at his presidential inauguration and accompanying press articles referred to his estrangement from her, he seemed a very private person and even the ANC's official website had little to say about his history. Kgalema probably realised then that he needed to be a bit more open about his private life. It was shortly after the story broke of the '24-year-old' with whom he was alleged to have been having an affair that I asked him about doing his biography, to which he agreed immediately.
5. It is customary for the subject of an authorised biography to provide a list of people to interview. However, because all those people on his list had worked with Kgalema in the unions, ANC and SACP, I interviewed many others who were not ANC members in order to strike that necessary balance.
6. At the time I worked as an organiser in another Cosatu affiliate, the Paper, Printing, Wood & Allied Workers Union (PPWAWU) and left the union in 1988, a year after Kgalema joined NUM.
7. Anthony Butler (2007: xiii), *Cyril Ramaphosa*, Johannesburg: Jacana.
8. Gevisser, xliii.
9. Arklay, 15.
10. Vick Allen (1992), *The History of Black Mineworkers in South Africa* (3 vols), Keighley: Moor.
11. Anthony Butler (2007), *Cyril Ramaphosa*, Johannesburg: Jacana.

An introductory reflection
1. This phrase was coined to capture the combination of political oppression and economic exploitation and implicitly all the social miseries the black working class suffered.
2. See Martin Legassick (2007), *Towards Socialist Democracy*, Pietermaritzburg: UKZN

Press, chapters 3 and 5, for a comprehensive discussion of this thesis and the related 'Colonialism of a Special Type' (CST) and 'Two-stage theory', in chapters 3 and 5. See also Darcy du Toit (1984), *Capital and Labour in SA*, London: Kegan Paul International, 185–7 and 411–15; Harold Wolpe (1988), *Race, Class and the Apartheid State*, Paris: James Currey, chapters 2 and 3; No Sizwe (Neville Alexander) (1979), *One Azania, One South Africa: The national question in South Africa*, London: Zed Press. 95–111; Alex Callinicos (1988), *South Africa between Reform and Revolution*, London: Bookmarks, for a critical discussion of the (1962) *The Road to South African Freedom*, London; Inkululeko Publishers, 67–72.
3 This demonstrates that apartheid was sustained by and inextricably intertwined with capitalism, which affects every single thing in the lives of the working class.

Chapter One
1 In an interview with Padraig O'Malley in 1992, Kgalema said he had a sister. In fact he was referring to his cousin Catherine, youngest daughter of his mother's eldest sister Mantimu. He has also referred to Stadie, a paternal aunt, as his sister. In both cases the sense is 'sister-like'.
2 See Peter Delius (1983), *The Land Belongs to Us*, Johannesburg: Ravan, 1–10; Peter Delius (1996), *A Lion Amongst the Cattle: Reconstruction and Resistance in the Northern Transvaal*, Johannesburg: Ravan, 9–49; Peter Delius and Michelle Hay (2009), *Mpumalanga: An Illustrated History*, Johannesburg: Highveld. In *Putting a Plough to the Ground: Accumulation and Dispossession in Rural South Africa 1850–1930* (1986), William Beinart, Peter Delius and Stanley Trapido conclude that no other country in Africa experienced such systematic, comprehensive and violent displacement of rural societies as South Africa. Delius is probably the best historian on the Polokwane and Limpopo regions and is exceptionally good on Sekhukhuneland and the resistance to both Boer and British colonialism in that key area, including that of the ANC, SACP and migrant workers over decades.
3 Delius, *Lion Amongst the Cattle*, 1.
4 Ibid, 80–1.
5 'Funeral Programme of Comrade Mahwidi John Phala', 8 August 2009, 5. Phala was on Robben Island with Kgalema, where they shared a cell in F section.
6 Ibid, 1.
7 Delius, *Lion Amongst the Cattle*, 4–5.
8 'Funeral Programme', 3: 'Sebatakgomo is an ages-old battle cry amongst the BaPedi to indicate enemy intrusions amongst the people. It is a battle cry that is used to this day, and when it is heard, particularly at night, the entire village rises to its feet.'
9 Botshabelo ('place of refuge' in Sotho), in the then Eastern Transvaal, was the name given to the new mission station established by Alexander Merensky and Albert Nachtigal of the Berlin Missionary Society.
10 The old man's original name was Madingoane and surname Makena but because there were too many family members with the same name in his home, which created confusion when they received letters in the post or messages, he decided to use his name as his surname. Makena is still the clan surname.
11 Under apartheid, Marapyane fell under Bophuthatswana. Kgalema says Lucas Mangope, its then president, used to tell municipal officials to 'leave them [the Madingoanes] in that zoo of theirs because they have title deeds.' The hard reality is that conditions on the farm have been a sorry picture of poverty and neglect. They have lacked the most basic services such as an in-house supply of water and flush sanitation. Asked in 2006 why he could not have done more to help his family, Kgalema's answer at first sounded surprisingly insensitive but upon reflection quite poignant: 'I am not in public office

Endnotes

to work for my family.' He believes that unless the family lives on the farm there will be no development. On the other hand they do not live there precisely because of the conditions, lack of jobs and money, and the fact that all their appeals for help from their Moroka local municipality have failed.

12 According to Seswai Mahlamola Nkadimeng, the couple got married and lived in Dichoeng (Jane Furse). Kgalema and his brother Ernest say they got married in Marapyane. But I tend to go with the Seswai's version, based on that of his aunt Mankwane, who incidentally grew up with Madingoane's children and helped bring up Kgalema's mother and her sister Dikeledi. It is this marriage to Sehole that introduces the Bakgatla (Tswana) dimension in Kgalema's history, though there have been long links between the BaPedi and the Bakgatla. Delius holds that despite those connections stretching back to about 1650 they must not be stressed too much because from about 1800 the Pedi have emerged as a much more politically powerful and distinct entity. Interestingly, Kgalema's Bakgatla heritage seems to have been stressed much more than his BaPedi ancestry. I have even heard African people say he is Tswana, yet both his maternal and paternal side originally spoke Sepedi. When Kgalema became the new president in 2008 some in the media claimed that 'Motlanthe was the first Tswana-speaking President of South Africa' (see www.enotes.com/topic/Kgalema_Motlanthe).
13 Benoni Old Location is the old location of Etwatwa, from where 151 656 people were moved to Daveyton when it was established in 1955.
14 Two schools were built in his honour, Kgalema Lower Primary and Madingoane Higher Primary. Madingoane Street in Daveyton was named after him.
15 Interview with Kgalema's aunt Deborah (77), Johannesburg, 22 November 2009. She was very knowledgeable about the family, having lived with them for years as a child. (Unless otherwise stated, all interviews in this book are with the author.)
16 Unless otherwise stated, all quotations of Kgalema come from interviews with the author.
17 Eddie Webster, interview, 22 November 2009. Webster sees Trevor Huddleston, who had a big influence on Kgalema, as personifying just such a progressive outlook.
18 Despite the weaknesses and failures of the boycott it was a huge consciousness-booster and a great lesson for mass struggles. For a useful critique of the boycott see Robert Fine and Dennis Davis (1990), *Beyond Apartheid: Labour and Liberation in South Africa*, Johannesburg: Ravan, 182–7.
19 Sydney Motlanthe, interview, 18 October 2010.
20 Ibid. But Sydney also recalls the many times when Kgalema was working at the city council and gave him and Ernest money. 'You see, we grew up in the Church with all the values that you can expect from there, like helping people in need, respect for all people, self-respect and so on.'
21 Cousin Catherine stayed with the Motlanthes in Alexandra and took Kgalema to and from Pholosho Primary School. The society was formed while Kgalema was on Robben Island. He does not appear to have had any direct influence in the decision to form it but it is an initiative after his own heart.
22 'Mmope-Kgalema Burial Society', section 2 (2.3), 2.
23 Ernest Motlanthe, interview, 22 September 2009. Ernest comes across as particularly loyal to Kgalema and proud of his achievements.
24 Paul Langa, who served time with Kgalema on Robben Island, recalls that he has never seen anybody so meticulous about how their clothing must be ironed. He liked to do the job himself. He had many preferences that set him apart from most people, that stemmed from his view of how one should live – with order, structure, discipline, cleanliness and neatness – but, Paul says, never is he judgemental about others who live differently.
25 Kgalema's deep involvement with the Church was typical of many earlier ANC leaders. He notes: 'ANC leaders since its birth in 1912 were Church and community leaders.

In fact that is how they got elected, because they were known Church and community leaders.' Such people appear to have a more orderly lifestyle and a principle of selfless service to whatever other cause they adopt as adults.

26 Kgalema Motlanthe, interview with Padraig O'Malley, 14 July 1992.
27 See Paulose Mar Paulose (undated), 'Encounter in Humanization: Insights for Christian-Marxist Dialogue and Cooperation', Kerala: Christian Sahitya Samithy. This is a novel attempt to marry the Marxist and Christian notions of social justice, in the belief that this can strengthen both Marxism and Christianity.
28 The dissolution of the Stalinised Comintern did not change the fundamental political line of Stalinism practised in the Soviet Union and Eastern Europe until the collapse of the Berlin Wall in 1989 and the cataclysmic events in Eastern Europe thereafter.
29 Kgalema's spirituality is not consciously a religiously inspired one but rather of a kind that I can best describe as a deeply human-centred life force. Yet he continues to have an interest in religious institutions. Travelling overseas he will not miss an opportunity to visit churches such as St Paul's Cathedral in London. He is fascinated by the power the Church wields. For a socialist (as he assured me in 2006 that he was) he has an extraordinarily wide, considerate mind on religious matters (Ebrahim Harvey (2006), 'Few problems, no worries', interview with Kgalema Motlanthe, *South African Labour Bulletin*, May/June 2006, 4–7). This is true of most subjects he engages with. Thabo Makunyane, who was with Kgalema on Robben Island, puts it well: 'He was more of a man of the Marxist dialectic but when he does refer to some positive Christian values he does not embrace it because it comes from some deity out there or because it is supposedly the will of God, but because of its intrinsic worth as a lesson for life' (Thabo Makunyane, interview, Johannesburg, 8 February 2010).
30 It was after St Peter's was converted into a seminary that Kgalema often went there and even stayed over weekends. He can remember when the old Liberal Party decided to disband in the 1960s: 'When the Liberal Party decided to close shop they held their last meeting there. I was in St Peter's when that happened.'
31 We cannot say with certainty whether it would have emerged in the first place had the ANC and PAC not been banned, but that it had a significant impact on South African politics is beyond doubt, a fact that is not sufficiently appreciated now because the BC movement has for a long time been in utter disarray.
32 This is the only time he has worked in the private sector. There is an irony in the fact that all the men in Kgalema's family except himself worked for the Anglo American Corporation (AAC) at some stage. During the period that his father and brothers worked there, AAC held unparalleled sway over not just mining but most other major sectors of the South African economy. The company epitomised the growth of South African capitalism. Rather than work for them Kgalema ended up leading the biggest union of mineworkers in the history of South Africa, which dominated AAC mines and the mining industry, trained and educated black mineworkers, and represented them at the Chamber of Mines in wage and other negotiations.
33 When he joined MK around 1974 Kgalema was about twenty-five. Though he had been reading much he had not really read or studied Marxist theory systematically. At that point he would have known little about the dangerous pitfalls of urban guerrilla warfare in a highly developed capitalist society with a very powerful state. He says it was much more the abhorrence of naked racism against black people that drove him to join MK.
34 The group included Mabetoa, Robbie Kgame and Oupa Mthimkhulu (the brother of Phil Mthimkhulu).
35 Section 10 rights fell under the infamous 1952 Native Laws Amendment Act, which 'limited Africans with a right to live permanently in the urban areas to those who were born there, those who had lived there continuously for fifteen years, and those who worked continuously for the same employer for ten years'. Those who did not qualify

were treated as 'temporary sojourners' in an urban area and could not remain there longer than 72 hours without securing special official permission.
36 Kgalema and his group were all still young and excited at taking up arms, not seeing that having a weapon is one thing but being armed with correct theory was far more important, facing apartheid. The 'armed struggle' failed utterly in South Africa and was arguably not really why the Nationalist Party opted for negotiations. Yet the origins of MK and countless official ANC statements declare that MK was formed to force the enemy to the negotiation table, and never to build the capacity for mass insurrection in order to overthrow the state. In fact the ANC was never truly a revolutionary movement because it never sought the overthrow of South African 'racial capitalism', which represented the real origins of the terrible exploitation the majority black working class was subjected to for over a century.
37 Mabetoa has never stopped appreciating the financial assistance Kgalema gave him to pay for his studies one year at the University of South Africa. It was a 'princely sum of R140, which was then a lot of money,' he says. Because apartheid blocked black people from education and skills, Mabetoa regarded the gesture as both educationally and politically motivated.
38 See 'ANC profile of Kgalema Molanthe' at http:/blogs.timeslive.co.za/ Hartley/2008/0924/anc-profile-of-kgalema-motlanthe-full-text.
39 The day after his arrest, on 14 April, the *Rand Daily Mail* lead headline read: 'SA smashes guerrilla network in Swaziland'. Zuma and Thabo Mbeki, who were working closely together in Swaziland, were arrested. The Swazi police had earlier planned to deport them to Botswana via Jan Smuts airport in Johannesburg, Since police at John Vorster Square were in touch with the Swazi police and had the photos of Mbeki and Zuma they would certainly have been detained at the airport. That plan was stopped by the urgent intervention first of Stan Mabizela, a leading refugee in Swaziland at the time, and then the ANC president, Oliver Tambo.
40 Jacob Zuma, interview, Pretoria, 22 September 2010.
41 Nelson Mandela (1976), 'Clear the obstacles and confront the enemy', in Mac Maharaj (ed) (2001), *Reflections in Prison*, Cape Town: Zebra, 7–20.
42 'Special Feature: ANC Conference', Deputy President, Kgalema Motlanthe, *Financial Mail*, 12 December 2007.

Chapter Two
1 Charlene Smith (1997), *Robben Island*, Cape Town: Struik, 98.
2 George Jackson (1971), *Soledad Brother: The Prison Letters of George Jackson*, Middlesex: Penguin. Jackson was eventually killed in prison by white racist warders.
3 Smith, 102–3.
4 Murphy Morobe, interview, Johannesburg, 12 August 2009.
5 Paul Langa, interview, Johannesburg, 23 September 2009. Langa was arrested in 1977 for the attack on the Jabulani police station. His underground job on the Island was to store and retrieve political literature and correspondence.
6 Ibid.
7 Fran Lisa Buntman (2003), *Robben Island and Prisoner Resistance to Apartheid*, Cambridge: Cambridge University Press, 171–2.
8 Ibid, 125.
9 Most times when Govan Mbeki came to Johannesburg he stayed with Kgalema in Dobsonville. When Kgalema could not fetch him from the airport he arranged for him to be fetched. Walter Sisulu was also drawn to Kgalema and the two grew very close, many ANC leaders have said. This would have been helped by Kgalema's deep respect for all the older stalwarts of the ANC. Buntman states (135) that Lawrence Phokanoka

did not respect Mandela on the Island but was close to Gwala and Mbeki. Kgalema was different. Though he too became close to both Gwala and Mbeki he always had great respect for Mandela. Whether he respected leaders or not was regardless of political and ideological debates; he valued them for their consistent contribution to the struggle and their sacrifices over a long period.

10 Buntman, 123.
11 Murphy Morobe, interview, 12 August 2009.
12 Thabo Makunyane, interview, Johannesburg, 10 November 2010. He was then the mayor of Polokwane.
13 Maurice Cornforth was a noted philosopher, especially on the Marxian concepts of dialectical and historical materialism. He was a member of the British Communist Party until his death in 1980, and deeply critical of Stalinism in the former Soviet Union.
14 Mahwidi John Phala, from Sekhukhuneland, was also imprisoned with Kgalema. He was an old ANC stalwart and founding member of Sebatakgomo. He passed away in 2009. Kgalema was very fond of him and spoke at his funeral.
15 George Mashamba worked with Kgalema in the ANC underground before his arrest in 1976. He is a leading member of the SACP.
16 George Mashamba, interview, Johannesburg, 12 November 2009.
17 Paul Langa, interview, 23 September 2009. Langa works in intelligence in the ANC and in government.
18 A book on the rich social life of Robben Island is indeed sorely needed, alongside the political emphases that books on the Island have had thus far – but the history of the Island is so steeped in politics, even then such a book will be quite heavily politicised.
19 Paul Langa, interview, 12 November 2009.
20 Ibid. Kgalema, forever modest, clarifies that they did not exactly rewrite the sports constitution but dealt with some of the weaknesses and tried to strengthen it. He was on the sports committee, a coordinating body, for most of the years he was there.
21 The importance of this point is that many migrant workers who were attracted to Marxist ideas still believed in traditional practices. Peter Delius in *A Lion Amongst Cattle* draws attention to the fact that Boshielo spent time training to be a herbalist ('*muti* man') but not to the fact that he did this to counteract the negative influences of such healers. The point Kgalema makes in relating the story of Boshielo is that Marxists in this country have had to adapt their role in part to the cultural and often contradictory consciousness of workers.
22 Department of Manpower, Central Organisation for Trade Testing, 19 March 1984. Bafana Sithole spoke at length about how much more concerned Kgalema was with the education of prisoners who were either illiterate or with little formal education than he was with his own. Though he tried to study towards a BCom degree he was always concerned with helping these prisoners. When he was either denied study or could not study for lack of funds he spent much time trying to teach them.
23 Prisoner Studies' Report, Robben Island, 4 January 1986. These are the English translations from the text, which was always written in Afrikaans because the warders were by then almost all white Afrikaners from poor working-class backgrounds.
24 Board of Prisoners Report, 24 July 1984.
25 Saths Cooper, interview, Johannesburg, 15 July 2011.
26 Saths Cooper, email correspondence, 25 July 2011.But Mandela also refers to the BC movement's 'emphatic rejection of Marxism' in an article he wrote on the Island. See Maharaj (ed) (2001), *Reflections in Prison*, Cape Town: Zebra, 41–2.
27 Ben Turok, interview, 28 January 2010.
28 A study of the ANC's literature since its birth and before it was banned, during exile and after 1990 reveals a mix of Marxist, African nationalist, social democratic, liberal, conservative and even reactionary thought, and virtually every conceivable shade across

the spectrum. But it seems such a very broad and undefined sweep has been at the expense of the ANC's own supporters, the vast majority of whom are drawn from the black working class and who are steeped in ever-growing unemployment, poverty and inequalities.
29 Buntman, 157.
30 Legassick, 396.
31 Professor Ismail Mohammed is an ANC MP who lived in Newclare, Johannesburg.
32 Among others, by Butler, 228. Whenever I asked Kgalema's about the claims that he was the protégé of Mbeki, Gwala or any other leader, his immediate response was not to affirm this but to say that various people at different times influenced him but never without an element of critical engagement. After all, he was no longer in the faith-based Anglican Church but in the school of revolutionary politics and Marxist dialectics. As a keen learner he has always had a growing mind of his own.
33 George Mashamba, interview, Johannesburg, 15 November 2010.
34 Raks Seakhoa, cited in Anthony Sampson (1999), *Mandela: The Authorised Biography*, London: HarperCollins, 291.
35 Ibid.
36 Ibid, 293.
37 Ibid. The high organ became the highest ANC structure on the Island after the arrival of the 'Rivonia trialists'. Buntman (97) reveals that until this structure was formed the disciplinary committee was the highest decision-making ANC structure in the general cells. That committee continued that role in the general sections but under the final authority of the High Organ.
38 Ahmed Kathrada, interview, Johannesburg, 21 October 2009.
39 Ahmed Kathrada, cited in Gail M Gerhart and Clive L Glaser (2010), *From Protest to Challenge, Vol. 6: Challenge and Victory, 1980–1990*, Bloomington: Indiana University Press, 497.
40 Ibid.
41 Sampson, 95.
42 See Cosatu 9th National Congress 2006, Book 1, Secretarial Report. Cosatu began to raise serious questions about the NDR in the light of, on the one hand, growing poverty and unemployment in post-apartheid South Africa, and on the other hand the resultant growing militancy in the unions and townships. In its political report (p 21) it asked: 'What is the relationship between the struggle for socialism and the national democratic revolution, given the reality that the ANC is pursuing a market path?' At the same congress Cosatu resolved that 'the working class must redirect the NDR towards socialism'. But this is the belated realisation of what were in fact congenital problems all along with an essentially non-socialist NDR, despite all the theoretical twists and turns over the years. We return to this key question in chapter five.
43 Ibid, 185.
44 Ibid.
45 Ahmed Kathrada, cited in Gail M Gerhart and Clive L Glaser, 497.
46 Cosatu 9th National Congress 2006, Book 1, Secretarial Report, 275.
47 Cited in *M&G*, 5 May 2000.
48 Cited in *M&G*, 12 May 2000.
49 Neville Alexander, cited in Fine and Davis, 271.
50 Fine and Davis, 276.
51 See Ebrahim Harvey, 'It's Time for the SACP to Step Out of the ANC's Shadow', *M&G*, 2 October 1999.
52 Maxim Gorky's *The Mother* was the 1906 novel on which Bertolt Brecht based his 1939 play *Mother Courage and Her Children*, one of several he wrote to counter the rise of fascism and Nazism. Maybe Kgalema was overkeen to get Mapula to read but his

commitment to broadening her horizons was commendable, especially at a time when many men, even progressive ones who were seriously involved in the struggle, often did not care much about their wives in that regard and may have felt threatened by having more knowledgeable and hence assertive partners. Kgalema clearly felt differently.
53 Saths Cooper, interview, Johannesburg, 15 July 2011.
54 Ibid.
55 Thabo Makunyane, interview. I was struck by how every person I interviewed who was with Kgalema on Robben Island had only positive things to say about him. This makes it hard for me to sound like a critical biographer but I must be true to the information!
56 Chuck Korr and Marvin Close (2008), *More Than Just a Game: Football v Apartheid*, London: Collins.
57 Andre Odendaal, who helped the research, says the book was based more on the 1960s. Yet the authors do also deal with the 1970s and 1980s, when Kgalema and his group were there.
58 Korr and Close, 257.
59 Bafana Sithole, interview, Johannesburg, 3 September 2009.
60 Thabo Makunyane, interview, 10 November 2009.
61 Director Matlala, interview, Johannesburg, 22 July 2009.
62 S'bu Ndebele, interview, Pretoria, 2 December 2009.
63 Bafana Sithole, interview, Johannesburg, 27 August 2009. Sithole was imprisoned with Kgalema.
64 It is a unique sense one gets from Kgalema and it is probably why Jesse Duarte said that he is not a typical politician. Ssomeone once said to me that he is either a great pretender – with his repeated claim that he is not interested in power for himself and the constant humility, decency and lack of ambitious drive many others talk about – or he is indeed the 'real deal', on a mission to transform politics into a noble profession and rid it of the filth that today oozes from our body politic.
65 Buntman, 268.
66 Moral issues seem to loom large for Kgalema. 'Moral rectitude' is something he sometimes referred to in interviews. However, it appears he and other ANC leaders link this to 'revolutionary morality', a phrase which in definition and practice is far from clear and raises debates. It is even more problematic if it means – and it often comes across like that – 'my party, right or wrong'. These are questions which fall into ethical and especially political philosophy. Whether we can also reconcile an often abstract moralistic approach to Marxist materialist philosophy, which will directly and indirectly link moral conduct to material conditions and class struggles, is another huge question. The changes the ANC has undergone since it came to power are a pertinent example here. It would be mistaken and dishonest, for example, to lambaste ANC cadres who went into business or government for moral lapses without examining what a switch from poverty to huge salaries and benefits can and has done to the moral fibre of people after 1994 and related ANC policy shifts. It was, after all, Marx who first asserted that conditions determine consciousness and if that premise is true naturally a change in material conditions will lead to a change in consciousness and as a result moral lapses will inevitably occur.
67 Daphne Mashile-Nkosi, interview, Johannesburg, 12 July 2009. Mashile-Nkosi is the widow of Stan Nkosi, Kgalema's great friend.
68 It is not absolutely certain that the marriage would have worked well if Mapula had shared more of Kgalema's interests by being more politically minded and more committed towards her own education, but it could well have done so.
69 Mapula Motlanthe, interview, 22 August 2010.
70 Kgomotso would have longed to catch up with his father after the decade he was away, since he was just five years old when Kgalema was jailed.

Endnotes

71 This is Mapula reflecting on the period since Kgalema's release in 1987.
72 Daphne Mashile-Nkosi, interview, Johannesburg, 22 July 2010.
73 Everyone, especially those who were with Kgalema and Stan Nkosi on Robben Island, speaks of their relationship in ways that make it worthy of further enquiry. A relationship that becomes very close between men who are temperamentally and personally very different is something worth dwelling on and learning from.

Chapter Three

1 See Chapter 10 of Jeremy Baskin's *Striking Back: A History of Cosatu* for a more detailed account of these dramatic events, which shook and shocked the entire labour movement inside and outside South Africa.
2 Kgalema has remained very close to Motlatsi, even though he is the boss of Teba, the mine's recruiting agency and the former deputy chair of Anglogold Ashanti. While others on the left may be cynical and regard this as evidence of how yesterday's union leaders are today part of the new black elite, his respect for them has remained consistent. Never has he been judgemental, sarcastic or envious about how their careers have prospered. Instead he sincerely wishes them well and tries to understand these changes in more objective terms.
3 Cyril Ramaphosa, interview, Johannesburg, 22 July 2010.
4 Vic Allen, personal email communication, 22 February 2010. Many people have echoed my own sense that Kgalema can be a bit too self-effacing at times, which could be a weakness, especially if issues need more assertive handling.
5 Thuli Mofutsanyane, interview, Johannesburg, 12 March 2010.
6 Allen, Vol. 3.
7 Cyril Ramaphosa, interview, Johannesburg, 22 July 2010.
8 Ibid.
9 Director Matlala, interview, Johannesburg, 12 September 2009.
10 Paul Nkuna, interview, Johannesburg, 21 May 2010.
11 Many factors appear to have boosted NUM's resolve to begin the strike. Three main ones were the ultra-low wages that had always been the lot of black miners, the deplorable working conditions and safety record, and more recently the rise of the mass movement, including the birth of Cosatu in 1985, since the Vaal uprisings of 1984. That the regime was in talks with Mandela and the ANC was meeting leaders from various constituencies in exile also contributed to a sense of imminent regime change and thus an increased determination to win union demands, especially since NUM had just months before the strike adopted the Freedom Charter. Jeremy Baskin says that what incensed NUM was that their members and other black miners were paid a pittance 'in spite of gold being the highest foreign exchange earner for the country.' NUM thus had a strong sense that it could win its demands. Ever since its February congress, its battle cry had been 'Mineworkers Take Control'. Kgalema says that though initially the slogan applied to the management of the hostels it soon became one that NUM readily applied to other aspects of their struggle.
12 Director Matlala, interview, Johannesburg, 22 October 2009.
13 Baskin, 227.
14 Hein Marais (2010), *South Africa Pushed to the Limit: The Political Economy of Change*, Cape Town: UCT Press, 428.
15 Ibid. See *South African Labour Bulletin* (1988), Vol. 13, No. 6, 72–104 for an explanation of the technological changes that reduced jobs on the mines.
16 Howard Gabriels, interview, Johannesburg, 22 April 2010.
17 Ibid.
18 See Allen, Vol. 1, 143–5 and Du Toit, 3–33 for an understanding of both the geological

conditions on the gold mines and South Africa's position in the growing world capitalist economy, which together necessitated large supplies of cheap black labour.
19 Baskin, 232. There were countless examples in the years after Cosatu's launch in 1985 when it failed to provide solidarity in action with one or more of its affiliates during a strike, making a mockery of its own slogan.
20 Ibid, 238.
21 Ibid, 232.
22 Baskin, 237.
23 Ibid, 237.
24 Howard Gabriels, interview, Johannesburg, 22 April 2010.
25 Baskin, 236.
26 Ibid.
27 Ibid.
28 Ibid, 237.
29 Ibid, 227.
30 Jesse Maluleka, interview, Johannesburg, 12 August 2009.
31 Allen, Vol. 3, 611.
32 Ibid, 423.
33 Ibid.
34 Manne Dipico, former premier of the Northern Cape, was incensed by Allen's remarks especially since he did not interview anyone in the union on the subject.
35 Butler, 228.
36 Cyril Ramaphosa, interview, Johannesburg, 22 July 2010.
37 Manne Dipico, interview, Johannesburg, 4 December 2009.
38 Allen, Vol. 1, xv.
39 Allen, Vol. 3, 609–10.
40 Kgalema was not inclined to criticise those he worked closely with in NUM, his intimates – an occasional lapse in how he served the organisation.
41 Baskin, 219.
42 Laloo Chiba, author's interview, 22 October 2010, Johannesburg. Chiba said how fortunate he felt when Kgalema, who was then president, came to visit him in Milpark hospital early in 2009. Kgalema loyally supports stalwarts of the ANC and is especially caring towards the elderly, in this way acknowledging the sacrifices they made over decades in the liberation struggle.
43 James Motlatsi interview, 22 August 2009, Johannesburg.
44 Allen, Vol. 3, 500.
45 Ibid, 502.
46 If we look at his record since he was released from the Island, Kgalema has repeatedly been thrown in at the deep end at critical moments in NUM, the ANC and later in government.
47 Dipico, interview, Johannesburg, 4 December 2009.
48 Ibid.
49 Khetsi Lehoko, interview, Cape Town, 29 January 2010.
50 Howard Gabriels, interview, Johannesburg, 22 April 2010.
51 *South African Labour Bulletin*, Vol. 16, No. 3, 93–5.
52 Gwede Mantashe, interview, Johannesburg, 30 March 2010.
53 Paul Nkuna, interview, Johannesburg, 21 May 2010. Kgalema has consistently believed that people have the right to express dissenting views.
54 Thuli Mofutsanyane, interview, Johannesburg, 12 March 2010.
55 Director Matlala, interview, Johannesburg, 12 September 2009.
56 Cyril Ramaphosa, interview, Johannesburg, 13 June 2010.
57 Director Matlala, interview, Johannesburg, 22 October 2009.

Endnotes

58 Cyril Ramaphosa, interview, Johannesburg, 13 June 2010.
59 Not much has been said about this matter but I am convinced that the fate and future of NUM was wedded to the ANC through the conscious efforts of Kgalema, probably more than anyone else. Kgalema played no small part in NUM's all-out campaign for an ANC victory in the 1994 elections. It is also true that even before Kgalema joined NUM the union had already effectively backed the ANC by adopting the Freedom Charter in early 1987.
60 The Workers' Charter (WC) supporters, led by Numsa, were defeated at the July 1987 Cosatu congress by those for the Freedom Charter. The WC – unlike the ambiguity in the Freedom Charter – was explicitly socialist and believed that the struggle for national liberation was inextricably linked to the struggle for socialism. It rejected a two-stage approach. Had Cosatu instead adopted the WC we can only speculate how that would have influenced the alliance with the ANC and SACP. The victory of the Freedom Charter signalled within Cosatu the decisive ascendancy of ANC politics in it. From then on it was the ANC and its alliance with Cosatu and the SACP all the way. Accepting the Freedom Charter 'was a victory which left many within Numsa, CWIU, Ccawusa and NUTW unhappy and believing that they had been bullied into submission. The mood of the congress thereafter was deeply divided' (Baskin, 221–2). The victory of the 'populists' over the 'workerists' was therefore shaky. Maybe these political differences and tensions have to some extent bedevilled the quest for solidarity in Cosatu since then, especially the evident lack of solidarity between affiliates during various strikes and industry disputes, an important area that must be properly researched.
61 Barbara Hogan, interview, Johannesburg, 12 November 2009.
62 *Inzile* was the colloquial term for an activist who did not go into exile.
63 Ferial Haffajee, 'The quiet man with paisley tie heads the NUM', *Weekly Mail*, 31 January 1992.
64 'I am still just a member of the NUM team', interview with Snuki Zikalala, *South African Labour Bulletin*, January 1992, 93–5.
65 The SACP decided in 1990, following its unbanning, that members should decide for themselves whether to go public about their party membership and activities.
66 Cited in Haffajee above. Haffajee herself states that 'his dislike for the adversarial colours his plans for the union.'
67 Director Matlala, personal email communication, 7 August 2012.
68 Director Matlala, interview, Johannesburg, 22 October 2009.
69 Kate Philip, interview, Johannesburg, 14 October 2009.
70 Ibid.
71 Thuli Mofutsanyane, interview, Johannesburg, 12 March 2010.
72 Gwede Mantashe, interview, Johannesburg, 30 March 2010.
73 James Motlatsi, interview, Johannesburg, 22 August 2009.
74 Sactwu in 1993 was the first Cosatu affiliate to form an investment company. When MIC was formed in 1995 it worked jointly with Sactwu but differences between them led to a parting of the ways.
75 Paul Nkuna, interview, Johannesburg, 21 May 2010.
76 NUM gave the R3 million to form the MI and thereafter the MIC. Because NUM is the sole shareholder of MIC, the R3 million has been referred to as a 'shareholder loan'. However, since NUM has nothing to do with MIC, the loan – in order to entrench and sustain the 'Chinese Wall' between them and avoid conflicts of interest – was repaid to the MIT and not to NUM. Clifford Elk, the first CEO of MIC, said that 'the first distribution by MIC of funds back to MIT would have been to repay this shareholder loan.'
77 But Baleni recently conceded that though NUM prevented its entities, such as the MIT, from doing business in the mining industry 'this did not preclude them from investing

upstream or downstream of the industry, where the NUM does not organise' ('In bed with mine houses', *City Press*, 26 August 2012). In same article Baleni went further to say that mining is very closely tied to the rest of the economy: 'To prevent the inclusion of its various commercial entities from any association with mining would in effect bar these entities from any transactions, given how closely interlinked mining is with all sectors in the South African economy.' For example, Remgro, the MIC's fellow shareholder in FirstRand, owns about 5 per cent of Impala Platinum. Furthermore 'WDB Investment Holdings, the MIC's empowerment partner in FirstRand and Masana Petroleum Solutions, has interests in Kalahari Resources and Anglo Inyosi Coal' (ibid).

78 Kuben Pillay, interview, Johannesburg, 12 November 2009.
79 Ibid.
80 Paul Nkuna, interview, Johannesburg, 21 May 2010.
81 Ebrahim Patel, interview, Cape Town, 28 January 2010.
82 See 'NUM congratulates MIC' at www.num.org.za/index.php?option=com_content&task=view&id=474&Itemid=72.
83 Kate Philip, interview, Johannesburg, 14 October 2009. Philip worked for 14 years in NUM. A fiercely independent, critical and assertive thinker she ruffled feathers not only in the industry but in NUM itself, especially because of her views on NUM's investment company, the MIC.
84 Ibid.
85 Directors of MIC have three forms of remuneration for executives: salary, a bonus for performance and a retention mechanism which states that the longer they stay with the company they will get a vested interest that they can cash in on a rolling three-year basis, based purely on the growth of the company and their contribution to it. If you consistently 'out-perform' for five years, as they put it, in the third year you get a special bonus which is a percentage of your salary times the growth, meaning that in that year you could get three times your salary.
86 Kuben Pillay, interview, Johannesburg, 12 November 2009.
87 Kate Philip, interview, Johannesburg, 14 October 2009.
88 Ebrahim Patel, interview, Cape Town, 28 January 2010.
89 Ibid.
90 Nkuna basically told me to mind my own business and that I was not one of the stakeholders MIC reported to.
91 Dale McKinley (1999), 'Socialist Unionism' or 'Social Capitalism', in *South African Labour Bulletin*. Vol. 24, 6, September, 85–90.
92 Roger Southall (2007), 'Empowering the Working Class? COSATU and BEE', unpublished paper.
93 Irene Charnley, interview, Johannesburg, 22 June 2009.
94 Ibid.
95 Saths Cooper, interview, Johannesburg, 28 June 2011.
96 Raymond Suttner, personal communication, 17 June 2009.
97 Seeng Letele, from Lesotho, worked as a human resources manager in NUM at the time. Other than this concern she only had the highest praise and respect for Kgalema and spoke of how he arranged for her and others to meet Mandela when she made the request, and when her son struggled to get a visa to Sweden he quickly had the problem solved.
98 James Motlatsi, interview, Johannesburg, 22 August 2009.
99 Ebrahim Patel, interview, Cape Town, 28 January 2010.
100 Ibid.
101 Howard Gabriels, interview, Johannesburg, 22 April 2010.
102 Cyril Ramaphosa, interview, Johannesburg, 22 July 2010.
103 Kate Philip, interview, Johannesburg, 14 October 2009.

Endnotes

104 Jesse Maluleka, interview, Johannesburg, 12 August 2009.
105 Frans Baleni, interview, Johannesburg, 18 September 2010.
106 Gino Govender interview, Johannesburg, 15 September 2009. Govender recalled how Kgalema's humility was epitomised by these words in the poem: 'If you can talk with crowds and keep your virtue, / Or walk with Kings – nor lose the common touch.'
107 Gwede Mantashe, interview, Johannesburg, 30 March 2010.
108 As an example of Maharaj's claim that there was no real underground structures in place, he said: 'We couldn't talk about making a township like KwaMashu ungovernable – that's mass action – and in the meantime, our armed formations or the political underground were not there to support the creation of people's committees' (Padraig O'Malley (2007), *Shades of Difference: Mac Maharaj and the Struggle for South Africa*, Johannesburg: Penguin, 248). Raymond Suttner's book, *The ANC Underground in South Africa*, provides a much more informed, interesting and dynamic account of the nature of the underground during the late 1980s, the period in question (Raymond Suttner (2008), *The ANC Underground in South Africa*, Johannesburg: Jacana).
109 O'Malley, 308.
110 Ibid, 287–90. Maharaj makes his difficult, even hostile, relationship with Mbeki evident in these pages.
111 Gugu Mtshali, interview, Johannesburg, 23 July 2010.
112 Ibid.

Chapter Four

1 Thabo Mbeki, interview, Johannesburg, 22 June 2011. RW Johnson claims that Thabo Mbeki wanted Joel Netshitenzhe: 'Mbeki put up Joel Netshitenzhe instead, but Cosatu pushed forward Kgalema Motlanthe. ... Prudently, Netshitenzhe withdrew' (RW Johnson (2010), *South Africa's Brave New World, The Beloved Country since the End of Apartheid*, London: Penguin, 80). Kgalema and also Netshitenzhe strongly denied any knowledge of this (Joel Netshitenzhe, telephonic conversation, 15 November 2011) and Mbeki says: 'No, there is no such thing because it was actually a decision the ANC took to head-hunt him'.
2 Jacob Zuma, interview, Pretoria, 22 September 2010.
3 Jessie Duarte, interview, Johannesburg, 22 September 2009. Jessie Duarte said that Sisulu often came to visit Kgalema first at Shell House and later at Luthuli House, and that they would sometimes sit in his office for the whole day, talking about the ANC and government. The close relationship between Sisulu and Kgalema has hardly been mentioned in the media or the literature. Neither of them pushed for publicity.
4 Mathews Phosa, interview, Johannesburg, 13 November 2010. The literature and interviews all make it clear that of senior ANC leaders it was Mandela and Sisulu in particular who were keen on Kgalema becoming the ANC's next SG in 1997. Mbeki's biographer, Mark Gevisser, is thus incorrect in claiming 'that with Mbeki's patronage, Motlanthe would be elected ANC secretary-general' (Gevisser (2009), 251). Besides, where was the patronage Gevisser refers to?
5 Frans Baleni adds this account: 'Madiba ended up telling us a story of a young man from a rural village who was looking for a wife. He travelled from one village to another but he could not find one. However, when he arrived back home he saw that he had a neighbour who matched all the criteria he had in mind. In that way Mandela told us that the secretary-general the ANC needed was right here and that in the same way that the man was looking for a wife the ANC was looking for a bride' (interview, Johannesburg, 12 March 2010).
6 Jacob Zuma, interview, Pretoria, 27 September 2010.
7 Richard Calland (2006), *Anatomy of South Africa: Who Holds the Power?* Cape Town: Zebra, 128.

8 Ibid, 129.
9 Patrick Bond, *Unsustainable South Africa: Environment, Development and Social Protest*, London: Merlin, 203. This draft strategy was a particularly crude manifestation of monetary class-based municipal services in townships, released by the ministry for reconstruction and development. The quantity and quality of services delivered was determined by how much money you could pay.
10 Bond gives a wealth of information and good analysis of these important developments. Despite his analytical weaknesses of ANC politics, Bond is probably South Africa's leading radical scholar of urban protests on basic services infrastructure.
11 Asked about the assault on the dignity of black South Africans who, over a decade of ANC rule, were still without water or adequate amounts of it and the total absence of sanitation or poor levels of it in many parts of the country, he replied: 'Our first major achievement was the liberation of our people and the restoration of their dignity. I mean liberation from a legalised system of racism and oppression, but I agree there are countless ways in which the dignity of human beings can be undermined.' He told how an old man in a public hospital on the East Rand was in a toilet that had no paper. He had to call home on his cellphone to ask them to phone the hospital and get them to supply it. This example showed that the public sector urgently needed to be revamped to provide decent services.
12 My sense is that Kgalema has long believed, almost as Moses Kotane did, that the ANC was not only the heart of the liberation movement during apartheid but that it continues to be the heart of the ANC alliance in post-apartheid South Africa. How such a staunch belief in the ANC, despite its serious limitations on socialism, tallies with his Marxist convictions is a puzzle. It seems to be part of the broader conundrum of ANC politics. If there is an answer, it may partly reflect the uninspiring party the SACP has been, even before 1990. Yet the SACP have certainly taken up some important campaigns and will remain key in any realignment of socialist forces.
13 Kgalema was never really satisfied with the appointment of Smuts Ngonyama as head of the presidency and its spokesperson, to be based alongside himself at Luthuli House. He queried the purpose, need and wisdom of this move. In the past, the SG of the ANC had functioned as its spokesperson. The new scheme inevitably created confusion and overlaps between Kgalema's office and that of Ngonyama. But it seems that he did not voice his reservations in case they raised problems for the ANC.
14 Frans Baleni, interview, Johannesburg, 12 March 2010. Mantashe is also emphatic about Mbeki's domination of Luthuli House: 'Kgalema presided over years of demobilisation and his office was pushed to the margins, systematically. Just look how Smuts [Ngonyama] overshadowed his role, as SG of the ANC. I found a shell [evidence of war] here and asked him how he survived for all these years. That is why we entered Polokwane with a rescue plan after Mbeki's utter domination' (Gwede Mantashe, interview, Johannesburg, 19 February 2010).
15 Report of the Secretary-General, 51st ANC National Conference: Stellenbosch, 16 December 2002, Sect 1 (195).
16 'This is where we stand', *City Press*, 15 December 2002.
17 Xolela Mangcu (2008), *To the Brink: The State of Democracy in South Africa*, Scottsville: University of KwaZulu-Natal Press, 128.
18 Thabo Mbeki, interview, Johannesburg, 22 June 2010.
19 Karima Brown, interview, Johannesburg, 28 November 2009.
20 'Biggest challenge facing the ANC', *Sowetan*, 18 July 2000.
21 It was interesting to see a few ANC leaders who in the run-up to Polokwane – in anticipation of the defeat of Mbeki and especially after his defeat there – suddenly seeing much that was wrong with his presidency over the years and urging greater democracy in the ANC.

Endnotes

22 'Mbeki's man' is only one example of glibness in South African journalism. For informed reporting and analysis journalists need to do much more serious reading and research on the topics they cover in their stories – in politics, for example, on a very complex pre- and post-1990 society. Comments on the concepts and history of Marxism and 'communism' are often particularly shallow.
23 'Mbeki inherited his problems from Mandela', *M&G*, 22 March 2000.
24 'Ultra-left' as a term of abuse is part of a strategy used over the decades by Stalinists to dismiss and disarm radicals who campaign for genuine socialism and against rule by a bureaucratic elite over the labouring masses. Interestingly, whereas before 1994 it was a term reserved for the independent left – outside the ANC alliance – after Gear's adoption in 1996 and especially after the 2000 anti-privatisation strike it was increasingly used by some ANC leaders against Cosatu and the SACP.
25 *Star*, 2 October 2000.
26 Gwede Mantashe, interview, Johannesburg, 19 February 2010.
27 Ibid.
28 Ibid. Mantashe went on to say: 'That is why he lets you, a strong and consistent critic of the ANC, write his biography, because he wants an honest, frank and critical analysis of his life and the ANC. That takes a lot of courage but that is Kgalema for you.'
29 'This is where we stand', *City Press*, 15 December 2002.
30 Jacob Zuma, interview, 27 September 2010.
31 Irene Charnley, interview, Johannesburg, 22 July 2009.
32 Gevisser (2007), 670. Gevisser put it bluntly: 'Mbeki introduced a white paper which gutted the RDP of its Keynesian underpinnings and committed the government to fiscal discipline.'
33 See the ANC's 1994 *Reconstruction and Development Programme*, 'RDP financing' (6.5.1 to 6.5.18) for details of the fiscal situation that this RDP base document sketched. Section 6.5.7 specifically states: 'The existing ratios of the deficit, borrowing and taxation to GNP are part of our macroeconomic problem.' So, despite assertions to the contrary, it is untrue that the fiscal provisions in the White Paper were completely new and a radical departure from the base document.
34 Gear still stirs many fierce debates because its opponents and defenders are equally tenacious. It is the one major policy issue after 1994 that signalled the ascendancy of policy technocrats in government over the mass membership of the ANC and civil society. But the fact is that the members of the ANC, SACP and Cosatu failed dismally to stop its implementation because by then the aura of the most senior ANC leaders, such as Mandela, Sisulu and others had not yet faded and their own strength had declined, as had that of broader civil society.
35 Patrick Bond (2005), *Elite Transitions: From Apartheid to Neo-liberalism*, Pietermaritzburg: University of KwaZulu-Natal Press, 99.
36 Though he changed his mind on Gear he never once publicly criticised NUM and Cosatu's hostility towards it in 1996 or 1997.
37 Ibid.
38 Gevisser, 2007, 672.
39 Zwelinzima Vavi, interview, Johannesburg, 18 July 2010.
40 Mandela himself also admitted at Cosatu's annual congress in September 1997 that the government failed to consult adequately on its macroeconomic strategy. He also said that the plan could be revised if it did not meet its transformational goals. But less than a year later, in July 1998, Mandela slammed Cosatu and the SACP for attacking Gear: 'Gear, as I have said before, is the fundamental policy of the ANC. We will not change it because of your pressure. If you feel you cannot get your way [then] go out and shout like opposition parties. Prepare to face the full implications of that line' (*Business Day*, 2 July 1998).
41 Kgalema interview with Padraig O'Malley, 4 August 1997.

42 Ibid.
43 Kgalema interview with Padraig O'Malley, 15 September 2000.
44 Zwelinzima Vavi, interview, Johannesburg, 18 July 2010.
45 'Cosatu strike futile, says ANC, PAC', *Star*, 2 October 2002.
46 'The lies that ultra-left tells us', *Star*, 3 October 2002.
47 'ANC offensive against far leftists', *M&G*, 2 November 2001.
48 Kgalema Motlanthe interview with Padraig O'Malley, 14 July 1992.
49 See Kgalema Motlanthe's interview with Snuki Zikalala, *South African Labour Bulletin*, January 1992, Vol. 16, No 3, 93–5.
50 'Relationship dangerously undefined', *Business Report*, 13 July 2000.
51 Ibid.
52 Bafana Sithole, interview, Johannesburg, 13 August 2009. One has to exercise caution about the phrase 'balance of forces' because it can be 'ANC-speak', a glib response to more complex things including the lack of political will to begin to change that balance of forces.
53 Kgalema Motlanthe interview with Padraig O'Malley, 15 September 2000.
54 In 2006, when Mbeki wanted disciplinary action taken against the former deputy minister of health, Nozizwe Madlala-Routledge, Kgalema refused. She had lambasted the government's stance on HIV/Aids, especially the approach of her then boss, the minister of health, Tshabalala-Msimang. Kgalema supported not only her right to criticise Tshabalala-Msimang's handling of the pandemic but basically agreed with her. This is how his clash with Mbeki was captured when he took over from Mbeki in September 2007: 'Adding to his popularity within the party was his dismissal of Mbeki's call to take action against axed deputy health minister, Nozizwe Madlala-Routledge. He said that he did not see any need for her to be disciplined as she was not in breach of the ANC constitution. This came after a National Working Committee meeting where Mbeki wanted action against Madlala-Routledge, arguing that she had undermined not only him but the ANC as a whole' ('Kgalema Motlanthe: The new South African president', *Propaganda Press*, 22 September 2008, http://propagandapress.org/2008/09/22/kgalema-motlanthe-biography).
55 James Myburgh, 'Who is Kgalema Motlanthe?', *Politicsweb*, 25 September 2008.
56 Ibid.
57 Ibid.
58 Ibid. Myburgh, who suggests that Mbeki was probably manipulating Kgalema behind the scenes, concludes in this article: 'It is not clear to what degree Motlanthe took up these issues on HIV/Aids, Zimbabwe and cadre deployment, out of conviction – or whether he was just behaving like a loyal apparatchik dutifully defending and implementing the ANC "line" set by Mbeki.'
59 Zwelinzima Vavi, interview, Johannesburg, 18 July 2010.
60 Jaspreet Kindra, 'We would not like to burn our bridges', *M&G*, 11 May 2001.
61 Report of the Secretary-General, 51st ANC National Conference: Stellenbosch, 16 December 2002, Sect 1 (7).
62 Bafana Sithole, interview, Johannesburg, 13 August 2009.
63 Report of the Secretary-General, 51st ANC National Conference: Stellenbosch, 16 December 2002, Sect 1 (10).
64 Noor Nieftagodien, interview, Johannesburg, 12 November 2009.
65 Karima Brown, interview, Johannesburg, 28 November 2009.
66 Kgalema Motlanthe, 'NGC 2000: Mid-Term Report and Review', 2.1.2 State of the Branches.
67 Report of the ANC National General Council, Port Elizabeth, 11–15 July 2000. In this cause, the ANC decided in 1997 to establish a policy institute and a political school, and they had not happened at national level by the time of writing, fifteen years later.

Endnotes

68 Patrick Bond, interview, Johannesburg, 3 January 2010. When Bond refers to Kgalema as a 'machine-man' he implies that his loyalty to the ANC is unquestionable but also conveys a sense of him as an apparatchik. Yet Kgalema's strong criticisms of the ANC in many reports also show him as very much 'his own man' and often courageously independent-minded.
69 Trevor Manuel, interview, Cape Town, 12 January 2010.
70 Essop Pahad, interview, Johannesburg, 23 February 2010.
71 Ibid.
72 Jacob Zuma, interview, Pretoria, 22 September 2010.
73 Trevor Ngwane, interview, Johannesburg, 15 October 2010.
74 'People's power in action', *Sunday Times*, 15 December 2002.
75 See Bond, the most prolific writer on basic services infrastructure in this country. He provides compelling information on the deplorable conditions in black townships and rural areas and the resultant social protests, which still continue today.
76 This was the kind of problem he wanted to avoid after Mafikeng: Mantashe as SACP chairperson did not reprimand the SACP conference in 2009 decisively when delegates booed Malema. But would the resignation of Mantashe as chairperson of the SACP be that easy, even if it is wise? An electoral congress of the SACP chose him. Does such a move – especially if it is among the top leadership of the ANC and SACP – not undermine a democratic decision taken by the membership of the SACP? Such a precedent could have serious consequences inside the party, a point Kgalema and the ANC do not appear to have seriously considered.
77 Mbeki, Zuma and other SACP leaders summarily ended their SACP membership in 1990.
78 Essop Pahad, interview, Johannesburg, 23 February 2010. Pahad, a senior member of the SACP for decades, says: 'Perhaps we rushed for mass recruitment too soon. What we should have concentrated on – upon reflection – is to say let us identify some of the best people inside the ANC, trade unions and other mass organisations and really build a real quality cadre so that we could prepare much better the ground for later mass recruitment. We would then today have had a better and stronger cadre and leadership. We also should have had a more rigorous induction and orientation for new recruits, even after the decision for mass recruitment was taken'.
79 Jeremy Cronin, 'Lenin Is Not a Statute', *African Communist*, 4th Quarter 1991, 11–18. Jeremy Cronin notes that the distinction between mass and vanguard was false because there were many dynamic linkages between the two forms. Cronin made one of the better interventions during this debate. Sadly, however, he fails to deal with the crucial question of the SACP's two-stage theory. He deals with the organisational form of the party after 1990 but says nothing about the SACP's approach to the revolution in South Africa and its lack for decades of a clear, firm socialist programme. You cannot separate the organisational form of a party from its programme.
80 Many of the SACP's problems since the ANC came to power in 1994 arose as a result of a serious lack of clear and strategic thinking. Among them have been the SACP's relationship with the ANC after the 1994 elections and how the party would go about achieving its objectives alongside the ANC.
81 Ben Turok, interview, Cape Town, 12 January 2010.
82 Jaspreet Kindra, 'Cuba, China, models for South Africa', *M&G*, 12 May 2000.
83 Karima Brown, interview, Johannesburg, 27 August 2009.
84 'Struggle for real freedom still continues', *Star*, 27 June 2000. Kgalema wrote the article on the 45th anniversary of the Freedom Charter.
85 Unsurprisingly, this speech caused a huge stir in the liberal media. The slightest leftist indication by the ANC often does this, yet liberals include the most fervent supporters of freedom of speech, ideas and democratic debate.

86 Jaspreet Kindra, 'Cuba, China models for SA', *M&G*, 12 May 2000.
87 'South Africa's tragic leap to the right', *M&G*, 23 June 2000.
88 Kgalema Motlanthe interview with Padraig O'Malley, 30 September 2004.
89 Ibid.
90 My abiding sense is that Kgalema is wedded to the notion that the ANC can fix any problem it has through democratic decision-making. But too many decisions have already been taken by the ANC leadership without the ordinary members, not least the key policy decisions by the ANC-led government after 1994 that were made outside of ANC policy and national conferences. Gear, for example, was taken to ANC conferences as a fait accompli. IGoli 2002 was decided by city officials and consultants far removed from the lives, interests and needs of members. The South African Municipal Workers Union complained bitterly of how iGoli was bulldozed through the 'negotiations' that government officials falsely claimed they were having with the union. Kgalema concedes that this plan (which he too had problems with) was never adopted by an ANC conference.
91 The real empowerment and control of membership is gauged by how far they could have taken decisive action. The way these problems persist shows that ANC members were not strong enough to take action and in some respects, as we have seen, decisions were taken by leadership behind their backs and without meaningful consultation.
92 In 2002, the year of Stellenbosch, he contended with a huge case of membership fraud in the Eastern Cape that reflected regional intrigues ('Rank and File can reclaim ANC', *Sunday Times*, 15 December 2002). Once fraud was established, he acted not only to stop it but had the main culprit suspended. At this level, at least, Kgalema did act against such fraud. In fact it is inconceivable that he would not do so once fraud was established.

Chapter Five
1 Sankie Mthembi-Mahanyele replaced Mtintso.
2 No doubt his eye for such class contradictions, which have steadily increased the distance between leaders and ordinary members, comes from his Marxist training. Probably no report before or since has so accurately captured the growing problems in the branches that threatened to erode the liberation movement values and the redistributionist ethos of the Freedom Charter and the RDP.
3 Ibid, 14.
4 Ibid.
5 Yet these voters still return the ANC to power in every election even when in socio-material terms they do not have much to show since 1994.
6 Report of the ANC NGC, 11–15 July 2000, 2.
7 'People's power in action', *Sunday Times*, 15 December 2002.
8 Ibid.
9 Tellingly, the ANC has failed to provide a coherent political and class explanation for these sins of self-enrichment and careerism and their persistence since 1990.
10 Karima Brown, interview, Johannesburg, 22 July 2010. Reaching that point, the left would argue, requires that the ANC undergo a basic transformation from a multi-class organisation to a dedicated working class or socialist party. As we have seen, Kgalema has claimed this to be within the capacity of the ANC.
11 Some of the developments prompted the fervour that paved the way for the 'Polokwane revolution' at the ANC's 52nd national conference in December 2007.
12 'Alliance battle is not over', *M&G*, 3 January 2003.
13 'Crooked timber of humanity includes the ANC', *Business Day*, 10 June 2010.
14 Essop Pahad, interview, Johannesburg, 16 August 2009.
15 Andrew Feinstein (2007), *After the Party: A Personal and Political Journey inside the*

ANC, Johannesburg: Jonathan Ball, 205.
16 Ibid.
17 It was a welcome relief recently to learn that President Zuma has ordered a judicial investigation into the arms deal, something that should have been done over a decade ago.
18 'The ANC's Oilgate', *M&G*, 3 May 2005.
19 'Oilgate company was ANC front', *M&G*, 15 July 2005.
20 'The ANC's Oilgate', *M&G*, 3 May 2005. Of the remaining R4 milllion Mendi Msimang, the ANC treasurer-general, says: 'I spoke to PetroSA and told them that I am taking responsibility for the R11 million we got but not for the R4 million that went whereto I don't know' (Mendi Msimang, interview, 18 August 2010).
21 'The ANC's Oilgate', *M&G*, 3 May 2005. Kgalema's name was not adequately cleared even years later. In his significant judgment in August 2009, Justice Ntsikelelo Poswa set aside a report by the public protector, Lawrence Mushwana, into the Oilgate scandal after the *M&G* challenged the report's findings. The judgment found that Mushwana failed to conduct a proper and thorough investigation, including whether PetroSA executives knew that funds were paid to the ANC and whether they were under pressure in that regard ('Motlanthe cleared by Mushwana', *City Press*, 5 March 2006).
22 *Star*, 18 January 2011.
23 Mendi Msimang, telephonic communication, 3 January 2012.
24 In fact the whole scandal about PetroSA giving the ANC money 'for elections' would not have blown up at all had the R11 million been returned to Majali as promised.
25 Ibid. The newspaper was ecstatic when Justice Ntsikelelo Poswa set aside the report of the then public protector, Lawrence Mushwana, on his 'investigation' into the Oilgate scandal. In his ruling Poswa was clear (vindicating the concerns of both the *M&G* and Kgalema) that PetroSA itself should have been properly investigated: 'In the current matter the very basis on which PetroSA made payment to Imvume was challenged by the *M&G*, contending that it was an improper siphoning of state funds from PetroSA to the ANC, via Imvume. Seeing that these are state funds the respondent was obliged to investigate that complaint.' Mushwana did not think so.
26 Stefaans Brümmer, personal communication, 30 January 2012. One message, addressed to Steyn Speed who worked in Kgalema's office, read: 'Please note that we would like you to give an organisational response, but also to give Motlanthe the opportunity to respond personally should he wish to do so.'
27 The IIC's inquiry related to irregularities in the OFFP, which had been founded to assist Iraq, which had suffered severely as a result of the USA-inspired decision by the UN's Security Council in August 1999 to impose sanctions on the country. Its brief was to investigate many allegations that certain companies and individuals had violated the UN resolution that strictly forbade any company making kickback payments to the Iraqi regime during the life of the programme.
28 Kgalema recalls that when he met Aziz again during this trip, Aziz told him that Iraq was certain that the US was going to attack them, partly because Saddam Hussein was a good national leader but had no idea how the world worked. He was keen to present the façade that as a well-armed country he could take on any army on earth, when he in fact knew that Iraq was no match at all against the US.
29 'Oilgate company was ANC front', *M&G*, 15 July 2005.
30 See Independent Inquiry Committee Report on Programme Manipulation (2005) (IIC report), 112.
31 IIC report, 113.
32 Aziz was a prisoner in Iraq at the time of writing, sentenced for authorising executions, among other crimes.
33 IIC report, 113.

34 Some interviewees asked me if Mbeki and Smuts Ngonyama put Kgalema under pressure to work with and support Majali in Iraq because the ANC stood to benefit handsomely if Majali was successful. Majali would have been key to resolving this question but he is no more. Various attempts to secure an interview with him before his death were in vain.
35 Adv. Michael Donen, letter to the Director-General for the Presidency, Vusi Mavimbela, 28 August 2009.
36 Ibid.
37 He adds that there is no evidence that Majali actually paid surcharges. That may be true but it seems there is evidence that he undertook to conditionally pay the surcharges. That he ended up perhaps not paying is another matter but the intention to pay, it seems, was there.
38 Why, supposing he felt a letter to Aziz was necessary, would he ask Hemphill to help him write it? It does not make sense to me that the SG of the ruling party of South Africa had to ask a businessman he hardly knew to help him write a letter to the deputy prime minister of Iraq.
39 Cited in Jeremy Gordin (2008), *Zuma: A Biography*, Johannesburg: Jonathan Ball, 83.
40 Kgalema Motlanthe Affidavit, 'In the Matter between the State and Kunene and Two others', In the Specialised Commercial Court, 9 February 2007.
41 'Spooks haunt our democracy', *M&G*, 22 May 2009.
42 'Spy-war emails – what they really say', *M&G*, 15 December 2005.
43 Jackie Selebi, 'Investigation into the origins and veracity of the "e-mails" letter to Kgalema Motlanthe, 21 October 2005.
44 'Billy Masetlha: Vindicated and loyal as ever', *M&G*, 22 May 2009.
45 'Spy-war mails – what they really say', *M&G*, 15 December 2005.
46 Thabo Mbeki, interview, Johannesburg, 22 September 2010
47 'The oligarch, the ANC and the manganese deal', *M&G*, 10 November 2006.
48 Ibid.
49 Daphne Mashile-Nkosi, interview, Johannesburg, 23 August 2009.
50 Mendi Msimang, interview, Johannesburg, 12 November 2010.
51 Stefaans Brümmer, personal communication, 22 January 2010.
52 Vicki Robinson, personal communication, 19 November 2010, plus several emails from her and Brümmer.
53 Stefaans Brümmer, personal communication, 18 November 2010.
54 It would have been better, say, if Kgalema had asked Speed to write to the paper and state what his concerns were with their questions. Journalists in such a situation could reasonably wonder why Kgalema did not answer questions, especially when they had said they were well aware that questions around any business matters should be directed to Msimang but that 'the questions to Motlanthe arose only because of a specific set of (collateral) allegations' (Stefaans Brümmer, personal communication, 4 January 2011). That is understandable and fair.
55 'The oligarch, the ANC and the manganese deal', *M&G*, 10 November 2006.
56 Stefaans Brümmer, personal communication, 21 January 2010.
57 'ANC bigwigs in dodgy Land Bank loan deal', *Sunday Times*, 17 July 2005.
58 Ibid.
59 Ibid.
60 Ibid.
61 See 'Company Report: Pamodzi', *Financial Mail*, 3 October 2008.
62 'Motlanthe cleared by Mushwana', *City Press*, 5 March 2006.
63 Ibid.
64 Ibid.
65 But some members of the public believe what they read. This was one response in the public debate: 'You know Kgalema it's a bit hard to hear you when your mouth is so full

of gravy (check the Pamodzi deal above)! Seriously this farce has got to stop, these people are robbing the rest of us blind and doing it with the full support of the law.' http://southafrica.blogspirit.com/archive/2005/12/14/black-economic-enrichment.html.
66 This is how Ian Davidson of the DA put it: 'The refusal by the Parliamentary Questions Office to publish a question posed by the Democratic Alliance to President Kgalema Motlanthe, seeking answers about highly inappropriate dealings in which he is alleged to have been involved, highlights once again how parliamentary oversight mechanisms such as written questions have been undermined by the governing party in order to protect its political interests at all costs.' See www.da.org.za/newsroom.htm?action=views-news-item&id=6038.
67 Gordin, 212.
68 The *M&G* broke the 'Oilgate' scandal story just two months before the emails arrived. If Zuma's biographer Jeremy Gordin regarded 2005 as his *annus miserabilis*, then (though not as dramatically challenging) it was also Kgalema's in more ways than one.
69 Judge Chris Nicholson also found that it was 'bizarre to say the least that Zuma was not charged' in 2003 (ibid).
70 Ibid.
71 We have noted already how, for example, Zuma told Kgalema that when certain people went to Mbeki with negative stories about him he tended to believe them, which affected their relationship.
72 Thabo Mbeki, interview, Johannesburg, 22 September 2010. When asked if Kgalema and Msimang agreed that it was best for them to go and see Zuma, Mbeki said that 'they did not oppose the suggestion and that is why I never asked Zuma to come to the Union Buildings.'
73 Ibid. Zuma told Kgalema and Msimang that he felt strongly that it would have been better for Mbeki to speak to him direct instead of sending them. Zuma had a point; after all, he was Mbeki's deputy. He told his biographer Gordin how much he disliked Mbeki sending Kgalema and Msimang to ask him to resign (Gordin, 117). One gets a clear sense that after this the gloves came off. Gordin says Zuma was 'affronted and angry' (ibid, 118).
74 Ibid.
75 Gordin, 121.
76 Gordin, 281. And what exactly were the 'constraints within which government operates' which Zuma understands Mbeki based his decision on? This is far from self-evident and I have no explanation.
77 Thabo Mbeki, interview, Johannesburg, 22 September 2010.
78 Kgalema also said that 'his decision to replace him with Phumzile (Mlambo-Ngcuka) was not right and in fact proved counterproductive for him because it further alienated him and in fact also tended to alienate her.' He felt there were stronger candidates for the deputy presidency, including some women.
79 The decision to fire Zuma must have been complex for Mbeki, and not just because of the Shaik case. Many people believe the judgment might even have been convenient – that Mbeki was behind the NPA moves against Zuma, largely because he had come to learn that Zuma had presidential ambitions and wished to succeed him. Kgalema confirms that there were such rumours doing the rounds in some circles that Zuma expressed an interest in or wanted to become the next president of the ANC and the country: 'Thabo was part of a collective and largely operated in that context until he was rattled when he thought that JZ was campaigning to become the next president. He was not really campaigning, but generally speaking the thing you fear most is what you actually invite into reality. By this I mean when you are convinced somebody has got a hidden agenda and you set out to prevent it from happening that is precisely when you breathe life into it.'

80 Jacob Zuma, interview, Pretoria, 22 September 2010.
81 Mbeki was not really vanquished. Taking 42 per cent of the vote showed that he did have significant mass support for a third term as ANC president.
82 Jacob Zuma, interview, 22 September 2011. In this interview it was clear that nothing distressed and alienated Zuma – probably in his entire political life – more than Mbeki's dismissal of him and how he did it.
83 When Mbeki and other cabinet leaders expressed concern that Kgalema and others went to court to support Zuma, Kgalema's answer was pointed: 'If Zuma was not found guilty of any charges he faced what would our members think of the leadership if we did not support our deputy president while on trial? That is why some in the media said at the time that my presence in court meant that I am a strong Zuma supporter; but it had nothing to do with that as such but with the cardinal constitutional principle that no matter how serious the charges might be you are innocent until found guilty and you must be treated and seen to be treated properly and fairly in all matters. All that I did was to apply these constitutional principles. Nothing more.' He went on: 'I had big debates with Mbeki, Lekota and others at Mahlamba Ndolpfu at the time about my presence in court when Zuma appeared. When they asked why the ANC was getting involved in a criminal case I said, "But you were the ones who assured us that there was nothing untoward about the arms deal. But now this man is being charged by that same state in relation to the very arms deal you said was clean." Once it became clear where I stood, Mbeki never really tried to convince me to the contrary because he knew that we had a NGC 2005 resolution to support Zuma in his trial.'
84 Considering the contradictory statements in Mbeki's speech when he announced Zuma's dismissal and the circumstances under which Zuma came to be charged with rape and his subsequent acquittal, I have no doubt he was indeed the subject of a calculated attack by the state. Whether Mbeki was behind these moves against Zuma, and why, may never be settled; but Zuma was definitely victimised.
85 Gordin, 129.
86 Ibid, 281–2.
87 Ibid, 129.
88 There was a lot of rhetoric, as in this over-the-top remark by Zwelinzima Vavi: 'The trial of comrade Zuma is a classic attempt to drag the working class into a war whose terrain and outcome have been predetermined by neo-liberals using their hold over key components of the state machinery, in this case in particular the judiciary' (ibid, 125). Their sentiments were not matched by any ideologically coherent policy agreements with Zuma; and not once did he, while deputy president, come out to support Cosatu in any of the countless sharp policy differences they had with Mbeki.
89 Ebrahim Harvey, 'Jacob Zuma: Working class hero?', *M&G*, 29 September 2006.
90 These are the 'sins of incumbency' many talk about in South Africa today. When we see what the president, deputy president, MPs, ministers, provincial premiers, mayors and other senior people at all levels of the state earn and the perks they enjoy, there is a massive gap between their life style and the standards of living of the mostly poverty-stricken voters whose power at the polls put them in those positions. Seniors in the private sector are expected to get huge salaries and perks, but the ethical ground changes where politicians are serving an electorate mostly in the doldrums.
91 This is the insidious influence that money and other resources wield in every sector of our society including government. Capitalist and class ideology are indeed powerful material and social forces we have to contend with daily.
92 In 2010 I was told that the ANC had bought a farm near Johannesburg to house the school and institute. There has been no news about the farm in the media since then (at the time of this book in late 2012).
93 Kgalema seems to think that education and training by itself will solve all or most of

Endnotes

the ANC's problems. But the problems requiring education and training occur in a complex environment. The programme needs to be linked to building a strong, coherent organisation and a clear set of policies, programme and strategy, something the ANC has struggled with for a century precisely because of its 'broad church' character.
94 Gwede Mantashe, interview, Johannesburg, 18 November 2010.

Chapter Six
1 Section 27 (2) of the Constitution says that the state's fulfilment of socioeconomic rights depends on 'available resources'. Professor Themba Sono argues: 'To claim as our silly subsection 27 (2) does, is to hoodwink the populace. What if the state never has enough funds to fulfil these rights? Does it mean that these rights are held in permanent abeyance? Could such a right be a right then?' (*Star*, 25 April 2000).
2 Patrick Bond implies that the RDP White Paper deliberately omitted important lines from the original RDP document: 'The Base Document's statement of existing problems, its commitment to new policy directions and its many direct programmatic suggestions should still be considered as underlying the Government of National Unity's approach to restructuring and development' (Patrick Bond (2005), *Elite Transitions: From Apartheid to Neo-liberalism*, Pietermaritzburg: University of KwaZulu-Natal Press, 326).
3 Policies were adopted but without much discussion because there were no policy differences between Mbeki and Zuma.
4 Zuma's biographer Jeremy Gordin captured this moment thus: 'Right from the start, on Sunday morning, 16th December 2007, the chairman of the ANC, Mosiuoa "Terror" Lekota, never stood a chance. He would shout a rousing "amandla", clearly expecting an "awethu" in response. But the 4000 delegates, or what seemed like most of them, simply went on singing "Awuleth' mashini wami", Jacob Zuma's trademark song, and waving placards with Zuma's picture on them' (Gordin, 234). He notes: 'The delegates only fell silent when Motlanthe came to the podium' (ibid, 235).
5 Steven Friedman, interview, Johannesburg, 28 October 2010.
6 Adam Habib, interview, Johannesburg, 15 July 2010.
7 ANC, '52nd National Conference: Organisational Report', Polokwane, 17 December 2007, presented by Kgalema Motlanthe (Polokwane report). Though this report is constitutionally that of the NEC, which NEC members contribute to, it is finally brought together and written by the SG. Of all the officials and the NEC members it is the SG whose approach and input will matter most, simply because the person in office is in a position to know of and respond to every major ANC development nationally.
8 You cannot profess to subscribe to revolutionary politics and yet adopt economic and social policies that mostly benefit capital and not the black working class, the main body of supporters.
9 'Motlanthe looks a unifier', *Financial Mail*, 16 December 2007.
10 He also raised the email saga, which coincided and probably had links with the multifaceted adversities Zuma faced in 2005.
11 Factionalism in a multi-class, and popular, nationalist organisation where all are welcome is driven by ideological, class and programmatic differences. It appears also to coalesce with personalities and even subtly with ethnicities. A Marxist analysis will look at the competition between such things as arguments, class forces and social strata, and not moralise about conduct unbecoming as Kgalema and other ANC leaders often do.
12 Polokwane report.
13 Ibid. With all respect, it was easy to invoke the glory of past ANC leaders and use them as a benchmark. In those days the forerunners were not in power, tested by its numerous trappings and the resources and material privileges they would have had access to.
14 Jeremy Cronin, interview, Cape Town, 12 January 2010. Kgalema has this kind of

approach: 'If you can win more people over to moral rectitude all the better because you will triumph eventually.' Moral rectitude is a very abstract appeal that doesn't take us far. Jeremy Cronin says Kgalema is a powerful moral force, but the strength must surely lie in having clear principles, policies and programmes to fight for, rather than just behaving well. Yet Kgalema has been described as the moral conscience of the ANC, and certainly you are far more likely to be in the forefront of fighting the sins of incumbency when you are such a leader.

15 Polokwane report, 17.
16 In my view, that is precisely why there is no long-term unifying vision and programme between the ANC, the ANC Youth League (ANCYL) and Cosatu-SACP and why (many will argue) creating it is virtually impossible. No wonder the ANC alliance has been in chronic crisis ever since Gear in 1996.
17 I have not found a single ANC leader talking in public about these institutions. Allowing for other factors, policy is the heart of a political organisation because its interests, goals and programme are expressed through it.
18 Polokwane report, 22.
19 William Gumede (2005), *Thabo Mbeki and the Battle for the Soul of the ANC*, Cape Town: Zebra, 135.
20 Karima Brown, interview, Johannesburg, 19 October 2011. Steven Friedman has consistently argued that there was nothing particularly radical about the policy resolutions adopted at Polokwane and has shown that all of them were on the agenda since Mafikeng, one way or another. There were other fairly radical organisational developments at the conference and in the following year, but I largely agree with him about policies.
21 Yet social movements declined further after Polokwane precisely because activists there saw hope for a new radical direction in the ANC. Interviews with Trevor Ngwane and Dale McKinley, leading figures in social movements, showed that many of their own members, usually critical of ANC policies, were somewhat impressed with what they saw in Polokwane and then found it hard to organise people into their own movements.
22 'ANC must go back to the masses', Ebrahim Harvey interview with President Kgalema Motlanthe, *M&G*, 12 February 2008.
23 Ibid. On the other hand, before Kgalema took over from Mbeki in September 2008 he did concede that 'Polokwane would not have happened if the monopoly of ideas by a few was not evident'. This would suggest that indeed there was a political environment more amenable to freer discussion and debate or so people felt. Still, according to him, the cabinet remained the point where executive power was concentrated.
24 Gevisser, 327.
25 'ANC must go back to the masses', Ebrahim Harvey interview with President Kgalema Motlanthe, *M&G*, 12 February 2008.
26 Ibid.
27 Marais, 375.
28 'ANC Conference: Thabo Mbeki', *Financial Mail*, 14 December 2007. Some of Kgalema's closest comrades, like James Motlatsi, argued along similar lines. Kgalema, as we saw, said it was Mbeki's right to stand but not to canvass for himself; clearly the ANC needs to review its ethos on elections.
29 Thabo Mbeki, interview, 14 September 2011.
30 'ANC Conference: Thabo Mbeki', *Financial Mail*, 14 December 2007.
31 Marais, 364.
32 Moe Shaik, cited in Gordin, 231.
33 Polokwane report, 12.
34 Ironically, the last thing Zuma has done is pose a threat to capitalism.
35 When asked after he was elected deputy president whether he had any presidential

Endnotes

aspirations, Kgalema said he would rather coach Bafana Bafana – his way of declaring he was certainly not preoccupied with getting high office. Mark Gevisser, preparing for his biography on Mbeki, said Kgalema indicated in an interview that he began to show an interest in the possibility that he could become the president and, if he did, what he would try to do. Kgalema says flatly: 'No, he is mistaken. He asked me a number of questions of what went wrong with the Mbeki presidency. It was not about me at all. I was merely trying to share with him openly and honestly what I thought of where things went wrong and where Mbeki got sucked into a destructive role because it is one thing if you are a leader and want to remain in your seat but it's another matter when you get involved in canvassing for yourself. If you do that you can never hold the organisation together.' Gevisser backed down when he heard this response: 'He definitely said words along the lines of "If I were president…", although he might not have used those words exactly. Given the timing of the interview, I read this as a shift in his aspirations, albeit not necessarily a decisive one. … Of course, it is possible that he might have been using the phrase entirely hypothetically and metaphorically, and I might have misunderstood him' (Mark Gevisser, personal communication, 11 March 2011).
36 'Special Feature: ANC Conference: Zuma's A team', *Financial Mail*, 21 December 2007.
37 Verne Harris, personal communication, 5 February 2010. Harris is the director of the Nelson Mandela Centre of Memory and Dialogue.
38 Karima Brown, interview, 22 November 2011.
39 Adam Habib, interview, Johannesburg, 12 July 2010.
40 Gordin, 242.
41 Thabo Mbeki, interview, Johannesburg, 14 September 2011.
42 This is the name of the ANC's annual review, always given on 8 January, the date when the organisation began.
43 When Vavi says 'we', who exactly is he referring to? And was that not precisely the problem with that amorphous grouping in Polokwane – the 'coalition of the wounded' – whose only commonality appeared to be their dislike of Mbeki and determination to get rid of him? Yet to be fair to them we must concede that they seemed to have more in common than just a personal dislike for Mbeki. They felt that Mbeki was too dominant politically and was dictatorial even within the ANC and the broader alliance. As I have already said, though, did they ask themselves why they for years allowed that to happen to the oldest liberation movement in the country?
44 Report of the Secretary-General, 50th ANC National Conference, Mafikeng, 17 December 1997.
45 Ibid.
46 Report by the President of the ANC, Nelson Mandela, 50th ANC National Conference, Mafikeng, 16 December 1997. Mandela then was referring more to the ANC than to society at large. One can only wonder what he would say today when those problems have grown to truly destructive proportions.
47 On Malema wanting to remove some people already on the DC, Kgalema adds: 'If they wanted to propose new names we could have looked at it but they wanted to remove the names of DC members, which was also unethical and unprocedural. It was after this incident that the ANCYL attacked me in the press but I discovered that none of their structures had even discussed the matter.'
48 Some journalists, probably through no fault of their own, have lacked a full understanding of the mechanics involved.
49 'A minister cannot alone appoint a director-general,' Kgalema explains. 'There have to be two other ministers and a director-general from another department present on the interview panel. With that process I am satisfied because it is transparent and works well.' For administrative posts in the public sector there is an objective process that is followed, 'which is not and should not be affected by that kind of senior political deployment. This

is not to suggest that the ANC has not been sometimes guilty of deploying unsuitable people, but not the DC itself.'
50 He gives this example: 'Take the SABC. The ministry appoints people who do not go through the ANC's DC. We cannot and don't override the selection criteria and procedure of any state enterprise. All we do where we know of vacancies is to try and ensure that interested people apply properly and we look at their CVs to see if they meet the requirements. Those who do we encourage to apply, but the choice by the panel of selectors is from a pool of suitable candidates and never where we propose or impose a candidate we want. ... That is why I say what we do in the DC is unlike what people and the media imagine, except, of course, in cases of the appointment of political heads, which in any case is the norm with governing parties the world over. In those cases we make recommendations but on the whole the DC is not as powerful or arbitrary as it is often made out to be.'
51 A number of wrong people have been chosen, in the provinces and regions too. At last the ANC is addressing the problem, which is why, for example, the main thrust for revamping the health system now is to begin at managerial and executive level; people who manage hospitals must not only be professionals, they will also undergo the extra training they need for their particular job. Another area of concern is whether the ANC has been able to keep track of what is going on locally that may conflict with their guidelines on deployment, and how vigilant government at any level has been to guard against political appointments. All civil service posts should obviously be staffed by people who meet the professional requirements. The crisis in local government, aside from matters of policy, is very much the legacy of many years of incompetence and inexperience.
52 'ANCYL turns on Kgalema', *City Press*, 30 August 2009.
53 Ibid. In fact Kgalema's comments had nothing directly to do with the case against Zuma. They certainly did not mean that he agreed with how the NPA dealt with Zuma, as he strongly criticised the NPA for their cowboy style persecution of him. He points out: 'When people speak of the judiciary they include the directorate of special operations [DSO]. So attacks against the excesses of the DSO are seen as attacks against the judiciary. Our criminal justice system is young and we need to allow it to mature. We need to ensure that all these institutions enjoy respect from all South Africans.'
54 Ibid. When Shivambu made these allegations he was not even an ANCYL leader. Instead he was active in and a spokesperson for the Young Communist League.
55 Julius Malema, interview, 22 November 2010, Johannesburg.
56 Ibid. Malema did add that not once in all the encounters the ANCYL had with Kgalema did he seek to punish them for mistakes they made or to prove a point that he was in charge or tried to belittle them.
57 Julius Malema, interview, Johannesburg, 22 November 2010.
58 'A good compromise?', *News 24*, 18 March 2008.
59 Frank Chikane (2012), *Eight Days in September*, Johannesburg: Picador Africa.
60 His first clash with a major majority decision in the NEC was this one about going to parliament. It did show that he was not self-seeking. Besides, as I have seen, he never wanted to be put in a position that smacked of any unfair advantage he had over others, for whatever reason.
61 'I will rise to the challenge', Ebrahim Harvey interview with Kgalema Motlanthe. *M&G*, 25 January 2008.
62 Ibid.
63 All ministers are necessarily MPs except the president.
64 Thabo Mbeki, interview, Johannesburg, 14 September.
65 'I will rise to the challenge', Ebrahim Harvey interview with Kgalema Motlanthe. *M&G*, 25 January 2008.
66 It was during that two-month period between becoming an MP in May and a minister in

July that the ANCYL waged several venomous attacks against him.
67 'Alliance leaders pat him on the back', *M&G*, 22 June 2008. Malema was unrepentant, recalling the episode later on. 'I explained to Kgalema and have no regrets about that remark I made. He only made one point which was that we must not alienate ourselves from the forces he has worked with for many years because what we said about him can alienate and isolate us and that people do not know him in the way we spoke of him' (Julius Malema, interview, 22 November 2010).
68 Ibid.
69 Why did Zuma himself not immediately criticise Malema's remark, especially since it came across as a possibly violent threat?
70 William Gumede, interview, Johannesburg, 13 October 2010.
71 Gordin, 276.
72 Ibid, 277.
73 Billy Downer, 'The Rule of Law and Prosecutions: To Prosecute or Not to Prosecute', address to the Middle Temple South African Conference, 24 September 2010. This paper relies to a large extent on one that Wim Trengrove SC presented at a University of Cape Town seminar in April 2009, titled 'Zuma walks, Special Treatment for special cases: 'Are some more protected under the Constitution than others?'
74 Ibid, 7.
75 Ibid, 5.
76 Ibid.
77 Ibid, 7.
78 Ibid, 14.
79 Ibid.
80 Ibid, 19.
81 Ibid.
82 Ibid, 20.
83 Ibid.
84 Kgalema's assessment of this and other controversial legal matters is that law must keep pace with and reflect the development of society. Constitutional matters must in particular be subject to new lessons drawn from case law and actual experiences in a complex, constantly fluctuating and dynamic body politic and society at large.
85 The NPA and NDPP are key to a healthy jurisprudence, so much so that the ANC should seriously review making party political appointments there, as in many other areas of government. Thinking in the ANC is moving fast in that direction, or so it seems. Kgalema is certainly of the view that the ANC needs to 'use all the available skills and talents we have'. We need to professionalise the civil service in particular.
86 Trevor Manuel, interview, Cape Town, 12 January 2010.
87 Gordin, 285.
88 We can see that Kgalema has had a complex and intriguing relationship with Mbeki and acted very differently from those who were hostile before and after the recall. He has a remarkable ability few politicians have: he draws a distinction between personal relations and even the most serious political differences he may have with someone. He has repeatedly said that it is not the negative attitude of some people towards him that matters but his attitude to them in spite of it.
89 It was because Nicholson's opinion had no legal standing that the cabinet could remain, otherwise it would have had to dissolve immediately. That is exactly why it was difficult for the cabinet to enter into the matter and challenge the judgment.
90 Daphne Mashile-Nkosi, interview, Johannesburg, 16 November 2010.
91 It had still not been finalised at the time of writing in 2012.
92 Mapula Motlanthe, interview, Johannesburg, 12 November 2010.

Chapter Seven
1. 'Features', *Financial Mail*, 8 May 2009, see http://secure.financialmail.co.za/08/05/09/feautures/bfeat.htm.
2. Thabo Masebe, interview, Johannesburg, 19 August 2010.
3. Ebrahim Patel, interview, Pretoria, 12 March 2010.
4. Murphy Morobe, interview, Johannesburg, 12 November 2010.
5. Kate Philip, interview, Johannesburg, 22 October 2009.
6. Dale McKinley, interview, Johannesburg, 13 November 2009
7. Thabo Mbeki, interview, Johannesburg, 12 February 2011.
8. 'South Africa in "good hands"', says Mandela', *M&G*, 26 September 2008. Between the 1997 Mafikeng conference and the 1999 elections their positions in the ANC meant that Mandela and Kgalema had worked closely. Kgalema still visits him when he can.
9. Noor Nieftagodien, interview, Johannesburg, 22 July 2009.
10. Pitso Tsibolane, 'Kgalema Motlanthe on the Walls of History', 5 February 2009, see www.pambazuka.org/en/category/comment/53781.
11. Blade Nzimande, interview, Johannesburg, 6 November 2011.
12. Mark Gevisser, interview, Johannesburg, 21 November 2010.
13. In my view he is truly among the best to embody a culture of service to society but whether the ANC policies adopted after 1994 have served the interests and needs of the poor black majority is another matter.
14. *Daily Dispatch*, 26 September 2008.
15. Gordin, 285. After all, Mbeki had replaced Zuma with her when he was dismissed in June 2005.
16. All the constitutional requirements were fulfilled for the election of a president, except that under the circumstances it did not issue from a general election.
17. He was not the 'acting president', 'interim president' or 'caretaker president', as the media repeatedly said. The only time we have an acting president is when the deputy president acts for the president who is outside the country at the time. Nobody in the presidency put them right – did they perhaps not realise themselves? The *Telegraph* was one of the few publications that spelt out the true position: 'Motlanthe will be the president, not interim, of the republic until the elections' (*Telegraph*, 22 September 2008).
18. *ABC News*, 25 September 2008.
19. 'A leader in touch with his people', *Daily News*, 25 September 2008.
20. *Star*, 29 September 2008.
21. The rand fell by some 2.5 per cent against the dollar after his resignation, and the Johannesburg Stock Exchange dropped about 4 per cent, both recovering slightly when his resignation was reported as more to do with protocol and that he remained available to serve a new incoming administration. 'Scrambling to neutralise the damage, the ANC announced that Manuel would stay on' was how one publication captured the situation ('South Africa in political crisis as 11 cabinet ministers resign', *Ethiopian Review*, 23 September 2008, see www.ethiopianreview.com/content/4583).
22. Aubrey Matshiqi, cited in Fiona Forde, 'Judging the caretaker who kept the president's seat warm', *Sunday Independent*, 10 May 2009.
23. Ibid.
24. *Guardian*, 26 September 2008.
25. 'South Africa's Next President?', *Time*, 24 September 2008.
26. 'New President a 'Bridge-builder', *Australian*, 23 September 2008. Kgalema was indeed opposed to factions but he certainly did not sit neutrally by. When he concluded that Zuma was unfairly hounded by the NPA and Scorpions he spoke out. When he believed that Mbeki had a right to challenge the adverse findings of Judge Chris Nicholson he supported him. At first glance it often appeared that he was sitting on the fence when

he was SG; given the multi-class, heterogeneous nature of the ANC he was compelled to play a more unifying role, as every SG of the party has to do. But in many cases he was able to criticise or support a person, position or cause when policy or circumstances required – and often against the express wishes of Mbeki as state president.

27 'What kind of President will Kgalema Motlanthe be?', *Times*, 24 September 2008.
28 'The rise of a reluctant leader', *Times*, 28 September 2008. Speculation can make journalists over-interpret at times. Kalema says he made a 'minor protocol slip' at his inauguration when Chief Justice Pius Langa had to call him to shake hands with the chiefs of the security forces. Mkhaba suggests that the incident 'could well have signified Motlanthe's reluctance to ascend to higher office.'
29 'Talking straight to Motlanthe', *M&G*, 20 February 2009.
30 'I will rise to the occasion', *M&G*, 25 January 2009.
31 Ibid.
32 'In the ANC there is always a tomorrow', *M&G*, 3 September 2008.
33 Gugu Mtshali, interview, 28 February 2011.
34 Ambition itself is hardly blameworthy. What matters is how people behave for its sake. There is nobody I know of who can show Kgalema having at any time since he left Robben Island in 1987 operated in any unscrupulous way for self-advancement. On the contrary, he has often been extremely reluctant to pursue power.
35 Mpumelelo Mkhabela, 'The rise of a reluctant leader', *Sunday Times*, 2 April 2009.
36 Ebrahim Patel, interview, Pretoria, 23 March 2010.
37 Dan Nkambule, informal conversation, 12 December 2009. Even in the most powerful office Kgalema's tendency towards modesty springs from the virtual absence of ego in his psychological make-up. This trait may be partly why he generally treads with caution. He especially feels he does not have the right to impose decisions on others or rush into decisions that can harm others, in particular within organisational frameworks.
38 See www.sacp.org.za/doc/pr/2008/pr0925.html.
39 Kgalema has never turned down an invitation to speak at SACP events, and there have been many over the years.
40 *Cape Times*, 26 September 2008.
41 Thabo Mbeki, interview, Johannesburg, 12 February 2011.
42 'In the ANC there is always a tomorrow', *M&G*, 3 October 2008.
43 'Man in the middle', *Sunday Times*, 1 February 2009.
44 When Frank Chikane asked Kgalema before the inauguration whether members of his family would attend so that he could make arrangements for them, Kgalema said no (Frank Chikane (2012), *Eight Days in September*, Johannesburg: Picador; these excerpts appeared in the *Saturday Star*, 10 March 2012). His two brothers Ernest and Sydney did attend but even his children were not present, given the home scene.
45 Fiona Forde, 'The story behind the Motlanthe story', *Politicsweb*, 15 July 2010.
46 'President should have nothing to hide', *Financial Gazette*, 9 February 2009.
47 See www.anc.org/za/ancdocs/history/motlanthe/kmotlanthe.html.
48 'Blade plotting against Kgalema', *Sunday Independent*, 21 December 2008.
49 Ibid.
50 Malasela Maleka's email to me of 8 February 2011 includes his email to Monare with Nzimande's reply ('Article as discussed') to the story the *Sunday Independent* carried. When Monare was shown evidence that the article had been sent directly to him he responded: 'Granted, it is a serious matter given the controversy and seniority of those involved, but I ignore many press releases and op-ed offerings every week. It is not a sin if I can't recall something.' This seems unlikely, for a major story involving the state president.
51 Blade Nzimande, 'The tabloidization of the South African Media: A race to the bottom.' See www.sacp.org.za/pubs/umsebenzi/2009/vol8-03.html. Dated 18 February 2009.

When I asked Nzimande where the press ombudsman and Sanef were all along when this sleaze was carried and why they were not proactive in dealing with it, he said: 'Part of the problem, it would seem, is that unless a complaint is lodged, these institutions take no proactive action on their part' (Blade Nzimande, interview, Johannesburg, 6 November 2011).

52 Fiona Forde's stories alleging Kgalema's involvement with a 24-year old woman in January 2009 truly showed his mettle. For a few terrible weeks he faced a litany of slander, but remained calm and dignified throughout.
53 Cyril Ramaphosa, interview, Johannesburg, 27 July 2010.
54 'Mystery President', *Times*, 15 December 2008.
55 55 Ibid.
56 'Reclusive enigma thrust into political limelight', *N Press International*, 28 September 2008.
57 Ibid.
58 Ibid.
59 President Jacob Zuma, cited in the *Weekender*, 1–2 January 2009, 'Young lover's presidential playlist live on Kaya FM show.'
60 Redi Direko, for example, writing in the *Sowetan*, had this to say: 'I must say I never took Motlanthe to be a Casanova but hey, still waters run deep. How fascinating that his rivals could not find anything related to his work and leadership around which to betray him, but a woman' (Redi Direko, 'President's sex life no crisis', *Sowetan*, 6 February 2009).
61 Fiona Forde, interview, Johannesburg, 29 June 2010. Forde was sincerely apologetic: 'No newspaper wants to carry a big story about the head of state, only to end up apologising for getting things wrong. … I myself did not fabricate anything and the story was not written with malice at all and I drove no agenda. I will not throw away my reputation lightly. It killed me. But I deeply regret the hurt and harm I caused him and his family and I also don't think a journalist can come back from that. Please tell Kgalema that my regret is enormous and that I have absolutely nothing against him. And finally, there is probably nothing I regret more in my life than that story. I am trying to redeem myself.'
62 'Putting the record straight', *Sunday Independent*, 10 May 2009.
63 Kgalema was also upset that Raymond Louw said in *Business Day* that he was one of the people who had complained to the Press Ombudsman but who later withdrew the complaint: 'He does not say that I only withdrew when the paper offered to publish an apology. It therefore leaves the impression that it was a spurious complaint.'
64 Several attempts by myself to interview Moegsien Williams and Jovial Rantao, then editor and deputy editor of the *Star*, went unanswered. Earlier attempts to interview Maureen Isaacson also failed. The only journalist to grant me an interview was Moshoeshoe Monare, to his credit. He ceased being the group political editor immediately afterwards. After an altercation with Monare on a story they carried about the relationship between Kgalema and the education minister Blade Nzimande, the editors instructed everyone to stop all communication with me, including barring me from communicating with anyone in the group. Shockingly, they also wrote to the office of the deputy presidency and tried to discredit me but Kgalema was not swayed.
65 'Motlanthe won't sue her', *Times*, 9 February 2009.
66 'Kgalema Motlanthe on the walls of History', *Pambazuka News*, 5 February 2009.
67 'South African leader's sex life stirs salacious gossip and privacy debate', *New York Times*, 30 January 2009.
68 Ibid.
69 There was vigorous debate in the media about whether Fiona Forde in particular, and the *M&G* and other newspapers, had gone too far in surmises and revelations they made about Kgalema and his wife and later his alleged romance with the '24-year old', the false story Forde authored in the *Sunday Independent* on 25 January 2009.

Endnotes

70 Even though Kgalema emphasises 'moral rectitude', he still has failed to link the causes of moral degeneration in the ANC to its multi-class character and the related policy changes since 1994. The skirmish via the media was prompted by malicious factionalism in the ANC.
71 Mondli Makhanya, interview, Johannesburg, 27 November 2010.
72 Amina Frense, interview, Johannesburg, 28 June 2009.
73 'SA leader emerges in power shift', *OPB News*, 25 September 2008.
74 'Passing the power', *Saturday Star*, 10 March 2012.
75 Fiona Forde, cited in James Myburgh, 'Who is Kgalema Motlanthe?', *Politicsweb*, 25 September 2008.
76 'Call to bring back Scorpions', *Times*, 5 March 2012.
77 'South Africa's President Kgalema Motlanthe', *Newsvine*, 29 January 2009.
78 Ibid.
79 'Man in the middle', *Sunday Times*, 1 February 2009.
80 Steven Friedman, interview, Johannesburg, 29 February 2011.
81 Kgalema Motlanthe, address to Numsa Job Security Conference, Eskom Convention Centre, Johannesburg, 12–14 March 2009.
82 That is perfectly understandable because the exercise of state power is far more challenging in its terrain and responsibilities, as we have seen. Especially when the collapse of the former Soviet Union put socialist forces everywhere in a weaker position, pragmatism on leftist interests was inevitable. The working class in South Africa had not been provided with political and organisational alternatives and anyway most of them had traditionally supported the ANC despite worsening poverty and unemployment. The left do not allow for these realities. Pragmatism not only influences and sets the serious limits to exercising political power within a capitalist framework, but the very act of being pragmatic expresses an adverse balance of forces; it is a strategy against capital from a position of relative weakness. Trade unions in particular are caught up in pragmatism all the time. Nothing is more pragmatic than holding anti-capitalist beliefs and still having to negotiate better wages and working conditions. Such pragmatism amounts to reformism by way of incremental improvements for workers.
83 'Motlanthe near the end of a rough ride', *Star*, 6 February 2009. He may have had the US definition of 'lame duck' in mind ('an elected official … remaining in office in the interval between the election and inauguration of a successor'), but in South African usage this term means someone who is disabled or ineffectual.
84 When the Bill was introduced in 2006 it led to great protests from both media and civil society, claiming that it 'paved the way for pre-publication censorship and criminalized free expression'. See 'Controversial Films and Publications Bill signed into law' at www.ifex.org/south_africa/2009/09/02/fils_and_publications_amendment_bill. Kgalema earlier refused to sign the Bill because he was concerned that it might have unconstitutional provisions. He therefore referred it back to the legislature.
85 'Motlanthe feels the heat', *City Press*, 25 January 2009.
86 'Report Card', *M&G*, 19 December 2008. The unsourced claim by Moshoeshoe Monare, that the 30-minute delay during Kgalema's swearing-in ceremony on 25 September was because Kgalema sat with 'party bosses' trying to reach agreement on the cabinet, is completely untrue (*Star*, 6 March 2009). The delay was about entirely other matters.
87 Ibid.
88 Ibid.
89 'Mbeki suspends NDPP Vusi Pikoli', *Independent Online*, 24 September 2007, see www.iol.co.za/index.php?from=rss_South%20Africa&set_id=1&click_id=13&art_id=nw20070924144355971C413764. Frank Chikane sounded melodramatic when he told the parliamentary committee that was set up to decide on Pikoli's fate: 'When it was seen that the Scorpions might rock up in the middle of the night at crime intelligence

and create a major crisis for the country, the suspension was effected' ('Tragedy and farce', *M&G*, 23 January 2009). In court papers in 2009 Mbeki said he had suspended Pikoli because of his 'grave concerns' that Selebi's arrest would affect South Africa's security, especially if it was immediate. But he could have met with Pikoli, the minister of police and the NIA to discuss this hazard and find a solution. Instead, Pikoli's summary suspension simply reinforced the long-held view that Mbeki was protecting Selebi.

90 In July 2010 Selebi was sentenced to fifteen years for corruption, and released on medical parole in July 2012.
91 'The desperate bid to shield Selebi,' *M&G* 5 October 2007. As the political commentator Adam Habib points out: 'If the president suspended Mr Pikoli on the grounds that he had issued a warrant for the commissioner's arrest, then it suggests that an invasion is being made into an independent institution's operations. Intervening in the operations of the National Prosecuting Authority constitutes a violation of our Constitution' ('Rumours swirl over Pikoli's suspension', *M&G*, 30 September 2007).
92 'DA: Pikoli decision has hallmarks of a cover-up', *M&G*, 8 December 2008.
93 Ibid.
94 Ibid.
95 'We'll triumph over COPE', *M&G*, 9 January 2009.
96 'Pikoli axing: Cope joins chorus of criticism', *M&G*, 9 December 2008.
97 On the other hand it seems Pikoli also erred by refusing Mbeki the reasonable two weeks he requested before issuing the warrant for Selebi. Pikoli seemed insensitive to issues of national security, so Mbeki's concern may have been justified. For the commissioner of police to be arrested on serious charges does present a potentially difficult security situation. We do not know how the upper echelons of the police and ordinary police would have responded to such an arrest, especially those who supported Selebi and still had faith in him. Even if Mbeki was exaggerating the dangers of an immediate arrest, the delay would not have prejudiced the case against Selebi.
98 Ibid.
99 'Sacrificed for Zuma', *City Press*, 15 February 2009.
100 'Pikoli accepts R7.5 million golden handshake', *Sunday Times*, 22 November 2009.
101 'Motlanthe denies offering Pikoli a settlement', *M&G*, 15 December 2008.
102 Steven Friedman, interview, 29 July 2010. Kgalema has also repeatedly pointed out that Ginwala erred by making a recommendation that though he had some weaknesses Pikoli should continue in his job. 'But the Act does not envisage an inquiry to make a recommendation about the suitability or otherwise of the NDPP. It simply envisages the inquiry to make findings as to whether the person is fit and proper and then for the president, on the basis of such findings, to make a recommendation to parliament, meaning that not even the president has the power to finally decide the matter, which is good for democracy.'
103 Steven Friedman interview. Indeed South Africa was tiny in terms of China's world market, but for South Africa in a time of world recession the trade link with China meant a lot.
104 'Dalai Lama will steal limelight', *Star*, 24 March 2009.
105 Kate Philip, interview, 26 August 2009.
106 Ibid.
107 'Hogan's defiance slammed', *Star*, 26 March 2009.
108 Ibid. But the *Star* also reported government sources saying that Kgalema was unlikely to take any harsh steps against Hogan: 'He would at best censure her and then leave it to his successor to take a decision on her reappointment to the cabinet.'
109 Kgalema Motlanthe interview with Padraig O'Malley, 15 September 2000. In an insightful analysis of some leftist support for China, Martin Hart-Landsberg and Paul Burkett argue that China's 'post-1978 transformation to a market-based, foreign-driven,

export-led economy' and its 'uncritical celebration of China as development model' pose serious problems for the Chinese working class and civil society. (Martin Hart-Landsberg and Paul Burkett (2005), 'China and Socialism: An Overview', *Critical Asian Studies*, Vol. 37, No. 4, 597–628).

110 Kgalema also, surprisingly, tends to believe what the Chinese bureaucrats say about themselves and their role in Africa. 'In 1997, after fifty years of existence, the Chinese Communist Party admitted that they had failed to build a socialist state as they had attempted to bypass the primary stages of socialism. The Chinese believe in a hundred years' time they will have the base to build a truly socialist state – this is what could happen here too – and then you will have access to free health, education and so on.' Kgalema's view here fits in squarely with the two-stage theory. In the case of South Africa, CST became the rationale for two stages of revolution; in China it was the lack of capitalist development to lay the material basis for socialism. Both ideas were misleading, mechanistic and wrong.

111 China's huge economic growth has happened through super-exploitable cheap and abundant Chinese labour. The state's negative attitude towards trade unions and its suppression of civil society protests should be at the centre of the ANC's concerns in their political relations with China but the party appears either blind to those realities or believes that they are not as important as trade, economic and governmental relations.

112 'Hogan's defiance slammed', *Star*, 26 March 2009.

113 www.timeslive.co.za/local/article708651.ece/Hawks-shut-down-arms-deal-probe. In March 2011 the Constitutional Court found that the legislation that established the Hawks 'was inconsistent with the constitution and invalid to the extent that it fails to secure an adequate degree of independence.' The court thus ruled in March 2011 that the legislation be amended appropriately and allowed parliament eighteen months to take remedial action.

114 http://www.news24.com/SouthAfrica/News/Scorpions-not-part-of-police-20080507.

115 See heep://constitutionallyspeaking.co.za/president-must-refuse-to-sign-sabc-bill/.

116 'Controversial Bill amended, passed', *M&G*, 17 February 2009.

117 'Man in the middle', *Sunday Times*, 1 February 2009.

118 'Motlanthe feels the heat', *City Press*, 25 January 2009.

119 Cited in 'Man in the middle', *Sunday Times*, 1 February 2009.

120 Ibid.

121 Ibid.

122 See apology on page 21 in the *Financial Mail*, 27 November 2009.

123 'Motlanthe feels the heat', *City Press*, 25 January 2009.

124 Obviously Kgalema would not divulge details of what he believed was happening and who he thought was involved in spreading the lies and seeking to destroy him. Had he done so it might have been very damaging for the ANC, assuming those plotting against him were within the party, as many reports indicated.

125 Jabulani Sikhakhane, 'Cynicism aside, Motlanthe has ample reasons to dislike making omelettes', *Saturday Star*, 21 February 2009.

126 Ibid. Detractors could read this story as suggesting that Kgalema was not only faint-hearted but that he should not be ashamed to admit it, when in fact he was neither faint hearted nor ashamed of something he was not. I asked Carlin at the time if this was playing into their hands.

127 'We will triumph over COPE', *M&G*, 9 January 2009. In an interview, Kgalema denied ever saying this: 'Though it has always been a big passion of mine I've never said that I want to return to Luthuli House to do political education after the elections and will not be available for government posts'.

128 'Blade's out for Kgalema', *City Press*, 18 January 2009.

129 'JZ's Kgalema poser', *City Press*, 3 May 2009.

130 Ibid. The ANCYL was so keen, they called a meeting with Gwede Mantashe, reported thus: 'Malema said yesterday the Young Lions had a meeting with secretary-general Gwede Mantashe at which they asked him to tell the authorities, including the ANC president, that the youth will be highly disappointed if Kgalema is not appointed'. So much dirty water has flowed under the bridge of ruling party politics since then that, even though Zuma did appoint Kgalema as his deputy, after Malema's expulsion from the ANC the ANCYL was determined at the time of writing to remove Zuma in Mangaung in December 2012.

131 My own view is that this would be a bigger task than he realises, because the problems are those of the post-apartheid capitalist system. To solve them means fundamentally transforming the social and class relations in our society. No amount of moral tutoring can achieve that.

132 The Anglican archbishop Desmond Tutu chuckled when he was asked what he thought of the new president. 'I think he is … well, he is Anglican!' That is a very good point in his favour!' (*Cape Times*, 26 September 2008).

133 The Church and what it stood for made sense to him in the political and social context of apartheid, especially when he and his family grew close to its leading figures at St Peter's in Johannesburg. That is why, unlike many Marxists, he is especially careful not to disparage any religions.

134 Daryl Glaser, interview, Johannesburg, 22 August 2010.

135 Mark Gevisser, interview, Johannesburg, 20 August 2010.

Chapter Eight

1 Mondli Makhanya, interview, Johannesburg, 12 August 2010. Mondli Makhanya comments appreciatively that 'Kgalema is interested in acquiring power but not for himself at all. For him it is about what he can do with that power to achieve the objectives of the ANC or the government.'

2 As far as I know, this was the first time that a state president had gone on to become deputy president. If he were to be elected state president again, this would make an even more remarkable political record.

3 Though his name was reportedly on both Mbeki and Zuma slates in the run-up to Polokwane, the truth is that he was critical of many on both sides and never really comfortable with either group; as we have seen, he identifies with the ANC as a collective and decidedly not with cliques within it, however powerful. What Kgalema and the ANC should be doing is analysing the factions that have been tearing the ANC apart for the last decade, down to their roots. The clash between Zuma and Mbeki has seemed to be about access to state power and its huge resources, not underlying ideological and policy differences. In fact greed, along with class interests, is itself an ideological stance, so one could say that many people on both sides share the same basic view. As I see it, the two leaders have been backed for the sake of the individual self-interest of their followers and nothing much more. What reinforces the view that the conflict between Mbeki and Zuma was never a clash of ideologies is that since Zuma came to power in 2009 there have not been any major policy changes. The ANC needs to do more work to understand and relate the factionalist politics to the ideological, policy and programmatic changes it has itself undergone since its unbanning in 1990. Fragmented attempts to do so in its policy documents have not been adequate to sort out the many serious problems identified, which is why the party has been bedevilled by their stubborn persistence.

4 The fact that the state seems to have been used in other undesirable ways, which have also undermined both the ANC and the country, is a matter we return to later.

5 Moshoeshoe Monare, 'A silent majority who are opposed to Julius and JZ', *Sunday Independent*, 4 March 2012.

Endnotes

6 'Cosatu slams 5% pay rise for ministers', *City Press*, 14 November 2010. The presidential pension is equivalent to the salary of a sitting president. At the end of 2010 Kgalema received a salary of R2 130 000 (ibid.).
7 'Commission's report smacks of cheap political compromise', *M&G*, 4 May 2012. The *M&G* editor Sam Sole sees no problem here. Instead he maintains it is the media that stand to lose, and though self-regulation has many pitfalls he regards the view that it has failed as 'fuzzy opinion'. He goes on to say: 'Nowhere does the report discuss the reality that regulation beyond what is already contained in our law impinges on freedom of speech', yet South African law is far from able to protect people sufficiently from abuses by the media.
8 He is also keenly aware that the media are to be valued for the vital role they play in a constitutional democracy and wider society.
9 'ANC mum on reprieve for media', *Sowetan*, 18 October 2010.
10 'Cabinet Report Card', *M&G*, December 23 to January 2011.
11 'ANC in media parliamentary oversight call', *Star*, 27 February 2012.
12 Ibid.
13 'Print media guidelines "fair,"' *Times*, 26 April 2012.
14 Ibid. The recommendations, due for debate at an ANC policy conference in June 2012, are highly significant, especially in increasing the number of public members of the governing structures of the press council; introducing a hierarchy of penalties, including monetary fines, and suspension or expulsion from the jurisdiction of the press ombudsman; scrapping the waiver that barred those not satisfied with the ombudsman's ruling from approaching the courts for recourse; empowering the ombudsman to force newspapers to place apologies or retractions of a specific size on a specific page; increasing the number of public representatives on the press council to seven and decreasing the number of press reps to five. To remove a new model from the ambit of ANC party control through parliament is a huge step forward in addressing the concerns of the media. Supporting the plan for independent co-regulation, the media analyst Kupe criticises the very notion of media 'self-regulation' as a contradiction in terms; the central idea of regulation of any profession or service provided is that the regulatory body emerges from outside the profession or service in question in order to be more objective and conscientious. At the same time, the media can practise self-regulation internally but cannot continue to impose their self-comforting model on the rest of society, of which it is itself a pillar of power. Probably the biggest significance of the PFC report is the recognition of the need for greater public participation in the regulation of the media. That combined with the exclusion of the state and the decreased representation of the media in the new structure augurs well for a healthier and more effective regulation. Kupe comments: 'The ANC might have done us a favour by its intended media appeals tribunal, as we now have on paper something close to an ideal system of press regulation' (Tawana Kupe, 'Who will appoint civil society members of new press body?', *Sunday Independent*, 6 May 2012).
15 The state does not have the sole right to classify the information it possesses or seeks as so sensitive that the public cannot access it. How the state handles matters related to information, which is the lifeblood of civil society and the media, is a very major test of how far it is the true instrument of society or, on the other hand, serving those with their own authoritarian interests. There are also intrinsic links between access to state information and the fight against corruption in the government and public spheres; the greater the secrecy, the greater the likelihood of more crime and corruption and increased lack of accountability in government. In a constitutional democracy we also need to ask to whom the information held by government rightly belongs, with the Freedom Charter's goal in mind that 'the people shall govern', and the fact that government is meant to express the 'will of the people'.

16 Some like myself would not agree on abandoning it on that score. Surely that makes all the more reason to fight for such a clause. How can the ANC spearhead such legislation in a post-apartheid society, and Kgalema assent to it? The *M&G* (11 May 2012) reports: 'Legal experts have also challenged the ANC's claim that international precedents do not show a need for a public interest clause in legislation concerning the protection of state information.' Ben Turok took a principled decision to abstain from voting on the Bill in parliament. Instead of reflecting on why he did so, the ANC was hellbent on disciplining him. Kgalema did not support disciplinary action against Turok because he did not think it was necessary. We definitely need to review how MPs may vote on contentious matters.

17 In May 2012 the parliamentary committee proposed some amendments to the Bill and extended the deadline to the end of June for further submissions and public consultation. The Right2Know action group has in clear terms discounted or counter-argued the shifts made, clause by clause. My view is that there were some significant shifts in the latest version of the Bill, which is why Sanef also said it was 'a step in the right direction' ('Mixed response to Info Bill News', *News24*, 11 May 2012). The story continues at the time of writing.

18 My view is that there is a delicate balance to get 'right' between the judiciary and the ruling party (in effect, the executive), dictated to a large extent by the fact that the former has been largely white and the latter largely black, reflecting a range of realities South Africa inherited in 1994.

19 'In *Ready to Govern*, the ANC's policy guidelines for a democratic South Africa adopted in May 1992, it is said: "The bench will be transformed in such a way as to consist of men and women drawn from all sections of South African society. This will be done without interfering with its independence and with a view to ensuring that justice is manifestly seen to be done in a non-racial and non-sexist way and that the wisdom, experience and competent judicial skills of all South Africans are represented"' ('ANC statement on comments on judiciary', 10 January 2005).

20 He adds the example of Johannesburg High Court judgments 'which rule against the city evicting tenants for not paying rent or when a building is being occupied illegally. When the city gets an eviction order the court orders that it cannot evict unless it provides those affected with alternative accommodation. But the city operates on the basis of lists. So if you want to jump the queue the law is also being broken. These are areas that need to be reviewed.' My own view is that, given the history of housing in the city and the enormous disparities of race and class that have persisted after 1994, it is impossible to have apolitical judgments. Housing is still a profoundly political matter in South Africa.

21 In the same vein, he says that very senior posts in the police, intelligence and military services must as far as possible not go to any friends and associates. Of course, this may not always be achievable but his principle is important.

22 'Motlanthe praises judiciary', *Star*, 12 December 2011.

23 'ANC link to Sishen right', *Business Report*, 19 March 2010.

24 Although Kgalema did not want to embark on the topic, he did raise some concerns. His thrust was: If according to Kumba the Sishen mine belonged to the Sishen company and a mining licence cannot be fragmented and apportioned on mining land, how did it come about that for several years that was exactly what had happened before? ArcelorMittal SA (AMSA) had held 21.4 per cent of the Sishen mine. Why did Kumba allow AMSA to hold almost a quarter of the Sishen mine for years?

25 'Nothing for mahala', *Sunday Times*, 11 March 2012.

26 Kgalema said Mtshali did not meet with Oberholzer but was at another meeting at the same venue in Sandton, Johannesburg where he was having his meeting, and the *Sunday Times* story confused the two.

27 'Nothing for mahala', *Sunday Times*, 11 March 2012. Masebe's wording, that Kgalema did not meet Oberholzer 'in the *manner* suggested at all' (my emphasis) could be

interpreted to mean that he may have met him elsewhere or in other circumstances.
28 Ibid.
29 Madonsela indicated that the matter looked serious enough to warrant an investigation ('Madonsela will probe Motlanthe's partner', *Star*, 21 March 2012). She took much longer than anticipated to release the report. In August the media reported that the report was finished and about to be sent to Kgalema but this had not happened at the time of writing later that month.
30 'Motlanthe wants "serious allegations" to be investigated and his name cleared', *Star*, 13 March 2012.
31 Makhudu Sefara, 'Motlanthe, Zuma, in battle for credibility', *Star*, 30 March 2012.
32 Was this a botched attempt by the CIA and FBI and what do our own agencies know about it?' South African Institute of Corporate Fraud Management, 18 March 2012.
33 Ibid. From the outset the news story has felt like a premeditated gambit to harm Kgalema politically and by extension the South African government through the attack on Mtshali. About Mtshali's presence in the meeting the SAICFM maintain: 'The tone and circumstances of this meeting clearly reflect a person taken completely unawares. It reflects someone alarmed at what was transpiring and someone who does not sound like they have any idea as to what that meeting was all about. There is no way Mtshali from the transcription knew the details of the offer about to be made beforehand. The only evidence against Mtshali is that she was even in the room.'
34 'Football lessons for Motlanthe', *M&G*, 13 March 2009.
35 'Motlanthe slams party leaders', *Star*, 28 January 2010.
36 'Pilots query emergency landing', *Sunday Independent*, 6 September 2009.
37 Ibid.
38 Ibid.
39 'Motlanthe's forced landing a 'rumour'', *Star*, 13 September 2011.
40 'It's official: Gugu steps out at DP's side', *Saturday Star*, 5 November 2011.
41 Ibid.
42 'Gugu steals the show', *Star*, 10 February 2012.
43 Ibid.
44 'Cabinet report card', *M&G*, 23 December 2009.
45 We are limited in knowing what cabinet work involves because most of the business is not disclosed to the public and the minutes are confidential.
46 'Motlanthe tells ministers to explain silence', *Business Day*, 2 March 2010.
47 Ibid.
48 'Motlanthe cracks whip over queries', *Star*, 3 June 2010.
49 Ibid.
50 Ibid.
51 'Cabinet Report Card', *M&G*, 23 December 2010. In the end this is a problem the ANC must take a decision on. One thing is clear: without mechanisms to enforce compliance and the resolve to take strong punitive measures against those habitually irresponsible ministers, the problem will persist.
52 'Cabinet Report Card', *M&G*, 23 December 2009.
53 *Sunday Independent*, 3 December 2009.
54 'Cabinet Report Card', *M&G*, 23 December 2009.
55 A big problem here is that not a great deal is known about it in the public domain, including the media. The cut-out is so bad that the head of government's website on this initiative, Ian Houvet, told Patrick Bond who wanted more information: 'I am afraid the WoP website is for government officials associated with the WoP only and therefore access cannot be granted.' What could be so confidential about the work of government in fighting poverty to justify this unnecessary, counterproductive and in fact damning secrecy? Every bit of information that government possesses in the fight against poverty

must not only be easily accessible to the public but subject to its scrutiny, unless, of course, the government is not succeeding in this regard and therefore wish to conceal not only the depth of poverty but also its failures to effectively combat it. Kgalema and other ANC leaders never even allude to capitalism as a cause of poverty and unemployment. In my view, this glaring omission cannot change the hard facts of both the kind of society we live in and the economic policies the ANC has adopted since 1994.

56 'Motlanthe vows to end "turf wars" in anti-poverty fight', *Business Day*, 10 October 2012.
57 While appreciating the enormous role he plays, I see his response here as a weak, evolutionist view of history that believes change has to happen gradually in stages. This ignores the fact that the relationship between class and social forces makes radical change impossible. Kgalema and the ANC also do not ask how far the policies decided by the ANC after 1994 contributed to the current devastating degree of black unemployment, poverty and social inequalities.
58 To fulfil the role of acting president, a deputy president gets sworn in once for this task at the outset, which is applicable for the entire term. A great political advantage of this replacement system is that if deputy presidents become presidents later on they are thoroughly at home with the work to be done.
59 'Cabinet Report Card', *M&G*, 23 December 2010,
60 Jovial Rantao, 'As a nation who truly loves our Madiba, we have a right to know', *Saturday Star*, 29 January 2011.

Chapter Nine

1 Arrogance and vengeance are indeed expressions of the abused power. How state power, in particular, is wielded is critical in a constitutional democracy.
2 Kgalema tells a tale about a man who came as a refugee to a Jewish community and who told them that his king sent him. They said they could give him refuge but he must please not tell them about his king because they had one of their own. When that man died, another refugee came along and when he also wanted to talk about his king they said, 'Yes, we know him, he lived among us here.' In other words, your conduct is important. If it is exemplary and inspiring it will leave a proud legacy for those who come later. He told the story with the legacy of the previous iconic leaders of the ANC in mind, such as Walter Sisulu, Oliver Tambo and Chief Albert Luthuli.
3 Personal communication, 21 May 2012.
4 'Top two speak out', Adriaan Groenevald interviews Kgalema Motlanthe, *Business Report*, 7 June 2012.
5 It is futile to deny that South Africa has had a bigger crisis of governance under Zuma than under Mbeki. Virtually everywhere, things are falling apart. Some matters are still under judicial consideration, but there has been serious public concern at the appointment of the former crime intelligence boss, Richard Mdluli, and the mockery of the criminal justice system that his suspension thrice in as many months evoked; the inappropriate appointment of Menzi Simelane as national director of public prosecutions after the Ginwala Commission of Inquiry found him dishonest and unreliable; the suspension and eventual dismissal of the commissioner of police, Bheki Cele, after a board of inquiry found him guilty of maladministration and misconduct; the growing corruption in the police force, the loss of public confidence in it and the utter shambles it is in today; growing signs of the intelligence underworld influencing political developments; illegal interception by intelligence agencies; growing fraud and corruption in the ANC government; a judiciary under sustained attack; serious cases of financial mismanagement in various municipalities and provinces; a defence minister whose handling of the opposition in parliament and the media has been a disaster. All this

and much more has been wrong in the current administration.
6 It seems strongly that this has been the universal trend where liberation movements win state power. From that moment they appear to distance themselves from the party and the masses in it that put them in power. This has been the ANC's own trend since 1994. The sins of incumbency are a powerful force in shifting allegiance from the party to the government. State resources are not seen as the means to meet the basic needs of the masses but primarily the means to enrich party leaders who go into government.
7 In Zuma's case, he must be commended for deciding finally to dismiss Cele.
8 'Paralysis at the top – Vavi', *Times*, 27 October 2011.
9 'Donen did not clear ANC men', *M&G*, 9 December 2011.
10 Donen letter to Mavimbela, 28 August 2009.
11 Tokyo Sexwale, mentioned here, had been named in the report as a co-director of a foreign company, Mocoh, that was alleged to have paid some of the kickbacks. He too was cleared by the commission, who added that he had contributed valuably to their work.
12 Donen letter to Mavimbela, 28 August 2009.
13 Thabo Mbeki, interview, 22 September 2011.
14 Frank Chikane, interview, 22 August 2011.
15 The point remains: When a president establishes an inquiry on issues of profound public interest, it is only fair that if the report is either long delayed or not to be released he should give the country an explanation.
16 This story prompted the director-general in the presidency, Vusi Mavimbela, to ask Donen if the report could have been leaked. In his reply in August 2009 'Donen pointed out that the confidentiality of some of the documents in his chambers may possibly have been compromised by a break-in over a weekend in September 2008' ('The report Mbeki and Zuma hid from you', *Sunday Times*, 23 August 2009).
17 'The report Mbeki and Zuma hid from you', *Sunday Times*, 23 August 2009.
18 'Donen report will backfire', *M&G*, 21 October 2011.
19 Ibid.
20 Ben Turok (2008:22), *From the Freedom Charter to Polokwane: The Evolution of ANC Economic Policy*, Cape Town: New Agenda.
21 Cited in Anthony Sampson (1999:95), *Mandela: The Authorised Biography*, London: HarperCollins.
22 Julius Malema, interview, Johannesburg, 21 July 2010.
23 'Malema and Zuma in mining debate face-off', *Star*, 8 September 2010.
24 The ANC research report after a decision at the 2010 NGC to investigate the feasibility of nationalising the mining sector did not find this the best option. Instead the report advised developing the capacity of the state to play a greater role in the sector and the economy at large, primarily to promote job creation and social development through beneficiation and other measures ('Maximising the developmental impact of the people's mineral assets: state intervention in the mining sector', report prepared for the ANC Policy Institute, 17 February 2012). Until the unions themselves lead a struggle for nationalisation and are strong enough to win, we will be hearing a lot more about the ANC playing a bigger role in the economy. Even this course of action won't be easy to pursue in the midst of a world economic crisis that has shrivelled economic activities.
25 The constraints being what they are, we must explore alternatives. If a state-owned company yields positive results we must build on it. But it would be a competitor in the market and so complying with those rules and laws, making it highly debatable whether it would achieve the social objectives it set itself, especially when market conditions are tough. A big danger is that the company could quickly mean misappropriation of resources for a self-serving state bureaucracy, especially with the present massive corruption in high places.
26 The ANC, NUM and Kgalema have not clearly examined just what has state ownership

meant for such constituencies. All they ever do is to remind us of such state ownership.
27 This is only true technically. If these assets had really been socialised – the flipside of the coin of nationalisation as legal ownership – trade unions like NUM would be deeply involved in decisions about how these resources could benefit miners and other communities. Yet the unions do not exercise any social control over the assets and how they are processed. The mining law expert Peter Leon says: 'The Act does not enable the state to determine the use of mineral resources, there is nothing that stops mining companies from selling our mineral wealth to the highest bidder' (Peter Leon, 'ANCYL mining plan more than a surface concern', *Business Day*, 26 March 2010). The ANC, NUM and the government – including Kgalema – need to note this point, which seriously undermines their view that mineral resources actually belong to the state and hence 'the people.'
28 It seems that powerful interests, probably global, have absolutely opposed nationalising while others in the ANC alliance have tried to steer the debate away from nationalisation, towards other options. So much is at stake, the researchers themselves may be under pressure about their findings.
29 Kgalema himself not convinced about the SACP's argument because they failed to provide any evidence for it.
30 Jabulani Sikhakhane, 'ANCYL's mistake a boost for Zuma ahead of 2012', *Sunday Independent*, 21 August 2011.
31 'The ANC must go back to the masses', Ebrahim Harvey interviews Kgalema Motlanthe, *M&G*, 8 February 2008.
32 The rapid deterioration in the relationship between the presidents of the ANC and the ANCYL is probably the most dramatic ever seen since the latter was formed in 1944. Even in October 2009 Zuma praised Malema as a possible future president of the ANC. Just seven months later, in May 2010, the gloves came off between him and the ANCYL. It was a point of no return to the days when Malema had said that the ANCYL would 'kill for Zuma'. Just seven months later Malema said that Zuma 'was worse than Mbeki' ('Zuma worse than Mbeki', *Star*, 12 April 2012).
33 'Malema storms NGC', *Star*, 25 September 2010.
34 Kgalema was convinced that legal action only made matters more acrimonious and also thereby made a political solution even more difficult, which instead of bringing the parties sensibly together had the effect instead of polarising them further apart. 'There were adequate means within the constitution to resolve these disciplinary matters in a comradely and political manner without lawyers and without expelling anybody. If the ANCYL had read rule 25 of the ANC constitution, properly understood it and therefore relied on it – which is even more important than discussions towards a political solution of the disciplinary matters – there was no need for them to go to lawyers.'
35 Tokyo Sexwale and Mathews Phosa defended Malema during his disciplinary hearings, but officials and members of the NEC should not have been involved in disciplinary matters on which they could later be required to take a decision. Kgalema is firm on this point: 'NEC members are not supposed to get involved in disciplinary matters unless they are material witnesses. If they do then they must recuse themselves if and when the NEC reviews the findings.'
36 Kgalema says: 'Each one of them [in the national disciplinary committee] had to convince themselves and the ANCYL that they were not conflicted about what at various times they said about the ANCYL, its leaders and policies over the years.'
37 In fact Kgalema believes that Malema was deceived at the initial hearings into not taking the two-year suspension in 2010 seriously, thinking that he was just going through the motions and that nothing serious for him would come out of the plea bargain Mathews Phosa persuaded him to enter into and that eventually the matter would just go away. That was the trick, Kgalema says, because the penalty involved expulsion for five years

if during the suspension period he was found guilty of any transgressions the NDC decided were serious.
38 One theory is that some in the leadership were eager to lay charges because they wanted Malema expelled for reasons which had less to do with discipline and much more with their own designs on power. In this regard it seems Fiona Forde was right to perceptively point this out: 'History will show us that this week's ruling against Malema has less to do with party discipline and more to do with Zuma's own ambitions' (Fiona Forde, 'This is not ridding the ANC of rot, it is clearing Zuma's path', *Sunday Independent*, 13 November 2011).
39 Kgalema is also strongly opposed to using discipline to deal with essentially political issues.
40 Steven Friedman, 'Zuma is risking a Mangaung challenge', *New Age*, 24 April 2012. An example is Malema's criticism of the Botswana regime.
41 Rule 25.2 (a) of the ANC constitution prohibits using discipline as a weapon to stifle debate or to deny members their basic democratic rights. It disallows political differences and conflict to be resolved through disciplinary action. This point Kgalema has made many times in the case against the ANCYL and Malema in particular. Kgalema and Zuma have very different views on the ANC's character. Zuma has been determined to preserve the ANC, almost as if it cannot and should not change, whereas Kgalema believes that the ANC is not timeless and can change to whatever it wants to. This would certainly affect how they see the ANCYL and Malema's attempts to radicalise it. Zuma's conservative stance is: 'While the youth league should grow, the growth should not be at the expense of the character of the ANC. Our tools of mobilisation should not change the character of the national democratic movement' ('Fall into line, Zuma tells youth league', *M&G*, 17 June 2011).
42 'Malema willing to fight his expulsion in court', *Star*, 26 March 2012.
43 'ANC: We'll take Julius by the ear and bring him into line', *M&G*, 25 February 2009. The irony is that the ANC itself is in dire need of guidance about where it is taking itself and this country. The party is in its biggest crisis ever, with little or no clear vision for the future. How able is it, then, to guide the youth?
44 'Political solution sought over Malema', *M&G*, 25 November 2011.
45 Ibid.
46 With all the eyes on individuals, Kgalema is right in saying that people have been distracted from the implementation of policy. Outrage in 2012 over the Brett Murray painting *The Spear*, of Zuma's exposed genitals, saw huge protests down Commissioner Street in Johannesburg and outside parliament in Cape Town, with some people even wanting to kill the artist. Meanwhile millions of South Africans, including schoolchildren, still struggle daily with hunger, poor sanitation or none at all, lack of water and other basic services, devastating unemployment and poverty, all of which is seen in newspapers and on television. What can be more urgent and dignity-stripping than those conditions? Yet there are no comparable protests on these priorities.
47 S'Thembiso Msomi, 'Where is the ANC?', *The Times*, 28 March 2012.
48 *New Age*, 14 February 2011, 'The Black Jesus rises from political wilderness.'
49 Carol Paton, 'NUM needs to be ruthless about money and politics', *Business Day*, 29 May 2012.
50 Ibid.
51 'Gauteng slams Zuma allies', *Sunday Times*, 27 May 2012.
52 'A hurdle in Zuma's path', *Sunday Times*, 25 March 2012.
53 'Motlanthe appears ready to challenge Zuma', *Star*, 23 July 2012.
54 Since the 2009 elections and even while Kgalema was state president, most in the media have appeared to want Kgalema to stand against Zuma, which is probably why they have kept on daring him to throw his hat in the ring.

55 'Motlanthe: The reluctant challenger', *M&G*, 25 March 2011.
56 S'Thembiso Msomi, 'Serious clash of heads', *Times*, 16 November 2011. In saying that Kgalema 'has not publicly stated that he wants the job', Msomi has perhaps not quite understood that this is tantamount to Kgalema announcing his own candidacy for the election – the very notion that Kgalema condemns.
57 'Zuma challenged', *Sunday Times*, 2 October 2011.
58 Makhudu Sefara, 'The 2007 glue is wearing thin as succession looms', *Sunday Independent*, 17 April 2011. Sefara does not cite the source of this claim, unsurprisingly, because it is simply untrue.
59 The *Sunday Times* states that ANC structures 'may just feel that they can't risk having another five years with a president going in and out of court' ('A hurdle in Zuma's path', *Sunday Times*, 25 March 2012). Adriaan Groenewald, discussing Zuma's and Kgalema's credibility, says that 'the aura of integrity shines much brighter around Motlanthe than it does around Zuma. Recently approved ratings by TNS Research and an online survey among younger South Africans indicate more positive sentiment towards Motlanthe' ('Top two speak on status and service', Adriaan Groenewald interviews Kgalema Motlanthe, *Business Report*, 7 June 2012).
60 For decades the ANC's playing with words has been legendary. Kgalema said at a gala dinner in honour of the late Harold Wolpe, one of the best ANC theoreticians of all time: 'The ANC cannot afford to be reckless with words, because unfortunately, words are not like a finger ... once you have uttered a word you can't pull it back' ('Arrogance threat to ANC – Motlanthe', *Business Day*, 15 June 2012. Cited from an address by Motlanthe at the Liliesleaf Trust's Commemorative Gala Dinner in Honour of the Harold Wolpe Trust, 21 June 2012).
61 Ibid.
62 Pallo Jordan, 'In a century of movement', *M&G*, 23 December 2012.
63 The term comes from the 'The Second Transition? Building a national democratic society and the balance of forces in 2012', one of the ANC's Strategy and Tactics documents for the 2012 policy conference.
64 Kgalema Motlanthe, 'Reflections on the centenary of the ANC', speech delivered at UNISA, Pretoria, 29 January 2012.
65 '"Arrogance" threat to ANC – Motlanthe', *Business Day*, 15 June 2012.
66 What the ANC and Kgalema himself never properly defined at or after Polokwane was what exactly the renewal of the ANC's values and traditions would mean in the light of the many policy and ideological shifts the ANC had already undergone since its unbanning. To take just the goals and policies of the Freedom Charter and the RDP, the outright departures from or emasculation of many of these is evident in the economic and social policies the ANC adopted over that period.
67 Zuma, defending the ST document, has blamed the current social crisis on the backlog of the apartheid era, which is very misleading. He does, however, admit that the ANC made many compromises during the Codesa negotiations, which go far to explain the reason for the ST, which nevertheless left the black majority poorer and largely empty-handed. His radical talk on the ST sounds like the economic policy changes the ANCYL and Malema in particular campaigned for since 2009, which has ironically vindicated their stance, though the ANC is opposed to the outright nationalisation they sought.
68 Ibid.
69 Kgalema Motlanthe, cited in Sisulu, 634.

Bibliography

Adam, H and K Moodley (1981), *The Opening of the Apartheid Mind: Options for the New South Africa*, London: University of California Press

Adam, H and K Moodley (1993), *The Negotiated Revolution: Society and Politics in Post-Apartheid South Africa*, Johannesburg: Jonathan Ball

African Communist (1990), 'Will Negotiations Bring Peace to South Africa?', No. 122

African National Congress (1994), 'The Reconstruction & Development Programme', Johannesburg: Umanyano

Allen, V (1992), *The History of Black Mineworkers in South Africa*, Vols.1, 2 and 3 (2003), Keighley: Moor

Alexander, N, see No Sizwe

Arklay, T, Nethercote, J and J Wanna (eds) (2006), *Australian Political Lives: Chronicling Political Careers and Administrative Histories*, Perth: Australian National University, with the Australian and New Zealand School of Government

Baskin, J (1991), *Striking Back: A History of Cosatu*, Johannesburg: Ravan

Basson, A (2010), *Finish & Klaar: Selebi's Fall from Interpol to the Underworld*, Cape Town: Tafelberg

Bell, T (2001), *Unfinished Business: South Africa, Apartheid and Truth*, Cape Town: Redworks

Beinart, W, P Delius and S Trapido (eds) (1986), *Putting a Plough to the Ground: Accumulation and Dispossession in Rural South Africa 1850–1930*, Johannesburg: Ravan

Bond, P (2002), *Unsustainable South Africa: Environment, Development and Social Protest*, London: Merlin

Bond, P (2003), *Against Global Apartheid: South Africa meets the World Bank, IMF and International Finance*, Cape Town: UCT Press

Bond, P (2004), *Talk Left, Walk Right*, Pietermaritzburg: University of KwaZulu-Natal Press

Bond, P (2005), *Elite Transitions: From Apartheid to Neoliberalism*, Pietermaritzburg: University of KwaZulu-Natal Press

Bozzoli, B (1991), *Women of Phokeng: Consciousness, Life Strategy and Migrancy in South Africa 1900-1983*, Johannesburg: Ravan

Buntman, FL (2003), *Robben Island and Prisoner Resistance to Apartheid*, Cambridge: Cambridge University Press

Busin, V (1989), *Social Democracy and Southern Africa*, Moscow: Progress

Butler, A (2007), *Cyril Ramaphosa*, Johannesburg: Jacana

Calland, R and P Graham (2005), *Democracy in the Time of Mbeki*, Cape Town: Institute for Democracy in South Africa

Calland, R (2006), *Anatomy of South Africa: Who Holds the Power*, Cape Town: Zebra

Callinicos, A (1983), *Marxism and Philosophy*, London: Oxford University Press

Callinicos, A (1988), *South Africa Between Reform and Revolution*, London: Bookmarks

Callinicos, A (1992), *Between Apartheid and Capitalism*, London: Bookmarks

Chikane, F (2012), *Eight Days in September*, Johannesburg:

Picador Africa

Clark, S (ed) (1994), *Nelson Mandela Speaks*, Cape Town: David Philip

Clingman, S (2006), *Bram Fischer: Afrikaner Revolutionary*, Cape Town: David Philip

Cohen, MJ and J Major (2004), *History in Quotations: Reflecting 5,000 Years of World History*, London: Cassell

Coleman, K (1991), *Nationalisation: Beyond the Slogans*, Johannesburg: Ravan

Congress of South African Trade Unions (Cosatu) (2000), 'First term Report', August, Cape Town: Parliamentary Office

Delius, P (1983), *The Land Belongs to Us*, Johannesburg: Ravan

Delius, P (1996), *A Lion Amongst the Cattle: Reconstruction and Resistance in the Northern Transvaal*, Johannesburg: Ravan

Delius, P and M Hay (2009), *Mpumalanga: An Illustrated History*, Johannesburg: Highveld

Dennis, D (1984), *Black History for Beginners*, New York: Writers and Readers

Dolny, H (2001), *Banking on Change*, London: Penguin

Dubow, S (2000), *The African National Congress*, London: Sutton

Du Toit, D (1981), *Capital and Labour in South Africa: Class Struggles in the 1970s*, London and Boston: Kegan Paul International

Du Toit, P (2004), *The Great South African Land Scandal*, Johannesburg: Legacy

Everatt, D (2009), *The Origins of Non-Racialism: White Opposition to Apartheid in the 1950s*, Johannesburg: Wits University Press

Fanon, F (196), *Wretched of the Earth*, London: Penguin

Fatton, R (1986), *Black Consciousness in South Africa*, New York: State University Press

Feinstein, A (2007), *After the Party: A Personal and Political Journey Inside the ANC*, Johannesburg and Cape Town: Jonathan Ball

Feuer, LS (1984), *Marx and Engels: Basic Writings on Politics and Philosophy*, London: Fontana

Field, R (2010), *Alex la Guma: A Literary Political Biography*, Johannesburg: Jacana

Fine, R and D Davis (1990), *Beyond Apartheid: Labour and Liberation in South Africa*, Johannesburg: Ravan

Gelb, S (1991), *South Africa's Economic Crisis*, Cape Town: David Philip

Gerhart, GM and CL Glaser (2010), *From Protest to Challenge, Vol. 6: Challenge and Victory, 1980–1990*, Bloomington: Indiana University Press

Gevisser, M (2009), *Thabo Mbeki: The Dream Deferred*, Johannesburg: Jonathan Ball

Gordimer, N (1999), *Living in Hope and History: Notes from Our Century*, Cape Town: David Philip

Gordin, J (2008), *Zuma: A Biography*, Johannesburg: Jonathan Ball

Graham, P and A Coetzee (2002), *In the Balance: Debating the State of Democracy in South Africa*, Pretoria: Institute for Democracy in South Africa

Green, P (2008), *Choice, Not Fate, The Life and Times of Trevor Manuel*, Johannesburg: Penguin

Gumede, WM (2005), *Thabo Mbeki and the Battle for the Soul of the ANC*, Cape Town: Zebra

Harvey, E (2009), 'Whither the Independent Left', *The Thinker*, Vol. 3, 34–7

Habib, A & Bentley, K (2008), *Racial Redress & Citizenship in South Africa*, Cape Town: HSRC Press

Hermanus, M (1988), 'Mechanisation means retrenchment at

Western Areas', in *SA Labour Bulletin*, Vol. 13, 6, 77–9

Huddleston, T (1956), *Naught for your Comfort*, London: Collins

Innes, D, Kentridge, M and H Perold (1992), *Power & Profit: Politics, Labour and Business in South Africa*, Cape Town: Oxford University Press

Inquaba ya Basebenzi (Journal of the Marxist Workers' Tendency of the ANC) (1988), 'The Struggle for Power', June

Innes, D (1984), *Anglo American and the Rise of Modern South Africa*, Johannesburg: Ravan

Johnson, RW (2010), *South Africa's Brave New World: The Beloved Country since the End of Apartheid*, London: Penguin

Kathrada, A (2004), *Ahmed Kathrada Memoirs*, Cape Town: Zebra

Korr, C and M Close (2009), *More Than Just a Game: Football v Apartheid*, London: Collins

Legassick, M (2007), *Towards Socialist Democracy*, Pietermaritzburg: University of KwaZulu-Natal Press

Lenta, M (2007), 'SA: a nation built on the back of slavery', *Weekender*, Weekend Review, 24–25 March

Lodge, T and B Nasson (1991), *All Here and Now: Black Politics in South Africa in the 1980s*, Cape Town: David Philip

Machel, S (1981), *Sowing the Seeds of Revolution*, Harare: Zimbabwe

Maharaj, M (ed) (2001), *Reflections in Prison*, Cape Town: Zebra

Mandel, E (1992), *Power and Money*, London: Verso

Mandela, N (1976), 'Clear the obstacles and confront the enemy', in Maharaj (ed) (2001), 7–20

Mandela, N (1978), *The Struggle is My Life*, London: IDAF

Mandela, N (2010), *Nelson Mandela: Conversations with Myself*, London: Macmillan

Manganyi, NC (2004), *Gerard Sekoto: 'I am an African'*,

Johannesburg: Wits University Press

Mangcu, X (2008), *To the Brink: The State of Democracy in South Africa*, Scottsville: University of KwaZulu-Natal Press

Mangcu, X (2009), *The Democratic Moment: South Africa's Prospects under Jacob Zuma*, Johannesburg: Jacana

Manuel, T (1992), Keynote Address, in P Theron (ed), 'ANC National Meeting on Electrification', Centre for Development Studies, University of Western Cape, Cape Town

Marais, H (2010), *South Africa Pushed to the Limit: The Political Economy of Change*, Cape Town: UCT Press

Marks, S and S Trapido (1987), *The Politics of Race, Class & Nationalism in Twentieth Century South Africa*, London and New York: Longman

Marx, A (1992), *Lessons of Struggle*, Cape Town: Oxford University Press

Mashota, T (2004), 'We owe the ANC nothing', *Mail & Guardian*, Letters, 5–11 November

Mbeki, G (1991), *Learning from Robben Island: The Prison Writings of Govan Mbeki*, Cape Town: David Philip

McDonald, D and J Pape (2002), *Cost Recovery and the Crisis of Service Delivery in South Africa*, London: Zed

McDonald, D and G Ruiters (eds) (2005) *The Age of Commodity: Water Privatisation in Southern Africa*, London: Earthscan

Meli, F (1988), *A History of the ANC: South Africa Belongs to Us*, Harare: Zimbabwe Publishing

Meyer, JA and MG Califano (2006), *Good Intentions Corrupted: The Oil-for-Food Scandal and the Threat to the UN*, New York: Public Affairs

Michie, J and V Padayachee (1997), *The Political Economy of South Africa's Transition: Policy Perspectives in the Late 1990s*, London: Dryden

Miles, R (1989), *Racism*, London: Routledge

Bibliography

Modisane, B (1986), *Blame Me on History*, Johannesburg: AD Donker

Mokgatle, N (1971), *The Autobiography of an Unknown South African*, Johannesburg: AD Donker

Mulemfo, MM (2009), *The Story of Kgalema Motlanthe*, Johannesburg: Children's Illustrated Educational

Murphy, D (1998), *South from the Limpopo: Travels through South Africa*, London: Flamingo

Musson, D (1989), *Johnny Gomas: Voice of the Working Class*, Cape Town: Buchu

Naidoo, J (2010), *Fighting for Justice: A Lifetime of Political and Social Activism*. Johannesburg: Picador Africa

No Sizwe (Neville Alexander) (1979), *One Azania, One Nation: The National Question in South Africa*, London: Zed

O'Malley, P (2007), *Shades of Difference: Mac Maharaj and the Struggle for South Africa*, Johannesburg: Penguin

Orkin, M (1989), *Sanctions Against Apartheid*, Cape Town and Johannesburg: David Philip

Pallister, D, Stewart, S and I Lepper (1987), *South Africa Inc: The Oppenheimer Empire*, Johannesburg: Media House

Pinnock, D (2007), *Writing Left: The Radical Journalism of Ruth First*, Pretoria: University of South Africa

Plaatje, S (2007), *Native Life in South Africa*, Johannesburg: Picador Africa

Pottinger, B (2008), *The Mbeki Legacy*, Cape Town: Zebra

Price, RM (1991), *The Apartheid State in Crisis*, Oxford: Oxford University Press

Roberts, RS (2007), *Fit to Govern: The Native Intelligence of Thabo Mbeki*, Johannesburg: STE

Robinson, CJ (1983), *Black Marxism: The Making of the Black Radical Tradition*, London: Zed

Roux, E (1964), *Time Longer Than Rope: The Black Struggle for*

Freedom in South Africa, London: University of Wisconsin Press

Sampson, A (1999), *Mandela: The Authorised Biography*, London: HarperCollins

Satgar, V and L Zita (2009), *New Frontiers for Socialism in the 21st Century*, Johannesburg: Co-operative and Policy Alternative Centre

Saul, JS (1990), *Socialist Ideology and the Struggle for Southern Africa*, Trenton, NJ: Africa World.

Saul, JS and S Gelb (1981), *The Crisis in South Africa: Class Defence, Class Revolution*, New York and London: London Review

Saunders, C (1988), *The Making of the South African Past: Major Historians on Race and Class*, Cape Town: David Philip

Seekings, J and N Nattrass, N (2006), *Class, Race and Inequality in South Africa*, Scottsville: UKZN Press

Simons, J and R Simons (1983), *Class and Colour in South Africa 1850–1950*, London: International Defence and Aid Fund for Southern Africa

Simons, RA (2004), *All My Life and All My Strength*, Johannesburg: STE

Sisulu, E (2006), *Walter and Albertina Sisulu: In Our Lifetime*, Cape Town: David Philip

Smith, C (1997), *Robben Island*, Cape Town: Struik

Smith, D (1990), *Capitalist Democracy on Trial: The Transatlantic Debate from Tocqueville to the Present*, London: Routledge

Smith, J and B Tromp (2009), *Hani: A Life Too Short*, Johannesburg and Cape Town: Jonathan Ball

Southall, R and J Daniel, J (2009), *Zunami!: The 2009 South African Elections*, Johannesburg: Jacana

Sparg, M, J Schreiner and G Ansell (eds) (2001), *Comrade Jack: The Political Lectures and Diary of Jack Simons*,

Johannesburg: STE

Sparks, A (1994), *Tomorrow Is Another Country: The Insider Story of South Africa's Negotiated Revolution*, Johannesburg: Struik

Sparks, A (2009), *First Drafts: South African History in the Making*, Johannesburg and Cape Town: Jonathan Ball

Stedman, JS (1994), *South Africa: The Political Economy of Transformation*, Boulder: Lynne Rienner

Suckling, J and L White (1988), *After Apartheid: The Renewal of the South African Economy*, University of York: Centre for Southern African Studies

Suttner, R (2008), *The ANC Underground in South Africa*, Johannesburg: Jacana

Swilling, M, R Humphries and K Shubane (1991), *Apartheid State in Transition*, Cape Town: Oxford University Press

Trotsky, L (1947), *Stalin*, London: Hollis and Carter

Trotsky, L (1967), *The Transitional Programme for Socialist Revolution*, New York: Pathfinder

Trotsky, L (1972), *The Revolution Betrayed: What Is the Soviet Union and Where Is It Going?*, New York: Pathfinder

Trotsky, L (1985), *The History of the Russian Revolution*, London: Pluto

Turok, B (2003), *Nothing But the Truth: Behind the ANC's Struggle Politics*, Johannesburg: Jonathan Ball

Turok, B (2008), *From the Freedom Charter to Polokwane: The Evolution of ANC Economic Policy*, Cape Town: New Agenda

Turok, B (ed) (2010), *The Historical Roots of the ANC: Understanding the ANC Today*, Johannesburg: Jacana

Uhlig, MA (ed) (1986), *Apartheid in Crisis*, Harmondsworth: Penguin

Van Diepen, M (1988), *The National Question in South Africa*, London: Zed

Watson, RL (1990), *The Slave Question: Liberty and Property in South Africa*, Pietermaritzburg: Natal Witness

Webster, E (ed) (1986), *Essays in Southern African Labour History*, Johannesburg: Ravan

Webster, E and K von Holdt (eds) (2005), *Beyond the Apartheid Workplace: Studies in Transition*, Scottsville: University of KwaZulu-Natal Press

Wolpe, H (1988), *Race, Class and the Apartheid State*, Paris: Unesco

Wylie, D (2008), *Art and Revolution: The Life and Death of Thami Mnyele*, Johannesburg: Jacana

Index

A

African National Congress (ANC): xi, xiv–xv, xvii, xxii, xxiv–xxv, 4–5, 9, 14, 23, 38, 43, 47, 49, 52, 59, 63, 70, 72, 78, 80–1, 83, 88–91, 93, 95, 98–9, 103–5, 112, 114, 134, 176, 189–90, 201, 209, 214, 217, 220–3, 224, 247–8, 250–2, 272, 279–80, 288, 309, 327, 330, 350; Alexandra bus boycott (1957), 9; banning and unbanning of (1960/1990), 19–20, 23, 46, 51, 61, 90; branches of, 46, 166, 206, 222, 267, 283; Conference (1994), 126–7; deployment committee (DC), 235–7, 240–1; disciplinary committee of, 339; electoral slogans (1994), xxiii, 126; founding conference of (1912), 4; Freedom Charter (1955), 9, 45, 52–3, 55–6, 58, 75–6, 80, 87, 95, 98, 175, 177, 214, 223, 302, 334–6; ideology/policies of, 10, 35, 48, 59, 62, 135, 149, 216, 219, 223, 226, 267, 348; Luthuli House, 40, 51, 128, 130, 133, 136, 151, 178, 186, 213, 232–3, 241, 252, 257, 262, 270, 272, 277, 280–1, 283, 285–6, 291, 293, 296, 298, 329; Mafikeng Conference (1997), x, 124, 127–9, 134, 141–2, 145, 147, 156, 158, 162–3, 174, 176, 235, 346; Mangaung Conference (2012), 326, 331, 333, 343, 346, 349, 351; members of, x, 12, 15, 17, 27, 36–7, 39–40, 45–6, 49–54, 57, 60, 67, 71, 73, 78, 84, 91–2, 95, 100, 104, 114, 119–20, 123–6, 131, 135, 137, 140, 143, 147–9, 155–60, 163–7, 171–5, 178, 180–1, 187, 193, 195, 205, 207, 209–13, 216, 220–1, 227–8, 230–1, 233, 235–40, 249–50, 258, 265, 268, 272, 275, 285, 291, 294–5, 301, 305, 313, 316, 321, 328–9, 343–4, 351; national executive committee (NEC), 61, 79, 130, 133, 135, 138, 158, 160–1, 189–90, 206–7, 212, 215, 221–3, 234, 243, 249–50, 252–3, 260, 266; national general council (NGC), 131, 135, 149, 159–60, 176, 204, 206–7, 261; national working committee (NWC), x, 130, 133, 138, 160, 203–4, 212, 222, 235–6, 240–1;

Operation Vula, 119; opposition to, 49, 114; Policy Conference (1992), 126; political dominance of, 306, 308; Policy Institute, 224; Polokwane Conference (2007), x, 32, 128, 132, 136, 161, 187, 208, 210, 214, 218–19, 222, 225–7, 230, 232–3, 240, 243, 245, 250, 252, 257, 261, 267, 279–83, 285, 294, 300, 328, 344, 349; regional committees of, 90, 98; 'second transition' (ST), 350–1; Stellenbosch Conference (2002), x, 128–9, 136, 145, 156, 158–9, 162–3, 174–7, 212, 214, 222, 225, 245, 252; support for MAT, 303; supporters of, 21; Youth League (ANCYL), 57, 231, 239, 241, 244–5, 265, 277, 299, 333, 336, 338–44

African People's Democratic Union of South Africa: members of, 51

Alexander, Neville: 34

Alexander, Ray: 223

Allen, Vic: 78–9, 87; *History of the Black Mineworkers in South Africa*, xvi

Anglo American Corporation: 30, 323; subsidiaries of, 311

apartheid era, xxii, 7, 36, 75, 127, 140, 154, 171, 246, 278, 311

Arab Spring: Tunisian Revolution (2010–11), 317

Australia: 106; United Mineworkers of Australia, 107

Azanian People's Organisation (Azapo): founding conference (1978), 46; members of, 51

Aziz, Tariq: Iraqi Deputy Prime Minister, 183, 185

B

Baldwin, James: *Go Tell It on the Mountain* (1953), 20

Baleni, Frans: 88, 90, 117

Bantu Education: 8, 20

Barayi, Elijah: 90, 97; vice-president of NUM, 76

Biko, Steve: death of (1977), 19; role in formation of South African Students Organisation, 20

Bisho massacre (1992): 99

Black Consciousness (BC): 19–20, 41, 46; influence of, 34, 78

black economic empowerment (BEE): 67, 162, 173, 184; companies, 108, 191, 337

Blair, Tony: 153

Bloemfontein (Mangaung), 176, 230, 299, 312

Boipatong massacre (1992): events of, 98–9

Bond, Patrick: 59, 160

Boshielo, Flag: 4; leader of SACP, 44

Botswana: Botswana Democratic Party, 197; Gaborone, 25, 197; government of, 339

Bozalek, Lee: 69

Brown, Gordon: 153

Brown, Karima: 59, 130, 159, 168, 225, 230

Brümmer, Stefaans: 191, 194–5

Brutus, Dennis: 34

Bud-Mbelle, Russa: family of, 15

Budlender, Geoff: 30

Buntman, Fran Lisa: 39, 48

Bush, George W.: 153

Butler, Anthony: *Cyril Ramaphosa*, xvi

Butshingi, Ephraim: imprisonment of, 32–3

C

Camilla, Duchess of Cornwall: 320
Cape Town, 32, 69, 71, 119, 203, 253, 303
Carmichael, Stokely: 19
capitalism: xxiv, 57, 61, 83, 162, 169, 334; racial, xxii, 46–8, 168
Carolus, Cheryl: deputy secretary-general of ANC, 124
Castro, Fidel: visit to Soweto, 172
Catholicism: 8
Central African Republic: Bangui, 318
Chamber of Mines: 75, 101
Chancellor House: 195
Charles, Prince of Wales: 320, 324
Charnley, Irene: 94, 113, 138
Chetty, Shun: defence lawyer for trial of Molanthe, 30
Chikane, Frank: 274, 279, 332; *Eight Days in September*, 242
China: 169, 288–91
Christianity: 11, 313; Anglican, 8–9, 16, 18, 34, 37, 43, 73, 81, 300; Bible, 44; Dutch Reformed, 8; Lutheran, 5; Methodist, 8
Cleaver, Eldridge: 19
Clinton, Hillary: US Secretary of State, 324
colonialism: 48; British, 3; internal, xxii
Coloured People's Congress: 61
Comintern: dissolved (1943), 17
Communications Union: opposition to Telkom's sale of stake in Vodacom (2008), 295
Community of the Resurrection: members of, 16
Congress of Democrats: 61
Congress of South African Trade Unions (Cosatu): xiii–xv, 24, 52, 60, 62, 91, 95–6, 98, 127–8, 135, 145–7, 156, 161, 166, 176–7, 201, 203, 222, 225–7, 229, 282, 296, 308, 327; affiliates of, 92, 97, 108; Central Executive Committee, 90, 141; Congress (1987), 80; Congress (2006), 212; criticisms of use of finance by government officials, 314–15; founding congress of (1985), 77, 112; May Day rally (2000), 61, 135, 146, 169; members of, 12, 84, 91, 127, 140, 147, 166, 329, 331; opposition to iGoli 2002, 145; support for Jacob Zuma in, 211, 343; view of RDP Urban Development Strategy, 139–40
Congress of the People (Cope): 280, 283, 296; criticism of Ginwala Commission report, 286; formation of (2008), 71, 162
Constitution of South Africa (1996), 35, 57, 205, 219, 247, 292, 294, 304, 306, 309–10
Convention for a Democratic South Africa (Codesa): 75, 98, 104, 124, 126, 134, 149; founding of (1992), 97; negotiations, 99, 126, 166
Cooper, Saths: 46, 65, 114
Copelyn, Johnny: 104
Cornforth, Maurice: 42
Crawford-Browne, Terry: 291
Cronin, Jeremy: deputy general secretary of SACP, 337
Cuba: 169, 174, 259

D

Dalai Lama: 289–90

Dadoo, Dr Yusuf: 223
De Klerk, FW: 291; Nobel Peace Prize laureate, 288
Democratic Alliance (DA): 198; members of, 197, 199
Democratic Republic of Congo (DRC): 319; Gbadolite, 318
Desai, Ashwin: xxv
Dipico, Manne: 87–8, 92; alleged shares in Pamodzi Investment Holdings, 196–8; parliamentary adviser to Thabo Mbeki, 197
Directorate of Special Operations (Scorpions): 246, 283, 292–3; alleged role of personnel in 'email saga' (2005), 186, 188; raid on home of Jacob Zuma (2005), 201, 210–11
Donen Commission: 183–4, 186, 332; forming of (2006), 182; interim report (2006), 185, 331–3
Douglas, 323–4
Downer, Billy: Deputy Director of Public Prosecutions in Western Cape, 247–8
Duarte, Jessie: 298, 306
Durban, 210, 316

E
economy: 110–11, 336, 347
Elijah Barayi Memorial Training Centre: 106, 108
email saga (2005): 177, 200, 209; events of, 187–9, 199, 209; political impact of, 186–8, 190, 198, 222
Erson, Father Kingston: 16, 19, 71

F
Fanon, Frantz: *The Wretched of the Earth* (1963), 20
Feinstein, Andrew: *After the Party*, 178–9
FIFA inter-ministerial committee: members of, 323
Finland: 319
Fischer, Bram: 223
Forde, Fiona: 279; false news story by, 273, 276, 280–1, 297
Friedman, Steven: 220, 265, 281, 287

G
Gabriels, Howie: 76, 79, 83–4, 88, 94, 116
Gauteng Province, 73, 88, 90–2, 98–9, 101, 124, 127, 345
Ginwala Commission of Inquiry: 285; report of, 286–8
Golding, Marcel: 97, 101, 104; criticisms of ANC, SACP and Freedom Charter, 95; electoral campaign for secretary-general of NUM, 94–5
Gordin, Jeremy: 199; biographer of Jacob Zuma, 204
Gorky, Maxim: *The Mother*, 64
Gqabi, Joe: assassination of, 25; imprisonment of, 25
Griffin, Howard: *Black Like Me* (1961), 20
Growth, Employment and Redistribution Strategy (GEAR): 123, 125–6, 133, 139, 142, 144, 156–7, 177, 219; adoption of (1996), 126; criticisms of, 139–41, 163
Gumede, William: 224, 245
Gwala, Harry: 18, 78; imprisonment of, 66; influence of, 58; 'Man and His Country', 50

H

Habib, Adam: 220, 231
Hani, Chris: assassination of (1993), 99
Hartley, Ray: 264
HIV/AIDS: 123, 132–3, 139, 149–51, 229; antiretrovirals (ARVs), 150–2; AZT treatment, 149; education focusing on, 110; strategies for preventing, 322
Hogan, Barbara: 101; Minister of Health, 284, 289
Holomisa, Bantu: 71, 285
Huddleston, Trevor: *Naught for Your Comfort*, 19
Hussein, Saddam: 332

I

iGoli 2002: 123, 139; criticisms of, 145; provisions of, 144–5
Imperial Crown Trading (ICT): executive personnel of, 311
imperialism: Boer, 4; British, 4
Imvume Management: role in Oilgate scandal, 179–80
Indian Congress: 61
Inkatha Freedom Party (IFP): 99
'Inqindi and Marxism' (Inq-M): 52, 57–8; circulation of (1978), 51; focus of, 53–4; written responses to, 52–3
International Monetary Fund (IMF): 141, 154
Iran: arms deals in, 312–13; oil exports of, 290
Iraq: 186, 195; Ba'ath Socialist Party, 182–4; Baghdad, 183; Ministry of Oil, 183
Iraqi–South African Friendship Association: 184; establishment of (2001), 183

J

Jackson, George: *Soledad Brother*, 35
JB Marks Education Test: 106
Johannesburg: 3, 6–7, 20–1, 26, 30, 42, 68, 71, 76, 145, 253, 347; Alexandra, 3, 7–8, 10, 20; Park Station, 22; Soweto, 25–6, 51, 163, 172, 216; Yeoville, 106
Johannesburg Stock Exchange (JSE): 143
Jonas, Vuyisile: 116–17
Jordan, Pallo: 349

K

Kalahari Resources: 191, 311; application with mining license, 191–3; personnel of, 191, 195
Kalk, Willy: 82
Kasrils, Ronnie: 188
Kathrada, Ahmed: xii; imprisonment of, 34–5, 40–1
Khumalo, Sydney: 21
Kindra, Jaspreet: 146–7, 156
Kipling, Rudyard: 'If', 118
Kotane, Moses: 57, 223; secretary-general of ANC, 62
Kumba Mining: owners of Sishen Iron Ore Company, 311
KwaZulu-Natal: 75, 99

L

Land Bank: 196–8
Lansberg, Chris: 264
Langa, Paul: 38, 66
Leeukop Prison, 32–3, 69

Lehoko, Khetsi: NUM education coordinator, 92
Lekota, Mosiuoa: 161, 220; co-founder of COPE, 71
Lenin, Vladimir: writings of, 44
Leon, Tony: 188; leader of DA, 197, 199
Letele, Seeng: 114–15
Levin, Melissa: 128
Lomax, Louis: *When the Word Is Given* (1963), 20
Lonmin mine massacre (2012): 352
Luthuli, Albert: xii, 223, 262

M

Mabandla, Brigitte: removal of, 284; Justice Minister, 284
Mabanga, Thebe: 221
Mabetoa, Phineas: 14, 22, 26, 73
Madingoane, Kgalema Marcus: family of, 5–6
Madingoane, Masefako Sophia: family of, xv, 3, 5–7, 10–11, 22, 262
Madingoane, Rev. Ramatoto Johannes: 5
Maduna, Penuell: Minister of Justice, 246
Maharaj, Mac: 119
Majali, Sandile: 183, 331; death of, 180–1; role in Oilgate scandal, 179–80
Makhuru, David: 345
Makunyane, Thabo: 67
Malema, Julius: xviii, 265, 336–7; charges brought against, 339–40; criticisms of, 244, 314, 338–42; expulsion from ANC (2011), 326, 342–3; leader of ANCYL, 239; member of ANC NWC, 235
Maluleka, Jesse: 86
Mandela, Nelson: 29, 67, 94–5, 119, 124, 134, 180, 201, 223–5, 260, 325, 328; author of 'Inqindi and Marxism', 52; electoral victory of (1994), 226; imprisonment of, 34–5, 40–1, 55, 334; Nobel Peace Prize laureate, 288; president of ANC, x; release of (1990), 56, 73, 90
Mantashe, Gwede: 90, 118, 135, 164, 216; assistant to Molanthe, 102; chairperson of SACP, 165; secretary-general of ANC, 104, 165, 245, 249; secretary-general of NUM, 104
Manuel, Trevor: 160, 236, 249; resignation of, 263; South African Finance Minister, 263
Marais, Hein: 82
Marcus, Gill: Governor of Reserve Bank, 323
Marks, JB: 223
Marx, Karl: writings of, 44
Marxism: 17, 20, 42, 53–5, 58, 93, 300, 334; interpretation of Freedom Charter, 55; literature of, 47, 50; relationship with nationalism, 58, 60
Marxist-Leninism: 167
Marxist Workers' Tendency (MWT): criticisms of, 48–9
Masebe, Thabo: 288, 312, 325; spokesperson for Molanthe, 259, 273
Masefako, Sophia Mmateng: family of, 5
Maseko, Tim: South African Ambassador to Swaziland, 28

Index

Masetlha, Billy: 188; director-general of National Intelligence Agency, 187
Mashamba, George: imprisonment of, 32–3, 43
Mashile-Nkosi, Daphne: 71, 192; chair of Kalahari Resources, 191; family of, 74, 191, 194–5
Masondo, Amos: executive mayor of Johannesburg, 42
Mathakoe, Louis: family of, 6
Matlala, Director: 69, 80, 88, 96, 101–2
Matshiqi, Aubrey: 263–4
Mbatha, Khulu: 318–19
Mbeki, Govan (Oom Gov): 18, 50, 54, 57, 78, 91, 95, 99, 116, 119, 223; imprisonment of, 34–5; influence of, 40; *Learning from Robben Island*, 55–6
Mbeki, Thabo: xiv, 136, 138, 146, 161, 188, 215, 225, 227–8, 241–2, 246, 257, 260, 268, 278, 281, 286, 330, 332, 338; alleged dominance within ANC, 129–36, 139; challenge to verdict of trial of Jacob Zuma, 269–71; criticism of Cosatu and SACP, 147; dismissal of Jacob Zuma (2005), 177, 199–203, 205–10, 222, 230–1; economic policies of, 264; President of ANC, 127, 208–9, 239; President of South Africa, ix, xi, 78, 103, 128–32, 177, 186, 198, 242, 267, 275, 303, 328; relationship with Molanthe, 127–8, 138–9, 190, 209; resignation of (2008), ix, 208, 218, 242, 244, 249–50, 252, 261–3, 265–6; supporters of, 187, 189, 199, 219, 221, 231–4, 243, 269; view of Gear, 144; views on HIV/AIDS, 149–50
Mbelle, Isaiah Budlwana: family of, 15; secretary-general of ANC, 15
McCarthy, Leonard: 248
McDonald, Faith: 82
McKinley, Dale: 112
media appeals tribunal (MAT): opposition to, 305–6; proposals for, 303
Mhlaba, Raymond: 90, 119; criticisms of Molanthe, 163–4; imprisonment of, 54
Minerals and Petroleum Development Act (2004): 336
Mineworkers Development Agency: focus of, 106
Mineworkers Investment Company (MIC): 75, 110–12, 148; awards for performance, 108; financial investments, 105–7; launch of (1995), 104–5, 107; market value of, 107; personnel of, 106, 109, 111
Mineworkers Investment Trust (MIT): establishment of (1995), 105, 107; funding of, 105, 108; personnel of, 105, 109; projects, 108
Mkhabela, Mpumelelo: 265–7
Mlambo-Ngcuka, Phumzile: Deputy President of South Africa, 187, 262
Mmope-Kgalema Burial Society: formation of, 13
Mofutsanyane, Thuli: secretary of Molanthe, 96
Mohamed, Prof Ismail: 48–9

413

Mokate, Mapula: 64, 66, 116; background of, 22; divorce (2010), 73, 254; family of, 22–3, 63–4, 72, 253, 271–4; affair of, 64–6, 73; member of South African Municipal Workers Union, 23

Molanthe, Kgalema Petrus: ix–xiii, xviii, xxi, xxv, 11, 15, 17, 19–21, 24, 27–9, 37–9, 42, 50–1, 56, 59, 62–3, 67–8, 73, 78, 81–4, 86, 93, 96–7, 99, 102–3, 105, 110–11, 113–14, 116–18, 128–30, 137, 142, 146, 152, 160, 165–6, 174, 186, 202, 206, 215–16, 220, 237, 277, 283, 297–8, 300–2, 305, 315–16, 329, 340, 346–7, 352–3; alleged role in application for mining license for Kalahari Resources, 191–3; alleged shares in Pamodzi Investment Holdings, 196–8; ANC coordinator of PWV region, 91–2; arrest of (1976), 27; birth of (1949), 3, 7; chair of ANC DC, 235; chair of FIFA inter-ministerial committee, 323; chair of South African National AIDS Council, 322; co-chair of South Africa–Germany Bi-national Commission, 324; Deputy President of ANC, 240–2, 260, 275–6, 347; Deputy President of South Africa, 120, 199, 207, 218, 249, 281–2, 319–20, 327; director of MIT, 105; divorce (2010), 73, 254; education of, 8–10, 19–20, 44–5; ex-officio member of National Planning Commission, 322; family of, xv–xvi, 3, 5–8, 10–16, 22, 30, 63–4, 66, 71–2, 253, 262, 271–4; imprisonment of (1977–87), 12, 20, 22–3, 31–6, 43, 45, 63–4, 67–70, 116, 149, 334; interim President of South Africa, 198, 244, 257, 262–8, 275, 281, 316, 325; member of ANC NEC, 266; member of central committee of Cosatu, 90; member of MK, 119; member of NUM, xiv, 12–13, 39, 60, 76–8, 86–7, 104, 108, 115, 123, 127, 135, 148, 308; member of SACP, 163–5; NUM education coordinator, 92–4; personal interests of, 259; public image of, 60, 260–2; relationship with Gugu Mtshali, 254, 266, 311–13, 320; relationship with Thabo Mbeki, 127–8, 138–9, 190, 209; relationship with Zwelinzima Vavi, 233; role in founding of MIC, 75; secretary-general of ANC, x, 46, 60–1, 100, 104, 114, 123–5, 131, 135, 137, 139, 143, 147–9, 152, 155–7, 159–60, 163, 171–4, 193, 195, 205, 209, 216, 220–1, 231, 239–40, 268, 275, 321; general secretary of NUM, 89–90, 95, 97, 100–1, 104–5, 111, 127, 141, 143–4, 166; survivor of plane crash landing (2009), 318–19; trial of (1977), 30; views on ARVs, 150–2

Molanthe, Kgomotso: 22

Molanthe, Lekota Sydney: 11–12; family of, xv, 10, 13, 15–16

Molanthe, Louis Mathakoe: death of, 13; family of, 3, 10–12, 30

Index

Molanthe, Tlatlane Ernst: family of, xv–xvi, 8, 10, 13–16, 71
Moosa, Mohammed Valli: 119, 236
Morobe, Murphy: 47–8; imprisonment of, 36, 41
Mosoeu, Joseph: trial of (1977), 30
Mothopeng, Zeph: 34
Motlatsi, James: 90–1, 115; President of NUM, 76, 90
Motsoaledi, Elias: 4
Mpshe, Mokotedi: acting National Director of Public Prosecutions, 247–8
Mpumalanga, 3, 5
Msimang, Mendi: 191, 193, 202; treasurer-general of ANC, 181
Msomi, S'Thembiso: 346
Mtintso, Thenjiwe: deputy secretary-general of ANC, 174; South African Ambassador to Cuba, 174
Mtshali, Gugu: 120; background of, 254; director at ICT, 311; relationship with Molanthe, 254, 266, 311–13, 320
Mugabe, Robert: opposition to, 154; President of Zimbabwe, 153

N

Naidoo, Jay: head of RDP, 125; general secretary of Cosatu, 84
Natal: 27
National Council of Provinces: role in enactment of legislation, 308
national democratic revolution (NDR): xxii, 55, 351; conception of, 59; radical, 157
National Intelligence Agency: personnel of, 187–8
National Medical and Dental Association of South Africa (Namda): members of, 82
National Party: 56–7, 100; ideology of, 36; rise to power (1948), 7
National Planning Commission: members of, 322
National Prosecuting Authority (NPA): 187, 269; charges against Jacob Zuma, 201, 232, 246, 269–70; personnel of, 284
National Union of Mineworkers (NUM): x, xv, 37, 79, 89, 91, 99, 104, 106, 115, 283, 341; adoption of Freedom Charter (1987), 76, 80, 87; affiliates of, 76; central committee of, 94; Congress (1987), 76–7; Congress (1989), 85, 94; Congress (1994), 101; Cosatu House, 76; education unit, 76, 90–1, 116; elective conference (2012), 345; funding of, 105, 108; legal department, 76; members of, xiv, xvii, 12–13, 39, 51, 60, 69, 75–7, 79, 86, 88–90, 92–7, 100–4, 107–9, 111, 113, 117, 123, 127, 135, 141, 143–4, 148, 166, 308, 335, 345; strike (1987), 38, 75–6, 80–5
nationalism: 58; African, 57–62, 165–6; relationship with Marxism, 58, 60
Ndebele, Sibusiso (S'bu): 69; imprisonment of, 32–3
Nduli, Joseph: 28; arrest of (1976), 27
Nene, George: 21, 25
New Zealand: Rugby World Cup (2011), 319
Newton, Huey: 19

415

Ngcuka, Bulelani: National Director of Public Prosecutions, 187, 200, 247–8
Ngonyama, Smuts: 210, 296; head of presidency, 128–30, 182
Ngoyi, Lilian: 223
Ngwane, Trevor: 59; expulsion from ANC, 162
Nicholson, Chris: ix, 299; presiding judge in trial of Jacob Zuma (2008), 246, 248–9, 251, 269, 271, 278
Nieftagodien, Noor: 260
Nkadimeng, John Kgoana: 4
Nkambule, Dan: 268
Nkosi, Stan: 21, 25, 27–9, 42–3, 72–4, 79, 117; arrest of, 26; death of (2008), 253; family of, 74, 191, 194–5; imprisonment of (1977–87), 32–3, 66, 71; involvement with Kalahari Resources, 191; joined NUM (1987), 76, 84; trial of (1977), 30
Nkuna, Paul: 80; CEO of MIC, 106, 109, 111; Treasurer of NUM, 95
Northern Cape, 323
Nqakula, Charles: removal of, 284; Safety and Security Minister, 284
Nyanda, Siphiwe: 21, 25, 29, 189; self-imposed exile of, 28–9
Nzimande, Blade: 272–3, 299; general secretary of SACP, 164, 261; South African Minister of Higher Education, 322

O

Oberholzer, Barry: company director at 360 Aviation, 312
Oilgate scandal: 177, 199, 209–10; events of, 179–80, 183–4; participants in, 179–81, 185–6

P

Pahad, Essop: 137, 161, 178, 210
Pambi Trust: shares in Pamodzi Investment Holdings, 196
Pamodzi Investment Holdings: granting of loan by Land Bank (2005), 196; shareholders, 196–8
Pan Africanist Congress (PAC): 41; banning of (1960), 19–20, 23; members of, 51
Patel, Ebrahim: 115, 259, 267; Minister of Economic Development, 110
Pedi: defeat of resistance movement (1879), 4
PetroSA: 182; personnel of, 181; role in Oilgate scandal, 179–81
Phala, John: 42; death of (2009), 4
Philip, Kate: 289
Phokanoka, Lawrence: 4; influence of, 58
Pikoli, Vusi: 210, 280, 285–6; National Director of Public Proseuctions, 284
Pillay, Kuben: 107
Plekhanov, George: 50; *The Role of the Individual in History* (1898), 20
Polokwane (Pietersburg), 6, 128
Port Elizabeth, 119, 131, 159
Press Freedom Commission: establishment of, 306
Pretoria, 117, 140, 249, 320
Prisons Act: provisions of, 31
Promotion of Access to Information Act (2002): provisions of, 307

R

Rampahosa, Cyril: 78–9, 88, 91, 95–6, 103, 116, 231, 273; report to NUM Congress (1989), 85; secretary-general of ANC, 91, 94, 104, 124; general secretary of NUM, x, 75–7, 101, 104
Rantao, Jovial: 325
Rashid, Amer Mohammad: Iraqi Oil Minister, 183
Reconstruction and Development Programme (RDP): 125, 148, 163, 177, 214, 223; closure of (1995), 139; poor quality of housing created by, 351; personnel of, 125–6; Urban Development Strategy (1995), 125–6, 139–40, 219
Renova: 191–2
Renwick, Lord Robin: 328
Reserve Bank: 323
Rhodesia: 26
Robben Island, xv, 12, 16, 20, 22–3, 25, 29–30, 32–7, 39–44, 46–55, 57, 63, 66–71, 76, 78, 81, 84–5, 100, 113–14, 116–17, 127, 149, 160, 334
Robinson, Vicki: 191, 194

S

Sabatakgomo: formation of, 4
Sachs, Michael: 128
Saul, John: 169–70
Seepe, Jimmy: 129
Sefara, Makhudu: 312
Sehole, Louisa Mmope: family of, 5
Sekhukhune: 4
Sekhukhune II, King: 4
Sekhukhune Revolt (1958): influence of, 5
Seko, Isaac: imprisonment of, 32–3
Sekwati: 4
Selebi, Jackie: 188; head of South African Police Service, 285, 292
September, Reg: 223
Sexwale, Tokyo: 231, 331
Shaik, Schabir: relationship with Jacob Zuma, 186–7; trial of (2005), 186, 200–2, 208, 210
Sharpeville Massacre (1960): 23
Shiceka, Sicelo: 315–16
Shilowa, Sam: 98; general secretary of Cosatu, 97
Shivambu, Floyd: member of ANCYL, 239
Shubane, Kehla: imprisonment of, 32–3
Sikhakhane, Jabulani: 337
Simelane, Menzi: 287
Sishen Iron Ore Company: 311
Sisulu, Walter: x, xii, xv, 78, 90, 95, 99, 119, 124–5, 171, 223, 262, 328; death of (2003), 352; imprisonment of, 34–5, 54; influence of, 51
Sithole, Bafana: 40, 47–8, 66–7, 69, 104, 158
Slovo, Joe: 78
Smith, Charlene: *Robben Island*, 35
Smith, Ian: 154
socialism: 46, 53, 55, 61, 89, 145–6, 149, 157, 167–8, 170
Socialist International: membership of, 168
Sotho: language of, 3, 8
South Africa–Germany Bi-national Commission: members of, 324
South African Airways: 320

South African Broadcasting Corporation (SABC): 232, 283; executive board of, 242, 280, 293, 299
South African Broadcasting Corporation Bill: 294, 299; passing of (2008), 293; provisions of, 293
South African Clothing and Textile Workers Union (Sactwu): 104
South African Communist Party (SACP): xiii–xv, xxii, 5, 17, 47, 49, 52, 58, 60, 62–3, 72, 90–1, 95, 98, 114, 128, 134, 146–7, 161, 166, 168, 176–7, 201, 203, 211, 222, 225, 227, 229, 277, 288; branches of, 163; central committee, 100, 127, 163; Congress (2012), 165; ideology of, 10, 35, 157; members of, 12, 44–5, 48, 54, 57, 62, 91, 163–4, 261, 269, 329, 337; opposition to, 46, 114; opposition to iGoli 2002, 145; support for MAT, 303
South African Council of Churches: funding of, 70
South African Council of Higher Education (Sached): members of, 82
South African government, xiii, 11, 38, 70, 127, 130–1, 134, 138, 145–6, 158, 164, 171, 173, 178–9, 186, 189, 217, 222, 242, 252, 314, 331–2, 348
South African Institute of Corporate Fraud Management (SAICFM): investigation of 360 Aviation-Molanthe bribery allegations, 312–13

South African Municipal Workers Union: 23
South African National AIDS Council: 322
South African National Defence Force: 319–20; personnel of, 28
South African National Editors Forum (Sanef): 303; members of, 278; opposition to MAT, 305–6; role in creation of Press Freedom Commission, 306
South African Police Service: personnel of, 285, 292
South African Railway and Harbour Workers Union: 71
South African Students Organisation: formation of (1969), 20
South African World Cup Committee: 288
Soviet Union (USSR): 53
Soweto Uprisings (1976): 34, 44
Speed, Steyn: 318–19
Squires, Hilary: presiding judge in trial of Schabir Shaik (2005), 200–2, 210
Swaziland: 16, 26–8; Manzini, 22, 28
Sweden: 170

T

Tabra, Khalid: 183
Taiwan: 170
Tambo, Oliver: xii, 171, 223, 262
Tanzania: 26; Morogoro, 61
Taylor, Dora (Nosipho Majeke): *The Role of the Missionaries in Conquest* (1952), 20
Telkom: 296–7; sale of stake in Vodacom (2008), 295
Terrorism Act 83 (1967): 30

Tibet: 289
Tiro, Abram Onkgopotse: funeral of, 25
Trengrove, Wim: 248
Trotsky, Leon: writings of, 48
Tshabalala-Msimang, Manto: removal of, 284; Minister of Health, 150–2
Tsibolane, Pitso: 260–1, 277
Tucker, Raymond: 32, 69; defence lawyer for trial of Molanthe, 30
Tunisia: Revolution (2010–11), 317
Turok, Ben: 47, 167; nomination of Molanthe for President of South Africa (2008), 262
Tutu, Archbishop Desmond: 291; Nobel Peace Prize laureate, 288

U
Umkhonto weSizwe (MK): 21, 23, 25; formation of, 5; guerrilla attacks conducted by, 24; members of, 4, 24, 27–8, 32, 119
United Democratic Front (UDF): affiliates of, 71; members of, 285
United Kingdom (UK): xxi, 154
United Nations (UN): 319; Independent Inquiry Committee (IIC), 182–6; Oil-for-Food programme (OFFP), 180, 182, 185, 331
United States of America (USA): 35, 154, 290; Black Power movement, 19; Central Intelligence Agency (CIA), 313; Federal Bureau of Investigation (FBI), 313
Unity Movement: 20

V
Vaal Uprisings (1984): 44
Van der Merwe, Sue: Deputy Minister of Defence, 318–19
Vavi, Zwelinzima: 134–5, 141, 143, 145–6, 156, 283, 315, 331, 343; relationship with Molanthe, 233
Vodacom: 296–7; shareholders, 295
Von Leires, Klaus: Transvaal attorney-general, 30

W
Western Cape, 238, 247
World Bank: 141, 154
World Cup (2010), 323
World Youth Conference (1953):, 172

X
Xhosa: language of, 3, 52
Xuma, Dr AB: removed from power, 277

Z
Zikalala, Snuki: 95, 147
Zimbabwe: 25, 123, 132–3, 139, 152, 229, 284; Harare, 152; Matabeleland, 155; Movement for Democratic Change (MDC), 153–4; Zanu-PF, 153–5
Zokwana, Senzeni: President of NUM, 345
Zulu: 4; language of, 52
Zuma, Jacob: 28, 120, 124–5, 137, 161, 173, 188, 203, 205, 212, 225, 227, 242, 259, 265, 276, 278, 283–4, 287, 296, 302, 309, 321, 324–5, 342, 344–5, 351; Deputy President of South Africa, 177, 186, 230,

303; dismissal of (2005), 177, 199–203, 205–10, 222, 230–1; member of MK, 27; polygamous relationships, 316–17; President of ANC, 270, 272, 291, 301; President of South Africa, 40, 215, 218, 229, 241, 257, 264, 270, 297, 312, 326–7, 330–1, 337; raid on home of (2005), 201, 210–11; relationship with Schabir Shaik, 186–7; supporters of, 211, 219–20, 230, 232–3, 241, 243, 263, 269, 281–2, 285–6, 292, 343, 346; trial of (2008), 207, 246–7, 252, 261, 269–71, 287, 348

Zuma, Nkosazana-Dlamini: 229